JEWISH AND CHRISTIAN TEXTS IN CONTEXTS AND RELATED STUDIES

19

Executive Editor
James H. Charlesworth

Editorial Board of Advisors
Motti Aviam, Michael Davis, Casey Elledge, Loren Johns, Amy-Jill Levine, Lee McDonald, Lidia Novakovic, Gerbern Oegema, Henry Rietz, Brent Strawn

Persian Influence on Daniel and Jewish Apocalyptic Literature

Vicente Dobroruka

t&tclark
LONDON • NEW YORK • OXFORD • NEW DELHI • SYDNEY

T&T CLARK
Bloomsbury Publishing Plc
50 Bedford Square, London, WC1B 3DP, UK
1385 Broadway, New York, NY 10018, USA
29 Earlsfort Terrace, Dublin 2, Ireland

BLOOMSBURY, T&T CLARK and the T&T Clark logo are trademarks of
Bloomsbury Publishing Plc

First published in Great Britain 2022
Paperback edition published 2023

Copyright © Vicente Dobroruka, 2022

Vicente Dobroruka has asserted his right under the Copyright, Designs and Patents Act, 1988, to be
identified as Author of this work.

For legal purposes the Acknowledgements on p. xiii constitute an extension
of this copyright page.

All rights reserved. No part of this publication may be reproduced or
transmitted in any form or by any means, electronic or mechanical,
including photocopying, recording, or any information storage or retrieval
system, without prior permission in writing from the publishers.

Bloomsbury Publishing Plc does not have any control over, or responsibility for, any
third-party websites referred to or in this book. All internet addresses given in this book were correct at
the time of going to press. The author and publisher regret any inconvenience caused if addresses have
changed or sites have ceased to exist, but can accept no responsibility for any such changes.

A catalogue record for this book is available from the British Library.

Library of Congress Cataloging-in-Publication Data
Names: Dobroruka, Vicente, 1969– author.
Title: Persian influence on Daniel and Jewish apocalyptic literature / Vicente Dobroruka.
Other titles: Jewish and Christian texts in contexts and related studies ; v. 19. Description: London ;
New York : T&T Clark, 2022. | Series: Jewish and Christian texts in contexts and related studies ; 19 |
Includes bibliographical references and index. | Summary: "Vicente Dobroruka explores Iranian influence
on Second Temple Judaism, providing a new explanation of Persian culture and history in the context
of biblical accounts by focusing on the spread of Zoroastrian ideas in the period c.300 BCE – 200 CE.
Dobroruka begins his investigation with an overview of the problems posed by a dualistic worldview –
he examines the Indo-European origins of Zarathushtra and his ideas, the long-term implications for the
notion of free-will, and clarifies the lightness/darkness paradigm that originated in Persia. Following this,
Dobroruka discusses a variety of concepts that illustrate this influence, such as the role of matter and
the material world, aspects of dualism and the cosmic struggle, the perspectives on the rewards for the
just and the opposing punishments for the wicked, the idea of an 'Anointed One', shamanistic visionary
experience, the resurrection, and the concepts of Sheol and Paradise"– Provided by publisher
Identifiers: LCCN 2021054767 (print) | LCCN 2021054768 (ebook) |
ISBN 9780567205056 (hardback) | ISBN 9780567705280 (pdf)
Subjects: LCSH: Bible. Daniel–Criticism, interpretation, etc. |
Zoroastrianism–Relations–Judaism. | Judaism–History–Post-exilic
period, 586 B.C.–210 A.D. | Apocalyptic literature–History and criticism.
Classification: LCC BS1555.52 .D63 2022 (print) | LCC BS1555.52 (ebook) |
DDC 224/.506–dc23/eng/20211208
LC record available at https://lccn.loc.gov/2021054767
LC ebook record available at https://lccn.loc.gov/2021054768

ISBN: HB: 978-0-5672-0505-6
PB: 978-0-5677-0529-7
ePDF: 978-0-5677-0528-0

Series: Jewish and Christian Texts in Contexts and Related Studies, volume 19

Typeset by Newgen KnowledgeWorks Pvt. Ltd., Chennai, India

To find out more about our authors and books visit www.bloomsbury.com
and sign up for our newsletters.

To my father, Luiz Camillo Dobroruka

To my wife, Anna Beatriz

To Bernd, Hans, Elly, Rudi, Carol and Bubi the very best companions, now in garōdmān; may they continue to follow, inspire and advise me

Contents

Foreword *James H. Charlesworth*	ix
Acknowledgements	xiii
Abbreviations	xvii
Introduction: A review of some issues related to this research topic	1
1 Good and Evil in a clash of civilizations and ideas	21
2 The role of matter and the material world	51
3 Aspects of dualism: Pairs of opposites and the cosmic fight in Zoroastrian texts	83
4 GŠR, or crossing the bridge: A similarity with *Činwad*?	109
5 Visionary experiences: Striking parallels, first-hand accounts and pseudepigrapha	139
6 Meta-historical schemes	161
Conclusion: Towards a great future	199
Bibliography	209
Index of passages	231

Foreword: Persian perspicacity perceived in ancient Palestine history

In 536 BCE, Cyrus II, the founder of the first Persian Empire (the Achaemenid Empire), became King of Persia. He is called 'the anointed' or 'the messiah' in Isa 45:1.

כֹּה־אָמַר יְהוָה לִמְשִׁיחוֹ לְכוֹרֶשׁ אֲשֶׁר־הֶחֱזַקְתִּי בִימִינוֹ לְרַד־לְפָנָיו גּוֹיִם וּמָתְנֵי מְלָכִים אֲפַתֵּחַ לִפְתֹּחַ לְפָנָיו דְּלָתַיִם וּשְׁעָרִים לֹא יִסָּגֵרוּ׃

Thus says the LORD to his anointed, to Cyrus:

'His right hand I have grasped to subdue before him nations,
And to strip kings of robes,
to open before him doors;
and the gates shall not be closed.' (Isa 45:1 now poetically arranged)

One of Cyrus's first edicts was to allow the captured Israelites in Mesopotamia to return to their homeland and to Jerusalem. Within Babylon, Second Isaiah (Isa 40–54) had been added to the teaching of Isaiah (Isa 1–39) and Ezekiel shared his idiosyncratic thoughts. Then, Nehemiah, Ezra and Zerubbabel migrated homeward.

Soon, the earliest sections of the *Books of Enoch* were composed in the Land of Israel, now called Judaea, and Jewish interest in astrology and astronomy began in earnest and is evident in a large Qumran scroll that was abbreviated into chapters 72 to 82 in the *Books of Enoch*. Babylonian astrology most likely shaped these chapters. The author of chapters 89 and 93 cast aspersions on those who returned from Babylon; they were polluted and apostates. Clearly, Persian culture helped to shape the multifaceted world of Early Judaism (*c*.300 BCE–200 CE).

These apparently new insights are not necessarily so novel, as Mesopotamian culture has long been recognized in the biblical books (Old and New Testaments). For example, the Epic of Gilgamesh was obviously mirrored in Genesis 1–3 and a copy of Gilgamesh was unearthed in Megiddo, proving that Mesopotamian culture influenced those in the Promised Land long before Joshua, David and Solomon. Consequently, we have proof that influence from the East is obvious within Palestinian thought beginning about 1850 BCE, the supposed date when Abraham migrated from Babylon to Palestine, until the codification of the Mishnah not long after 200 CE and the codification of ancient traditions in the Babylonian Talmud.

Persian loanwords in early Jewish languages

Persian loanwords are found in Palestinian Aramaic and Hebrew. In the TANAKH (Old Testament), Persian loanwords are found in four late post-exilic books, namely Esther, Daniel, Ezra-Nehemiah and Chronicles.

The most obvious Persian loanwords in pre-70 CE Hebrew and Aramaic are the following:

ganzak: 'treasury'; cf. the noun גנזא, 'treasure'.
rabmag: 'high priest'. The compound noun is from Hebrew *rab*, 'great' and Persian *mag*.
apadana: 'audience hall'; cf. noun אפדנא and ܐܦܕܢܐ, 'palace'.
datta: 'what is given'; cf. the noun דת, דתא, ܕܬܐ, 'law'. The noun *datt*, 'law' is common in Daniel and Ezra-Nehemiah.
qinamon: 'cinnamon'; cf. the noun קנמון and the nouns ܩܘܢܡܐ and ܩܘܢܡܐ.

More importantly, Persian ideas and concepts significantly shaped Jewish thought and helped pave the stimulus for the development of apocalyptic theology. For example, old Iranian *pairidaēza* first denoted 'a wall enclosing a king's garden' or 'walled garden' as in Song of Songs (*pardes*). Eventually this noun signified 'paradise'. The Persian source seems to be *pardeiz*. In early Jewish apocryphal and apocalyptic texts 'paradise' was imagined to be on earth far to the north or to the east. In the Jewish apocalypses, paradise was situated in one of the heavens, subsequently in the Third Heaven and then higher heavens.

Similarly, *raz* is a Persian loanword in Hebrew and Aramaic and well known in Israel today. It means 'mystery'. All forms of Jewish mysticism, from about 300 BCE to the pre-Medieval *Sefer haRazim* (ספר הרזים) until today, were developed because of this word, *raz*, and the reflections it generated.

Fecund thought

The sources for Zoroastrianism post-date Zoroaster (Zarathushtra; c.628 BCE–c.551 BCE) by many centuries; the extant texts are medieval and show evolutions of thought. Apparently, this Persian genius taught a dualism that is both cosmological and ontological. Zoroastrianism is a religion (and philosophy) in which a tendency towards monotheism coexisted with an explicit dualism. Two beings are opposed. The celestial world is created by two powers or beings. The cosmological dualism is also ethical: truth versus falsehood, good versus evil and virtue versus vices. What enables this system to work are the choices by all, spirits and humans.

Zurvanism, the extinct 'heretical' branch of Zoroastrianism, has been incorrectly dated to the Christian period; most likely it emerged in the late Achaemenid Empire, between 550 and 330 BCE, and became more dominant during the Sasanian Empire, or 224–651 CE. In this aspect of Zoroastrianism, the god Zurvan (time) is the 'father' of twins: Ahura Mazda represents good and light. He is opposed by Angra Mainya who represents darkness and evil. Thus, a form of monotheism ultimately shaped an apparent absolute dualism.

The dualism of the Persian Zurvanites profoundly influenced the insights in Qumran thought. It significantly shaped the Essene's most definitive text, the *Rule of the Community*. In columns three and four of this scroll, the Angel (Spirit) of Light protects the Sons of Light against the Angel (Spirit) of Darkness who misleads all humans, especially the Sons of Darkness. This dualism is limited. Each Spirit or Angel is inferior, in time and power, to 'the God of Knowledge' who is the source of all, all powerful and eternal. This modified dualism influenced the author of the Gospel of John:

εἶπεν οὖν αὐτοῖς ὁ Ἰησοῦς,"Ἔτι μικρὸν χρόνον τὸ φῶς ἐν ὑμῖν ἐστιν. περιπατεῖτε ὡς τὸ φῶς
ἔχετε, ἵνα μὴ σκοτία ὑμᾶς καταλάβῃ· καὶ ὁ περιπατῶν ἐν τῇ σκοτίᾳ οὐκ οἶδεν ποῦ ὑπάγει.
ὡς τὸ φῶς ἔχετε, πιστεύετε εἰς τὸ φῶς, ἵνα υἱοὶ φωτὸς γένησθε.

Therefore, Jesus said to them:
'A little time the light is in (with) you.
Walk while you have the light,
In order that darkness does not overtake you.
And the one walking in darkness does not know where he goes.
While you have the light believe in the light,
So that you may become Sons of Light.' (John 12:35)

How did the Persians influence the Palestinian Jews? Zurvanite dualism could have influenced Israelites in Persia who subsequently returned to their homeland, shaped the thought of Palestinians as caravans crisscrossed ancient Palestine and shaped the discussions of other merchants and diplomats in numerous areas of the world. After the Persian invasion of Palestine in 40 BCE, causing the senate in Rome to appoint Herod the Great to be King of the Jews, this dualism would be present to influence later Essenes. They would have been in Judaea and might have helped shape the new thoughts within the early Christian community in Jerusalem, in which the first edition of the Gospel of John was most likely composed.

Vicente Dobroruka's insights

Since the 1960s, when I sought to explain Persian influence on Qumran thought, I yearned for a specialist on Old Persian to provide a study of how and in what ways Persian language, culture and thought had helped shape early Jewish culture and the origins of Christianity within Judaism. In the present monograph, Vicente Dobroruka provides this *desideratum* for specialists.

Dobroruka has published research that prepare him for this special task; note these articles:

2006: 'Chemically-Induced Visions in the Fourth Book of Ezra in Light of
   Comparative Persian Material'
2012: 'Hesiodic reminiscences in Zoroastrian-Hellenistic apocalypses'
2014: 'Zoroastrian apocalyptic and Hellenistic Political Propaganda'
2014: 'The order of metals in Daniel 2 and in Persian apocalyptic'
2019: 'Eunus: royal obverse, messianic preacher, firebreather and avenger of Syria'
2020: 'Mithridates and the Oracle of Hystaspes: some dating issues'

The evidence is now abundant that Persian language and culture helped Jewish culture in ancient Palestine. I shall leave it to others to discern how significant such influence was and whether Persia or Greece had the most profound influences within Palestinian Judaism before 70 CE.

I wish to express my appreciations to Dobroruka for contributing this book to my series and to Brandon Allen for helping me prepare the work for publication.

James H. Charlesworth
Princeton, NJ
30 May 2020

Acknowledgements

I would like to thank a number of people who inspired, helped or otherwise had some part to play in this project. First of all, James H. Charlesworth, who suggested the theme, and the book project, during a trip of mine to Princeton; without him, this would never have taken place. I am grateful to a large extent to John J. Collins (Yale, now retired), who urged me a long time ago to write this book – back then, in 2002 or 2003, it looked like a distant proposition, and I hope I came up with some work living to his expectations; Chris Rowland (Oxford, retired) and Martin Goodman (Oxford) have, during many years, insisted that I could take on the job.

I must not forget the great group of Iranologists I came to know in the course of these years, but especially after my stay in Cambridge during 2010 as Visiting Fellow; people from Clare Hall and from the Ancient India and Iran Trust have since been instrumental in everything I did – special thanks must go here to Almut Hintze, Nicholas Sims-Williams (School of Oriental and African Studies, London, retired) and his wife Ursula Sims-Williams (British Library, London), Sam Lieu (Macquarie University, Sydney) and Rastin Mehri (School of Oriental and African Studies, London). From the other side of the Atlantic, Touraj Daryaee (UCLA) and Yuhan Vevaina (Stanford) were crucial, either by means of comments or due to their published work itself. I can only say the same regarding Carlo G. Cereti (La Sapienza, Rome; as nice as a scholar and a friend as one can be), Domenico Agostini (The Van Leer Jerusalem Institute), Matteo Compareti (Berkeley, at the time of this publication), Miguel-Ángel Andres Toledo (Salamanca; another scholar whom I can only praise, personal and professional-like) and Dan Shapira (Bar-Ilan University, Tel Aviv).

Zeke Kassock (University of Mary Washington, Fredericksburg) deserves a separate note of gratitude not just for his support and friendship but also for all the toils in editing so much Pahlavi or Pazend material; this made my work and that of many other scholars in the field easier. It will be reckoned in the future that his contribution to Pahlavi students all over the world was immense. The informal title of *dānešmand* bestowed upon him is well deserved. Basil Lourié (St. Petersburg State University) helped me get more texts I could not find than I can remember, always in good humour and goodwill. Ms Simin Dokht Goodarzi from Tehran sent me much needed material, unavailable in the circumstances of writing this book.

This is not a side note, but since I work in the 'no-man's land' between Zoroastrianism and Second Temple Judaism, being part of the Enoch Seminar, the great scholarly group reunited by Gabriele Boccaccini (University of Michigan) allowed me to draft and expose to my peers many a chapter from this book. In this respect, there are people from the Enoch Seminar that in one way or another became invaluable critics and sometimes friends. I wish to thank André Gagné (Concordia, Toronto), Loren Stuckenbruck (Munich), Lorenzo DiTommaso (Concordia, Toronto) and, with special warmth, Michael E. Stone (Hebrew University, Emeritus). Besides the scholars above, others who dealt primarily with languages by their own sake were very important in shaping my ideas as a graduate and then as a colleague: I wish to say a very warm thank you to Alison Salvesen (Oxford); Charlotte Hempel (University of Birmingham); Emmanouela Grypeou (Stockholm University); Farhad Sasani, Marzi Razavi and Sara Kiani (Alzahra University, Tehran); and Charlotte de Blois (JRAS). Catarina Belo (Oriental Institute, Oxford, now professor at the American University, Cairo) was a great friend who helped me through DPhil and beyond: life would be far less colourful without her.

Patience does not describe the attitude of my editors at Bloomsbury. They put up with delays, health issues and all sorts of trouble always in a supportive and graceful manner. Dominic Mattos, Miriam Cantwell and Sarah Blake were the best editors I could deal with, as well as Brandon Allen at the final stages of the typescript.

Finally, I must express my gratitude to a number of students and colleagues who have discussed, shared or rejected some of the ideas contained herein: Raul Vitor Rodrigues Peixoto was not only an awesome student to supervise but also shared many of the subtleties of Pahlavi texts with me. I can only repeat this praise to Ayub Naser (now in Groningen, PhD), but this time regarding Farsi and Arabic, and to Tupá Guerra (University of Birmingham, PhD) for undiluted support in stormy weather. My junior research group, composed of Ana Carolina Bittencourt Leite, Andreza Carvalho, Débora Fontenele, Igor Leite, Paula Djanine, Samantha Alves de Sousa and Stephany Guedes Krause (in alphabetical order), were a family in their own right. The unflinching friendship of Ana Carolina Paranhos and Rodrigo Carvalho cannot be forgotten as well as that of Luiza Larangeira da Silva Mello – a talent whose growth I witnessed almost since her childhood.

Isabela Ramos had a very special role in revising and editing the first (readable) drafts of the typescript, and her support was also unwavering throughout good and bad weather. I hope she has profited (as a historian-in-the-making) as much as I did while working together; it was fun and very rewarding.

The originals have been extensively revised regarding English by Giovana Lins Braga and Letícia Santos, with the content normalized by Leticia; Giovana and Letícia worked long hours to get a passable draft. Giovana was already a trusted friend who will also make it to the academic professional cadre. My gratitude towards them is mandatory, and so is the careful and acute criticism by Matthias Henze. Matthias did more than just check on the development of this book; he was the most present friend when I was out of steam due to previous dishonest reviewing.

E. Tigchelaar showed me some issues in the Dead Sea Scrolls for which I am thankful.

Last but not least, here are a few people that made the difference from the beginning: Arno Vogel, for his advice and trust; and Marcelo Gantus Jasmin, Ilmar Rohloff de Mattos, Selma Rinaldi de Mattos and all the staff at the history department from the Pontifical Catholic University of Rio de Janeiro (PUC-Rio). I owe you more than you will ever know. I am glad to extend my thankful note to all my former teachers in that remarkable institution – and also to a gifted Orientalist who never had any trouble in wearing the mantle, Carmen Lícia Palazzo.

Any faults, mistakes and omissions in this book are, of course, entirely my own.

Were it not for the constant and unflinching companionship of Bernd, Hans, Achille, Ilse, Paula, Rudi, Tazio, Norma, Carolina, Bubi and Nimzo, this work would have been much harder to conclude. This is why it is, to a very great extent, theirs too, although some of them did not live long enough to get their own copies.

An amazing woman was, to a great extent, inspirational to this work: Christiane A. Blatter. May this book be up to the expectations you always held regarding my choices.

This work is dedicated to the most important and loving person I ever knew – my father, Luiz Camillo Dobroruka. It is also dedicated to my team of home companions, depicted above, now gone. May we all meet in *garōdmān* when the time comes; this would be the better life indeed.

Abbreviations

General

Akk.	Akkadian
Aram.	Aramaic
Arab.	Arabic
As.	Assyrian
ASC	altered state of consciousness
Av.	Avestan
BDB	*Brown-Driver-Briggs Hebrew and English Lexicon*
BW	*BibleWorks 7.0.* Version 7.0.012g. Copyright BibleWorks, 2006 (applies to versions of the Hebrew Bible, Peshitta, Vulgata, LXX and Greek NT, unless otherwise noted. They will be quoted in the original language in footnotes or in the main text, whenever especially relevant for the issue discussed)
CPD	David N. MacKenzie. *A Concise Pahlavi Dictionary*. Abingdon: RoutledgeCurzon, 2006. [reprint]
DSS	Florentino García-Martínez and Eibert J. C.Tigchelaar. *The Dead Sea Scrolls Study Edition* (2 vols). Leiden: Brill, 1999.
FPP	fantasy-prone personality
Gr.	Greek
HZ	Mary Boyce and Franz Grenet. *A History of Zoroastrianism* (3 vols). Leiden: Brill, 1975–91.
HB	Hebrew Bible
Heb.	Hebrew
het.	heterogram (Far. *huzvarish*)
IE	Indo-European
Kindle loc.	Sometimes electronic editions in the property of the author were used in the e-reader Kindle, which usually gives 'locations' (a sort of percentage of the physical book the reader would be in); however, I sometimes used printed sources for the same books, hence the simultaneous use of them throughout this book.

Throughout the book the reader will notice differences in writing the name of Zaraθuštra. This is an option I made long ago since that spelling seems to me to convey more of the ancient scripts in which he name of the religious leader was spelled. A note is in order here, because the use of 'Zoroaster' is restricted to Greek, Roman or East Roman usage. The rest of the variant spellings ('Zathustra', 'Zardošt', 'Zardosht', etc.) was kept as found in the original editions or sources, so as to not change their authors' way of seeing it.

LXX	Septuagint
MP	Middle Persian
MMP	Manichaean Middle Persian
ms.	manuscript
mss	manuscripts
MT	Masoretic Text
NP	New Persian (Farsi)
ODLA	*Oxford Dictionary of Late Antiquity*
OP	Old Persian
Oss.	Ossetian
*PIE	Proto Indo-European
Pz.	Pazand
RV	Rig Veda
Sans.	Sanskrit
SBE	*Sacred Books of the East*. Oxford: Oxford Uiversity Press, several editions since the end of the nineteenth century when this gigantic series enterprise was undertaken by Friedrich M. Müller. Several of them are still quite readable when not still the standard editions and are useful, especially when compared to more recent studies on a defined field.
Syr.	Syriac
PT	possessional trance
Ved.	Vedic
Vulg.	Vulgate

Primary sources

Hebrew Bible

Abbreviations used herein follow usual conventions of SBL and Sheffield University; being canonical and, thus, well-known works, it seems superfluous to put down such abbreviations here. Throughout this book quotations from Bible translations or secondary literature use interchangeably 'God', 'LORD', 'the Lord God' and 'Yahweh', among others, and I kept them in order not to meddle with other authors' texts. There is no religious, political or in any way disrespectful bias on this. See below a similar disclaimer regarding Persian sources in general.

Early Christian

OH *Oracles of Hystaspes*

Apocrypha and Pseudepigrapha

1 En.	Ethiopic Book of Enoch
2 Bar.	Syriac Apocalypse of Baruch
3 Bar.	Greek Apocalypse of Baruch
3 En.	Hebrew Book of Enoch
4 Bar.	Fourth Book of Baruch
4 Ezra	Fourth Book of Ezra
Apoc. Ab.	Apocalypse of Abraham
Ascen. Isa.	Ascension of Isaiah
Mart. Isa.	Martyrdom of Isaiah
Sib. Or.	Sibylline Oracles
T. 12 Patr.	Testament of the Twelve Patriarchs
T. Levi	Testament of Levi

Persian

Throughout this book quotations from Persian translations or secondary literature use, whenever possible, the MP forms, because they are the most usual in the context of our discussion – which is a late one, either due to our external criticism of primary sources or to more common usage by scholars (e.g. 'Ahuramazda' = 'Ohrmazd'; 'Angra Mainyu' = 'Ahriman'). When other forms appear in quotations, titles of works or sources in general I kept them as they appeared (i.e. literally) in order not to meddle with other authors' texts. Other names (usually proper names) are trickier as they came to English via Greek and Latin as a rule (unless we are dealing with very specialized literature on the subject). Well-known examples would be 'Zoroaster' for 'Zaraθuštra' or 'Hystaspes' for 'Vištasp'. But the Hellenized forms were kept, as a rule, for strict use of Zoroastrian names in Greek, Latin oracles or other texts (these normally present themselves in Christian garb as spurious late attempts to legitimate then rising Christianity with prophecy *ex-eventu*, using Persian household names such as the two quoted above). There is no religious, political or in any way disrespectful bias on this and the same applies to titles of Zoroastrian works unless their primitive form is subject to doubt or a common-English form took its place (e.g. 'Avesta' for 'Auuestā'). See above a similar disclaimer regarding HB sources in general.

AiP	Ardashir-i Papagan
AiZ	Ayadgar-i Zamaspik
AWN	Ardā Wirāz Nāmag
Bd	Bundahišn (Domenico Agostini and Samuel Thorpe. *The Bundahišn. The Zoroastrian Book of Creation*. New York: Oxford University Press, 2020)
BY	Bahman Yasht
CV	Conversion of Vištapa
DD	Dadestan-i Denig
Dk	Dēnkard
FiP	Frahang-i Pahlāvik
FrYt	Frawardin Yašt

GrBd	Greater Bundahišn (Behramgore T. Anklesaria. *Zand-Akasih. Iranian or Greater Budahishn. Transliteration and Translation in English*. Bombay: Feeroze Madressa, published for the Rahnumae Mazdayasnan Sabha by its Honorary Secretary Dastur Framroze A. Bode, 1956)
HN	*Hādōkht Nask*
KIns	Kirdēr inscription (general)
KKZ	Kirdēr inscription (Ka'ba-ye Zardošt)
KSM	Kirdēr inscription (Sar-e Mašhad)
KNRb	Kirdēr inscription (Naqš-e Rajab)
KNRm	Kirdēr inscription (Naqs-i Rustam)
JN	Jamasp Namag
MX	Mēnōg ī Xrad
NPi	Kirdēr inscription (Paikuli, Iraq)
OAv.	Old Avesta
PahRiv	Pahlavi Rivayat
Shahn.	*Shahnameh* (Abolqasem Ferdowsi. *Shahnameh: The Persian Book of Kings*. New York: Penguin, 2006)
SGW	*Škand Gumānig Wičar*
SKZ	Kirdēr inscription (with Narseh I)
SZ	Selections of Zadspram
Vd	Vendidad / Videvdat
WD	Wizirkard-i Denig
Y	Yasna
YAv.	Young Avesta
YH	Yasna Haptaŋgāiti
Yt	Yašt, or Yasht
ZA	Zend Avesta
ZN	Zardoštnama
ZWY	*Zand-i Wahman Yasn*
ZY	Zamyād Yašt

Other early Jewish and Christian literature

BJ	Josephus, *Bellum Judaicum*
CA	Josephus, *Contra Apionem*
V	Josephus, *Vita*

Classical

Arist., *Frogs*	Aristophanes, *Frogs*
WD	Hesiod, *Works and Days*
RGDS	Res Gestae Divi Saporis

Secondary sources

ActAnt	Acta Antiqua Academiae Scientiarum Hungaricae
Acta Iranica	*Acta Iranica, Encyclopédie permanente des Études Iraniennes*. Deuxième Série. Leiden: Brill.
AJCH	*American Journal of Clinical Hypnosis*
AJCHH	*Australian Journal of Clinical Hypnotherapy and Hypnosis*
AJT	*American Journal of Theology*
AJSR	*Association for Jewish Studies Review*
AMI	*Archäologische Mitteilungen aus Iran*
AMWNE	Daniel Hellholm (ed.). *Apocalypticism in the Mediterranean World and the Near East: Proceedings of the International Colloquium on Apocalypticism, Uppsala, August 12-17, 1979*. Tübingen: Mohr, 1983.
ANF	Alexander Roberts and James Donaldson (eds). *The Ante-Nicene Fathers. Translations of the Writings of the Fathers down to A.D. 325*. Edinburgh: T&T Clark, 1989.
ATR	*Anglican Theological Review*
Bib.	*Biblica*
BzI.	*Beiträge zur Iranistik*
BN	*Biblische Notizen*
BSOAS	*Bulletin of the School of Oriental and African Studies*
CBQ	*Catholic Biblical Quarterly*
CHIr	*Cambridge History of Iran*
CHJ	*Cambridge History of Judaism*
DDD	Karel van der Toorn, Bob Becking and Pieter W. Van der Horst. *Dictionary of Deities and Demons in the Bible* (2nd ed.). Leiden: Brill, 1999.
EA	*Ex Auditu*
EI	*Encyclopedia of Islam*
EIr	*Encyclopaedia Iranica*
ExpTim	*Expository Times*
FrGH	Felix Jacoby. *Die Fragmente der griechischen Historiker*. Leiden: Brill, 2003. [CD-ROM edition]
HPL	Ronald E. Emmerick and Maria Macuch. *The Literature of Pre-Islamic Iran: A Companion to A History of Persian Literature*. London: I.B. Tauris, 2009.
HTR	*Harvard Theological Review*
HZ	Mary Boyce and Frantz Grenet. *History of Zoroastrianism* (3 vols). Leiden: Brill, 1975–91.
IrAnt	*Iranica Antiqua*
IIJ	*Indo-Iranian Journal*
IJAIS	*Nāme-ye Irān-e Bāstān. The International Journal of Ancient Iranian Studies*
Int.	*Interpretation*

JA	*Journal Asiatique*
JAAR	*Journal of the American Academy of Religion*
JAAS	*Journal of Asian and African Studies*
JAOS	*Journal of the American Oriental Society*
JBL	*Journal of Biblical Literature*
JHS	*Journal of Hellenic Studies*
JKR	*Journal of the K.R.Cama Institute*
JNES	*Journal of Near Eastern Studies*
JRAS	*Journal of the Royal Asiatic Society*
JSAI	*Jerusalem Studies in Arabic and Islam*
JSIJ	*Jewish Studies, an Internet Journal*
JSOT	*Journal for the Study of the Old Testament*
JSP	*Journal for the Study of the Pseudepigrapha*
JSS	*Journal of Semitic Studies*
JTS	*Journal of Theological Studies*
LCL	Loeb Classical Library
LSJ	Henry George Liddell, Robert Scott and Henry Stuart Jones. *A Greek-English Lexicon*. 9th edn with revised supplement. Oxford: Clarendon Press, 1996.
Mnem.	*Mnemosyne*
MOTP	Richard Bauckham, Jim Davila and Alexander Panayotov (eds). *Old Testament Pseudepigrapha: More Non-Canonical Scriptures*. Vol. 1. Grand Rapids: Eerdmans, 2013.
NT	*Novum Testamentum*
NTP	Wilhelm Schneemelcher (ed.). *New Testament Apocrypha*. Vol. 2. London: Lutterworth Press, 1965.
NTS	*New Testament Studies*
OHIR	*Oxford Handbook of Iranian History*
OTP	James Charlesworth (ed.). *The Old Testament Pseudepigrapha* (2 vols). New York: Doubleday, 1983–85.
RB	*Revue Biblique*
SBE	Friedrich M. Müller (ed.). *The Sacred Books of the East*. Oxford: Oxford University Press.
SIr	*Studia Iranica*
TB	*Tyndale Bulletin*
TH	Daniel Theodotion's recension
Th.	*Themelios*
VT	*Vetus Testamentum*
WBCZ	*Wiley-Blackwell Companion to Zoroastrianism*
ZDMG	*Zeitschrift der Deutschen Morgenländischen Gesellschaft*

Introduction: A review of some issues related to this research topic

§1 A brief review of literature

This work presents my long-term thoughts and research on the theme of Second Temple Judaism and some aspects of Zoroastrianism that may have helped shape the former. Like so many things from each person's youth, as a student and then a junior researcher I took for granted some of these aspects as 'obvious' facts, which needed only to be bound together. As I grew older and gathered more primary and secondary literature (that have also become exponentially larger since the 1990s), I discovered that what I regarded as answers were, in fact, questions. This made the work even more pleasant to do, but whatever 'influence' I thought was obvious then proved to be just another problem to be tracked down and investigated (to be fair enough, more than three generations of scholars adopted the same procedure, even in their mature days; but then again not all that glitters is gold). My assumptions became more modest, and despite the title of this book, it is about 'parallels' rather than 'influence' that we will be talking about most of the time. I insist that this is for the better, at least for me: giving away some preconceptions made me better, and I never ceased to look after whatever Zoroastrianism could have in common with Second Temple Judaism.

That being said, as an 'introduction' to a work such as this book, many distinct approaches could be tried. I have chosen to follow the route of the six most relevant issues in the guise of sections or chapters.

This means that this introduction will present the most pressing issues all in one piece but divided in several subsections. This allows some freedom to go back and forth between specific literature, epistemological problems and personal doubts that together weave the cloth of which this book is the result. This format was *not* chosen for fancy reasons, or because it was ordered. I rather felt I should try to present matters in that format so as not to become enmeshed in the subtleties of Iranian studies that are of scarce interest to the average reader or the commonplaces of *Einfluß-Studien* regarding the possible relations between Persia and Second Temple Judaism.[1]

---

[1] Typical examples of the latter are Edwin M. Yamauchi. *Persia and the Bible*. Grand Rapids: Baker Book House, 1990; and Jon Berquist. *Judaism in Persia's Shadow*. Minneapolis: Fortress Press, 1995. A shorter – but in some ways smarter – attempt to address some of these issues had been done by David Winston. 'The Iranian component in the Bible, Apocrypha and Qumran: A review of the

A parallel discussion is that the very idea of the survival of the soul, in the sense that it was practised by Zoroastrians, may have a textual history of its own. That is to say that due to the comparatively poor quality and quantity of textual material along with the consequent discussions regarding their dating, we have to rely on ideas that are not necessarily dependent on the dating or even the existence of Zaraθuštra himself.[2]

§2 Did Zaraθuštra exist?

One may ask whether this is a history of ideas in the sense of 'small ideas' (i.e. in terms of everyday life and of what the common person may have thought or felt about a given issue) or if it is a history of 'great ideas' (and, as a consequence, of 'great men'[3]), since many of the characters named or taken in pseudepigraphic form are definitely not 'common men'[4] by any standard, even if they may have shared mental attitudes, tastes and, generally speaking, ways of living with their fellow men in a given time frame. But the mere fact that we have here a bunch of texts that determined, to an immense extent, what Iranians believed to a certain date (including our own contemporary) regarding eschatological issues, it would seem farcical to me to pretend that a study of the nomad commoner would mean the same as a study of Zaraθuštra (beginning with the very assumptions on his existence). The commoner may share with the remarkable many similar features of his life (collective mentality, folk tales, material life), while the opposite is not true. This holds true even more when dealing with religion-founders, mythical or historical.

The question of the role of the 'great man', once the main issue that historians did care about, became the only one during the last seven decades or so, mostly because of the deprecating stand taken by the French of the *Annales* on the theme. Histories of the masses, of collective *mentalitées*, of economic cycles and even of climate seemed always to take precedence regarding the once-recognized great figures of the past – but for some reason Ancient History seems to have been more or less forgotten by such fashions, as ancient historians and classicists remind us every now and then. In

---

evidence' in: *History of Religions* 5 (1966): 183–216. More recent works, of better quality and more insightful, will be mentioned as the text goes on.

[2] On the theme of Zaraθuštra's dating again, for a more conservative approach that locates him at the end of the Bronze Age, cf. Martin L. West. *The Hymns of Zaraθuštra: A New Translation of the Most Ancient Sacred Texts of Iran*. London: I.B.Tauris, 2010, Kindle loc. 188; and Martin L. West. *Old Avestan Syntax and Stylistics: With an Edition of the Texts*. Berlin: De Gruyter, 2011 (where he goes as far as to compare Avestan to Vedic tout-court, p. vi). For a bolder approach, cf. Helmut Humbach (in collaboration with Josef Elfenbein and Prods O. Skjærvø). *The Gāthās of Zarathustra and the Other Old Avestan Texts. Part I – Introduction – Text and Translation*. Heidelberg: Carl Winter – Universitätsverlag, 1994, pp. 3, 67, 73. Cf. also Helmut Humbach and Pallan Ichaporia. *The Heritage of Zarathustra. A New Translation of his Gāthās*. Heidelberg: Carl Winter – Universitätsverlag, 1994, pp. 10–15; and Jean Kellens. *Essays on Zarathustra and Zoroastrianism*. Costa Mesa: Mazda, 2000, p. xiii.

[3] I will follow the spelling that is closer to Avestan and MP, partly because it is closer to any other and partly because the name 'Zoroaster', as derived from Greek Ζωροάστρης or Latin *Zōroastrēs* (later form *Zōroastris*), can be used when referring to non-Persian, mostly Greek, Hellenistic or Roman sources.

[4] Karl Jaspers. *The Origin and Goal of History*. New Haven: Yale University Press, 1953, pp. 8, 22.

any case, I am not supporting the opposite view – that had in Karl Jaspers its greatest proponent – namely that there was an 'Axial time', or *Achsenzeit*, when simultaneously all over the Eurasian continent 'great men' appeared and changed forever, and at the same time, our modes of thinking and behaving.⁵

To hold such an opinion is, of course, entirely up to the individual, but definitely out of the scope of this book. Eventually, the above-referred *Achsenzeit* supposed that Zaraθuštra is to be included in the 'greats' of the middle of the First Millenium BCE⁶ – and this, in itself, is one of the main polemics among Iranalogists regarding the dating for the existence of the prophet Zaraθuštra, not to mention the main-picture discussion regarding the possibility of Zaraθuštra having never existed or that of his very name constitutes one of the big confusions in the history of religion.⁷

It is fair to say that part of the modern dating of Zaraθuštra is based on a sort of circular reasoning in order to place him together with the other 'big names' that would have composed the plethora of thinkers, reformers, tragedians, prophets and great names that have had, supposedly, marked the history of big ideas according to Jaspers himself and his followers.⁸

---

⁵ The bibliography alone on the theme occupies already some seventy pages on a critical work devoted to the theme: cf. Robert N. Bellah and Hans Joas (eds). 'Bibliography – Works on the Axial Age' in: *The Axial Age and Its Consequences*. Cambridge, MA: Harvard University Press, 2012, pp. 469–536.

⁶ The idea of *Achsenzeit* seems to have become a modern myth, one of those meta-historical standpoints that, once imagined, seem to have taken a life of their own; the literature on the 'Axial time' is long indeed and quite repetitive, with one remarkable exception – the critique of Jan Assman. 'Cultural Memory and the Myth of the Axial Time' in: Bellah and Joas. *The Axial Age and Its Consequences*, pp. 389–90. For a fresh approach to the theme of the ages of the world as Indo-Iranian myth, cf. Yuhan S.-D. Vevaina. 'Miscegenation, "Mixture", and "Mixed Iron": The Hermeneutics, Historiography, and Cultural Poesis of the "Four Ages" in Zoroastrianism' in: Philippa Townsend and Moulie Vidas (eds). *Revelation, Literature, and Community in Late Antiquity*. Tübingen: Mohr Siebeck, 2011, pp. 237–69.

⁷ Chief among modern Iranalogists who take this line of argument is Jean Kellens, in Jean Kellens and Eric Pirart. *Les textes vieil-avestiques* I. Text with foreword, translation and commentary. Wiesbaden: Reichert, 1988, pp. 4, 18–19. Common etymologies – that may lead to false cognates – are, mostly relating the prophet's name to camels, MP *uštar* (*CPD*, Ar. GMRA, 'wstl, NP *uštur*) plus derivative forms of Av. 'zarant', 'nervous', 'angry'; also Av. 'zarš', 'conducting', 'driving'; less reliable seems to be the link between the Vedic 'har' ('to desire') and Av. 'zara' (same meaning). The most popular etymology seems, however, to be MP 'zard', 'yellow', perhaps 'dirty' or 'dusty', plus *uštar* (also stemming from Av. 'zairi'; cf. *CPD*, 'zard', zlt', 'yellow' (see above); 'zarr', Ar. ZHBA, 'golden'; 'gard', glt', 'dust'): 'he who has a yellow [or dusty] camel'.

⁸ Dating of Zoroaster for Greeks is notoriously unreliable but does follow some patterns: the first one dating his existence according to *The Sack of Troy* (Zoroaster would have lived five thousand years before that, as quoted by Hermodoros in Diogenes Laertius's *Lives of the Eminent Philosophers* 1.2), or, alternatively, six thousand years before the invasion of Greece by Xerxes (Xanthus of Lydia, Eudoxos, Aristotle and Hermippus of Smyrna); the second (clearer but nonetheless prone to doubting as well) pointing to the times just before Darius I; the latter situates itself even in Zoroastrian sources (*WBCZ*, p. 3) putting Zoroaster as having lived '258 years' before Alexander the Great (this would mean *c*.588–590 BCE). The latter link would have seemed more plausible to ancient historiographers such as Ammianus Marcellinus, who relates Hystaspes (correctly singled out as Darius's father) to the mythical character, as the first king who adhered to Zaraθuštra's ideas. Cf. Abraham V. W. Jackson. 'On the Date of Zoroaster' in: *JAOS* 17 (1896): 1–22; Manfred Mayrhofer. *Zum Namengut des Avesta*. Vienna: Verlag der Österreichischen Akademie der Wissenschaften, 1977.

Regarding his geographical origins, it appears that Zaraθuštra is always linked to the easternmost parts of the Iranian plateau and beyond (i.e. to Central Asia).[9] He lived 77 years and 40 days according to some sources[10] and was apparently killed by a rival priest called Brādrēs.[11]

§3 What does 'influence' mean?

A book on the development of 'influences' of any thought system over another is the best way of describing the effort behind the present work – and also the best way to tell the reader what it was possible to do, what was not and what arguably never will be.

When we speak of 'influence', we are usually talking about an elusive thing – like its English derivative, 'influenza', a point not missed by John Pocock.[12] Worse still, the researcher may be incurring in a series of commonplace mistakes, well displayed and obligingly chastened by that great historian of great ideas, Quentin Skinner.[13] This happens because sometimes we are fortunate enough to be able to retrace a whole train of thought – who read what, in what period, and sometimes we can even track down different editions or similar nuances in the source investigated. But even in modern times it is not necessarily so: more than once we stumble upon an idea in 'X' that must be, cannot be indeed other than that old rationale first proposed by 'Y', in book, article or chapter 'Z'. This is why Pocock and Skinner are still (deservedly) remembered: for having cautioned us against such easy, taken-for-granted assumptions.

With the issue of Persian 'influence', the dreaded word, over Second Temple Judaism, it is precisely what happens. The Exile in Babylonia itself can be explained in more than one way – in terms of the sheer number of exiled, of the stories related to their remaining in Babylonia (this is the setting for Daniel 1–6, lest we forget) and what Jews may have absorbed there or in other places of the Diaspora.[14] However, this

---

[9] This is the location of the late form 'Goshtasp', cf. Shahn, pp. 369–70.
[10] HZ 1, pp. 188–9, with a vague reference to the 'tradition' but pointing more specifically to Yt 5.109.
[11] HZ 1, p. 192. A big deal of such polemics related to the dating of Zoroaster himself can be found in an article now quite old but with an interesting review of literature: Jarl Charpentier. 'The Date of Zoroaster' in: *BSOAS* 3 (1925): 4, where Charpentier contends vigorously against a dating in the sixth or seventh century for the flourishing of Zaraθuštra. The author also offers another spelling for the prophet's name, which according to him should be something like 'Zuraθuštra' (ibid., p. 748). Also of interest here is the picture presented by Late Antiquity writers that deal with dating and setting issues: cf. Jan W. Drijvers. 'Ammianus Marcelinus' Image of Sasanian Society' in: Josef Wiesehöfer and Philip Huyse (Hgs). *Ērān und Anērān: Studien zu den Beziehungen zwischen dem Sasanidenreich und der Mittelmeerwelt*. München: Franz Steiner, 2006, pp. 51, 59–65.
[12] John G. A. Pocock. *Politics, Language, and Time: Essays on Political Thought and History*. New York: Athenaeum, 1971, p. 204. The famous passage is that on Meinecke's feeble defence of the theory that Edmund Burke had read Hume without any hard proof of it but was nonetheless 'influenced' by Hume '"because it was in the air" [sic] and thus had infected Burke as a species of *influenza*'.
[13] Quentin Skinner. 'Meaning and Understanding in the History of Ideas' in: James Tully (ed.). *Meaning & Context: Quentin Skinner and his Critics*. New Jersey: Princeton University Press, 1988, pp. 29–32. Of special interest is Skinner's critique of the 'mythology of doctrines', which tends to make into wholesome doctrines issues that are, in fact, mere passing observations.
[14] Lester L. Grabbe. '"They shall come rejoicing to Zion" – or Did They? The Settlement of Yehud in the Early Persian Period' in: Gary N. Knoppers and Lester L. Grabbe with Deirdre N. Fulton (eds).

is not enough: time spent under Persian rule is the first factor to be taken into account, and yet it does not explain all we need – partly because of non-matching, conflicting or inexistent dating for the Persian sources.

That being so, I should – and the reader is well-advised to do so too – be very economical in using the term 'influence'. It is something that, in our case, has left its 'smell' on Second Temple Judaism, but we are not able to trace where it comes from. So, instead of catching Pocock's 'influenza', let us be careful here, as another possibility will be shown below.

§4 Jew and Zoroastrian in the Exile

Most people, scholarly minded or otherwise, will have no problems in agreeing that the resurrection of the dead appears first in what came to be known as the Hebrew Bible in Dan 12:2–3.[15] By the same reasoning, no rewards for the just could be expected in, say, Gen 37:35 when Jacob mourns for Joseph ('All his sons and all his daughters sought to comfort him; but he refused to be comforted, and said, "No, I shall go down to Sheol to my son, mourning." Thus his father bewailed him') or even more so in Eccl 9:3–5, 10:[16]

> This is an evil in all that happens under the sun, that the same fate comes to everyone. Moreover, the hearts of all are full of evil; madness is in their hearts while they live, and after that they go to the dead. But whoever is joined with all the living has hope, for a living dog is better than a dead lion. The living know that

---

Exile and Restoration Revisited: Essays on the Babylonian and Persian Periods in Memory of Peter R. Ackroyd. London: T&T Clark, 2009, pp. 117–22; for contacts between Jews and Zoroastrians, cf., among others, Christian Marek (in collaboration with Peter Frei). *In the Land of a Thousand Gods: A History of Asia Minor in the Ancient World*. Princeton: Princeton University Press, 2016. Marek refers here more specifically to 'influence' of the magoi to the Greeks (p. 154) and later to the Persian immigrants' interest in local cults and gods (pp. 162–3).

[15] John J. Collins. *Daniel, with an Introduction to Apocalyptic Literature*. Grand Rapids: William B. Eerdmans, 1984:

> On the surface, chs. 1 – 6 tell a series of stories about Jewish exiles in Babylon in the sixth century, one of whom was the recipient of the revelations which are presented in chs. 7–12. The impression that Daniel was the author of the book is derived from the first-person accounts in chs. 7–12 and the direct address of the angel in 12:4, 'you, Daniel, shut up the words, and seal the book.' By contrast, modern scholarship has held that Daniel is a legendary figure, that the stories in chs. 1–6 are no older than the Hellenistic period, and that the revelations in chs. 7–12 were written in the Maccabean period when the Syrian king Antiochus Epiphanes was persecuting the Jews.
>
> In short, the setting of the court tales in Dan 1–6 and the apocalypse proper (7–12) share a common 'pseudo-background', namely Babylon at the eve of its fall to the Persians. It is also noteworthy that a non-historical figure called 'Darius, the Mede' appears in Dan 5:31. Cf. also Rainer Albertz. 'The Social Setting of the Aramaic and Hebrew Book of Daniel' in: John J. Collins and Peter W. Flint (eds). *The Book of Daniel: Composition and Reception*. Leiden: Brill, 2001; and Lester L. Grabbe. 'A Dan(iel) for All Seasons: For Whom Was Daniel Important?' in: Collins and Flint. *The Book of Daniel*.

[16] *Qohelet*, or Ecclesiastes, can be dated roughly to the second century BCE – which means that it overlaps, in a sense, with the Danielic text as we came to know it, although proposing a much more conservative view of life and death.

they will die, but the dead know nothing; they have no more reward, and even the memory of them is lost. Their love and their hate and their envy have already perished; never again will they have any share in all that happens under the sun … Whatever your hand finds to do, do with your might; for there is no work or thought or knowledge or wisdom in Sheol,[17] to which you are going.

However, an entirely new and fresh perspective is revealed in Dan 12:2–3.[18] In fact, what would become 'canonical Daniel' will play a big role throughout this book.

Many of those who sleep in the dust of the earth shall awake, some to everlasting life, and some to shame and everlasting contempt. Those who are wise shall shine like the brightness of the sky, and those who lead many to righteousness, like the stars forever and ever.

But it must be noted that even if these 'developed afterlife' ideas are more common by far in Persian than in Jewish sources, that does not 'prove' a point, strictly speaking.

We may be facing other possibilities of development, and we should take them into account lest one is to incur what Bruce Metzger aptly called 'demonstrative borrowing', that is, to get some ideas (but not others), compare them with what we want to 'prove' and, *presto*, we have it done.[19] Frazer has done this – the results of his once-mandatory *The Golden Bough* are questionable by today's standards, despite the depth of his scholarship. Unfortunately, depth alone is not enough when dealing with material such as ours.

One view to be taken into account – already proposed by Herbert Rose in 1934[20] and familiar to Jungian students or patients – is that similar patterns of thought may be found in different, non-communicating cultures, thus 'proving' the universality of some traces in mankind. So, as Rose put it, we would have a 'polygenesis' of sorts, that is, the same ideas would have appeared in different places throughout the planet without a common root or cultural borrowings:

To my mind, the chief merit of such parallels is the very fact that they are taken from disparate cultures, such as never, on any reasonable theory, can have been part of one 'culture-circle', and therefore illustrate, not the historical development of a particular set of customs, but certain trends of human nature generally. They thus belong to the proper material of anthropology as such, and not to an outlying branch of history.[21]

To our modern perspective this looks almost too good to be true – and in fact, it is. What Rose claimed to be the explanation (namely what he calls 'human nature') is

---

[17] Heb. שְׁאוֹל; *BDB*, שְׁאוֹל, 'underworld', 'Hades', etc.
[18] For a simple and clear overview of traditional and heterodox Jewish views on survival of the soul, the world beyond and related matters, cf. Rifat Sonsino and Daniel B. Syme (eds). *What Happens after I Die? Jewish Views of Life after Death*. New York: URJ Press, 1990; and Simcha P. Raphael. *Jewish Views of the Afterlife*. Lanham: Rowman & Littlefield, 2009.
[19] Bruce Metzger. 'Forgeries and Canonical Pseudepigrapha' in: *JBL* 91.1 (1972): 8.
[20] Herbert J. Rose. *Concerning Parallels*. Oxford: Frazer Lecture, 1934.
[21] Ibid., p. 24.

precisely the problem, what needs to be explained rather than what explains. So I do not think it is a reasonable way of explaining why Dan 12:2 displays such common traces as other (maybe 'older') Persian materials claiming that 'human nature' is such that at a given time these or that ideas popped up.[22] Here we are again trapped in the *Achenzeit* theme, this time looking as if it were a device, so to speak, that would explain how certain themes make their first appearance as part of a *Zeitgeist*. I insist, however, that this is exactly what needs to be explained and not what explains the emergence of some concepts in a certain time and place.

These 'universal', 'human nature' or other teleological assumptions have no place in the current work, not because they are intrinsically wrong but because they are unscientific. Every man or woman has the right to cherish his/her own beliefs, but I underline the 'beliefs' here, which are the opposite of 'hard-proof' facts or deductions. There is nothing to *actually prove* that Persian ideas were taken by the writers of Daniel, or worse still, that these were 'in the air'.[23]

The other risk involved is that of taking similarities as borrowings 'by necessity'. One such fault of method could be given, for example, in the once fashionable claim that the DSS community was composed by the Essenes.[24] This may be so, but it is no longer held as a necessity for the researcher to hold true.

Looking back now, some seventy years after the DSS discovery, relatively few would make such a bold claim.[25] And yet, even if the Essenes never existed at all but were rather the fancy of Josephus and Philo to give their Greek audience a treat, which was repeated mindlessly by that great compiler, Pliny the Elder (d. 79 CE), the fact that they were once related 'hard-proof-like' to the scrolls is in itself a fascinating story, one that tells a lot about biblical scholarship in the middle of the twentieth century and also about the risks of the staunchest assumptions of the *Religionsgeschichtlicheschule* proposers. Speaking in a very sceptical way, there is no relation that can absolutely, doubtlessly be established between the ruins, the scrolls and the caves. Moreover, to

---

[22] On Jaspers and the meta-historical issues regarding the concept of *Achsenzeit*, cf. notes 3 and 4 (supra). It should be noted that the same reasoning has already become part of what the 'educated public' reads – a good example of that is the popular work on Jesus Christ by Paul Johnson. *Jesus: A Biography from a Believer*. New York: Penguin, 2010.

[23] A good case in question here goes back to the author of Ecclesiastes – there is an all-round flavour of Greek philosophical vulgarization in the text, which may well have been 'in the air' during the author's life. Another proposal is to claim that there is no influence (the dreaded word) of Greek thought in Ecclesiastes, first, because the Ecclesiastes author's train of thought can be found nearer, in Hebrew or Ancient Near Eastern sources, and, second, because there is no identifiable quotation of other Greek works in Ecclesiastes. We need not have a full-blossomed quotation, or borrowing, to prove this point, but at least identical, or very similar passages, should be looked out for. In their absence, there is room for much speculation – and even more so for vague and unproven assumptions.

[24] This view, as fairly well-informed readers know by now, was first hinted by Otto Eißfeldt ('Der gegenwärtige Stand der Erforschung der in Palästina neu gefundenen hebraischen Handschriften' in: *ThLZ* 75 (1949): 23–6) and then by Eleazar Sukenik; Edmund Wilson, fulfilling his duty as liaison officer between high scholarship and the average reader, duly made this into his best-selling book (*Os Manuscritos do Mar Morto*. São Paulo: Companhia das Letras, 2009, Kindle loc. 340). In an ironic way, this became the standard view of even respected scholars like Roland de Vaux (cf. *Archaeology and the Dead Sea Scrolls*. Schweich Lectures. London: Oxford University Press, 1973).

[25] The treatment of the matter in the small but well-researched book by Martin Goodman and Geza Vermès is a typical example of today's more cautious attitude (cf. *The Essenes according to the Classical Sources*. Sheffield: Oxford Centre Textbooks, 1990).

take that bunch of evidence and put them against classical sources is, in my opinion, to create a methodological mess that does not hold any solid ground in a debate.

That does not mean that scholars should just avoid tracing parallels between ideas that resemble one another; rather, I would advise any student to take this task very seriously. It is more a matter that not all that glitters is gold; nonetheless, gold does glitter.[26]

This is all the more true when we take into account that, in theory, very similar ideas *may* pop up in different times and cultures by pure chance. This is very odd, not to say bordering on the irrational sometimes – and by this very reason research looking for 'proven' parallels should be pursued. But in the absence of direct quotations, traceable loan-words or, for example, parallels in the Greek versions, the scholar should be reminded, as a sobering medication, that coincidences *do* happen in the history of religion as in other areas of research. It is our task to try to be as impartial as possible regarding such disarming thoughts – after all, parallels give a nice sensation that, in the end, all things have a design or serve a purpose. This may well be a conclusion (albeit a difficult one to reach), but never an assumption. A case related to this would be that of Zurvan, a deity above Ahuramazda and Ahriman, which is time embodied; this is the case of the testimonies from Late Antiquity, where 'Zarouam' [*sic*] is equalled to *Tyché*, the goddess of Fortune.[27]

It is my stance on the problem, then, that we are dealing with 'parallels' rather than 'influences'. It would be so much better if we had the latter proven and marked in stone, but that is not the case. However, chasing parallels does not require the induction of preconceived ideas into our object. After all, whereas we lack dating, documentation and almost everything 'concrete' on the Persian side (even for those who dwell in linguistic approaches, where there are no easy agreements either), parallels abound.

It is my point of view, as will be developed in many places in this book, that Persian (i.e. Zoroastrian) ideas are older than Second Temple Judaism, going back to the Late Bronze Age. But this is not a unanimous position among Iranologists, even if it is probably the most common. This point of view is what the reader can expect throughout this work, and parallels are useful not just in the absence of proper Zoroastrian documentation (this would lead us to an epistemological absurdity, where the question provides already the answer, so any investigation in the field would be, by the very nature of this fact, concluded before it started). Parallels enlighten us, but only if we take enough care not to mix our ingredients in the wrong order, so to speak.

§5 Some ideas regarding *PIE and the spread of ideas related to the afterlife

The problems related to the spread of ideas – not to mention the origin, if common or linked to a chain of borrowings – are manifold and involve the notion of *PIE

---

[26] De Vaux had in very early articles made the ungainly suggestion that Origen himself had visited the caves ('La grotte des manuscrits hébreux' in: *RB* 56 (1949): 236); fortunately, this idea was never mentioned again in his later works.

[27] Mary Boyce. 'Some Further Reflections on Zurvanism' in: Dina Amin and Manuchehr Kasheff (eds). *Iranica Varia: Papers in Honor of Professor Ehsan Yarshater*. Acta Iranica 30. Leiden: Brill, 1990, pp. 25–6.

mental-mythical complexes as related (opposed or in complementary form) to Jewish (i.e. Semitic) ones and will probably lack a definite solution. In this sense, the reception of the Danielic text – and thus of the ideas regarding resurrection and an afterlife 'proper' – is easier to deal with, both because of the DSS Para-Danielic material and of other sources that quote Daniel (e.g. AJ 10.263).[28]

This is something that needs to be tackled – and will be – but whenever such issues appear I shall redirect the reader immediately to a work of that kind. It is an amazing field of its own, ranging from the archaeological[29] to the linguistic[30] fields. I will draw on such works, many of them by now staple reading, but will not, by myself, push forward on these areas.

When examined against a Danielic background (easier to be dated, even if in more conservative terms that put the text in the same setting of the narrative – something almost abandoned approximately in the past seventy years[31]), the Zoroastrian counterparts furnish a lot of material (on the other hand, more difficult to date even if one is to rely on the narrative content rather than 'hard-proof' evidence such as colophons and similar references,[32] and this is, to my view, a particular case in the long 'history of the great ideas',[33] specifically of religious ideas).

---

[28] Such efforts, exotic or far-fetched as they may seem at first hand, should not be dismissed carelessly. A scholar of the calibre of Jacques Duchesne-Guillemin was one of the foremost proposers of the West-East way of travelling for the 'apparently' Iranian-origin mythical complexes, although his defence sounds rather clumsy (Jacques Duchesne-Guillemin. 'Apocalypse juive et apocalypse iranienne' in: Ugo Bianchi and Maarten J. Vermaseren (eds). *La soteriologia dei culti orientali nell'Impero romano: Atti del Colloquio internazionale su la soteriologia dei culti orientali nell'Impero romano, Roma, 24–28 settembre 1979*. Etudes préliminaires aux religions orientales dans l'Empire romain 92. Leiden: Brill, 1982, p.758). Philippe Gignoux is also to be taken seriously, notwithstanding the acrimony of his polemics with Geo Widengren and, to some extent, with Boyce; cf. Philippe Gignoux. 'L'apocalyptique iranienne est-elle vraiment la source d'autres apocalypses?' in: ActAnt 31.1–2 (1988): 67–78, 68). Even stronger points are made by him in 'Sur l'inexistence d'un *Bahman Yasht* avestique' in: *JAAS* 32 (1986): 53–64.

[29] For more general questions in that field, I suggest the reader go to Kamyar Abdi. 'The Iranian Plateau from Paleolithic Times to the Rise of the Achaemenid Empire' in: Touraj Daryaee (ed.). *The Oxford Handbook of Iranian History*. New York: Oxford University Press, 2012, Kindle edition; and, for even more generic issues, cf. Elena E. Kuzmina. *The Prehistory of the Silk Road*. Encounter with Asia. Philadelphia: University of Pennsylvania Press, 2008, especially ch. 3, 'The Eurasian Steppe in the Bronze Age'.

[30] A fine general introduction yet specialized and nicely woven is the one by Ludwig Paul (ed.). *Handbuch der Iranistik*. Wiesbaden: Reichert, 2013. A more recent approach for the general reader can be found in Touraj Daryaee. *Sasanian Iran. 224–651 CE: Portrait of a Late Antiquity Empire*. Costa Mesa: Mazda, 2008. The classical work in this field still is the one from Arthur Christensen. *L'Iran sous les Sassanides*. Copenhague: Ejnar Munksgaard, 1944.

[31] Harold H. Rowley. *Darius the Mede and the Four World Empires in the Book of Daniel*. Cardiff: University of Wales Press Board, 1959, pp. 5, 7, 9–11.

[32] As such, it is fair to say that I am following in the footsteps of the works of Benjamin W. Fortson IV (*Indo-European Language and Culture: An Introduction*. Second edition. Chicester: Wiley Blackwell, 2010), James P. Mallory and Douglas Q. Adams (*The Oxford Introduction to Proto-Indo European and the Proto-Indo-European World*. New York: Oxford University Press, 2008) and Martin L. West (*Indo-European Poetry and Myth*. New York: Oxford University Press, 2008), to quote two of the more recent scholars on the subject who have never been afraid to toe the more traditional line or argument – that is, positing *PIE and a world of loosely connected cultural practices linked to it.

[33] As it has been undeniably done by Skinner ('Meaning and Understanding in the History of Ideas') when dealing with meaning of ideas *as they were put down in a text*; in his own words, 'It is the

In other words, works of social, cultural or material history of the period spanning from roughly 1500 BCE to 1000 CE are not only necessary but are also indispensable and as recommended as any other type of literature. But it will play second fiddle here, I must repeat.[34]

§6 An overview of dating issues

Again we face here the subtleties of content versus hard data; this means that even if defining a position that Zaraθuštra did exist as an historical individual, whose compositions does show a second millennium BCE world, there is always the counterargument that one should either

1. Rely on the testimony of datable Classical sources (e.g. Herodotus, I.131-140); the earliest mention of the name Zaraθuštra or similar occurs in a Greek source, from the mid-fifth century BCE;[35]
or
2. Trace the dating of Zoroastrian ideas based almost exclusively on internal criticism.[36] This seems a tenable position but is far from bulletproof; the fact that the earliest extant mss related to Zaraθuštra is from the tenth century, in Sogdian (British Library BL Or.8212/84), originating from the caves of Dunhuang, China, does not help. The next of kin is a ms. dated from 1323 CE, acquired by a British personal collector from the widow of Dastur Darab, the priest that between 1758 and 1760 taught Avestan to Anquetil du Perron. It appears that the same scribe made one copy of the Vd (1324) and two extant copies from the Y (1323).

---

context of religious, political and economic factors which determines the meaning of any given text, and so must provide the ultimate framework to understand it' (p. 29). It should be noted here that no matter how much of Skinner's ideas may be correct, a common objection to his methodology – namely that language is always in a 'fluid state' – is even more applicable to our texts, given that MP, with all its limitation in terms of lexemes and its various archaisms, is particularly prone to misinterpretation if we overestimate the feasibility of using Skinner's methods.

[34] Cf. Kuzmina, *Prehistory of the Silk Road*.
[35] I subscribe to the views expressed by Almut Hintze. 'Zarathustra's Time and Homeland: Linguistic Perspectives' in: *WBCZ*, p. 32: 'That outside the *Avesta* there is no evidence for the person Zarathustra from the presumably prehistoric times of the religion's inception, the question of his time and homeland is essentially that of the date and provenance of the earliest expression of Zoroastrianism, the *Avesta*.' Cf. also Peter Kingsley. 'Meetings with Magi: Iranian Themes among the Greeks, from Xanthus of Lydia to Plato's Academy' in: *JRAS* (Third Series) 5.2 (1995): 173–209.
[36] There is always the possibility of dating Zaraθuštra according to the message he conveyed in the Avesta, but then one should follow an order that is not the one in which the Yts are presented; following the 'chronological order' of the mythical explanation of the *dēn* to Zaraθuštra, it is reasonable to begin with Yt 27.13 (the *Yaθa Ahū Vairiiō* prayer); the spread of the righteous teachings by Zaraθuštra himself comes at Yts 19.80–81 and 13.94. In terms of linguistic analysis and the many layers proposed by scholars, cf. Prods O. Skjærvø. 'The Antiquity of Old Avestan' in: *IJAIS* 3.2 (2003-4): 15–41; and Almut Hintze. 'Avestan Literature' in: Ronald E. Emmerick and Maria Macuch (eds). *The Literature of Pre-Islamic Iran: Companion Volume I to A History of Persian Literature*. London: Taurus, 2009, pp. 34–7.

So, this leaves us with few options in terms of external evidence; the first problem we have to face is that related to dating of copies and several different levels of redaction therein.[37] Any sort of dating is, in this sense, tentative; that is because, weird as it may seem, most of the manuscripts we have (and here palaeographical material is very important because it can be dated to very early periods e.g. the Kirdēr inscription or those of Behistun) can only be traced to the ninth century or from even later periods.[38]

Now, sometimes we can rely on colophons as in the case of ms. DH,[39] but most of the time it is puzzling that it is only after the Arab conquest that we find significant output of texts systematizing Zoroastrianism[40] – or, as this term never appears in the manuscripts themselves, we have texts organizing what the faithful call simply *dēn*, the word used to define both the doctrine, practice and associated literature, be it poetry or prose, designed to explain or even to debate (as in the case of ŠGW) with members of other faiths the finer points of what we call now Zoroastrianism.[41]

From a Western perspective, the development of Iranian studies as an area of its own (i.e. not to be confused with the 'Persian mania' of the eighteenth century) began roughly by the time of the Enlightenment as European intellectuals were drawn towards what seemed then a revolutionary approach, which would discredit once and

---

[37] This problem has a very objective treatment in a work that became referential to the matter: Harold W. Bailey. *Zoroastrian Problems in the Ninth-Century Books*. Oxford: Clarendon Press, 1943. As Bailey himself said, this is a field where so little is known with any degree of certainty that it leaves much room for the flights of imagination (ibid., p. vi). Also of interest are, both from Alberto Cantera, '*Abastāg ud Zand*: Das Avesta und dessen Pahlavi-Übersetzung' in: *Studien zur Pahlavi-Übersetzung des Avesta*. Wiesbaden: Harrassowitz, 2006, pp. 13–15; and 'Die Überlieferung des Avesta und dessen schriftliche Fixierung', in: *Studien zur Pahlavi-Übersetzung des Avesta*, p. 118.

[38] It should be noted that this too has its pitfalls, as one can see in the overly optimistic interpretation of some OP terms in Fridrich-Wilhelm König. *Relief und Inschrift des Koenigs Dareios I. am Felsen von Bagistan*. Leiden: Brill, 1938, p. 80; for a more sobering approach, see Georg G. Morgenstierne. *Indo-Iranian Frontier Languages II: Iranian Pamir Languages*. Oslo: 1938.

[39] With colophons referring it to 1321, 1351 and 1331; cf. Carlo G. Cereti (ed.). *The Zand-i Wahman Yasn: A Zoroastrian Apocalypse*. Roma: Istituto italiano per il Medio ed Estremo Oriente, 1995, p. 3.

[40] In this sense the specific discussion positing the anteriority of Persian apocalyptic related to Jewish-Christian material is but a particular case of a more generic discussion regarding other genres that comprise Zoroastrian religious texts as a whole. The fact that these texts have been collected, copied or even composed *after* the Arab invasion and conquest should not surprise us, as it can be seen as a last-ditch effort to preserve not just the *dēn* but also a whole way of life.

[41] This text is a case in point where we have reasonable dating for the material both in terms of internal as well as external evidence, we know the author by name and even that the text is of Iranian provenance.

> (35) (As to me), I am Mardānfarrox son of Ohrmazddād. I have written this composition because in (our) times I have seen sectaries of many kinds, of many religions and of many different practices. (36) And from childhood on I have always sought and investigated the truth with a fervent mind. (37) For this very reason I have gone to many countries, up to the shore of the sea.

Cf. Carlo G. Cereti. 'Some notes on the *Škand Gumanig Wizār*' in: Dieter Weber (ed.). *Languages of Iran: Past and Present*. Ranian Studies in Memoriam David Neil Mackenzie. Wiesbaden: Harrassowitz, 2005, pp. 1–4.

for all Christian faith and together with it would relegate religious thought to the dark, dusty and unholy depot of surpassed ideas.[42]

In 1727, a piece of the Avesta was noticed in the Bodleian Library, Oxford.[43] As nobody could read it at that time, it was left as it was, untouched, for a while – until a young Frenchman had his attention drawn to it and began a passionate adventure that took him to India. His name was Abraham Hyacinthe Anquetil-Duperron,[44] and his endeavours were only made possible by the colonialist designs of the times; indeed, his exploits – and, to the chagrin of Saidists,[45] his taking the stand for the Parsees[46] – would intermingle with the turbulent sparks begun by the Colonial Wars between France and the fledgling British Empire in India and went on throughout the French Revolution and the Napoleonic Wars. As Norman Cohn put it,

> This chance encounter [i.e. Anquetil-Duperron's with the Avestan fragment], in 1754, of a young man with a scrap of writing in an unknown language was momentous, for it launched the process to which we owe our now very comprehensive knowledge of Zoroastrian beliefs.[47]

To be fair, some of Anquetil-Duperron's first attempts to get his hands on Avestan look, by today's standards, incredibly naïve, but not all of his enterprise can be dismissed. While researching a MP lexicon (and one that is of paramount importance to this day, the lexicon that concentrates a good deal of what we now call 'heterograms', words written in Pahlavi but spoken in a different manner – e.g. m^el^ekh, spelled $sh\bar{a}h$, 'king'[48]), Anquetil-Duperron's attempts, as in the example below, may look weird – but cannot be dismissed as entirely ill-founded:

---

[42] This was the expectation of many an intellectual during the Enlightenment; cf. the biography of Anquetil-Duperron (Raymond Schwab. *Vie d'Anquetil-Duperron: Suivie des usages civils et religieux des Parses*. Paris: Librairie Ernest Leroux, 1934, pp. 92–8).

[43] Norman Cohn. *Cosmos, Chaos and the World to Come*. New Haven: Yale University Press, 2001, Kindle loc. 5235.

[44] Cf. Schwab. *Vie d'Anquetil-Duperron*.

[45] By this term I refer to the followers of the infamous book by Edward Said, *Orientalism* (Harmondsworth: Penguin, 1985), which did so much damage to a whole generation of scholars with its countless mistakes and demagogical/Marxist appeal. It is not my intention to discuss [sic] the position of Said, but regarding Anquetil-Duperron's biographer, Raymond Schwab, it is remarkable that Said misquotes him (Schwab) in favour of his own positions. It seems pretty clear that Said did not bother to read Schwab's *Vie d'Anquetil-Duperron*, but then he quotes Schwab's best-known book, *La renaissance orientale* (Paris: Payot, 1950), entirely out of context and saying the opposite of what it means. Cf. Said's *Orientalism* and Schwab's *Renaissance orientale*.

[46] 'Parsees' or just 'Parsis' are late-generation Zoroastrians living in India, who emigrated from Persia and who remain in India to the present day. Their 'migration', as so often happens, has its own foundational myths and truths; cf. Alan V. Williams. *The Zoroastrian Myth of Migration from Iran and Settlement in the Indian Diaspora: Text, Translation and Analysis of the 16th Century Qesse-ye Sanjan 'The Story of Sanjan'*. Leiden: Brill, 2003, p. 205.

[47] Cohn. *Cosmos, Chaos and the World to Come*. Kindle locs 5242–3.

[48] These constitute a big part (perhaps half) of the vocabulary in MP. They come mostly from Aramaic, thus the (once) popular term of 'Arameograms' for them, but some simply have no discernible meaning and as such can be read as a sort of ideograms. 'Heterograms' is the term now universal among scholars, or in Farsi, *huzvarish*.

The knowledge of the Frahang i Pahlavīk was brought to Europe by Anquetil du Perron [sic]. In the second volume of his *Zend-Avesta* of 1711 he published (pp.476-526) a version of the Frahang which had been prepared for him by his teacher Dastur Darab from an original manuscript stated to be 400 years older. In the manuscript of the Dastur, now kept in the Bibliothèque Nationale of Paris under the No. Suppl. Pers. 417, the Pahlavi words are arranged in an orthographical order, based on signs rather than letters. The words are given in Pahlavi writing, in Avestan writing (Pāzand) and in Arabic writing (Pārsī). In his edition, Anquetil presents the material in three columns: one with a Latin transcription of the Pahlavi word, based mainly on the Pāzand, one with a Latin transcription of the Pārsī (close to New Persian), and one with a French translation, presumably of the Pārsī. Thus a typical lemma reads like this: 'Aïoman. Tschaschm. Oeil'.[49]

It should be remembered that, shortly after Anquetil-Duperron's death, in 1805, linguistics was a cutting-edge science and many names that are still revered flourished: the brothers Jacob and Wilhelm Grimm, Hans-Christian Andresen, Thomas Young (d. 1829, the first man to have a degree of success in deciphering hieroglyphs) and, most famous of them all, Jean-François Champollion. It remains my personal opinion that, in terms of sheer achievement, what Anquetil-Duperron, the quiet, unassuming Catholic, did is on par with Champollion's exploits. But the flamboyant nature of the latter – and the West's long-standing fascination with things Egyptian, as compared to the more down-to-earth Persian materials in art, literature and history,[50] made Anquetil-Duperron's achievements pale by comparison to those of his later countryman. It is in my best hopes that future generations will do him justice.

However, it is somehow ironic that it took approximately 180 years for Champollion to have his own biography written in a decent, elaborate manner;[51] compare that with the first work *only* about Anquetil-Duperron, written in 1934.

---

[49] Henrik S. Nyberg (ed.). *Frahang i Pahlavīk, Ed. with Transliteration, Transcription and Commentary from the Posthumous Papers of Henrik Samuel Nyberg by Bo Utas with the Collaboration of Christopher Toll.* Wiesbaden: Harrassowitz, 1988, p. vii. Cf. also Jacques Duchesne-Guillemin. 'Zoroastrian Religion: Iranian Religion under the Selucids and Arsacida' in: E. Yarshater (ed.). *CHIr Vol. 3: The Selucid, Parthian and Sasanid Periods, Part 2.* Cambridge: Cambridge University Press, 1983, p. 874. Other important efforts in making sense of that part of vocabulary were those by Martin Haug. *The Pahlavi Language. [From the Pahlavi-Pazand Glossary Edited by Destur Hoshangji and M. Haug].* Stuttgart: Carl Grüninger, 1870; and Heinrich F. J. Junker. *The Frahang I Pahlavīk.* Heidelberg: Carl Winters, 1912 (2 vols). It should be noted that Zeke Kassock provided many students I supervise and myself with a handmade list of heterograms, not (yet) for sale, and this proved most useful.

[50] In that respect one cannot fail to note the enthusiasm with which things Oriental were received, reinvented and circulated in the West: the example of Montesquieu's *Lettres Persanes* (from 1721) should suffice. In this sense it stands in a long line of French sympathizers of Persia as they conceived it, since the Renaissance. Cf. Ibn Warraq. *Defending the West: A Critique of Edward Said's Orientalism.* New York: Prometheus Books, 2007, Kindle loc. 2268.

[51] I refer specifically to Andrew Robinson's *Cracking the Egyptian Code: The Revolutionary Life of Jean-François Champollion* (Oxford: Oxford University Press, 2012). It is worthy of mention that Robinson also wrote a biography of Champollion's rival, Thomas Young (*The Last Man Who Knew Everything.* Oxford: Oneworld, 2006).

The passage below will, I hope, make it clear where we are starting from in terms of Iranology as the science which allowed them to toy with the 'influence' issues. Cohn, in the 'afterword' to his *Cosmos, Chaos and the World to Come*, puts it in a nicer way than most writers could:

> The attitude of the philosophes was very different. Already in his *Essai sur les moeurs* (published in 1756, but composed from 1745 onwards) Voltaire had confidently looked forward to seeing the divine inspiration of Moses called in question by Zaraθuštra. When Anquetil returned with his copy of the Avesta, such expectations were intensified. Within a year the German-French philosophe Friedrich Melchior Grimm summarised what was expected: '... a faithful translation of these books would doubtless throw much light on the books of Moses and the object of Monsieur Boulanger's researches'. As everybody knew, Boulanger's researches were concerned with 'the absurdity and incoherence of Christian doctrine'. In a private letter Voltaire admitted that he was impatient for the publication of Anquetil's book precisely because he expected the parallelisms between the Avesta and Genesis to undermine Christian faith. When, in 1771 – nine years after Anquetil's return – the book at last appeared, it bore the intimidating title *Zend-Avesta, ouvrage de Zoroastre, contenant les idées théologiques, physiques, et morales de ce législateur, les cérémonies du culte religieux, qu-il a établi etc.* – and contained not a word that could be used to impugn the biblical account of Creation.[52]

In short, the link, possible link, or even imaginary link, between Persian/Zoroastrian studies (these different issues could not be properly differentiated at the time of Anquetil-Duperron's life) and the very foundations of Judaism and Christianity was spotted from the start: it is remarkable that the very first person to bring any sort of reliable information on Zaraθuštra's teachings for almost 1,500 years should be linked to the so-called Enlightenment scholars' permanent effort to discredit Christianity. It is even more remarkable that he lived and died as a faithful Catholic, who despised the French Revolution while keeping deep respect for his own country's laws, under whose protection he lived.[53]

§7 Jews and Zoroastrians during the Exile

With that foreground in mind, that is, of the beginnings of the study of Zoroastrianism as a discipline in its own right, one expects an investigation of how, where and by whom Jewish contemporaries came into contact with Zoroastrianism.[54]

---

[52] Cohn. *Cosmos, Chaos and the World to Come*, Kindle locs 5282-91.
[53] Schwab. *Vie d'Anquetil-Duperron*, pp.122-4.
[54] Besides Cohn's works, which deal with the subject in a more matter-of-factly way, others following this trend could be quoted here – Löwith, Popper and, more recently, Dumas-Rengoat. The proposition announced here will be discussed in deeper fashion at the end of this book, since it is not unanimous nor without implications – 'Jews in contact with Zoroastrianism' implies an

The danger here lies ironically in the fact that Zoroastrians had no systematic theology, so to speak, in the manner that Jews, Christians and Muslims have their own.[55] It is thus no coincidence that beginning of modern Iranian studies coincide with the meeting of Parsees in India and that much of that field became entangled with theological issues that tried to deal with Zaraθuštra as a big, lofty reformer, on one hand, and in a mirror-like game, imposing the same categories of the three Abrahamic faiths to Zoroastrianism, on the other.[56] With such methods, then, it is no surprise to find in Iranian ideas whatever one may want to fit in other theological schemes (i.e. a kind of 'selective approach'; in this respect Zoroastrianism and Second Temple Judaism are far from being the only pair that suffered from the consequences of that habit[57]). So, we should be very careful in approaching Iranian

> order of things, one to which I subscribe but that nonetheless has alternatives. This idea has serious implications when one takes into account that the 'official history' of Zoroastrianism was 'reformed' by Kirdēr – this is a version which emphasizes violence and expulsion of those not conforming to the dēn:
>
>> A single religious authority has shaped our understanding of how Zoroastrians regarded the adherents and institutions of other religions. The *mowbed* Kerdir [sic] who served three successive kings of kings in the third century – Shapur I (r. 241–70), Ohrmazd I (r. 270–71), and Wahram I (r. 271–74) – was the only priest in the Sasanian period prolifically to have produced inscriptions. On the stone walls of the so-called Kaaba of Zoroaster, alongside an inscription of Shapur I and beneath relief sculptures of early Sasanian rulers, he recounted his career as the supervisor of the institutionalization of Zoroastrianism throughout the nascent empire. This inscription was duplicated on the neighboring reliefs of Naqsh-e Rustam and on the image of Wahram I at Sar Mashad, where Kerdir appears alongside the king of kings as a partner in rule. According to the *mowbed's* account of his own activities, he erected fire temples everywhere from the heart of Iran in Babylonia to its limits in Peshawar. He organized the performance of the Yasna and instructed believers in the principles of the Good Religion. He also claimed to have suppressed the other religions in Iranian territory: 'The Zoroastrian religion [*dēn mazdēsn*] and the priests held great authority in the empire [*šahr*]. The gods, water, fire, and domestic animals received satisfaction, and Ahreman and the demons received blows and suffering. The doctrine [*kēš*] of Ahreman and the demons was expelled from the empire and became unbelief. The Jews, Buddhists, Brahmins, Nazarenes, Christians, Baptizers, and Manichaeans were struck in the empire. Idols were destroyed, and the residences of demons were eliminated and became the place and seat of the gods.' On the basis of this account, historians have argued that Kerdir oversaw a persecution of the named groups, inaugurating a project whose aim was the elimination of religious others, towards which subsequent Zoroastrian religious authorities worked until the end of the empire. If such was the goal, the flourishing of Jewish and Christian communities from the third century through the seventh suggests that they made little headway against these groups. The prophet Mani was slain at the behest of the court for rivaling the ritual power and cosmological knowledge of Zoroastrians, but there is no persuasive evidence for action against Christians or Jews during the era of his tenure. Nevertheless, histories of Zoroastrian interactions with Christians, Jews, and others in the Sasanian period often begin with, and rely on, Kerdir's self-representation as a paradigmatic example of how his fellow religious authorities, whether in the third century or the sixth, treated or wished to treat rival religious groups. He has provided the archetype of the persecutory Zoroastrian. (Cf. Richard E. Payne. *A State of Mixture: Christians, Zoroastrians and Iranian Political Culture in Late Antiquity*. Oakland: University of California Press, 2015, Kindle loc. 768)

[55] Michael Stausberg. 'Zarathustra Post-Gathic Trajectories' in: *WBCZ*, Kindle loc. 4385.
[56] Ibid.
[57] Cf. James Barr. 'The Question of Religious Influence: The Case of Zoroastrianism, Judaism, and Christianity' in: *JAAR* 53.2 (1985): 201–35; Shaul Shaked. 'Iranian Influence on Judaism: First Century B.C.E. to Second Century C.E.' in: W. D. Davies and Louis Finkelstein (eds). *CHJ Vol. 1*,

ideas as sources for other theologies in order to avoid anachronism and end up 'proving' what was, indeed, a collection of precariously mounted and arranged texts (if not a free creation during Sasanid times). To be fair, the amount of manuscripts available to the scholar of Iranian ideas, related or not to the figure of Zaraθuštra himself, is very small compared to what is available to scholars of the other three Abrahamic faiths.[58]

This poses another question, perhaps the one most ardently debated among Iranologists during the last decades: since we do know for sure (i.e. in terms of external evidence) texts that came to us from the tenth century onwards (the Sogdian fragment) or else from the fourteenth century onwards, one has to rely on linguistic evidence to plead a case for the antiquity of Zoroastrian literature (or for that matter, for Zoroastrianism at large) or else posit that what we have is not just a concoction but perhaps a wholesale fabrication of two mobads, Tōnsar or Tansar (a semi-legendary one[59]) and Kirdēr (on this one we have lots of information, no matter how accurate they may be). The organization of the Avesta is traditionally ascribed to Tōnsar; the cementing of State and Zoroastrian clergy, with a greater degree of precision, to Kirdēr.

On another front I have, quite effortlessly and without any definite intention, gathered a group of students I supervised over the years that deal with MP, Persian apocalyptic and similar material. Whenever credit is due to sparks they started or ideas they suggested; it will be given in footnotes or in the main text.[60]

Introduction: The Persian Period. Cambridge: Cambridge University Press, 1984, pp. 308–25; Shaul Shaked. 'Eschatology i. In Zoroastrianism and Zoroastrian Influence' in: *EIr* 8.6 (1998): 565–9; Rose. *Concerning Parallels.*

[58] A different matter altogether, which will be dealt with in late chapters, is the usage of (pseudo) Zoroastrian names, characters and doctrines by Greeks and Romans (which includes a good deal of Christians in Late Antiquity).

[59] Touraj Daryaee. 'The Sasanian Empire 224-651 CE' in: *OHIR*, p. 188:

> Even before Kerdir [sic], another priest named Tosar (Tansar) was responsible for sifting through the documents and oral tradition to come up with a Zoroastrian doctrine, which had been dispersed and in a state of flux since the time of Alexander the Great's destruction of the Achaemenid Persian Empire in 330 BCE. The Sasanian sources state that Tosar was responsible for the codification of the Avesta, the collection of Zoroastrian hymns that later were put into writing, and that Kerdir brought about the organization of the church and a religious hierarchy.

[60] I am referring particularly to Mrs Miriam Bergo Tremblay (whose work with the 'Oracle of Hystaspes', first under my supervision and then with Lorenzo DiTommaso and André Gagne at Concordia, Canada, has forced me to read quite a bit on the subject); Adriano Carlos de Oliveira worked on a BA Honours monograph whose theme was Zoroastrianism in Bactria, 'cleansing' of corpses and the impact of such customs on the Greeks; Rodrigo Nunes was, at the time of this writing, researching at a BA level the demonization of Alexander the Great in the ZWY and related sources; and last but not least my PhD student Raul Vitor Rodrigues Peixoto pursues a research related to the sequences of metals in 1En and in Persian sources, and he made me take a closer look at the Ethiopic material he translated. To all these people I am grateful for making me move ahead and read things I would not normally read were it not for the fact that I had to supervise them.

§8 Conclusion

In tackling the manifold issues discussed in this introduction, maybe it was not scholarship or knowledge that was lacking – but simpler things, like pausing to think if we were asking the adequate questions to our sources.

After all, the questions related to religious syncretism in Antiquity are, to a great extent, much more our own business as twentieth- and twenty-first-century scholars than of the men and women who lived in the crossroads (both temporal and spatial) of Judaism and Zoroastrian paths. This was first suggested by Metzger, who went further in his admonitions to make us realize that a great deal of the sources we have to deal with are of a relatively late date – from the second to fifth centuries CE[61] (not considering that manuscripts are much later than that, in the Zoroastrian case), with all the ensuing problems.[62]

Perhaps this has nothing to do with scientific research – such a position, which may be held as naïve, is a private matter, not the stuff of research proper.

Or is it?

I suppose it is to be taken very seriously, because, even taking a fundamentalist point of view respectfully, I cannot understand why a given set of godly revelations had, by definition, to be Semitic *or* Indo-European. Moreover, people tend to forget that these terms are useful (most of the time at least) to distinguish cultural blocks or groups, *never* ethnicities.[63] So, I confess that, both as a public researcher and privately, I failed to make any sense of *why* Daniel has to be 100 per cent 'Semitic inspired word' without any trace of Persian concepts.[64]

I picked up Daniel[65] because this is a particularly sensitive source – it is canonical, it is apocalyptic and without Danielic themes, less would be left to build upon for the NT's own eschatological hopes. Thus, the NT, if it existed at all, would be something very different from the corpus that came down to us.

With pseudepigrapha these issues are far less severe; after all, from a fundamentalist point of view, they are not 'inspired', so who cares? This may have been a blessing in disguise, because as biblical scholarship rose to a very high status in the nineteenth century, the ensuing research on apocrypha and pseudepigrapha was left relatively to its own devices. Not so with Daniel. Two or three ironies lie behind this fact.

---

[61] Metzger. 'Forgeries and Canonical Pseudepigrapha', p. 6.
[62] Cf. Jacob Neusner. 'Zoroastrianism in the Comparison of Religions' in: Acta Iranica 25 (1985): 436–7, where Neusner recognizes that parallels between Zoroastrianism and Judaism, no matter how plentiful they may be, are a starting point, not an answer to a question.
[63] Arnaldo Momigliano. 'Time in Ancient Historiography' in: *Essays in Ancient and Modern Historiography*. Middletown: Wesleyan University Press, 1987, p.180.
[64] The same reasoning could be applied to gods or goddesses in the *PIE pantheon that are known to be of Semitic provenance; Aphrodite would be a case in question. Cf. Fortson IV. *Indo-European Languages and Culture*, p. 48.
[65] And related material, such as e.g. 2Br and 4Ezra, later apocalypses that depend nonetheless on Daniel.

The first is that, revered as a prophet, there is in fact a 'tomb of Daniel' located, alas, in modern-day Iran.[66] The second is that the forefather of all Western studies in Avestan, MP and the like, Anquetil-Duperron, who professed Catholicism staunchly, as a matter of fact, abused for failing to show – in scholarly terms – that Christianity was a mere warmed-up version of the teachings of Zaraθuštra.[67] And third, Zoroastrians themselves, although having to deal with a plethora of legal and ritualistic issues of their own, until today, never seemed to care much for the religious duel about who influenced who and what came first. This belongs much more to modern worries in the field of (religious) ideas.

In this sense, two reference works that almost immediately became mandatory are Touraj Daryaee's *The Oxford Handbook of Iranian History* (New York: Oxford University Press, 2012) and Michael Stausberg and Yuhan Sohrab-Dinshaw Vevaina's (with the assistance of Anna Tessmann) *The Wiley Blackwell Companion to Zoroastrianism* (Malden: John Wiley & Sons, 2015).

That Christians and Jews suffered – like any religious minority at any given time – at the hands of the Sasanian is well known and need not be demonstrated.[68] What is surprising is that, in modern times, they have both produced superb scholars and at the same time kept their religious identity, without big worries of the kind that afflict Jews and Christians on the similarity/parallelism/borrowings between Zaraθuštra's teachings and those of other religious thinkers. To sum up the effort described above, I picture this book roughly as dealing with *common* themes between Second Temple Judaism and Zoroastrianism (as it came down to us, ancient testimonies and very late

---

[66] The location is usually given as Susa, as one refers to the most ancient reference to this by Benjamin de Tudela when travelling to the East (between 1160 and 1163 CE).

[67] Cf. Cohn. *Cosmos, Chaos and the World to Come*, Kindle locs 5286–99:

> In a private letter Voltaire admitted that he was impatient for the publication of Anquetil's book precisely because he expected the parallelisms between the Avesta and Genesis to undermine Christian faith. When, in 1771 – nine years after Anquetil's return – the book at last appeared, it bore the intimidating title *Zend-Avesta, ouvrage de Zoroastre, contenant les idées théologiques, physiques, et morales de ce législateur, les cérémonies du culte religieux, qu-il a établi etc.* – and contained not a word that could be used to impugn the biblical account of Creation. The resentment of the philosophes was boundless. Its first expression took the form of an open letter to Anquetil, published in London but written in French. The author of that letter was William Jones – who was later, when he himself had become an eminent orientalist, to apologise for it. But in 1771 Jones was simply a student, and a brash one at that. It was suggested at the time that he had lived in France and had frequented journalists whose ideas were borrowed from the philosophes. That is more than likely; for in effect Jones was acting as spokesman for that formidable section of the French intelligentsia. 'We would never have believed,' he wrote, 'that the least skilful charlatan could have written the stuff and nonsense which fill your last two volumes ... Either Zaraθuštra lacked common sense or he did not write the book which you ascribe to him ... It follows either that you do not have the knowledge you boast of having, or that that knowledge is vain, frivolous and unfit to occupy the mind of a man of forty.'

The plethora of insults to Anquetil-Duperron is almost endless, but I guess this sample is enough to give an idea of the *Zeitgeist* [sic] against which he had to publish his results.

[68] As opposed to the relative peace and quiet for non-Zoroastrian minorities in Persia during Arsacid times; cf. Parvaneh Pourshariati. *Decline and Fall of the Sasanian Empire: The Sasanian-Parthian Confederacy and the Arab Conquest of Iran*. London: I.B. Tauris, 2011, p. 323, n. 1848; for a balanced view of such persecutions, see Payne. *A State of Mixture*.

mss). 'Common' does not imply influence or even contact, although this (mutual) borrowing is our starting hypothesis.

These three areas would be

(1) the idea of a Paradise regained;
(2) the resurrection of the dead; and
(3) the Final Judgement.

Incompatible areas would be as follows:

1. The dualism, explicitly or tacitly implied by the notion of two deities, Ahuramazda and Ahriman.
2. The process and ending by which the world was created; it appears as the work of a God and His speech-acts in the Genesis/Jubilees tradition. In Zoroastrianism deities exist before the creation and as such, creation itself is the place by definition where Good can take Evil and defeat it.

Partially compatible areas are the notion of 'Good' and 'Evil' taking into account the following:

1. 'Good' and 'Evil' are not entirely similar because of the manifold origins of Evil in Second Temple texts – the theological explanation may be the Fall, the serpent, the murder of Cain, the transgression of the angels as it appears in the Enochic tradition.
2. The fact that being religions with well-defined boundaries of what is expected of their practitioners (which is different from what they in fact did, as Edward Sanders remarks correctly), both developed in due course a sophisticated code of conduct for the respective communities.

And in our 'Conclusion', the most important area in common, and the one that arguably left a most lasting heritage: the notion of time – especially historical time – as a process, with a beginning and an end. That Creation had this purpose is evident in Daniel and Para-Danielic literature, almost in the same fashion as in Zoroastrian texts (but then again the dating issues on the texts from the latter prevent us from moving too far).

An area of great promise for research is the one related to legislation and codes of conduct, especially regarding purity laws, between Jews living in Ērān (and even Anērān) and Zoroastrians. This seems to be of immense urgency to all those interested in Talmudic law, which is a sort of 'Irano-Judaica'; a plea in that direction has already been made as early as 1968, by Daniel Sperber.[69] More recently, the work of scholars such as Dan Shapira, Shaul Shaked and Yaakov Elman made this effort remarkable.[70]

---

[69] 'Bab Nahara' in: *IrAnt* 8 (1968).
[70] Yaakov Elman. '"Up to the Ears" in Horses Necks (B.M. 108a): On Sasanian Agricultural Policy and Private "Eminent Domain"' in: *JSIJ* 3 (2004): 95–7; cf. also Antonio Panaino. 'Trends and Problems

Since this book is by its very nature a product of our own *Zeitgeist* – as it had to be – I hope one day younger researchers pick up things from where my generation stopped or, at least, take a minute to check out what happened in between Anquetil-Duperron's work and their own fathers'; I shall be rewarded looking from the other side of the *Činwad* bridge, hopefully. And it is in this respect that I also wish to clear up – much in manner that Franz Cumont, Joseph Bidez and Albert de Jong have done in the recent or pre-Second World War years – the distinction between what, with any degree of certainty, belongs to Zorastrianism 'proper' and what was perceived as such by Greeks and Romans.[71]

Concerning the Mutual Relations between Pre-Islamic and Jewish Cultures' in: Antonio Panaino and Andrea Piras (eds). *Melammu Symposia IV. Schools of Oriental Studies and the Development of Modern Historiography. Proceedings of the Fourth Annual Symposium of the Asasyrian and Babylonian Intellectual Heritage Project held in Ravenna, Italy, October 17–21, 2001*. Milano: Università di Bologna & ISIAO, 2004.

[71] These terms are not synonyms, but whenever one talks about religious phenomena in ancient Persia, no matter what dating is assumed for Zaraθuštra, or even if we are dealing with his very existence, external evidence (e.g. the inscription in Behistun) points towards a well-established place for the cult of Ahuramazda during the Exile. The issue of dating the life of Zaraθuštra – if indeed he was a historical character – is complicated, but normally the following stands are taken: the Hellenized form Ζωροάστρης appears in a fragment by Xanthus, the Lydian (FrGH 765F32), who locates Zaraθuštra six thousand years before Xerxes crossed the Hellepont in order to invade Greece; Ctesias, in his *Persika*, for all its faults, re-evaluates this dating and puts Zaraθuštra only four centuries before Xerxes (FrGH 688; here he was a king of Bactria – all traditions locate Zaraθuštra in the Eastern parts of Persia, even in Central Asia; cf. also Friedrich-Wilhelm König. *Die Persika des Ktesisas von Knidos*. Graz: Archiv für Orientforschung, Beiheft 18, 1972); Eudoxos of Cnidus, a friend contemporary to Plato, also takes Xanthus's dating but marks Plato's death as the identifying event (347 BCE); Hermodorus of Syracuse, writing after Alexander the Great, reformulates the date to five thousand years before the Trojan War. The examples of Greek philosophy taking a stand in recognizing dualistic or antagonistic forces operating in the world is quite large, but fragment 34 Rose, of Aristotle, is again of interest here since it also locates Zaraθuštra six thousand years before Plato's death; of interest here are also the names quoted by Diogenes Laertius. *Lives of the Eminent Philosophers* 1.2. The same reasoning applies to the Pseudo-Zoroastrean literature 'dated' to the time of Cyrus (e.g. the treatise *On Nature*, in: Joseph Bidez and Franz Cumont. *Les Mages Hellenisés: Zoroastre, Ostanès et Hystaspe d'après la tradition grecque*. Paris: Belles Lettres, 1973 (2 vols), vol. 2, p. 158).

1

Good and Evil in a clash of civilizations and ideas

§1 A brief disclaimer

This book is about two ancient civilizations, the Jews and the Persians, who have both left their mark on Western thought in a myriad of ways. For this project, I am particularly interested in the moment of the encounter Biblical scholars call the Late Second Temple, for it was precisely at this period that the Jewish intellectuals were heavily influenced by Persian thinking. Such influence can be readily found in most versions of the Bible and we feel its impact to this very day, especially when we observe the substantial imprint Zoroastrianism has left in both Western and Eastern world views.

For starters, I present you with the big question: when did people first start to wonder about the origins of Good and Evil as a struggle sentenced to a beginning and fated to an end? When did Jews begin to ask this question and who did they turn to for answers? These concerns will be addressed throughout the book by the means of a comparative reading of the Zoroastrian and the biblical texts in order to promote a better understanding of this essential enquiry.

The point of starting with a discussion of what 'Good' and 'Evil' mean in both Zoroastrianism and Second Temple Jewish texts – with an emphasis on Daniel and apocalyptic literature – lies within the understanding that these are the primary sources in which we can find more poignant contrasts between these two concepts. These two groups of texts, regardless of source-dating issues, are responsible for most of the spiritual *Bildung* of Eurasia from, broadly speaking, the oriental side of the Iranian plateau westwards.

It is true that the importance of each of these groups in their own *zenith* is widely different. Zoroastrianism was never a 'missionary' religion aiming to convert others; it was much more of an ethnical cult with its centre in 'Eran', that is, 'the land of the noble'.[1] Judaism was, on the other hand, a doctrinal religion – at least for a while and in some of its varieties. The Jewish historian Josephus, writing in Greek in the first century, gave us a vivid glimpse of that when he travelled to Rome: there he contacted two 'proselytes',[2] one actor named Aliturus and the wife of

---

[1] CPD, 'Ērān', Eran; land of the Aryans; land of the heroes ('ēr').
[2] LSJ, προσήλυτος, II, one who has come over to Judaism, convert, proselyte.

Nero, Poppaea.[3] Additionally, Josephus tells us in detail about the conversion of a whole buffer state between the Roman Empire and Parthia, the realm of Adiabene,[4] which would prove to be, however, a one-off occurrence.

Similar themes can be found in the NT when Jesus rebukes the Pharisees, who 'traverse sea and land',[5] into proselytizing. Jesus was a Jew, of course, and we can gather from his attributed utterances that he wanted followers to his name; but then again other Jews had similar goals, and to that we have many witnesses and reports, such as Josephus, Philo and the DSS.

None of that can be found among Zoroastrians though. The folklore involving the *magi* and Zoroaster regarding the birth of the Messiah are late Christian concoctions, which are very important but not in the least loyal to what we know from 'true' Zoroastrianism. It has been said that the role of Zoroastrianism by far surpasses the number of its faithful at any given time and disregards the diffusion of its Scriptures, which is why it is often questioned as an influence in the formation of the Islamic religion.

The notion that Zoroastrianism may have had a big role in the formation and development of Second Temple Judaism – thus in Christianity itself – relies, then, in a pair of religions that have many basic 'creed' issues in common. It also relies, as we shall see, on the precedence of Zoroastrianism in relation to Second Temple Judaism. Now, in which aspects they offer more 'parallels', since it is quite unwise to talk about 'influence', is yet to be thoroughly agreed upon.

Regarding the written nature of its sacred texts, we have almost nothing but a few inscriptions in OP from the sixth century BCE, and even these are not clear regarding the nature of Zoroastrianism then. We will never truly know if Cyrus and Darius, who were practitioners of Zoroastrianism as we know it, are from centuries later.[6] Nonetheless, the name of Ahuramazda[7] appears enough in these inscriptions to allow at least for the belief in a kind of monolatry: perhaps Cyrus and Darius worshipped other gods too, but they knew Ahuramazda.

Looking the other way around – from the point of view of the exiled Jews – Cyrus was held in such high esteem that Isaiah called him the 'messiah', although the Hebrew term originally meant nothing more than someone anointed for a given post.[8] In that light, another question arises: why has this term grown so much as to acquire the fantastic, supernatural qualities it already had before Jesus entered the scene? Here

---

[3] V, 16. The description given by Josephus of the lavish gifts and her connection to Aliturus make a good case for her being a proselyte, although this is not explicitly stated by Josephus. However, other noblewomen in Rome were definitely so, such as Fulvia (AJ 18.82).
[4] AJ 20.32–40.
[5] Matt 23:15.
[6] This is a thorny issue – some claim that he was, otherwise his liberal and fair conduct cannot be easily explained; on the other hand, other scholars claim – rightly – that no primary sources state that either he or Darius were Zoroastrians. My opinion is that this debate rests on another discussion on the dating of Zoroastrianism; and this, ultimately, leads us to late mss.
[7] CPD, 'Ohrmazd': *Ahura Mazda*; in astrology, Jupiter. 'Ohrmazd', that is, a later form of 'Ahuramazda' is similar to many words borrowed from OP to MP, a contracted form of the same word.
[8] BDB, 'מָשִׁיחַ', anointed; Messianic prince related or not to Davidic dynasty and many correlates.

again, Max Weber goes straight to the point, arguing that the needier a society is, the more supernatural its hopes become.[9]

Was Zoroastrianism then a messianic religion? Judging from what we have in proper Zoroastrian texts (which, no matter how Sasanian they claim to be or their setting in Sasanid times, begin to appear only in the fourteenth century[10]), it can be considered, indeed, a messianic religion. It has a detailed counting of the beginning of the world when Creation by Ohrmazd had a very specific purpose and of an ending of all times, to which at least three different versions survived. In all of them, humankind is redeemed.

Now, we have reasonably solid clues to guide our investigation: the mention of Ohrmazd before the end of the Jewish Exile in Babylon; the many related texts – of which Daniel is remarkable not only for its setting but also for becoming a template of sorts for other apocalypses; and, finally, the forms of Judaism that bear unmistakable similarity to Zoroastrianism. Nonetheless, it is worth remembering that similarity is not the same as equality: in theory and often in practice, scholars find themselves with similar tales at opposite ends of the world, with no way of linking them through a common channel of transmission.

Ideally, a social history of the relations between Jews and Persians (the most important ethnic group to hold Zoroastrian beliefs and practices) would provide the answer to these questions, and there are in fact excellent works on the Jews during the Exile,[11] after the Exile[12] and even more during the Hellenistic period (i.e. after 323 BCE). Many of those mention the commonly shared vicinities between Jews and Zoroastrians in Asia Minor and even in Syria, yet these sources are few, scattered and lack continuity. Regardless, they remain worthy of analysis precisely due to the lack of primary sources and/or first-hand accountings.

---

[9] Max Weber. *The Sociology of Religion*. London: Methuen, 1965, pp. 259–60.

[10] Apart from what is called among scholars the 'Pahlavi Psalter', a twelve-page fragment of the Psalms, derived from the Syriac. This was found at the oasis of Turfan, in Central Asia. Since its script is less clear and developed than Book Pahlavi (on which we have most of the older mss), it is possibly from the sixth or seventh century CE. Two good introductions to the subject are Jan P. Asmussen. 'The Pahlavi Psalm 122 in English' in: *Dr. Unvala Memorial Volume*. Bombay: Published by Kaikhusroo M. Jamaspasa for Dr. J.M. Unvala Memorial Volume Sub-Committee, 1964, pp. 123–6; and Richard N. Frye. 'A Brief Note on the Pahlavi Psalter and Bare Ideogramms' in: *Sir J. J. Zarthoshti Madressa Centenary Volume*. Bombay: Trustees of the Parsi Punchayet Funds and Properties, 1967, pp. 70–4.

[11] Jonathan Stökl and Caroline Waerzeggers (eds). *Exile and Return: The Babylonian Context*. Berlin: Walter de Gruyter, 2015, is a very handy book, and three chapters in this book are especially useful: Laurie E. Pearce. 'Identifying Judaeans and Judaean Identity in the Babylonian Evidence'; Jonathan Stökl. '"A youth without blemish, handsome, proficient in all wisdom, knowledgeable and intelligent": Ezekiel's Access to Babylonian Culture'; and Lester L. Grabbe. 'The Reality of the Return: The Biblical Picture versus Historical Reconstruction'.

[12] This is of imperative importance to us, for it was after the Exile that Jewish apocalyptic took shape, in chronological terms at least – I have never seen this questioned; the main issue of this book, that is, the link between Daniel and later related literature, with special regard to apocalyptic, is another matter altogether in this sense. *Exile and Restoration Revisited* has at least four chapters that are worth reading to deepen our understanding. These are the following: John S. Bergsma. 'The Persian Period as Penitential Era: The "Exegetical Logic" of Daniel 9.1-27'; Tamara C. Eskenazi. 'From Exile and Restoration to Exile and Reconstruction'; and two by Lester L. Grabbe. '"They shall come rejoicing to Zion" – or Did They? The Settlement of Yehud' and 'Was Jerusalem a Persian Fortress?'.

On the other hand, when we look at the post-Exilic texts, references to Persians are plentiful: Isaiah, Tobit, Ezra, Nehemiah and, perhaps the most important of them all, Daniel. Other bits of information can also be found on the DSS, on the *Magi* of Matthew and at the list of provenances in Acts. Never mind the greater number of sources available, careful analysis is advised, for not all textual similarities indicate solid evidence of Zoroastrian influence.

Among these historical characters' narratives, Daniel's had the most promising career – not only was he a royal servant who managed to grasp prestige while keeping Jewish *kosher* precepts at all times, but he also provided the matrix of things to come – other apocalypses that correlate, on a varying degree, to Zoroastrianism as we know it from late manuscripts and some references in Antiquity.

One thing is, all in all, certain: the Greek and Roman knowledge of Zoroastrian ideas would play a quite different role in Christian literature, at a much later date. Their usage of its precepts is somewhat similar (the Oracles of Zoroaster and of Hystaspes testify to that) yet not related to first-hand knowledge of Avestan doctrine which may have influenced Second Temple Judaism. Nonetheless, thanks to the works of historians such as Theopompus, we retain a precious clue on the antiquity of Avestan doctrines amongst Greek folk. Furthermore, commentaries of other intellectuals such as Plutarch, Pliny the Elder and Diogenes Laertius provide scholars with other demonstrations of Greek prowess on transforming bits and pieces of local knowledge into a world of their own, as they did with virtually every foreign culture that came into contact with them.

All the issues highlighted so far will play a noticeably big role in the formative years of Christianity. Alongside those matters, some more questions shall be discussed further on, namely what was the effective role of Persian lore in Second Temple Judaism and in which ways that doctrine was 'misused' for the sake of complying with Greek and Roman definitions of cultural heroes, their origins and their roles.

§2 '*Huīh*' and '*Petyārag*': Zoroastrian views on Good and Evil

One of the most common presumptions regarding religious thought is that, necessarily, religions imply the idea of eternal life and of rewards or punishments in the world beyond.[13] Regarding Zoroastrianism, these ideas would be presented to the masses through understandable terms – good deeds, good thought, election and grace, reincarnation and so forth – but many other religious systems took no interest in such criteria. Some of them propose the complete denial of any validity to the world we live in, such as Buddhism, while others consider this world of ours as a stage to be completed before the next, such as Spiritism.

---

[13] Respectively, as the title of this chapter, 'huīh' and 'petyārag'; *CPD*, 'contentment, happiness', '[of a] good nature', MP, 'hw-'; *CPD*, 'evil', 'misfortune'; 'adversary'. *Petyāragīh* would be an onslaught of the evil forces. Av. 'paityāra', NP *patyāra*.

Thus, many religions survived humanity's shenanigans very well throughout centuries without these assumed notions. For instance, most civic cults in Greece and Rome did not have such concepts at all, apart from their mystery cults which are another matter altogether.[14] Moreover, other religious practices held a more practical nature and worried more about daily issues than about the definitive salvation of the soul or eternal life. In fact, we can say that the very idea of an eternal life emerges relatively late in the comparative history of religions.[15]

Most scholars have come to the conclusion, at some point, that those uncanny concepts are very likely the works of Zaraθuštra himself, yet some of them still doubt this idea. I side with the opinion of many other scholars, such as Mary Boyce and Martin L. West, that the existence of a man from the Late Bronze Age who has left many biographical imprints in the Avesta is readily depicted on the very core of Avestan texts. The same thing cannot be said about Moses, for one, as his historicity is much less certain in comparison to Zaraθuštra.

Even though the earliest ideas related to an afterlife that is blissful for the good and awful for the bad as they wait for the final judgement (something non-existent in Egyptian funerary texts, for instance) can be properly traced to the Avestan corpus, they cannot be haphazardly attributed to Zaraθuštra.[16] Hence, an important distinction has to be made: even though notions of good and evil are present in every conceivable society, it is not mandatory that Good should be rewarded with eternal bliss or that Evil must be punished until the end of times. Yet, both these ideas can be found in Iranian perspective which was, in due time, attributed to Zaraθuštra.[17] In fact, most

---

[14] Walter Burkert. *Ancient Mystery Cults*. Cambridge, MA: Harvard University Press, 1987, pp. 2–20, where the unjustified assumption that mystery cults are, by definition, Oriental, is challenged.

[15] A good introduction to such matters is provided by Richard King. 'Mysticism and Spirituality' in: John Hinnells (ed.). *The Routledge Companion to the Study of Religion*. Second edition. Abingdon: Routledge, 2010, pp.323–38.

[16] Contrast this to Egyptian religion and its emphasis on not doing wrong to judge a soul after death, rather than accounting for its own merits; this is clear in Egyptian funerary texts from the Old Kingdom onwards, too many to be cited here individually. For a recent evaluation of Egyptian afterlife expectations, cf. Bojana Mojsov. 'The Ancient Egyptian Underworld in the Tomb of Sety I: Sacred Books of Eternal Life' in: *The Massachusetts Review* 42.4 (2001): 489–506.

[17] Here, too, the political dimension may be found in the discussion of how old Zoroastrian documents are in fact. This, in turn, turns us to a discussion regarding Indo-European or *PIE origins – a touchy matter these days. The traditional, that is, orthodox, position among scholars is still that proposed by Boyce, who followed Nyberg and in turn has been followed by Cohn, Hintze and the biggest part of Zoroastrian scholars themselves:

> The prophet Zarathushtra, son of Pourushaspa, of the Spitaman family, is known to us primarily from the *Gāθās*, seventeen great hymns which he composed, and which have been faithfully preserved by his community. These are not works of instruction, but inspired, passionate utterances, many of them addressed directly to God; and their poetic form is a very ancient one, which has been traced back (through Norse parallels) to Indo-European times. It seems to have been linked with a mantic tradition, that is, to have been cultivated by priestly seers who sought to express in lofty words their personal apprehension of the divine; and it is marked by subtleties of allusion, and great richness and complexity of style. Such poetry can only have been fully understood by the learned; and since Zoroaster believed that he had been entrusted by God with a message for all mankind, he must also have preached again and again in plain words to ordinary people. His teachings were handed down orally in his community from generation to generation and were at last committed to writing under the Sasanians, rulers of the third [*sic*] Iranian empire. The language then spoken was Middle

of Zoroastrian cosmogonical myths can be traced back to the issues regarding that duality.

Some would state that Near Eastern religions – and even Indian ones – did not regard time as something with a beginning and an end. Indeed, the general mindset was that mankind is supposed to, with time, either be reborn,[18] live a tasteless afterlife[19] or, sometimes – and this is an important proto-form – experience the μακάρων νῆσοι (makárōn nêsoi), 'Isles of the Blessed', where there would be for the chosen few an eternity marked by the absence of displeasure and, more clearly, by an even climate.[20]

In Avestan texts[21] the very notion of a natural landscape, carefully manicured as being free of the 'unpleasant' part of living with animals, appears in Y 7.8:[22]

Persian, also called Pahlavi; and the Pahlavi books provide invaluable keys for interpreting the magnificent obscurities of the Gathas themselves. (Mary Boyce. *Zoroastrians, Their Religious Beliefs and Practices*. London: Routledge & Kegan Paul, 1979, p. 17)

The very same idea, namely that Zaraθuštra had a concrete, physical and thus historical existence (the same idea expressed by Martin L. West), has been seen before. It has become a touchy issue because of the subsequent political derivations that can be made out of this for modern purposes (the polemics between Carlo Ginzburg and Georges Dumézil in the eighties of the last century). Cf. also Vevaina. 'Miscegenation, "Mixture", and "Mixed Iron"', p. 250; Kianoosh Rezania. 'Zurvan: Limitless Time or Endless Time? The Question of Eternity and Time in Zoroastrianism' in: *JKR* 68 (2008); and Boyce. 'Some Further Reflections on Zurvanism', p. 27.

[18] The many followers of Pythagoras are too varied to be quoted here; for a general idea of the theme I suggest that the reader go to Carl Huffman (org.). *A History of Pythagoreanism*. Cambridge: Cambridge University Press, 2014.

[19] Homer. *Odyssey*, 11.

[20] Here the most quoted reference among many in Greek or Hellenistic thought is that of Plutarch in his *Life of Sertorius*, 8, which insists on the moderation of the climate and the fact that these islands are but a few days' sail from Hispania (i.e. Spain). This is even more evident on the confused mix between earthly egalitarian paradise (such as the one proposed, apparently, by Aristonicus in Asia Minor) and the proper literary reference to that, preserved in a very small fragment of Iamblichus, in Diodorus Siculus (it should be something relative to Hesiod's 'Golden Age' and a whiff of Plato's *Republic* – in Book II, pp. 55–60, Diodorus resumes Iamblichus's account on their expulsion of such islands, at the South of the Ocean, and how they shipwrecked in India to tell the story:

Ἑπτὰ δ' ἔτη μείναντας παρ' αὐτοῖς τοὺς περὶ τὸν Ἰαμβοῦλον ἐκβληθῆναι ἄκοντας, ὡς κακούργους καὶ πονηροῖς ἐθισμοῖς συντεθραμμένους. πάλιν οὖν τὸ πλοιάριον κατασκευάσαντας συναναγκασθῆναι τὸν χωρισμὸν ποιήσασθαι, καὶ τροφὴν ἐνθεμένους πλεῦσαι πλέον ἢ τέτταρας μῆνας· ἐκπεσεῖν δὲ κατὰ τὴν Ἰνδικὴν εἰς ἄμμους καὶ τεναγώδεις τόπους· καὶ τὸν μὲν ἕτερον αὐτῶν ὑπὸ τοῦ κλύδωνος διαφθαρῆναι, τὸν δὲ Ἰαμβοῦλον πρός τινα κώμην προσενεχθέντα ὑπὸ τῶν ἐγχωρίων.

[21] These are 'represented' with events, people and habits unequivocally of the Late Bronze Age, that is, c.1500 BCE–1100 BCE; traditional scholarly thinking agrees that these were oral compositions kept so for more than a thousand years and put into writing during the Sasanid period (i.e. after the third century CE). This is a tenable idea when we think of Homer (the *Iliad* and the *Odyssey* being a mix of Late Bronze Age themes, the 'Dark Centuries' before the *poleis* and even later concoctions discovered in Hellenistic times); it is even more reasonable when compared to the oral preservation of Vedic texts.

[22] The term 'Yasna' can refer to the essential collection of Zoroastrian texts or to a liturgical ceremony using them as well. It comprises seventy-two books. Y 3–8 are collectively attributed to Sraosh, or Sraosha, one of the major divinities in the Zoroastrian pantheon. *Sroš*, or its variations, is the divinity related to human conscience. Cf. Prods O. Skjærvø. 'The Avestan Yasna: Ritual and Myth' in: Claus V. Pedersen and Fereydun Vahman (eds). *Religious Texts in Iranian Languages: Symposium Held in Copenhagen May 2002*. Copenhagen: Det Kongelige Danske Videnskabernes Selskab, 2007, pp. 57–84, for a recent evaluation of this material; and also Dastur F. M. Kotwal and James W. Boyd. *A*

And I offer with a complete and sacred blessing to these places, districts, pastures, and abodes with their springs of water, and to the waters and the lands, and the plants, and to this earth and to heaven, and to the holy wind, and to the stars, and the moon, even to the stars without beginning (to their course), the self-appointed, and to all the holy creatures of Spenta Mainyu,[23] be they male or female, regulators (as they are) of the ritual order.[24]

The very idea of 'paradise' in this paragraph is clearly related to the idea of good conduct being rewarded[25] with a 'pleasant' afterlife. Etymologically, 'paradise' is commonly referred to as having its origin on the Heb.[26] root *pardes*, which was already being used by the Assyrians as *paradesu*.[27] The Vendidad, a Zoroastrian legal treatise to deal especially with the matters of demons, mentions several times the blessings of paradise, for example, Vd 3.24:

Unhappy is the land that has long lain unsown with the seed of the sower and wants a good husbandman. For him, who would till the earth, O Spitamā[28] Zarathustra, with the left arm and the right, with the right arm and the left, the earth will bring forth plenty of fruit.

Another passage relevant to this discussion is Vd 9.46, where the idea of a permanent place of pleasure and delight related to the realm of nature emphasizes again the possible results of the final combat between Good and Evil:

And the Druj[29] shall flee, like an arrow well darted, as hastily as would the previous season's green freshness covering the Earth.

Finally, the appearance of the very same theme in several other Yts is equally remarkable, for example:

Persian Offering. The Yasna: A Zoroastrian High Liturgy. Studia Iranica –Cahier 8. Paris: Association pour l'avancement des études iraniennes, 1991, pp. 96–7.

[23] One of the great, or more important, divinities in the cohort of Ahuramazdā, *Spenta Mainyu* being a sort of Holy Spirit.

[24] Lawrence H. Mills. *Avesta – Yasna: Sacred Liturgy and Gathas / Hymns of Zarathushtra.* Oxford: Oxford University Press, 1887. (*SBE*)

[25] 'Good' can be understood not only in simple terms of correct conduct (e.g. not lying, not cheating, not killing, etc.) but also in more specific terms, related only to each religion's quite developed ritual codes – in Zoroastrianism one finds discussions quite similar to Jewish Talmudic ones in that regard.

[26] *BDB*, פרדס; zend *pairi-daêza*, 'enclosure'; NP, Aram. *parṭêz*, etc.

[27] A case of the concept being much more important in the Iranian world but with a different root that goes back to Av. *garō.dəmāna*, with many changes in several Iranian languages until our MP *garōdmān* ('paradise').

[28] That is, from the Spitama family (*CPD*).

[29] *CPD*, 'drozan', lying, liar; 'drozih', falsehood. Lies and lying are among the worst mistakes or sins for Zoroastrians, regardless of the age of the text in question.

FrYt 13.79: ... *reverence, by name, to the waters; reverence, by name, to the trees.*[30]

HN 13 ... *withholding charity to the needy, cutting down trees ... then, one feels obliged to chant the Gāθās.*

Hence, nature, as part of the material creation, remains unsoiled and perfect in the realm of paradise. Now, the later development of this place of bliss and perfection for the good and lawful as a model for a definite resting place for all the dead is merely the branching of the original concept. Nature and its creations appear either symbolically as aforementioned or as the concrete reality of the impending post-war world. They can also appear (and this notion is very important when compared to Homeric poetry) as a place where the glorious deeds of oneself in battlefield are sung and remembered.

Thus far, we have seen a short string of themes related to one another in terms of precise commands which are either positive, 'do this', or negative, 'do not do this'. But what do these commands lead to? Here we come to one of the most interesting crossroads that Zoroastrianism presents us with: the obedience to these prescriptions leads, at the same time but in different mythical complexes, both to the individual salvation of the soul and to the final victory of Good against Evil, which has cosmic dimensions.

Equally as significant is the old *paradesu* (which is comparatively simple and is not the result of any cosmic struggle, not for Mesopotamian peoples or in Syro-Phoenicia) transforming into an all-encompassing world of bliss, to last forever after Evil (in all of its sorts) disappears from this world. This is an idea that would have a great future and would, ultimately, lead to the secular speculative philosophies of history from the eighteenth century. In turn, these ideas, put into practice in the twentieth century, would lead to massacres on a previously unimaginable scale, all in the name of one worthy cause: paradise on earth.

At this point religion becomes secular, but with the same doctrinal background of pre-election, predestination and the need to act together with the 'correct' side. However, it is important to distinguish pragmatic and systematic programs of world 'cleansing' in the twentieth century from the cosmic ideas in Zoroastrianism, from Second Temple Judaism afterlife concepts and from the related writings in the NT.

One heroic/epic episode in the notion of Good overcoming Evil is portrayed as a race between horse-drawn chariots, which is in turn linked to the right choice of patrons by Zaraθuštra, namely Y 49.7–9. It is, in a sense, the repetition of the idea of Homer choosing Agamemnon as the leader of the Argives – he is not the bravest or the wisest and not even the most famous, but he has superior means of waging war than that of most of the Greeks: his fleet is bigger.[31]

The themes of Zarathustra's [*sic*] revelatory experience, the protological (i.e., original) establishments of eschatological (final) reciprocities, and chariot-race

---

[30] Jean Kellens and Eric Pirart. '*Yazamaidē, nāmēni, āpō; Yazamaiē, nāmēni, urvarō*' in: *Les textes vieil-avestiques*. Wiesbaden: Reichert, 1988 (vol. 1 of 3).

[31] Homer, *Iliad*, 2.100–124; for a more complex analysis of Agamemnon's leadership, cf. Bernard Sarachek. 'Greek Concepts of Leadership' in: *The Academy of Management Journal* 11.1 (1968): 40.

imagery are collocated in Y 43.5: 'Holy did I think Thee, O Lord Mazdā, when I saw Thee first at the birth of existence, when Thou didst establish words and deeds as having payments, evil for evil, good reward for good, through Thy skill at the final (race-course) turn of existence.' After Zarathustra requests of Mazdā that He impart correct discernment/choice (Y 49.6), two actual patrons, brothers, are addressed in terms of Right and Wrong as choices with their reciprocities, including bliss. Y 49.7c–d: 'Which tribe, which family would be with the laws, and will bring the community good reputation?' Y 49.8: 'For Frašaoštra establish the most blissful co-union with Rightness in Thy good Dominion; for that I entreat Thee, O Lord Mazdā, and for me, too. Forever let us be Thy envoys!' Y 49.9b–d: 'He whose speech is true does not make a connection/union with a wrongsome person, since the ones yoked up for the best prize are those yoked (conjoined) to Rightness in the race, O Djāmāspa!' The latter name, having -aspa- 'horse' occurs in a word-play with 'race,' as again at Y 46.14a–c, where Zarathustra's chief patron is named, again in a context of eschatological reward (and, as in Y 30.11, abiding fame): 'Zarathustra, who is thy righteous ally with regard to great patronage? Or who wants to be famed? That's Vīštāspa in the race!' Here we also have a simple example of the institution of reciprocity, which characterizes the Old Iranian relationship between poet-priest and patron.[32]

The text above mixes a Late Bronze Age scenario and, amazingly, the role of the poet in illiterate IE societies – or societies that knew the use of script but only for management purposes, like Linear B in Mycenae. The poetry he declaims is truth itself, not a simile to truth and even less an 'idea' of truth, as will happen in Classical Greece.

Still tracing parallels to the Homeric world, the righteous ally in this Avestan text is the one with some additional measure of force that distinguishes him from others: Vīštāspa, famed in a race that will eventually be an eschatological race or, in its later variants, a race involving only the horses, not horse-drawn chariots anymore. This too reflects a sort of forgetfulness or misuse of IE warrior practices – in Homer (as we know it) the usage of war chariots is laughable. In the Iliad 6.230, Diomedes and Glaucus use their chariots – a reminiscence of Bronze Age warfare – but even the poet does not understand their role anymore: the chariots are kept, the two heroes rush towards one another on each chariot and then jump down and begin the preliminaries of their duel while discoursing about each one's lineage.

In Zoroastrianism, the role of the first patron of Zaraθuštra is at first made clear in a carriage race, which remains an important tenet of the Zoroastrian faith. However, even if the war chariot itself would be left behind, its role in the origin myths of Zoroastrianism remains intact. This is, I would argue, one more reason to believe in the texts that have been preserved in oral form up to Sasanid times. Homer, by contrast, underwent many changes before the 'canonical' text of the Iliad and Odyssey came to be established.

---

[32] Martin Schwartz. 'Dimensions of the Gāthās as Poetry' in: WBCZ, p. 53. This dimension of patron and poet/craftsman resembles very closely the one in the Homeric world e.g. Iliad 5.59–64 and Odyssey 3.425; 19.56–58; many more examples could be given in the Iliad and Odyssey alone.

Later in Zoroastrian thought, we find a variation of the chariot race in the guise of a battle between two stallions, which only underlines the mainstream hypothesis of Zoroastrianism being a Late Bronze Age, Central Asian religion in its origin, given the importance of horses, chariots and related themes.[33] This is linked to the idea that the material world itself is the way to defeat the forces of *druj*, that is, those related to *Angra Mainyu*. It is similar to the hero's prowess in the world of Homer: 'winning' means making one's own name eternal or having their deeds remembered forever, much like the Homeric hero would be.[34]

The big difference arises, however, when what is at stake is no longer the heroic deed in itself, as in Homeric and *PIE patterns of celebration and orality, but rather that such deeds can even be despised, as, for example, in the 'cow complaint's' chant, Y 47.[35] In a sense, this is a substitution of ancient deities by new ones, who embody new concepts (the most common being those of good deities in one religion becoming demons or lesser divinities) or slightly modified ones, as would happen to *Mithra* – embodiment of warriors, justice, law, agreements and of good faith.

---

[33] Again, we find here cosmological lore enmeshed with anthropomorphic animal deities and the perennial theme of the fight between good and evil, light and darkness, all based fundamentally on the role played by the star Sirius (*Tištriia*), as well explained by Antonio Panaino. 'Cosmologies and Astrology' in: *WBCZ*, pp. 246–7:

> Sirius was considered the chief of the astral army, and directly compared to the role assumed by Zarathustra among human beings. Thus, *Tištriia* played a remarkable role in the framework of the Indo-Iranian mythological theme of the fight against a demon who had imprisoned the waters (Ved. *Indra*). *Tištriia*, rising over the Iranian lands for a whole month of thirty days changes his own body every ten days; first, he appears in the body of a fifteen-year-old virile boy, then in that of a golden-horned bull, and finally in that of a beautiful white horse with golden ears. Assuming the form of a stallion, he asks human beings for sacrifices and then approaches the Vourukaa Sea. The demon *Apaoša*, in the form of a terrible black horse, aggressively runs against him. Both horses, ramping against each other, fight in order to take possession of the Vourukaa Sea, which seems to assume the form of a mare. After three days and nights of combat *Tištriia* is defeated and compelled to run away from the sea, sadly lamenting his defeat. Then, the *yazata* [*CPD*, 'god', 'soul'] declares that his failure was due to the lack of sacrifices by humans, who did not offer him the due worship in which his own name should have been pronounced (*aoxtō.nāman- yasna-*). At this point, it is *Ahura Mazdā* who offers such a sacrifice in order to strengthen his champion. Thus, *Tištriia* can charge again against *Apaoša* and, after an undetermined period of time, he wins at midday. Now, *Tištriia* enters the Vourukaa, agitating its waters. The star Sirius raises from the sea, followed by *Satauuaēsa*, and the clouds also ascend from the mountain Us.haṇdu, which lies in the middle of the waters. *Apąm Napā*, 'the Son/Nephew of the waters', an important divinity of Indo-Iranian origin, concurs to distribute waters and rains on the material world.

[34] Fortson IV. *Indo-European Languages and Culture*, p. 44; Georges Dumézil. *Naissance d'archanges (Jupiter, Mars, Quirinus III): Essai sur la formation de la théologie zoroastrienne*. Paris: Gallimard, 1945; cf. also Georges Dumézil. *Romans de Scythie et d'alentours*. Paris: Payol, 1978; and more specific than those two, *Heur et malheur du guerrier: Aspects mythiques de la fonction guerrière chez les indo-européens*. Paris: P.U.F., 1969.

[35] A short but remarkable piece of literature known as part of the third *gāθā*. '47.3: Of this Will Thou art the bounteous father / (the Will) which fashioned for that (pious) man the gladdening cow / while for her pasture Thou didst establish peace and piety / because he took counsel, Mindful One, with Good Thought' (Helmut Humbach. 'Interpretations of Zarathustra and the *Gāthās*' in: *WBCZ*; West. *The Hymns of Zoroaster*, Kindle loc. 1632).

§3 Supporting sides

It was in the Iranian plateau that Zoroastrianism first developed as an 'ethnic' religion and came to be identified with the indigenous kingdoms that replaced Hellenistic empires (i.e. the Parthian and Sasanid kingdoms). Furthermore, theological discussions regarding the notions of purity and impurity, from the supposedly more ancient texts to the more recent ones, become increasingly important. Whether this has anything to do with the similar development in rabbinic Judaism is far from certain.[36] In any event, we are pointing here to similar developments that happened in a loosely defined time frame rather than positing influences of one religion on the other.

In Avestan texts, both in the OAv. and the YAv.,[37] we have two possibilities of understanding what 'good' means: it either encompasses Ahuramazdā and his fellow deities or it regards the relationship between man and matter.[38] However, it is in a ninth-century polemical text, SGW (lit. 'The Exposition that Dispels Doubts'), that we find this everyday idea of Good and Evil best developed – perhaps even in comparison to the Greek notion of 'nothing in excess', although this does not prove or point towards mutual influence.[39]

The golden measure of Zoroastrianism could be seen, by non-believers, as very extreme: its sets of rules only grew more with the passing of time and the catalogue of purity/impurity resembles very much that of Talmudic Judaism and perhaps even of Late Second Temple Judaism. It is very possible that this implies a great influx of ideas between the Jewish community in Babylonia and their Zoroastrian masters, but that theory is still far from being proved.[40]

---

[36] Philippe Gignoux. 'Dietary Laws in pre-Islamic and post-Sasanian Iran" in: *Jerusalem Studies in Arabic and Islam* 17 (1987): 16–42. In recent years few scholars have dedicated more efforts to discuss religious law issues related not just to Babylonian Jewry but also to late Zoroastrian prescriptions than Yaakov Elman's 'Does Pollution Fill Space?' in: *ARAM Periodical* 25.1-2 ('Zoroastrianism in the Levant and the Amorites') (2014).

[37] The difference between the two is the following: both are Indo-Iranian languages, the OAv. referring linguistically to the second millennium BCE and the YAv. to the first millennium BCE (both were preserved in late copies, as usually happens with the textual sources we are working with). However, it should be noted that 'the Old Avestan texts express the same worldview as the Young Avesta, making allowance for differences in time and place, and the ritual they accompanied may have been an early version of the later *yasna* ritual' (Prods O. Skjærvø. 'The *Gāthās* as Myth and Ritual' in: *WBCZ*, p. 62).

[38] A discussion on this point can be found in Philippe Gignoux. 'On the Notion of Good Measure (*paymān*) and Other Related Philosophical Concepts from the *Dēnkard* III' in: K.R. Cama Oriental Institute, Third International Congress. Bombay, 2001. Cf. also Philippe Gignoux (ed.). *Mazdéens et chrétiens en terre d'Iran à l'époque sassanide*. Serie Orientale Roma. Roma: ISMEO, 2014.

[39] Shaul Shaked. *The Wisdom of the Sasanian Sages (Denkard VI)*. Boulder: Persian Heritage Series, 1979, p. xl.

[40] Contrasting views on this point can be seen by Jacob Neusner on one side and the pair Prods O. Skjærvø/Yaakov Elman on the other: Neusner advocated to the end of his life the autonomy or non-connection of Jewish purity laws and their development, Skjærvø and Elman the opposite, the latter being especially favourable to the notion of Zoroastrian-Jewish legal thinking intermingling. Cf. Michael Stausberg. 'Zoroastrian Purity Rules and Purification Rituals' in: *Die Religion Zarathustras: Geschichte – Gegenwart – Rituale*. Band 3. Stuttgart: Kohlhammer, 2004; and Alan V. Williams. 'Purity and Pollution: The Body' in: *WBCZ*, p. 345. Another good article on the subject was written by Samuel Thorpe. 'Zoroastrian Exegetical Parables in the *Škand Gumānīg Wizār*' in: *Iran and the Caucasus* 17.3 (2013). The author of the SGW is Mardanfarrokh-i Ohrmazdad,

A more important development in the notion that human beings must take sides on this cosmic struggle leads, perhaps for the first time in human history, to the greatest issues related to divine rule and free will, which are of utmost importance in Second Temple Judaism and the DSS. The first issue consists of a composite of lofty ideals that include respect for human and animal life, which makes for one reason why Zoroastrianism became again fashionable in the nineteenth and twentieth centuries – namely its 'green' worries that appealed to modern sensibilities.[41]

As for the second issue, much less attractive yet arguably better anchored in a careful and unbiased reading of the sources, it is one of the dangers scholars face when dealing with Zoroastrianism, as discussed in the Introduction: the *Gāθās* – or the five hymns attributed to Zaraθuštra himself – have been proposed by Helmut Humbach to be *maŋθras* that reflect not prayers from men to gods but rather hymns from gods to other gods.[42]

The late treatise on the nature of Good and Evil, the SGW, regardless of timely misinterpretation of its apologetic nature by all sorts of religions, offers similar ideas to be found in Second Temple literature and even in Greek writings, about how to behave properly regarding the material world.[43] That is, for the author, a way to prevent demons from imparting excess, lust and vice in men.[44] Chapter 300 of the Dk III gives us a particularly fine example of this matter in the shape of a list consisting of both correct and wrong tenets believers should live by, which were not that different from those found in other places in the Hellenistic or in the Roman world.[45]

---

a rare occasion when the Iranologist has a declared and very likely real author, as opposed to pseudepigrapha or pseudonymity.

[41] Richard Foltz's *Spirituality in the Land of the Noble: How Iran Shaped the World's Religions* (Oxford: Oneworld, 2004) is a work that touches these issues with more detail.

[42] Helmut Humbach. *The Gāthās of Zarathustra and Other Old Avestan Texts. Part I – Introduction – Text and Translation*. Heidelberg: Carl Winter Universitätsverlag, 1991, pp. 81–6; Helmut Humbach. *The Gāthās of Zarathustra and Other Old Avestan Texts. Part II – Commentary*. Heidelberg: Carl Winter Universitätsverlag, 1991, p. 23, n. 7; also Yuhan S.-D. Vevaina. 'Textual Taxonomies, Cosmological Deixis, and Canonical Commentaries in Zoroastrianism' in: *History of Religions* 50.2 (2010): 111–43.

[43] OHZ, Kindle loc. 7749:

> In the *Škand-gumānīg Wizār* we find the central question of the problem of evil: Why does the creator *Ohrmazd* not keep *Ahreman* back from evil doing and evil seeking, when He is the mighty maker (*tuwān kardār*)? The answer is this, that the evil deeds (*wad-kunišnīh*) of *Ahreman* are owing to the evil nature (*wad-gōhrīh*) and evil will (*wad-kāmagīh*) which are always his, as the Lie (*druj*). The omnipotence (*wisp-tuwānīh*) of the creator *Ohrmazd* is that which is over all that is possible to do (*wisp šāyēd*) and is limited (*sāmānōmand*) thereby. (SGW 3.2, 4–6; cf. Jean de Menasce. *Une apologétique Mazdéene du IX*ᵉ *Siècle. Škand-Gumānīk Vičār. La Solution Décisive des Doutes*. Fribourg: Librairie de l'Université, 1945, pp. 38–9)

[44] Carlo G. Cereti. '"And the *frawahrs* of the men [...] agreed to go into the material world": Zoroastrian Cosmogony in the 3rd Chapter of the *Greater Bundahišn*' in: Maria Macuch, Mauro Maggi and Werner Sundermann (eds). *Iranian Languages and Texts from Iran and Turan: Ronald E. Emmerick Memorial Volume*. Iranica 13. Wiesbaden: Harrasowitz, 2007, p. 28.

[45] An especially interesting passage in chapter 429 of Dk IV is that concerning the nature of balance and good sense in Iran: 'Iran has always exalted Good Measure and scorned excess and deficiency' (MP, *Ērān hamē paymān stāyid frehbud id abēbūd nikōhīd*).

> Exposition in the good religion about that unconscientious man who possesses the skill of the immoral *Druj* and fights on the side of the sinful *Ahriman*. And the man who is connected with the evil one fights with the support of the *Druj*. (300) Again a man may be

§4 Zarathustra as patron and predecessor of Greek thinkers

Should the core precepts of Zoroastrianism – that the material world is the stage where a cosmic struggle is being waged, and that Zaraθuštra is the prophet who received this message and organized its spread – prove to be correct, the whole idea of practising good would take an entirely different meaning and much of the ethical ideas traditionally attributed to Zoroastrianism or to Zaraθuštra would need to be moved forward in time. In other words, although Greek traditions, such as that of Plutarch, insist on the struggle between Good and Evil as integral to Zaraθuštra's teachings, we cannot rely on these sources alone.[46] Later proper Zoroastrian sources greatly contributed to the brief abstract given by Plutarch:

> The great majority and the wisest of men hold this opinion: they believe that there are two gods, rivals as it were, the one the Artificer of good and the other of evil. There are also those who call the better one a god and the other a daemon, as, for example, Zoroaster the sage, who, they record, lived five thousand years before the time of the Trojan War. He called the one Oromazes and the other Areimaniusc; and he further declared that among all the things perceptible to the senses, Oromazes may best be compared to light, and Areimanius, conversely, to darkness and ignorance, and midway between the two is Mithras; for this reason the Persians give to Mithras the name of 'Mediator'. Zoroaster has also taught that men should make votive offerings and thank-offerings to Oromazes, and averting and mourning offerings to Areimanius. They pound up in a mortar a certain plant called omomi, at the same time invoking Hades and Darkness ... However,

> connected with the evil *Druj* but may not be so with *Ahriman*; a man may not be connected with the immoral (*Druj*) and may be so with *Ahriman*; and may not be connected with either the immoral *Druj* or *Ahriman*. [Sur ce dont l'excès est plus destructeur de la substance (*mâtag*) de la Mesure que ne l'est de defaut; sur ce dont le défaut est plus destructeur que l'excès; sur ce qui comporte excès / et non défaut; sur ce qui comporte défaut et non excès; et sur ce qui ne comporte aucunement excès ou défaut.] (Jean de Menasce. *Le Troisième Livre du Dēnkart: Traduit du pehlevi*. Paris: Klincksieck, 1973, pp. 293–4)

> In an older English translation by Peshotan D. B. Sanjana, trans. Ratanshah E. Kohiyar. *Denkard, Book 3. Vol. 7* (Avestan compilation by Joseph Peterson, http://www.avesta.org/denkard/dk3s.html; original, Bombay: 1894):

> Be it known that the man who aids unwise and wicked conduct like that of the unconscientious *Druj* and evil *Ahriman* fights with the assistance of the defiling *Ahriman*. The man who possesses the power of the demons wages satanic war in this world with the aid of the evil *Druj*. The man who is connected not with the evil *Druj* but with *Ahriman* is a still greater cause of disturbance in the world. The man who is not connected with Ahriman is charitable to those who deserve charity and does other good deeds. The man who is connected neither with the evil *Druj* nor with *Ahriman* is a follower of *Ohrmazd*'s Mazdayasnian faith and recites the sacred Manthras.

[46] Cf. an exceptionally fine introduction to that matter by Marco Frenschkowski. 'Christianity' in: *WBCZ*, pp. 457–75. Besides the work of Joseph Bidez and Franz Cumont quoted in note 52, this topic has been continuously debated since the time of Theodor Nöldeke ('Syrische Polemik gegen die persische Religion' in: Ernst Kuhn (ed.). *Der Festgruß an Robert von Roth zum Doctor-Jubiläum 24. August 1893*. Stuttgart: W. Kohlhammer, 1893, pp. 34–8).

they also tell many fabulous stories about their gods, such, for example, as the following: Oromazes, born from the purest light, and Areimanius, born from the darkness, are constantly at war with each other; and Oromazes created six gods, the first of Good Thought, the second of Truth, the third of Order, and, of the rest, one of Wisdom, one of Wealth.[47]

Plutarch's testimony, despite coming from the Parthian period from a Mediterranean point of view, points to a much older theme which he quotes from Theopompus at some length (although we only have fragments of the latter[48]):

> Theopompus says that, according to the sages, one god is to overpower, and the other to be overpowered, each in turn for the space of three thousand years, and afterward for another three thousand years they shall fight and war, and the one shall undo the works of the other, and finally Hades shall pass away; then shall the people be happy, and neither shall they need to have food nor shall they cast any shadow. And the god, who has contrived to bring about all these things, shall then have quiet and shall repose for a time, no long time indeed, but for the god as much as would be a moderate time for a man to sleep. Theopompus says that, according to the sages, one god is to overpower, and the other to be overpowered, each in turn for the space of three thousand years, and afterward for another three thousand years they shall fight and war, and the one shall undo the works of the other, and finally Hades shall pass away; then shall the people be happy, and neither shall they need to have food nor shall they cast any shadow. And the god, who has contrived to bring about all these things, shall then have quiet and shall repose for a time, no long time indeed, but for the god as much as would be a moderate time for a man to sleep.[49]

Summing up Plutarch's ideas, which are much more in line with what we now know about Zoroastrianism, according to what Theopompus describes as Zoroastrianism, we have, first, a period of 'sleep' or spiritual existence (*mēnōg*[50]); second, a period of fight whose outcome is already known; and third, apart from the bliss awaiting those worthy of paradise, we have periods of three thousand years in each stage of the cosmic struggle. The idea that 'Hades will pass away' is here merely a Greek way of expressing the end of after-death suffering.

Part of the wording is uncertain according to the LCL edition but in no manner affects the general meaning of the text in comparison with Avestan ideas. This is one of the cornerstones for those that hold orthodox views regarding the dating of Zoroastrian ideas: if Plutarch, writing towards the end of the first century CE or during the 120s CE at the latest, is quoting an earlier source, it is very difficult to dismiss Avestan ideas as an invention to the Sasanid Era, whether in part or in total.

---

[47] Plutarch. *De Isis et Osiride*, pp. 46–7.
[48] FrGH 115.
[49] Gr., 'καὶ τοὺς μὲν ἀνθρώπους εὐδαίμονας ἔσεσθαι μήτε τροφῆς δεομένους μήτε σκιὰν ποιοῦντας· τὸν δὲ ταῦτα μηχανησάμενον θεὸν ἠρεμεῖν καὶ ἀναπαύεσθαι χρόνον'.
[50] CPD, 'mēnōg', 'mēnōgīg', 'mēnōgīh': 'spiritual', 'heavenly', 'spirit', 'spirituality'.

After that passage – and much in conformity to the style of the *Moralia*, of which *De Isis et Osiride* are but a part – Plutarch goes on to discuss other cosmogonic themes and ideas. Similar topics can also be found in Pliny, with remarkably acidic criticism on the very origin and usage of the term 'magic' (originated, as it were, from the *Magi*) considering the sources he uses.

> Without doubt magic arose in Persia with Zoroaster. On this our authorities are agreed, but whether he was the only one of that name, or whether there was also another afterwards, is not clear. Eudoxus, who wished magic to be acknowledged as the noblest and most useful of the schools of philosophy, declared that this Zoroaster lived six thousand years before Plato's death, and Aristotle agrees with him. Hermippus, a most studious writer about every aspect of magic, and an exponent of two million verses composed by Zoroaster, added summaries too to his rolls, and gave Agonaces as the teacher by whom he said that he had been instructed, assigning to the man himself a date five thousand years before the Trojan War. What especially is surprising is the survival, through so long a period, of the craft and its tradition; treatises are wanting, and besides there is no line of distinguished or continuous successors to keep alive their memory. For how few know anything, even by hearsay, of those who alone have left their names but without other memorial – Apusorus and Zaratus of Media, Marmarus and Arabantiphocus of Babylon, or Tarmoendas of Assyria? The most surprising thing, however, is the complete silence of Homer about magic in his poem on the Trojan War, and yet so much of his work in the wanderings of Ulysses is so occupied with it that it alone forms the backbone of the whole work, if indeed they put a magical interpretation upon the Proteus episode in Homer and the songs of the Sirens, and especially upon the episode of Circe and of the calling up of the dead from Hades, of which magic is the sole theme. And in later times nobody has explained how ever it reached Telmesus, a city given up to superstition, or when it passed over to the Thessalian matrons, whose surname was long proverbial in our part of the world, although magic was a craft repugnant to the Thessalian people, who were content, at any rate in the Trojan period, with the medicines of Chiron, and with the War God as the only wielder of the thunderbolt.[51]

---

[51] Pliny. *Natural History*, 30.2:

> Sine dubio illic orta in Perside a Zoroastre, ut inter auctores convenit. sed unus hic fuerit an postea et alius non satis constat. Eudoxus, qui inter sapientiae sectas clarissimam utilissimamque eam intellegi voluit, Zoroastrem hunc sex milibus annorum ante Platonis mortem fuisse prodidit, sic et Aristoteles. Hermippus qui de tota ea arte diligentissime scripsit et viciens centum milia versuum a Zoroastre condita indicibus quoque voluminum eius positis explanavit, praeceptorem a quo institutum diceret tradidit Agonacen, ipsum vero quinque milibus annorum ante Troianum bellum fuisse. mirum hoc in primis, durasse memoriam artemque tam longo aevo commentariis intercidentibus, praeterea nec claris nec continuis successionibus custoditam. quotus enim quisque auditu saltem cognitos habet, qui soli nominantur, Apusorum et Zaratum Medos, Babyloniosque Marmarum et Arabantiphocum, Assyrium Tarmoendam, quorum nulla exstant monumenta? maxime tamen mirum est in bello Troiano tantum de arte ea silentium fuisse Homero tantumque operis ex eadem in Ulixis erroribus, adeo ut totum opus non aliunde constet, siquidem Protea

On that note, as it often happens in Pliny's writings – which are mostly based on other sources and not on eyewitness accounts – we have the usual Hellenistic (and partially Latin) mumble of discrepancies: Pliny is talking about a 'Zoroaster' that his audience will find palatable and nice and yet, at the same time, he is talking about magic. 'Magic' here is enmeshed with an interesting observation that would have a long career on its own: 'Zoroaster' left two million verses in written form, which can be considered 'a great sum' in the realm of ancient writers. Pliny does not state this but affirms that Hermippus, whom he claims to have studied these verses, is writing after the episode of the Trojan War.

These writings – concerned again with Good and Evil – would form an important part of the investigation by later Greeks. Pliny goes on ascertaining that Homer, should all this be true, would have given much more attention to the popularity that magic acquired amongst the Greeks. Moreover, the ascribing of such teachings to a certain Ostanes highlights once more the use, or rather misuse, of what the Greeks thought were Zoroastrian teachings. That would not only lead to some misunderstandings of what Zoroastrianism was about but also provide, at the same time, early examples of Greek (i.e. Pagan, at this point) appropriation of foreign ideas, which would reappear later refashioned very much alike the Sibylline Oracles.

All that material – either in the form of praise as it appears in Plutarch or in reprobation and utterly confusing scepticism as it appears in Pliny – appears to exemplify the common usage of the figures of Oriental sages about whom very little was known by the end of the first century CE (the time when Plutarch also wrote his *Natural History*, completed by 77 CE).

In both cases, which are the most notorious treatments of Zoroaster/Zaraθuštra in the Western world, there are several reinterpretation problems. For instance, they relate not only to partial or complete ignorance of his teachings but also reflect the usual way Graeco-Roman lettered men reacted to the idea of 'alien wisdom'. As a modern author succinctly put it, Greek and Roman men of culture, from the fifth century BCE onwards, seem to prefer a fantastic, quasi-magical explanation and examples for phenomena and knowledge coming from the East or even from their most extreme borders.

The approach to the same topic in Plutarch and Pliny may differ in perspective but diverges more pointedly in terms of quality: while quoting Theopompus, Plutarch leads us towards a very precise notion of basic Zoroastrian cosmogonic themes. Diverse treatments given to those materials can also be found in several authors who currently deal with the most relevant basic research on that matter. Their biggest challenge is to understand the fantastic element surrounding the imagination of the Greek reader which would, in many cases, replace factual knowledge.[52]

> et Sirenum cantus apud eum non aliter intellegi volunt, Circe utique et inferum evocatione hoc solum agi. nec postea quisquam dixit quonam modo venisset Telmesum religiosissimam urbem, quando transisset ad Thessalas matres, quarum cognomen diu optinuit in nostro orbe, aliena genti Troianis utique temporibus Chironis medicinis contentae et solo Marte fulminante.

[52] Albert de Jong. *Traditions of the Magi: Zoroastrianism in Greek and Latin Literature.* Leiden: Brill, 1997. Antonio Panaino. 'Astral Characters of Kingship in the Sasanian and Byzantine Worlds' in: *La Persia e Bisanzio. Atti dei convegni Lincei (Roma), 201.* Bologna: Università degli Studi di Bologna, 2004, pp. 555–94. More recently, the work of Brent Landau dealing with the Magi cannot be dismissed

§5 Staraθuštra's legacy regardless of dating issues

Nonetheless, one thing is for sure: within Iranian texts attributed to Zaraθuštra the history of religions faces a turning point when the traditional struggle between order and chaos acquires a fixed timetable, which would vary according to the version of the legend one was dealing with. That notion has become fairly canonical; hence, the greatest issue here is pinpointing the exact period in which that particular idea surfaced, given the extensive problems scholars face regarding manuscript's dating.

The world described in Avestan poetry, regardless of its age and correct attribution to Zaraθuštra, is a world in which the struggle between Good and Evil (e.g. between Light and Darkness) is frequently described as the struggle between poets. Moreover, this struggle is perpetually present in both the daily lives and efforts of the faithful and in the cosmic dimensions of the world. Light and Darkness stand as symbols of that struggle, but even those have other meanings since the natural (i.e. physical) world is in itself a creation of Ohrmazd – after the three thousand years of creation in a 'sleeping' state, *mēnōg*, as we saw above. Ohrmazd takes the battle to the only field in which he knows Ahriman can be defeated: a natural, physical, newly created world. That will also be Ohrmazd's answer to the question of the resurrection of the dead, for it would be no more difficult for him to 're-create' the physical world than it was to create it out of the spiritual sleep in the beginning of the cosmic battle.

All this means that the proclaimer of *aša*,[53] of 'righteousness', is to be seen as a winner, as a person to be respected due to great virtue of character. A good example of that can be found in the *Gāθās* 46–48, where the disdain of the winning poet regarding the rulers of chaos is remarkable: 'Differently from Genesis, at the outset of the Gāthās the cosmos has already been made and consists of two worlds (*ahu*[54]), the one of thought and the one of living beings or "the one with bones".'[55]

> The reinvestment of Ahura Mazdā is achieved by the combined efforts of the gods supporting the cosmic order over the daēuuas, old gods who chose the wrong side in the in the cosmic battle (1.30.6, 2.44.20); the poet's scorn of the rulers of chaos, which deprives them of fame, hence also power ...; and the ritual competition.[56]

---

and has opened up an entirely new field of work with the new manuscript examined (*Revelation of the Magi: The Lost Tale of the Wise Men's Journey to Bethlehem*. New York: HarperOne, 2010, Kindle edition). The work of Bidez and Cumont (*Les Mages Hellenisés*), for all its limitations to the modern reader, is a classic in its own right and should be the ideal starting point to all investigations related to the usages of Zoroastrian lore.

[53] CPD, 'ašō', righteous (from Av. 'ašawa').
[54] CPD, 'axw(ān)', world(ly).
[55] Skjærvo. 'The *Gāthās* as Myth and Ritual', Kindle loc. 2162.
[56] Karl Hoffman. 'The Avesta Fragment FrD.3' in: *IIJ* 10.4 (1968); Prods O. Skjærvø. 'Praise and Blame in the Avesta: The Poet Sacrificer and His Duties' in: *JSAI* 26 (2002); also by Skjærvø is the more introductory work *The Spirit of Zoroastrianism* (New Haven: Yale University Press, 2011). Related to that theme it might be useful to take a look at Carlo G. Cereti and David N. MacKenzie. 'Except by Battle: Zoroastrian Cosmogony in the 1st Chapter of the *Greater Bundahishn*' in: Carlo G. Cereti, Mauro Maggi and Elio Provasi (eds). *Religious Themes and Texts of Pre-Islamic Iran and Central Asia: Studies in Honour of Professor Gherardo Gnoli on the Occasion of his 65th Birthday on 6th December 2002*. Wiesbaden: Reichert, 2003, p. 31.

The idea that winning a poetry contest has any part in the preservation of the soul is not strange to the Late Bronze Age epic. In fact, a person's name being preserved due to their deeds in life is a feature commonly found in the Homeric world. Also, the struggle between Good and Evil represented as a horse race is likewise a usual reinterpretation of a contest between two deities, two individuals or two differently ordered worlds. On that note, it is purposeful to compare the *Gāθās* Y 1.34 with the accomplishments of Homeric heroes[57] even though the heroic exploits in Homer would be dismissed as plain robbery in the Avestan world. Undoubtedly, the life perspective attributed to Zaraθuštra and to Zoroastrians remained exceedingly competitive, from the very genesis of the world to its unavoidable end.

At this point, those affairs function as a powerful reminder of the importance of words in IE societies which, although capable of writing, insisted on singing their words in order to perpetuate memory, scorn, cowardice and other important features, for heroic triumphs were an essential part of their collective memory. The same phenomenon has been registered in Vedic India, in the whole complex of Druidic lore from Anatolia to Scotland and, of course, in the Homeric world. If not deliberate, it would be a great coincidence for all that parallel poetry to exist in so many similar societies. Notably,

> Stanzas 1–2 ... address the very basic theme of the choice between Right and Wrong. This theme is illustrated poetically via an extended metaphor, that of a race between two chariots, a figure whose origin, as is seen from Vedic Sanskrit and from Greek poetry, is Indo-European, including the metaphor of a chariot of Rightness. Only the righteous team survives the race, as that chariot, remaining firmly yoked at the finish, enters the divine paradisiac abode in abiding fame, while the pole of the chariot of Wrongness (under what must be assumed as the pressure it undergoes at the last turn in the course, as precedented by recorded real situations) snaps with fatal results.[58]

§6 Combats, free will and the world beyond

As seen above, a remarkable feature in the *Gāθās* is that at the outset of the battle between Good and Evil the world already existed. Truly, two worlds had already been made: one consisting purely of thought, and the other, the one filled with living beings, was literally named 'the one with bones'.[59] As Prods O. Skjærvø noted, this is a world that was made in a workmanlike fashion: it was created not out of nothing but rather fashioned as an artisan would have done it (*Gāθās* Y 1.31.7; 2.44.5; Yt 5.85).[60]

---

[57] Skjærvø. *Spirit*, pp. 214–15.
[58] Schwartz. 'Dimensions of the *Gāthās*', p. 51; and Fortson IV. *Indo-European Languages and Culture*, p. 50 (related to Roman practices of ritual chariot-racing too); cf. also Calvert Watkins. *How to Kill a Dragon*. New York: Oxford University Press, 1995, p. 9: 'The metaphor of the ruler as driver, charioteer recurs in the Old Irish text *Audacht Morainn* §22 and frequently in the Rigveda.' More parallels regarding the heavenly chariot in the RV 4.53.4 and the *Homeric Hymn to Selene* 32.11.
[59] YH 37.2.
[60] Skjærvø. 'The Avestan Yasna', p. 72.

With the help of the human sacrificers, Ahura Mazdā heals the world ... of the illnesses brought upon it by darkness and evil, embodied in Wrath ..., who is overcome by Sraoša, 'the one who overcomes the obstacles' .... Wrath, the night sky, is cut off (the cosmic loom), and the 'covering' (viiā) of Good Thought, the pure sun-lit sky, is spread out (3.48.7), for the sun to travel across. The visible sign of Order, the sun, reappears (1.32.2, 2.43.16, 46.3), achieved by the sacrifice and songs of the saošiiaṇts (opponents of Wrath, 3.48.12), whose 'guiding thoughts' (xratu) are the oxen that pull the wagons of the new days ..., while the supporters of chaos try to prevent the sun from rising ... and, with their bad xratu,[61] merely increase Wrath (3.49.4) and with it make the world sick (1.30.6).[62]

Here a typical false dilemma regarding free will is noticeable: men are free to choose Evil, but their personal reward is, in the end, greater if they choose Good. The outcome has already been defined by the sheer sagacity of *Ahura Mazda*, the Good god: he made a treaty (*paymanag*[63]) with Ahriman, the Evil god, and defined that their combat would last nine thousand years (twelve thousand in other versions), but the outcome would always favour *Ahura Mazda*.

Ohrmazd in his omniscience knew that the Evil Spirit exists, what he was planning to do in his jealousy, how he would mix creation from the beginning to the end, and with how many instruments; so he fashioned the creatures spiritually with the necessary instruments. For three thousand years, the creatures were only spiritual; that is, they were unthinking, unmoving, and intangible.[64]

Creation remained in this 'primeval', or motionless, state (*mēnōg*), for the first three thousand years of this theogony. Then, Ahuramazda offered peace to Ahriman, who disdainfully rejected it. After a while, Creation entered motion and Ahuramazda was able to finally create his creatures for the combat (as did Ahriman, in his ignorance of the outcome of the combat).[65]

---

[61] CPD, 'xrad': 'wisdom', 'reason', but 'xraftsar' (from Av. *xrafstra*): 'reptile', 'noxious creature' – reinforcing the idea of a good and a bad 'xrad', so it seems.
[62] Skjærvø, 'The *Gāthās* as Myth and Ritual', Kindle loc. 3176.
[63] CPD has similar forms: 'paymān': 'measure', 'period'; 'moderation'; 'treaty'; 'paymanag': 'period', 'measure', 'proportion'.
[64] Bd 1.12–13.
[65] Bd 19–25:

> 19. Then Ohrmazd, knowing the nature of creation and the end of the affair, went to meet the Evil Spirit. He proposed peace and said: 'Evil Spirit, give aid to my creatures and offer praise, so that, as a reward, you may become immortal and ageless, without sensation or decay. 20. If you do not provoke a battle, you will not become powerless yourself and you will bring benefit to us both.' 21. The Evil Spirit snarled: 'I will not help your creatures and I will not offer praise! No, I will destroy you and your creatures for ever and ever! I will incite all your creatures to hate you and to love me.' 22. The explanation is that he believed that Ohrmazd had offered peace because he was helpless against him. He did not accept it, and made his vow. 23. Ohrmazd said: 'You are not omnipotent, Evil Spirit. You cannot destroy me nor can you prevent my creatures from returning to my possession.' 24. Then Ohrmazd in his omniscience realized: If I do not set a time for our battle, he will be able to do to my creation

The same circumstances are replicated in Second Temple Judaism, particularly in apocalyptic literature, with the additional aspect that the later the texts are, the better their thematic development. For illustration, let us compare a 'founding' passage in Daniel and its outcomes in later apocalypses, in several passages in 2 Bar. (1–6 provide a good example) and in 4 Ezra (chs 4–6; 7:19–30; 8:1–3; 10:19–59; 11). Daniel does not know, in the sequence of visions 7–12, most of what he sees and requires an explanation (as opposed to ch. 2 in which a Pagan king, Nebbuchadnezzar, is the one who has the vision and Daniel, through God's will, merely repeats it):

> Dan 7:1: In the first year of Belshazzar king of Babylon, Daniel had a dream and visions of his head as he lay in his bed. Then he wrote down the dream, and told the sum of the matter. 2. Daniel said, "I saw in my vision by night, and behold, the four winds of heaven were stirring up the great sea. 3. And four great beasts came up out of the sea, different from one another. 4. The first was like a lion and had eagles' wings. Then as I looked its wings were plucked off, and it was lifted up from the ground and made to stand upon two feet like a man; and the mind of a man was given to it. 5. And behold, another beast, a second one, like a bear. It was raised up on one side; it had three ribs in its mouth between its teeth; and it was told, 'Arise, devour much flesh.' 6. After this I looked, and lo, another, like a leopard, with four wings of a bird on its back; and the beast had four heads; and dominion was given to it. 7. After this I saw in the night visions, and behold, a fourth beast, terrible and dreadful and exceedingly strong; and it had great iron teeth; it devoured and broke in pieces, and stamped the residue with its feet. It was different from all the beasts that were before it; and it had ten horns. 8. I considered the horns, and behold, there came up among them another horn, a little one, before which three of the first horns were plucked up by the roots; and behold, in this horn were eyes like the eyes of a man, and a mouth speaking great things. 9. As I looked, thrones were placed and one that was ancient of days took his seat; his raiment was white as snow, and the hair of his head like pure wool; his throne was fiery flames, its wheels were burning fire. 10. A stream of fire issued and came forth from before him; a thousand thousands served him, and ten thousand times ten thousand stood before him; the court sat in judgment, and the books were opened.

A few differences are noticeable in this passage: Jewish visionaries either receive God's explanation (Daniel), or these explanations are useless but promote inward changes on the visionary (4 Ezra), or God explains the defeat of His chosen people in propitiatory terms, that is, mercifully in order to appease the believers. In Zoroastrianism there is no need for such explanations, for the faithful know from the very beginning the outcome of the cosmic fight and the subsequent destiny of humanity.

> as he vowed, and the strife and Mixture will be forever. During the Mixture, he will be able to mislead the creatures and make them his own. Just so, now during the Mixture, there are many people who commit more sins than good deeds; that is, they always do as the Evil Spirit desires. 25. Ohrmazd said to the Evil Spirit: 'Let us set a time, so that by this pact our battle will be limited to nine thousand years.' For he knew that in this time he would render the Evil Spirit powerless.

§7 On bones, primaeval androgyny and free will

If we are talking about resurrection of the flesh, especially in pastoral-hunting societies, the roles of the bones of animals and men are equally important. Early archaeological evidence shows that in the past, perhaps during Palaeolithic times, burials involved particular arrangements of the corpses throughout the rituals. On the other hand, if one's body was to be cremated the idea of a burial ceremony was reverted, but the bones still retained their importance. Essentially, the notion that the bones are hard and 'inside' the flesh, thus allowing the rest to take shape, was something widespread even to pre-scientific minds. Also, in cultures that have developed a strong tie with shamanistic practices, the role of bones is even bigger. Nonetheless, the reference to the 'bones' as a vital force in the world to come is something altogether strange to the world view of Semitic scriptures.[66] For instance, in the book of Genesis, God fashions the world out of nothing (or so a great deal of scholars put it), but there is no reference of Him ever 'seeing' His Creation. That highlights a remarkably similar anthropomorphic feature: that God needs to create light in order 'to see' what He is doing, much like men themselves would (cf. e.g. Gen 7:1 – Hb. ראיתי. In the Qur'an God fashions man out of a clot of blood (Sura 23:14, Ar. ملقنا لنطفه, 'then We made this drop into a clot.')).[67]

The issue of bones equalling life fully refers to a culture that was originally that of hunters-gatherers, with a strong shamanistic trait. In fact, more than one shamanistic ritual involves the shaman himself going to the underworld after some initiation that entailed being placed inside an animal's hide.[68] The evidence of such ethos abides when we think about the demon of death in Zoroastrian culture, called the 'bone-breaker' or the one that unties the bones and thus brings death.[69] A good example of that belief could be found in Dan 12:2, in which the resurrection process involves coming back from the dust of the bones.

---

[66] The most passages here are, arguably, Ezek 38:11 and even more so Ps-Ezek in the DSS (4Q385-388).
[67] Quranic references were taken from https://quran.com/, given its vast resources for comparison of translations and location of passages. I usually follow, among the several translations in the site, those of Sayyid Abul Ala Maududi.
[68] Mircea Eliade. *Shamanism: Archaic Techniques of Ecstasy*. Princeton: Princeton University Press, 1962, pp. xviii, 93, 108, 396-7; Karl Meuli. 'Scythica' in: *Hermes* 70.2 (1935): 133-4: 'Das Sitzen auf dem Fell eines Tieres, dessen Bedeutung uns hier nicht aufzuhalten braucht, kommt z. B. auch bei yakutischen und samojedischen Schamanen vor'; Vevaina, 'Theologies and Hermeneutics', p. 214: 'The religion (*dēn*) is bound (*paywast*) to the sacred word (*mānsr* from Av. *maθra-*, compare Skt. mantra-, lit. "instrument of mind") and is in harmony with it in the same way as flesh (*gōšt*) is with skin (*pōst*) and as a vein (rag) is with its enveloping hide (*čarm*) (Dk 6.324).'
[69] Skjærvø. 'The *Gāthās* as Myth and Ritual', p. 63:

> 'The text also reflects the evolution of *Ahura Mazdā*'s ordered world, from the birth of the first ordered existence, when *Ahura Mazdā* recited the Ahuna Vairiia (Y 27.13) and dispelled chaos the first time (Y 19.15), via Zarathustra's first battles with the forces of darkness and evil …, to the final healing of the world, when the *Airiiaman Išiia* (Y 54.1) will be set in motion by the successful poet-sacrificers, the *saošiiaṇts*, upon which *Ahura Mazdā* will have absolute command, the Dark Spirit and his ilk will be deprived of any command and will hide forever, and *Ahura Mazdā*'s creation will have life and bones forever (compare Y 8.5-6; FrW 4.1-3, compare 3.48.5, 5.53.8, YH 41.3, Vd 19-21. (Variations in spelling, here and elsewhere, due to the original sources or authors' preferences)

The Promethean myth itself is a strong reminder of this, when Prometheus changes the flesh that should be due to the gods by bones covered with fat.[70]

Finally, the reminiscence of the IE familiar theme of the primeval twins is yet another way of depicting the fight between Good and Evil in a very concrete and portrait-like way: 'The two twinned Spirits – a better one and a bad one, opposite in mind, word, and deed – were heard in a dream. Of these two, the beneficent one chose (decided) rightly, not the maleficent one.'[71] This theme can be found in several IE myths and it even makes an appearance in Plato's *Symposium* through the speech of Aristophanes which, although satirical, retains many of the essential elements of the primeval androgyny theme.[72]

> Hence I shall try and introduce you to his power, that you may transmit this teaching to the world at large. You must begin your lesson with the nature of man and its development. For our original nature was by no means the same as it is now. In the first place, there were three kinds of human beings, not merely the two sexes, male and female, as at present: there was a third kind as well, which had equal shares of the other two, and whose name survives though the thing itself has vanished. For 'man-woman'1 was then a unity in form no less than name, composed of both sexes and sharing equally in male and female; whereas now it has come to be merely a name of reproach. Secondly, the form of each person was round all over, with back and sides encompassing it every way; each had four arms, and legs to match these, and two faces perfectly alike on a cylindrical neck. There was one head to the two faces, which looked opposite ways; there were four ears, two privy members, and all the other parts, as may be imagined, in proportion.

> And Zeus, afraid of their might and a seasoned veteran after the Titans affair, said,

> 'I will slice every person in two, and then they must go their ways on one leg, hopping.' So saying, he sliced each human being in two, just as they slice sorb-apples to make a dry preserve, or eggs with hairs; and at the cleaving of each he bade Apollo turn its face and half-neck to the section side, in order that every one might be made more orderly by the sight of the knife's work upon him; this done, the god was to heal them up. Then Apollo turned their faces about, and pulled their skin together from the edges over what is now called the belly, just like purses which you draw close with a string; the little opening he tied up in the middle of the belly, so making what we know as the navel. For the rest, he smoothed away most of the puckers and figured out the breast with some such instrument as shoemakers use in smoothing the wrinkles of leather on the last;

---

[70] Meuli. 'Scythica', p. 134, on the fantastic powers obtained via the time spent in the animal hide.
[71] Schwartz. 'Dimensions of the *Gāthās*', p. 63.
[72] Geo Widengren. 'Les ages du monde selon hésiode' in: Geo Widengren et al. (eds). *Apocalyptique iranienne et dualisme qoumrânien*. Paris: Adrien Maisonneuve, 1995, pp. 44–7. Widengren also quotes a seldom remembered legend where Zeus is also androgyne (Kern fragment 168, where Zeus is both the Universe and the creator of the same Universe – an implicit form of androgyny).

though he left there a few which we have just about the belly and navel, to remind us of our early fall. Now when our first form had been cut in two, each half in longing for its fellow would come to it again; and then would they fling their arms about each other and in mutual embraces yearn to be grafted together, till they began to perish of hunger and general indolence, through refusing to do anything apart. And whenever on the death of one half the other was left alone, it went seeking and embracing either any half of the whole woman (which now we call a woman), or any half of the whole man on which it might happen. In this plight they were perishing away, when Zeus in his pity provided a fresh device. He moved their privy parts to the front – for until then they had these, like all else, on the outside ... Each of us, then, is but a tally of a man, since every one shows like a flat-fish the traces of having been sliced in two; and each is ever searching for the tally that will fit him.[73]

However, it is very possible that this passage is merely a variation of a conflict that takes place amongst astral bodies in more common aspects of mythology.[74] In such cases, the result would be the same but the basis of the fight itself would configure a somewhat different world view.[75] All in all, Zoroastrian thought would remain with one unanswerable question: if the result of such conflict between Good and Evil (let us remember, a pair of twins) is known beforehand, what is the need for the common man to side with one instead of the other? That very same problem regarding the antagonism between free will and an omniscient God appears time and time again within Judaism, Christianity and Islam.[76]

Another interesting matter regarding the same discussion is this: humankind had, in *PIE societies and texts, a protoform akin to the gods, with particular reference to androgyny and omniscience. The myth of a macrocosmos repeated in the microcosmos, that is, each man and woman is found from Central Asia to Europe with remarkable consistency. The combat myths (i.e. in the beginning of time and in its end) share common traits amidst *PIE and Semitic societies, but a very important difference is clear: since Semitic societies did not fully develop an 'end of times' once-and-for-all myth, scholars have to focus solely on the implications of their creational myths.[77]

---

[73] Plato. *Symposium*, 189 D–191 E.
[74] Such is the case of Hermaphroditos, 'son of Hérmes and of Aphrodíte. He was passionately loved by the spring-nymph Salmakis, so much so that their bodies merged and united forever, thus giving rise to an androgynous being. *The cult of this twin divinity (which may have ancient oriental antecedents) reached Athens by way of Cyprus.'* Cf. Manfred Lurker. 'Hermaphróditos' in: *The Routledge Dictionary of Gods and Goddesses, Devils and Demons*. London: Routledge, 1987, p. 79 (emphasis mine).
[75] Cf., among others, Panaino. 'Astral Characters of Kingship', pp. 555–7; and also, by the same author, 'Iniziazione e dimensione esoterica nella tradizione mazdaica: Riti e simboli' in: *Sulla soglia del sacro: esoterismo ed iniziazione nelle grandi religioni e nella tradizione massonica. Firenze 1-3 marzo 2002. Atti del Convegno di Studi*, a cura di A. Panaino. Milano: Mimesis, 2002, pp. 105–10.
[76] An important issue that is better discussed in Chapter 3 of this book, more devoted to the questions regarding dualism, monism and similar issues especially because of their importance in the DSS.
[77] In some sections of the HB previous to Daniel, we have a glimpse of God's omnipotence but not much more than glimpses: Deut 32:8 would be one such (when El Elyon divides the nations between his sons, and Yahweh, in this case a subordinate god, receives Israel), but there is nothing 'universal' or 'cosmic' in that. Closer to such notions would be Pss 29:3 and 93. On that theme, much has been written, but a very summary bibliography must contain the following: Bernhard

In Indo-Iranian societies, however, the idea of the passing of time having some sort of predefined meaning, to flourish completely at the end of the one cosmic fight, is the focus.

The problem that arose simultaneously with the texts examined in the passages just above was thus that of free will versus the need to 'choose sides' in this fight. The greatest question remains complex and unanswered: what is the role of free will in a religion system whose main deity already knows the final destiny of everything, including men? Once formulated, this baffling question will be at the forefront of theological worries of the three Abrahamic faiths.

Whether those discussions came to be as a result of Persian influence or not seems a likely possibility, but, as stated earlier, it is risky to define these coincidences as more than 'parallels'. Even that being the case, the parallels themselves are striking: in Judaism, Christianism and Islamism the same puzzling question pervades theological thinking up to this day. If God (or one God) is absolutely good and only good things come to be from his actions, then what is the role of evil in the world?

§8 Good and evil as perceived in Daniel: Some concrete thoughts

One of the most interesting related issues regarding Daniel is that, as opposed to ch. 2 where the last empire (the Greeks, or Diadochi, or any variation on the theme) is something bad in itself, in the apocalypse proper we have more detailed information regarding why, precisely, this last empire is evil. Additionally, the fight between Good and Evil is done, to a certain extent, by proxy using other angels.

That works as an interesting reminder of how the world that apocalypticists had before their eyes was much larger than that of the prophets or of the pre-Exilic Hebrews at large: when asking the poorly defined (to Daniel himself) being who touches him, Daniel receives the reply that his people's angel has to leave in order to fight his equivalent, in an angelic fight, Persia (Dan 10:20):

> Then he said, 'Do you know why I have come to you? But now I will return to fight against the prince of Persia; and when I am through with him, lo, the prince of Greece will come.'

The term used in Theodotion's Hebrew recension is not exactly depictive of an angel but rather of two שרים or 'princes'. Notwithstanding, it is clear from the visionary context that we are dealing with other-worldly beings here. If the angel was referring to humans – or concrete, non-heavenly beings – other non-heavenly terms would have

---

W. Anderson. *Creation versus Chaos: The Reinterpretation of Mythical Symbolism in the Bible*. Minneapolis: Fortress Press, 1987, pp. 99–110; Mary K. Wakeman. *God's Battle with the Monster*. Leiden: Brill, 1973, especially pp. 56–119; Herbert G. May. 'Some Cosmic Connotations of Mayim Rabbim, "Many Waters"' in: *JBL* 74 (1955): 9–21; and Carlos Kloos. *Yhwh's Combat with the Sea: A Canaanite Tradition in the Religion of Ancient Israel*. Leiden: Brill, 1986.

been used, like *kittim*, which was the name used to describe, progressively, what was west of Cyprus and later attributed to the Romans or any other enemy coming from the Mediterranean. In an intentionally comic fashion, this term would be used at least up to the First World War to refer to English vessels in the Mediterranean near Palestine.

§9 Pairs of opposites in Second Temple Judaism and Daniel

References to the contrast between light and darkness can be found in other texts that compose the DSS, such as in 1QM, known as the 'War of the sons of Light against the Sons of Darkness', in several quite fragmentary texts from Cave 4, and in the document named 'Covenant of Damascus', or CD, given the reference to that city. It is no surprise that in an environment much worried with legal prescriptions and a perfect calendar, observation contrasts between light and darkness will appear almost everywhere.

Now, it should be clear that not every mention to opposites, or pairs of opposites, is fatally related to a common source. Such is the case in the DSS, as it appears that most worries related to that duo of light and darkness in such texts deal with very concrete problems that affected the existence or coexistence of several Jewish sects, or groups, from the fourth century BCE onwards. Nonetheless, this is no affirmation that the contact with Persian ideas (which were in any case contemporary to Jewry in Exile long before that time) had a role to play in the formation of many concepts in Second Temple Judaism or that it was, definitely, responsible for them.

The idea of the survival of the soul is a case in point. However, it seems that to try to find these influences within the DSS is quite hazardous, for opposites do not imply necessarily theological dualism.[78] Here, as with many other texts, we may be able to find ideas that are remarkably similar to Persian ones, which still does not mean that we can trace their origin.

Another promising path is to investigate the role of some very definite ideas – of a finite time versus a cyclical one – as they appear in older Jewish texts, such as the ones found in the Pentateuch. 'Time' with a fixed span appears in 1 En. 5:8–10 and the translation generally accepted for this Ethiopic text clearly states that God already set up a time frame for the fight between Good and Evil. Even so, here and there in the HB and in the OTP one gets different impressions as to the certainty and the implications of this fight (usually carried on by God's angels or, in some Psalms, between God himself and a monstrous creature that, apparently, was not His creation).

> And then wisdom shall be given to the elect. And they shall all live and not return again to sin, either by being wicked or through pride; but those who have wisdom

---

[78] This is one of the most important distinctions – or agreements, depending on the scholar – regarding Second Temple Judaism and Zoroastrianism: dualism supposes 'two irreductible principles as the cause of the constitutive elements of all that which does or seems to exist in the world. It is more than dichotomy, polarity, or duality' (Ugo Bianchi. 'Dualism' in: Mircea Eliade (ed.). *Encyclopedia of Religion*. New York: Macmillan, 1987, vol. 1, pp. 506–12).

shall be humble and not return again to sin. And they shall not be judged all the days of their lives; nor die through plague or wrath, but they shall complete the [designated] number of the days of their life. And peace shall increase their lives and the years of their happiness shall be multiplied forever in gladness and peace all the days of their life.

On the other hand, Deuteronomy – the fifth book of the Jewish Torah – is the front runner regarding the notion of a time that is not exactly circular but implies a recurrent pattern. That pattern mixes the mistakes of the Hebrew people with the forgiveness of God, repentance, renewal of the covenant and with other mishaps on the part of the Hebrews soon after.[79] This notion is by far simpler and may have been, accordingly, more popular among the common folk.

Thus, we cannot speak of one single attitude regarding time on the part of Second Temple Jews, but rather of numerous attitudes that make the Deuteronomic pattern.[80] Other ideas are plainly close to Zoroastrian ideals, such as the notion of resurrection of the dead in Dan 12:2, while other concepts seem to be different from both mainstream Judaism and Zoroastrianism, such as the case of the famous wisdom literary text pseudepigraphically attributed to Solomon. Hence, a late daily text like Ecclesiastes (*Qohelet*) had the following to state:

2. Vanity of vanities, says the Teacher, vanity of vanities! All is vanity. 3. What do people gain from all the toil at which they toil under the sun? 4. A generation goes, and a generation comes, but the earth remains forever. 5. The sun rises and the sun goes down, and hurries to the place where it rises. 6. The wind blows to the south, and goes around to the north; round and round goes the wind, and on its circuits the wind returns. 7. All streams run to the sea, but the sea is not full; to the place where the streams flow, there they continue to flow. 8. All things are wearisome; more than one can express; the eye is not satisfied with seeing, or the ear filled with hearing. 9. What has been is what will be, and what has been done is what will be done; there is nothing new under the sun. 10. Is there a thing of which it is said, 'See, this is new'? It has already been, in the ages before us. 11. The people of long ago are not remembered, nor will there be any remembrance of people yet to come by those who come after them. (Eccl 1:2–11)

This passage could summarize the world view of some post-Exilic Jews, and even pre-Exilic tales (that may have had their final redaction later[81]) display a similar point:

---

[79] Cf., among others, Christoph Bultman. 'Deuteronomy' in: John Barton and John Muddiman (eds). *Oxford Bible Commentary*. Oxford: Oxford University Press, 2001, p.137; Sandra L. Richter. *The Deuteronomistic History and the Name Theology*. Berlin: Walter de Gruyter, 2002, pp.7–11 (the book also deals with the relations between Deuteronomistic propositions and their Mesopotamian background); and Alexander Rofé. *Deuteronomy: Issues and Interpretation*. London: T&T Clark, 2002, for a more general introduction to Deuteronomy problems.

[80] That is, one that is not cyclical but rather repetitive in its pattern – the chosen people sin, God punishes them, they repent, God accepts this repentance until the next chain of events in this pattern.

[81] The final text resumes material from about 400 BCE to 250 BCE.

Gen 35:37
>All his sons and daughters tried to comfort him, but he refused to be comforted. 'No,' he said, 'I will go down to Sheol in mourning and join my son.' Thus his father wept for him.[82]

These simple references show that in texts antecedent to Daniel, or at least in the other settings where the narrative takes place, there is no world-beyond that even pretends to be worthwhile. There is the notion of a resting place for the dead, but it seems rather vague with no reference to sensory experience in the world beyond, and, dreadfully, the texts may even present contradictory references to the narrative in *Qohelet*. No smell, no taste, perhaps not even sound as we can deduct from two very different sources that nonetheless resemble each other regarding the experience depicted: first, the witch of Endor in 1 Sam 28:7,[83] and then Isaac's mourning of his son Jacob in Gen 37:35. Even among the Greeks we find a similar phenomenon within a passage in the *Odyssey* 24.10–20:

>Past the streams of Oceanus they went, past the rock Leucas, past the gates of the Sun and the land of dreams, and quickly came to the meadow of asphodel, where the ghosts dwell, phantoms of men who have done with toils. Here they found the ghost[84] of Achilles, son of Peleus, and those of Patroclus, of flawless Antilochus, and of Aias, who in beauty and form was best of the Danaans after the peerless son of Peleus.
>
>So these were thronging about Achilles, and near to them drew the ghost of Agamemnon, son of Atreus, sorrowing; and round about him others were gathered, the ghosts of all those who died with him in the house of Aegisthus, and met their fate.

Similarly, pairs of opposites appear in the HB from the very beginning within the book of Genesis and eventually would be found repeatedly in canonical and non-canonical texts alike. Quotations from the temptations of Job suffice as examples, but more can be found in non-exhausted samples, such as Pss 37; 74:12-14; and Isa 5:20; 45:7. Another famous case would be that of Moses not being allowed to enter the Promised Land and, again, Saul consulting the Witch of Endor.[85] On the other hand, perspectives like the one displayed in *Qohelet* exemplify comparatively late points of view in Second Temple Judaism, where no afterlife rewards are involved either.

In the Persian world, regardless of the fact that the *Gāθās* may be compositions intended to be recited by gods to other gods[86] or that they may reflect Zaraθuštra's lofty ideals, we deal with an entirely different proposition intended to be read by the faithful.

---

[82] *BDB*, שאל or שאול.

[83] Saul, in disguise after his own banning of witches, looks for a spirit (רוח) who can 'divine' the future for him (*BDB*, קסם, so in Targumim, also in Heb. קיסמא, 'divination').

[84] In Gr., ψυχή.

[85] The whole story seems to be the most colourful of its genre in the HB – Saul in despair despite being blessed by God (e.g. 1 Sam 9:7) and confirmed by Samuel (1 Sam 9:24).

[86] As advocated by Humbach in his work, seen above.

In Zoroastrian texts – even if they may be late concoctions in the Sasanid period[87] – some remarkable and distinctive traits must be compared with Second Temple texts, as well as with older ones such as the Pentateuch. In the Avesta, time has not only a beginning but also a definite end, and there is also a clear-cut competition between Good and Evil, no matter how they are embodied.

The reinterpretations can vary greatly from a race between chariots, a fight amongst stallions or even the daily plight of the faithful to support *aša* against *druj*, but one thing is certain: the idea of competition is very clearly displayed. It is very much like the world of Homeric poetry where, in the end, eternity is a sort of reward for the righteous. Yet, in the world of Achilles and Hector no righteousness was implied; rather, the heroic deed in itself was the most valued.

If we were to compare that to the world of the HB, even before Second Isaiah, nothing similar could ever be found. There, righteousness is an end in itself with no afterlife worth living, for rewards or punishments would be given by God throughout bodily life. Whether these influences actually manifested themselves is still up for discussion, but if we take a closer look to the parallels offered, it's very possible to identify some notions of rewards for the good and punishments for the evil.

Those notions take very different shapes in Zoroastrianism and in Second Temple Judaism and can even be misleading in some cases. A great example of that can be found in 1QM and in the DSS where these pairs of incompatible stances are not always portrayed in competitive terms. A 'final triumph' of Good versus Evil is a theological proposition alien to most of the HB and quite limited in non-canonical Second Temple texts. Without a doubt, it would sound incredibly strange that Ahuramazda knew from the start that the forces of Good would surely triumph.[88]

§11 Good and Evil as a literary genre: How this applies to Persian apocalyptic

'Apocalyptic' is a modern definition applied to a particular corpus of texts and was a label unknown to its audience in Antiquity. Whether the same restriction applies to the great Zoroastrian apocalypses (i.e. ZWY and AWN) is still unknown and it falls, likewise, within the list of unanswered questions regarding the composition and the

---

[87] An issue that is pivotal to all argumentation here – basically, there are three positions held among scholars: those who hold that Avestan texts and related material are oral compositions from the Late Bronze Age, put into written form during Sasanid times; those who argue that these texts are more or less contemporary to Cyrus or, at least, Darius I; and finally, those who think that they were composed, written and given a stylish patina all during the Sasanid period. I align myself with the first group.

[88] A comparatively non-explored path that can lead to Persian traces is precisely that of free will versus predestination: this is one of the most controversial digressions among the DSS. Again, for the monotheistic faiths, a God that is omniscient is not compatible with human wrongdoings (e.g. 1 En. 5:1–10), nor with the heritage of sin (examples abound in the NT with Jesus healing the blind – Matt 9:27–28; 12:22). The most famous of them all, Mark 8:23; cf. also Luke 7:21–22; John 5:3, is perhaps the passage that best deals with the issue of evil in the world and it is the one Jesus regards as the most resourceful way out of the *melée*.

reception of those texts. Nonetheless, we should examine whether the conventional definition of 'apocalyptic' alludes to Zoroastrian texts, at least in theory.

Modern scholarship today understands 'apocalyptic' in the terms of a 'literary genre'. In the words of John J. Collins defined after the colloquium of Uppsala in 1979:

> One revelatory genre of literature with a narrative structure in which the revelation is mediated by a being from another world to a human recipient, revealing a transcendent reality which is both temporal, insofar as search eschatological salvation, also space insofar as it involves another world.[89]

However, this definition has some problems like any other systematizing effort. The main ones are the following:

1. Emphasis on the eschatological aspect of this type of literature.
2. The fact that the categories proposed above do not always suit the non-Judaeo-Christian apocalypses (e.g. the Persians).
3. The similarities between Jewish apocalypses and Persian material.
4. Throughout antiquity and during much of the Middle Ages, the apocalypses were not consumed as a stand-alone genre (i.e. as tragedy or historiography, or wisdom literature), which strengthens the problems related to the public reception of such texts to their authorship and even to whom their intended audience was.

Most of the remarkable parallels present themselves in the apocalypse called 4 Ezra, and they also present themselves other Persian texts (e.g. JN, WD, ZN, the 'Conversion of Vishtapa', the composite apocalypse that forms our ZWY, a section of the Dk reporting a visionary experience of Vištasp, a reference in the AWN and passages of the Vd).[90]

§12 Conclusion

Altogether, we have seen the following:

1. An apocalyptic world view is one where time is filled with meaning and the consequential fulfilment of that meaning is the outcome of a cosmic struggle – one, and only one, cosmic struggle.[91]

---

[89] Collins. *Daniel, with an Introduction to Apocalyptic Literature*, p. 4.
[90] All these will be dealt with in depth in a separate chapter.
[91] Vedic variants of the theme suppose the movement over and over again in cyclical style, it is true; we cannot ignore them since the matrix that is similar to Hesiod, the metals in Daniel and the ZWY and other important issues are also present there. But besides pure and simple similarity, the kind of combat they depict (no matter how much Late Bronze Age-like they may seem) is in no way conclusive. We may find the liberation of the individual soul from Samsara (the wheel of life) in its various guises, and this is a sort of apocalyptic – but too far away from the purpose of this book.

2. This 'single-combat' world view, if we may call it so, is probably of *PIE origin, given the many Late Bronze Age traits present – which are shared, for example, with Homer.
3. The idea of a single, final combat between two armies, men or creatures is not present in Judaism before Daniel – regardless of the dating issues on both Zoroastrian and Danielic sources.
4. The dating of Zoroastrian texts is, to put it mildly, a problem in itself. Supposing, like most scholars in the field of Iranology do, that they emerged during the Exile and within shared vicinities of Jews and Persians (e.g. in Asia Minor), resulting in mutual eschatological influence, it still does not solve the problem of the specificities of Daniel (with emphasis in Dan 7 and Dan 12:2). In fact, the opposite idea is brought into discussion: understanding that the final judgement and the resurrection of the dead rose out of the blue in Daniel seems very unwise because for all the dating issues we have, it is by no means impossible that Avestan texts (i.e. sacred scriptures of Zoroastrianism) may have been preserved orally up to Sasanid times and only then put into writing. Therefore, the Greek stories concerning Zoroastrian written sacred texts (as in Plutarch, Theopompus and Pliny, seen above) can be innocuously exchanged for the idea that Zoroastrian doctrines came first, and only afterwards Daniel and apocalyptic literature surfaced at large as well as communities that share common ground regarding this strict division between Good and Evil.

2

The role of matter and the material world

§1 When matter matters

This chapter discusses, essentially, what academics nowadays label 'the other god', that is, a divinity that is utterly and completely opposed to another one, from the beginning of times to the foreseeable ending of their fight. Many examples could be found within different cultural traditions, such as Near Eastern religions which emphasized cyclical destruction in annual rhythms. Apart from the Yahweh-cult – not yet monotheism but rather a monolatry – many of the existing religious systems were polytheisms.[1]

On that note, Zoroastrianism stands out in a variety of aspects, most remarkably in the setting of the fighting arena between Good versus Evil, as well as in the overall timing of the conflict. Alternatively, this poses a difficult question for all monotheistic faiths, Abrahamic or not: why would a God that is good allow evil in the world He created? This is a question of utmost importance given the role of Creation in both Zoroastrianism and in Second Temple Judaism. The answer, which ultimately makes us question the ethics of monotheism, has been manifold, but the focus here is the possible relation between the ethics in Zoroastrianism and the Second Temple Jewish texts, mostly apocalyptic.

Apocalyptic texts of most kinds, except for Vedic ones, are an ideal arena to analyse how this question – which is central to monotheism – develops. It should be noted that while we have few Zoroastrian apocalypses (in the strict sense of the term, there are only two, the ZWY and the AWN), there are plenty of Jewish apocalypses, many of them presenting relations to the Danielic corpus or attempting to deepen questions raised by Daniel[2] – 4 Ezra is the best example in this sense. Others took a life of their

---

[1] There is plenty of bibliography on the subject, which was a very 'hot' topic in the seventies of the last century. For a general and recent overview, cf. Michael S. Heiser. 'Monotheism, Polytheism, Monolatry, or Henotheism? Toward an Assessment of Divine Plurality in the Hebrew Bible' in: *Bulletin for Biblical Research* 18.1 (2008): 1–30.
[2] Many of the issues raised in Danielic literature – by this I encompass the canonical book of Daniel – in both its Hebrew and Greek variations, and the myriad non-canonical Danielic texts whose sheer volume is staggering: but most of those lie well outside our scope because they are so much later than Second Temple apocalypses proper (many examples of those are found in Lorenzo DiTommaso. *The Book of Daniel and the Apocryphal Daniel Literature*. Leiden: Brill, 2005). DiTommaso also deals with Second Temple non-canonical Daniel (such as the fragments found in the DSS), but these will be dealt with separately in the next chapter.

own and embedded themselves in the apocalyptic sections of most Testaments, except for those which are plainly Christian or those with Christian interpolations.

Subsequentially, another important group of texts formed, namely the one scholars nominated DSS. This denomination makes perfect sense in geographic terms, but it goes no further than that for content clarification. Since their 'discovery' around 1947, a great deal of attention has been paid to their 'apocalyptic content' even though it did not quite fit the canonical presentation of the apocalypses possibly composed, and almost certainly used, by the group associated with those texts.

This will be discussed in depth in Chapter 4, but for the moment, let us stay with the denomination of the 'Qumran sect'.[3]

In the DSS, mentions to pairs of opposites are plentiful – light versus darkness, the elect versus the damned, the Teacher of Rightfulness versus the Wicked Priest[4] and so on. These opposites were essentially tools for explaining evil in the world and for separating the few (which are good and chosen) from the many (which are the non-elect or wicked). These criteria also apply to non-DSS Jewish apocalyptic texts, and, in fact, the NT texts will take them a step further, such as Matt 22:14, John 13:18 and many other passages with similar struggles between the few good against the many wicked.

Nonetheless, Judaism and Christianism – in the many different guises in which we came to know them – emphasize the same thing: that the struggle between Good and Evil, as hard and long as it may seem, is not an endless, fruitless, Sisyphus-like effort. On the contrary, the battle will come to an end and the *material* world, since it has a deep-ingrained moral sense within these religious doctrines, will come out renewed.[5] At this point, it is crucial to evaluate the part each supreme divinity held in the Creation, maintenance and usage of the Judaeo-Christian material world.[6]

That discussion on matter entails a plethora of studies comparing similar problems in Mishnaic/Talmudic Judaism (especially among Babylonian communities) and Zoroastrian proposals on similar matters. Even so, it is vital for understanding how the approach to the regulation of the material world directly influenced other mundane

---

[3] Just as a quick reference regarding a problem to be developed in the next chapter and in Chapter 5 of this book, cf. Albert Baumgarten. 'Who Cares and Why Does It Matter? Qumran and the Essenes, Once Again!' in: *Dead Sea Discoveries* 11.2 (2004): 174–90, especially 174 and 177. For the moment, suffice it to say that Baumgarten had the intelligence to remember the sociological work of Ludwig Fleck (i.e. positing that analysis of data only makes sense when in a given context), with the ensuing results for and against the Essene-Qumran ties. Cf. Ludwig Fleck. *Genesis and Development of a Scientific Fact*. Chicago: University of Chicago Press, 1979, especially pp. 28–38.

[4] These are somewhat fanciful characters that promoted a big deal of the discussion on the origins and role of the DSS; again, let us see what can be regarded as a 'war of opposites' in Chapter 4.

[5] In this sense, what happens in GrBd 34.10, Rev 21:1–15 and 4 Ezra 14:27 is remarkably similar in the promises of redemption; let us remember that an earlier version of the Bd is harder on sinners who will be punished by the river of molten metal rather than be purified by it. But in all three examples we have a deity that is forgiving enough to renew His own Creation.

[6] This extends to the Muslim world, too, and the best author in this field is undoubtedly Richard C. Foltz: these three books are mandatory for discussing Scripture and environment. Cf. *Spirituality in the Land of the Noble*; *Animals in Islamic tradition and Muslim Cultures*. Oxford: Oneworld, 2006; and, as editor, of *Environmentalism in the Muslim World*. New York: Nova Science, 2005. Foltz started his career analysing the amazingly diverse world of religions along the Silk Road and Zoroastrianism, and then Islam at large in his later years.

worries that would be dealt with in terms of civil law in the Roman Empire, both Eastern and Western.[7]

It also puts in perspective dating issues of the texts themselves, such as the 'good' presence of the dog (whose domestication can be reasonably well traced[8]), and even the 'good' vulture, in itself a somewhat noxious creature that nonetheless was created by Ohrmazd so that it could serve the 'good' purpose of Creation.

§2 Creation in Zoroastrianism

Zoroastrians believed,[9] since our earliest records of them (whether these records, the *Gāθās*, are as old as they purport to be is an entirely different matter i.e. if we are looking at internal criticism or just at the dating of the most ancient ms.[10]), that originally there was no material world although there were two absolutely incompatible divinities, as different as light can be from darkness.[11] Ohrmazd and Ahriman, representing Good and Evil (and, some would argue, the very primeval and cyclical forces of cosmic order and chaos of other Near Eastern religions in a different guise), engage in a very peculiar battle, even for modern theological and meta-historical parameters. This conflict had a beginning and, as Ohrmazd knew from the start, would have an end with his own forces emerging victorious.

---

[7] Cf. Maria Macuch. 'Law in Pre-Modern Zoroastrianism' in: *WBCZ*, p. 239:

> The study of Zoroastrian law presents one of the most intriguing challenges to the scholar of Mazdaism (Zoroastrianism). The difficulties of the task are numerous, not only since no legal codex, digest, or systematic work has survived, but also because of the countless problems involved in understanding legal language and institutions. Information on law is scattered throughout the extant Iranian texts, covering a time span of almost 2,000 years, reaching from Old Iranian (Avestan) material to Middle Persian (Pahlavi) and Persian treatises of the Islamic period, but significant lacunae in the transmission of the sources make it impossible to reconstruct legal history from its simple beginnings in a pastoral society in the 1st millennium BCE to its most sophisticated known form in the jurisprudence of the Sasanian state (3rd–7th centuries CE).

Note the position on the antiquity of Zoroastrianism taken by Macuch.

[8] The first fossil that is undisputedly a domestic dog dates from thirty-six thousand years ago. Cf. Evan Irving-Pease et al. 'Paleogenomics of Animal Domestication' in: Charlotte Lindqvist and Om P. Rajora (eds). *Paleogenomics: Genome-Scale Analysis of Ancient DNA*. Cham: Springer, 2018. In a pastoral society such as the one portrayed in the Avesta, the dog is supremely useful and is one of the high points in Ohrmazd's creation: cf. also Mahnaz Moazami. 'The Dog in Zoroastrian Religion: "*Vidēvdād*" Chapter XIII' in: *IIJ* 49.1/2 (2006): 127–49.

[9] Most of the texts here quoted come from Mary Boyce's very useful manual on the subject – *Textual Sources for the Study of Zoroastrianism*. The English version used is, whenever possible, that of West. *The Hymns of Zaraθuštra*; otherwise, I will be using Lawrence H. Mills et al. *The Zend Avesta*. Oxford: Clarendon Press, 1895 (3 vols). (*SBE*)

[10] To this debate, one should mention the position of radical conservatism of West (cf. *The Hymns of Zaraθuštra*, p. 3).

[11] From this extreme literarity, the forms that law (especially in the form of ordeal trials) became the way par excellence to define guilt and innocence are understandable; the importance of this idea cannot be overestimated considering the role of a final 'ordeal' in Second Temple Judaism and, by derivation, Christianity. Cf. also Francis G. Downing. 'Cosmic Eschatology in the First Century: "Pagan", Jewish and Christian' in: *L'antiquité classique* 64 (1995): 99–109.

A perfect example of their utter incompatibility comes in Y 30.1–7:

1. Now I will proclaim to those who will hear the things that the understanding man should remember, for hymns unto Ahura and prayers to Good Thought; also the felicity that is with the heavenly lights, which through Right shall be beheld by him who wisely thinks.

2. Hear with your ears the best things; look upon them with clear-seeing thought, for decision between the two Beliefs, each man for himself before the Great consummation,[12] bethinking you that it be accomplished to our pleasure.

3. Now the two primal Spirits, who reveal themselves in vision as Twins,[13] are the Better and the Bad, in thought and word and action. And between these two the wise ones chose aright, the foolish not so.

4. And when these twain Spirits came together in the beginning, they created Life and Not-Life, and that at the last Worst Existence shall be to the followers of the Lie, but the Best Existence to him that follows Right.

5. Of these twin Spirits he that followed the Lie chose doing the worst things; the holiest Spirit chose Right, he that clothes him with the massy heavens as a garment. So likewise they that are fain to please Ahura Mazda by dutiful actions.

6. Between these twin the Daevas[14] also chose not aright, for infatuation came upon them as they took counsel together, so that they chose the Worst Thought. Then they rushed together to Violence,[15] that they might enfeeble the world of men.

7. And to him (i.e. mankind) came Dominion, and Good Mind, and Right and Piety gave continued life to their bodies and indestructibility, so that by thy retributions through (molten)[16] metal he may gain the prize over the others.

---

[12] The idea of a final conflagration by fire was very popular from the Hellenistic period onwards; commonly quoted sources are Berossos (AJ 1.70), Seneca (NQ 3.13), Pliny (NH 7.73) and a host of other authors, a good deal of them Stoics but not all.

[13] As discussed in Chapter 1.

[14] A very clear explanation on the matter is given by Helmut Humbach ('The *Gāthās*' in: *WBCZ*, p. 42 (differences in spelling derived from Humbach's readings)):

> Having approached with the evil purpose of getting hold of the offerings intended for *Ahura Mazdā* (Y 32.1) the *daēuuas* are addressed by the prophet as 'seeds from Bad Thought' (Y 32.3), which certainly stands for underlying 'seeds from the Harmful Spirit'. This poetic license is due to considerations of rhythm and, therefore, does not allow any conclusion as to what the prophet may actually have taught his adherents. Much more consistent in this respect than the Gathic is the Young Avestan scheme according to which it is not Bad Thought but the Harmful Spirit who is the chief and, in consequence, the producer of the *daēuuas*.

[15] CPD, 'must', 'snāh', 'tundīh' (MP).

[16] This is one of the main final judgement themes in Zoroastrianism, one which related the cosmic ending of the fight to the soteriology of individuals, the other being that of the crossing of the Činwad bridge (dealt with in Chapter 4 of this book). Here it has the main important parallel in GrBd 34.10. This is a main theme in Second Temple Judaism apocalyptic – the use of metals not just to signify monarchies ruling this world (as in Dan 2) but even more as a way of separating the elect and saved from the bad, who are damned.

Examining this passage, we conclude that Ohrmazd knew that the harm done would be great, but it would not be eternal. In this discovery lies perhaps the greatest contribution of Zoroastrian doctrine in the history of religious ideas – the single one thought that went far beyond specialized knowledge in the field of religious studies: the duality of 'Life' and 'Not-Life',[17] which has impacted common man like few others throughout human history. This notion may be a radical proposition and perhaps an exaggeration, given that material creation is also life since it exists and lives; yet the fact that it may be considered noxious constitutes an overall different matter.

Altogether, it is correct to posit that God, as understood by Second Temple Jews and later by Christians, is the source of Creation as a whole, which is good because it exists. In this sense, even a demon can be considered 'good' since it is God's creation and God has no adversaries (the Augustinian notion that since God cannot create anything bad, Evil is rather the absence of God than someone else's working is still some five centuries away). Here and there the HB left traces of a primordial combat such as is common in Near Eastern creational myths, but nothing compared to the 'match' between Ohrmazd and Ahriman. Y 45.2 summarizes this idea:

> I will speak of the Spirits twain at the first beginning of the world, of whom the holier spoke thus to the enemy: 'Neither thought, nor teachings, nor wills, nor beliefs, nor words, nor deeds, nor selfs [sic],[18] nor souls of us twain agree.'

Now, how does this translate into proper material struggle? How did the material world begin and how will it end for these two fundamentally incompatible forces?

§3 Creation and counter creation: A Zoroastrian match

In the Greater *Bundahišn* (GrBd), we find a treatise dedicated essentially to the Creation and to the myths surrounding it.[19] Within its writings there are more explanations regarding the development of the struggle between Ohrmazd and his archenemy, Ahriman, both not alone: Ohrmazd created six good spirits in order to help him build the material world and take care of it (the *Spentas*), and so did his evil counterpart. GrBd 1a.1–13 describes this process:

> 1. When the Evil Spirit was inactive owing to stupor, as I have written above, he lay in stupor, for three thousand years.

---

[17] *CPD*, 'zīndagīh', 'zī(w)išnīh' (MP): life versus not-life or death, who has even a demon of its own, 'Astwihād'. Death itself in a more usual sense is 'marg', 'margīh' (all MP).

[18] *CPD*, 'grīw', 'xwad', 'xwēštan' (MP); selfhood relates to the two last ones, 'xwadīh'. In the sense of our passage, they can be safely translated as 'essence' or 'selfhood'.

[19] The edition here used is that of Behamgore T. Anklesaria. *Zand-Akasih: Iranian or Greater Bundahishn*. Bombay: Published for the Rahnumae Mazdayasnan Sabha by its Honorary Secretary Dastur Framroze A. Bode, 1956.

2. During that inactivity of the Evil Spirit, Ohrmazd created the creation in material life; for, He created forth Fire out of Endless Light, Ether out of Fire, Water out of Ether, and Earth and all corporeality of Matter out of Water.

3. As one says, in the Scripture: 'First, the entire creation was a drop of Water;' that is, everything was from Water, except the seeds of men and animals; for, those seeds are of the essence of Fire.

4. He, first, produced the Sky, in order to withhold the Evil Spirit; there is some one who says: 'the foremost'-; secondly, He produced the Water, in order to smite the 'druj' Thirst; thirdly He produced the Earth, all corporeality; fourthly, He produced the Tree, for the help of the good-created Beneficent-Animal; fifthly, the Beneficent Animal, for the help of the Holy Man; sixthly He produced the Holy Man, for the destruction and inactivity of the Evil Spirit and all the Devs; then He produced the Fire, the Khvarag; He attached to it the ray from Endless Light, so good is its astral body as is the Fire's desire; then He created the Ether, in the astral form of a young man of fifteen years, which bears and preserves everything: this Water, Tree, Beneficent Animal, and Holy Man.

5. I will mention their whereabouts.

6. First, He produced the shining and visible Sky, which is very distant, and of steel, of shining steel, whose substance is the male diamond; its top is connected with the Endless Light; He produced all the creations, within the Sky, the fortification, resembling a bag within which is laid every implement which was requisite for the contest, or resembling a dwelling wherein everything remains; the prop of the base of the Sky, whose width is as much as its length, its length as much as its height, and its height as much as its capacity, is entirely like the desert, the chasm, and the forest; the Spirit of the Sky is meditative, speaking, active, knowing, beneficent, and discriminating; he accepted the work of lasting fortification against the Evil Spirit, that is, he did not let him go back, like the valiant warrior, who has put on armour, so that he may be saved fearlessly from the battle, the Spirit of the Sky so preserves the sky; He produced Delight, for the help of: the Sky; for, with Delight, He created it forth, wherein, even now, in the mingled state, the creation lives in Delight.

7. Secondly, He created the Water out of the substance of the Sky; so much as a man, who lays his two hands on earth, and walks with hands and feet, and the water stands up to his stomach; up to that height, did the water flow; He produced, for its help, the Wind and the Rain, that is: the cloud, snow, and lightning.

8. Thirdly, out of Water, He produced the round Earth, having distant roads, without descent and without ascent, whose entire length is equal to the width, and the width to the magnitude, arranged in the middle of this Sky.

9. As one says: 'He, first, created forth a one-third of this Earth, as hard as the eagle's crest; secondly He created forth a one-third of this earth, stuffed with dust; thirdly, He created forth a one-third of this Earth, felt topped.'

This account of the Creation leaves nothing to chance. However, when we come to the theory of a mixed source for the final redaction of the Pentateuch – that may have taken its present shape during the Exile or soon after[20]– we are, again, with our hands tied when it comes to Persian sources: too few, too late. These manuscripts (i.e. from the Bd or the GrBd) are currently so scarce that it is virtually impossible to 'retro-construct' levels of redaction. One feels the presence of orality here and there and some typical themes of the primeval combat; yet very little of that is conclusive.

Even so, despite the paucity of manuscripts, some features are striking: whatever it is that Ahuramazda creates, he does so already with the (future) duel with Ahriman in mind. Following water, fire is created – with the explicit aim of containing Ahriman – and everything is done with 'Delight' (*CPD*, '*huniyāgīh*', '*urwāhm(an)īh*'). After each day of the Creation, the Jewish God is pleased, but in the Zoroastrian myth Delight is something essential, even during the 'mixed' state of the material world (*CPD*, '*gumēzagīh*').

10. He produced, within the earth, the substance of the Mountains, which, thereafter, increased and grew out of the Earth; for the help of the Earth, He produced iron, brass, brimstone, borax, limestone, and also all the principles of the hard earth, distinct from those of Istakhr,[21] for, they are of a separate origin; so hard did He create the Earth, in the semblance of a man, when he had donned dress over dress, on all the sides, close over the body; and Water remained, everywhere, underneath this Earth.

11. Fourthly, He produced the Tree; first, it grew up in the middle of this Earth, several feet high, without branches, without bark, without thorn, fresh and sweet; it had, in its germ, all kind of force of the trees; He produced the Water and the Fire, for the help of the Tree; for every bark of the trees has a drop of Water at

---

[20] Literature on the composition and sources for the Pentateuch abound; for the issues that concern us most here, cf. Peter Frei. 'Persian Imperial Authorization: A Summary' in: James Watts (ed.). *Persia and Torah: The Theory of Imperial Authorization of the Pentateuch*. Atlanta: SBL Press, 2001, p. 6; for a more recent approach, cf. David M. Carr. 'Changes in Pentateuchal Criticism' in: Magne Sæbø; Jean L. Ska; Peter Machinist (eds). *Hebrew Bible / Old Testament. Vol.III: From Modernism to Post-Modernism. Part II: The Twentieth Century – From Modernism to Post-Modernism*. Göttingen: Vandenhoeck & Ruprecht, 2014.

[21] The reference to *Istakhr*, or *Eṣṭak̠r* (near the cliffs of *Naqš-e Rostam*), does not necessarily derive from a late redaction of this part of the text: the location was already important as Achaemenid royal residences (Cf. Donald Whitcomb. 'The City of Istakhr and the *Marv Dasht* Plain' in: *Akten des VII. Internationalen Kongresses für Iranische Kunst und Archäologie, München, 7-10 September 1976*. Berlin: D. Reimer, 1979, pp. 363–70). The religious role of *Eṣṭak̠r* as an important centre for fire-worshipping is well attested in ancient sources as diverse as Berossus (*Babyloniaka* 3.65) and al-Tabari (in the beginning of his monumental work). The role of *Eṣṭak̠r* as a centre for fire-worshipping has long been assumed to be contested during Sasanian times or even earlier (Strabo, *Geography* 12.8, or even long before him Herodotus, *Histories* 1.131), but in modern times this is a position that became orthodox teaching until very recently. For the traditional view downplaying fire *temples* as opposed to fire *cult*, cf. Mary Boyce. 'Iconoclasm among the Zoroastrians' in: Jacob Neusner (ed.). *Studies for Morton Smith at Sixty*. Leiden: Brill, 1975, vol. 4, pp. 94–9; for a modern reassessment of this position, cf. Michael Shenkar. 'Rethinking Sasanian Iconoclasm' in: *JAOS* 135.3 (2015): 471–98, especially 471–5, where the general phenomenon of iconoclasm in Abrahamic faiths is assumed by Shenkar, but Boyce's stance on the issue in the 1975 article is questioned. For more general points in the fire cult, cf. Klaus Schippmann. *Die iranischen Feuerheiligtümer*. Berlin: Walter de Gruyter, 1971.

the top, and Fire before it at a distance of four fingers; it grew forever with their strength.

Here we find one of the most widespread mythological themes, the 'cosmic tree', which follows the creation of water. Note that this tree is also in the 'mixed state' before the final purification and defeat of Ahriman.

> 12. Fifthly He created the sole-created Gav in Eranvej, in the middle of the earth, on the shore of the river Veh-Daitya. that is, the middle of the earth; she was white and shining like the Moon, and her height was three reeds of average length; He produced the Water and the Tree, for her help; for she had strength and growth, from these, in the mingled state.
> 13. Sixthly, He created Gayomard shining as the Sun; his height was four reeds of average length; his width was symmetrical as the height; he was on the shore of the river Daitya, that is, the middle of the earth; Gayomard was on the left side the Gav on the right side; their distance from each other, their distance, too, from the water Daitya, was as much as their own height; he was possessed of eyes, ears, tongue and mark; Gayomard's possession of the mark was this that mankind were born of his seed, in his semblance; He produced, for his help, repose giving Sleep; for Ohrmazd created forth the Sleep, in the astral form of a tall man, fifteen years of age and radiant; He created Gayomard, with the 'Gav' out of the Earth; He created forth the sperms of men and animals, out of the Light and verdure of the Sky; as these two sperms are of the principle of Fire, not of the principle of Water; He produced them in the material body of the 'Gav' and Gayomard, so that the complete propagation of men and animals arose there from.

A very peculiar aspect in this myth of Creation – especially as refashioned in the MP lore – is that Gayomard is the sixth Creation,[22] and the idea that humankind 'came from his seed' is also seen as a form of justification for endogamic marriage among Zoroastrians. This myth of Creation also shows parallels to Scandinavian myths and has been linked to *PIE origins.[23] Moreover, his name is a careful choice in the following of the primeval Ox and it lasts thirty years more, a symbolic number that equals the numbers of years when Baraθuštra first conversed with Ohrmazd.[24]

---

[22] Cereti and MacKenzie. 'Except by Battle', pp. 31–59.

[23] The best work to defend this point of view is still Arthur Christensen. *Les types du premier homme et du premier roi dans l'histoire légendaire des Iraniens*, pt. I *Gajōmard, Masjay et Masjānay, Hōšang et Taxmōruw*, vol. 1. Leiden: Brill, 1918–34.

[24] I tend to favour Carlo Cereti's ('Personal Names Ending in ت in the *Šāhnāma*' in: Touraj Daryaee and Mahmoud Omidsalar (eds). *The Spirit of Wisdom [Mēnōg ī Xrad]: Essays in Memory of Ahmad Tafazzoli*. Costa Mesa: Mazda, 2004, pp. 43–57, especially p. 48) observations on the subject, summarized here:

> According to later Iranian tradition, he is the first man and the first king, a powerful civilization hero. In the YAv the name Gaiia- is often found coupled with 'marətan-', 'mortal, human' so that Av. 'Gaiia- marətan-' can be rendered as 'mortal life'. Taking together the evidence provided by NP. *Kayumart/ț, Gayumart/ț*, Ar. *Jayūmart*, and MP (Phl) g'yw(k)mlt'

The presence of the metals is an early detail, one that will be lengthily developed over time. A good deal of apocalyptic judgement and cleansing has either to do with metals – for they represent kingdoms or kings on Earth – or with adversaries to a God that is also the Creator. Indeed, the differences on the roles of metals, branches of the tree and kingdoms in Dn and in the ZWY is dismal – another problem to postulate dating.

In short, the section of the GrBd that we just saw is clearly very different from the Jewish myth of Creation: *it is only through the material world that Ahriman can be defeated.* Thus, far from being a 'prison for the soul' or anything of the sort, the material world is the *only* battlefield where Ahriman can be overthrown, at a cost. The true beginning of their fight is described in detail within GrBd 4.10–11:

> 10. Then, the Evil Spirit, with all the dev [*sic*]²⁵ [agents, rose] against the Luminaries; he saw [the] Sky, [which he showed to them spiritually, as it was not produced material;] with malicious intent he made an on rush, [drew the Sky, which was at the Star station, down towards the void which, as I have written at the commencement, was under the base of the Luminaries and the Planets, so that] he stood [above the Star station,] from within the Sky, [up to] a one third; like a serpent, he [forthwith wished] to drag. the Sky underneath the Earth [and to break it]; he entered, in the month of Frawardin, and the day of Ohrmazd, at noon; the Sky was as afraid of him as a sheep of a wolf; he, then, came to the Water, [which, I have said,] was arranged underneath this Earth; he, then, pierced and entered the middle of this Earth; then, he came to the Tree;. then, [to] the Gav and Gayomard; then, he came [up] to the Fire; so that, like a fly, he went to all the creations.
> 11. He made the world so much invisible, at noon, that [the Sky held the darkness, below and above the Earth,] just like a dark night.

§4 Creation and Creator in Zoroastrianism and Judaism

As already mentioned, the chief issue to be discussed in this chapter is the role, or even morality, of the material world in two very different religious systems, namely Zoroastrianism and Judaism. These two have naturally different cosmogonies, but in both cases there is an originating god that entrusts humans with the maintenance of the world. However, in the case of Zoroastrianism, as we have seen, the main problem resides on 'why' humans should choose sides on a battle already predetermined. Besides, morally speaking, are humans even capable of doing good for Good itself?

---

a pronunciation 'Gayōmarθ' can be reconstructed; MMPers. Gehmurd rests on a different etymology.

Cf. Manfred Mayrhofer. *Die altiranischen Namen, Iranisches Personennamenbuch*. Band I, Fascs. I-II-III. Wien: Österreichisches Akademie der Wissenschaften, 1979, Band I, p. 45.

[25] CPD, 'dēw', 'dēwesnīh' (MP): 'idolatry', 'devil worship'. The use of the singular may have been intentional and inclusive of the plural forms of this practice.

In GrBd 34.10, or even in the more rigorous Bd 29-33, individual eschatology mingles itself with the cosmic struggle (and, for that matter, with the disappearance of the Činwad bridge itself). So, for all purposes, a rough taxonomy can be devised between Zoroastrianism and Second Temple Judaism creational myths – bearing in mind that it is improper to use the term 'monotheism' to describe the religion of the Jews before Isa 45:5, which is an Exilic text.[26] In Zoroastrianism, material creation is, essentially, something good which is corrupted by a counter-god, while in Second Temple Judaism (it is correct to locate the final redaction of the Pentateuch as we have it to the Exile period, too[27]), Creation is good in itself but, since God has established very strict laws of coherence, there are animals forbidden to be eaten (Lev 11:13, 47; Deut 14:12) actions forbidden to be taken (Deut 14:21); even in the NT, nature is chastised by Jesus more than once (Luke 8:32; Mark 5:13). Indeed, even a tree unwilling to do as Jesus wished goes punished in Matt 21:19 and in Mark 11:20.

On that note, in a clash of free will versus providence, are humans capable of acting well and doing good deeds unsupervised? Or do they act well only due to either the premonition of an Almighty God or the fear of being punished? A compromise position is that, yes, humans are capable of doing good or bad, and all of such predispositions have been foreseen, but humans do not know. That is a clever way of clearing good, all-encompassing and creative gods from allowing evil: they knew what people could do and the subsequent consequences of those actions, but mankind was, in a way, 'blindfolded' to that reality.

Hence, we humans act in good or bad ways with no idea of the consequences. The original Greek concept of 'hamartia'[28] is very much an illustration of that – but in Greek tragedy the main concern is not the ways of the world and Creation but rather the opposite: when Oedipus does all the deeds that lead to his fall, it is a proof of mankind's incapacity and smallness compared to what the gods have in store for them.[29]

---

[26] There is little doubt in academic circles that we are dealing with three different units in the book of Isaiah and at least with three different authors: the first, who gave his name to the book, lived in the eighth century BCE and chs 1–39 are his. Then, from chs 40 to 55 we have someone else writing using his name but introducing wholly new ideas regarding the cult of the Israelites' God; this person lived during the Exile. Finally, chs 56–66 are so varied in style and content that they may be ascribed to someone else or even to a group of people. Cf. the two volumes by Joseph Blenkinsopp on this (*Isaiah 40–55: A New Translation with Introduction and Commentary*. New York: Doubleday, 2002; and *Isaiah 56–66: A New Translation with Introduction and Commentary*. New York: Doubleday, 2003). Of interest here are also two volumes by Continuum: Robert K. Gnuse. *No Other Gods: Emergent Monotheism in Israel*. London: Continuum, 1997; and John Goldingay. *The Message of Isaiah 40–55: A Literary-Theological Commentary*. London: Continuum, 2005 (2 vols). For the best discussion on the issues raised by Deureto-Isaiah (the name by whom the author of Isa 40–55 is usually called), the two massive volumes by John Goldingay and David Payne (*A Critical and Exegetical Commentary on Isaiah 40–55*. London: T&T Clark, 2007) are mandatory. Cf. also note 1 in this chapter for a contemporary overview of Second Isaiah and 'monolatry' issues.

[27] Cf. John J. Collins. *The Bible after Babel: Historical Criticism in a Postmodern Age*. Grand Rapids: William B. Eerdmans, 2005, p. 34.

[28] LSJ, ἁμαρτία: 'failure', 'fault'; later in the Greek versions of the OT and in the NT, 'sin'.

[29] Bibliography here is immense (and usually refers to Aristotle's *Poetics*), but a fine introduction to the theme can be found in a still useful article: Leon Golden. 'Hamartia, Ate, and Oedipus' in: *The Classical World* 72.1 (1978): 3–12, especially 5–7; Tom C. W. Stinton. 'Hamartia in Aristotle and Greek Tragedy' in: *The Classical Quarterly* 25.2 (1975): 221–54, especially 221–3; also the book by William K. Wimsatt and Monroe C. Beardsley. *Hateful Contraries: Studies in Literature and*

When examined apart from other myths (especially Creation myths), the world of theatrical polytheism hardly matters due to the lack of explanations regarding some other-worldly morality in a way that is tangible to human minds. In those texts, humans face the full extent of the consequences to their actions and, more often than not, end up in disgrace.

Creation in Jewish texts can be, occasionally, confusing (like Pss 29:3 and 93, which suggest that there existed something before God himself), but that complication is exceedingly rare. Regardless of the sources generally accepted for the Pentateuch, Creation is an act of God, but it has one big problem regarding the 'stubbornness' of His chosen people. These problems are solved by a concept named 'Deuteronomistic pattern': God loves His chosen people, His people make mistakes, God chastises them, they repent and then God is back to being all-loving. Just like that the turn (not a cycle, it must be clear, since we are talking about different events here) is completed, until the next round of sinning and forgiving.

However, in Second Temple apocalyptic, such hopes and explanations take a slight turn towards more chaotic states of mind. For example, the visionary in 4 Ezra does not understand why is it that Jerusalem was destroyed (4 Ezra 3:28, among many others), and another visionary in 2 Baruch answers that in fact nothing was profaned by heathens (the Temple was already empty, as in the tradition represented by 2 Bar. 6:4–9 with parallel in BJ 6.300 and Tacitus, *Histories* 5.13). Many likewise scenarios resemble what happens to Job – in the end, it was of meaningless suffering for the reader but particularly important for the relation between Job and God himself.

Given that no contemporary scholar posits these writings later than the sixth century BCE to the fourth century BCE (i.e. during the Exile, in broad terms), the relation between the Jewish God and His Creation remains unaltered. In order to do as he pleases towards Job, 'Ha-Satan'[30] has to fulfil two requests: first, he needs the permission of God to do so, and, second, more importantly, he can harm Job all he wishes, but he cannot take his life.

This is an interesting feature, and it may be related to some sort of 'interval' between the shady, unhappy (but real) *Sheol* of the Israelite kings Saul, David and Solomon, and the promises of resurrection in Daniel and in subsequent literature. Satan is forbidden to take the life of Job, and even though an omnipotent God could easily rectify this decision, he could not do so given the theological terms at the date of the composition of Job. By the end of the story, Job receives back many times what he lost, but his deceased loved ones are not revived. That happened most likely because this possibility was not (yet) in the theological framework of Judaism nor in Exilic or post-Exilic Judaea.[31] That particular storyline is of utmost importance for any discussion

---

Criticism. Lexington: University Press of Kentucky, 1965; and for more recent approaches, Eli Rozik. *The Roots of Theatre: Rethinking Ritual and Other Theories of Origin*. Iowa City: University of Iowa Press, 2002. Rozik discusses the role of the concept in comedy as well, in the chapter 'The Ritual Origin of Comedy'.

[30] *BDB*, הַשָּׂטָן: 'adversary'.

[31] As can be clearly seen in the canonical books of Ezra and Nehemiah (e.g. Ezra 2:70; 3:1; Neh 8:2, etc.).

on resurrection since the story of Job is already quoted in Ezekiel (14:14), which, in turn, has a dubious passage related to bones that may be a predecessor to more precise apocalyptic ideas (Ezek 6:5; 24:4).

§5 Dualism, 'the other God' and individualism in Zoroastrianism and Qumran texts

The variety of Judaism found in the DSS lends itself pretty well for a comparison – sometimes hurried and unwise – with Zoroastrianism, given the dualistic traits of many of the texts in both religions.[32] Now, how would this comparison look against a more common-ground tradition like, say, the canonical Daniel scripture and its many pseudepigraphic variants?

Thereupon, recurrence to three main chapters in Daniel is mandatory: Dan 2, 7 and 12. Both Hebrew, Greek and later variants propose similar contrasts on the meaning of human history despite the (apparent) lack of understanding by humans themselves. In ch. 12 there is, perhaps, the most revolutionary idea in the whole book, that of rewards and punishments on a day to come. Briefly examining this in Greek and Hebrew, we would have, for our purposes, a suitable background against which to examine the DSS later.

§6 Final combats in Zoroastrianism: Another perspective

One distinguishing feature of Zoroastrianism versus Judaism/Christianity is that 'evil' things, animals or deeds are conceived as inherently separate from their 'good' counterparts, with the exception of the vulture who, even 'looking' filthy as he does, is a creation of Ohrmazd. That happens because, according to Zoroastrian funereal rites, the 'impure' corpse shall not touch the 'pure' earth, not until only its bare bones are left (Bd 24.31–36):

> 31. All other wild animals and birds were created to oppose the demons and vermin. 32. As it says: 'The birds and wild animals oppose the vermin and sorcerers.' 33. It also says this: 'All birds are clever, but the crow[33] is the cleverest.' 34. It says about the white falcon[34]: 'It kills winged snakes.' 35. Magpies kill locusts and were created

---

[32] On the side of the 'orthodoxy', that is, of the scholars that posit an early date, we find Boyce, Norman Cohn and, more recently, Martin West versus the ones that presume that Zoroastrianism, as we know it, is a Sasanid fabrication or, even more, that Zaraθuštra himself either is a very recent figure (say, from the sixth century BCE) or never existed at all. Among these, we shall find Philippe Gignoux, Jacques Duchesne-Guillemin and Prods O. Skjærvø. For a good overview on the general problems that arise in dualist religions in Antiquity (supposing that Zoroastrianism is one of them, something which is in itself a heated topic of debate), cf. Yuri Stoyanov. *The Other God*. New Haven: Yale University Press, 2000, especially chapter 1, 'The Bridge of the Separator'.

[33] CPD, 'warāy'.

[34] Bd 19.21–24.

to oppose them. 36. The vulture whose thought dwells on the old and dying – that is, the dālman – was created for eating corpses.

This unwavering antagonism would sometimes lead to severe historical misunderstandings, not to mention the heavy persecution of Christians by Zoroastrians in Sasanid Persia. The idea of a Creator of all things, good *and* evil, who was at the same time this grand redeemer who would save good and bad alike, was very peculiar to the believers of those doctrines. This testimony on the martyrdom of Christians under Shapur II (309–379 CE) is quite eloquent on how difficult these world view conflicts could be at times:

> In the thirty-seventh year of our persecution [under Shapur II in the fourth century] a cruel command was issued, and the mobads[35] were given power over all Christians to torment them with tortures and pains and to kill them by stoning and execution. The good shepherds who did not hide during this persecution were accused by the servants of evil, who said to the judges: 'The Christians destroy our doctrine and teach people to serve only one God, not to pray to the sun,[36] not to worship fire, to pollute water by hateful washing, not to marry, not to beget any sons or daughters not to take the field with the kings, not to kill, to butcher and eat animals without qualms, to bury the dead in the earth and to say that God, not Satan,[37] has created snakes, scorpions and all the vermin of the world. They also spoil many servants of the king and teach them magic, which they call writings.' When the evil judges heard this, they flew into a great rage that burnt in them like fire in wood.[38]

Readings related to free will versus divine action are somewhat different from the Ohrmazd–Ahriman cosmological battle. The idea that the universe has a moral purpose, and thus every human being has to choose a side, presents a brilliant parallel, but it goes not much further than that regarding the Zoroastrian theme of enemies of the *dēn*.[39] The apocalypse ZWY, on the other hand, is very clear about who the enemies

---

[35] CPD, 'mowbed': 'Mazdean' (i.e. Zoroastrian) priest. Plural should be 'mowbadan'; mobads is a concession in translation.
[36] The source describing the alleged persecution is suspicious for us here: after centuries of a common shared environment between Zoroastrians, Jews and Christians, a complaint such as this – that Zoroastrians worship the sun and have two main gods – in barely credible.
[37] Observe how in this passage Satan is equated to Ahriman (this confusion also appears in Danielic Sogdian fragments).
[38] Excerpt from the 'Chronicle of Arbela', from the second century CE, quoted and analysed by Josef Wiesehöfer. *Ancient Persia*. London: I.B. Tauris, 2011, p. 156. The nature of this persecution may have been more imagined than real; Kirdēr, the principal *mobad*, to promote himself – and the organization of something resembling a Zoroastrian doctrinal compilation – may have been eager to advertise his deeds in terms of zeal. This is possible because we have no similar complaints – at least not in the volume proposed by Kirdēr – in Jewish or Christian chroniclers. Cf. also Philippe Gignoux. *Le mage Kirdīr et ses quatre inscriptions*. Paris: Diffusion de Boccard, 1989, pp. 693–5; and also Adam H. Becker. 'Political Theology and Religious Diversity' in: Geoffrey Herman (ed.). *Jews, Christians and Zoroastrian. Religious Dynamics in a Sasanian Context*. Piscataway: Gorgias Press, 2014, pp. 18–19, 23.
[39] The title of 'enemies of the dēn' is of widespread use but is particularly detailed in ZWY 1–4.

and who the friends of the *dēn* are, but in a different fashion from Daniel: metaphors in the ZWY, when they appear at all, are quickly explained.

The first list of enemies, in ZWY 2:1, is related to the rebel Mazdak:

In the zand of the Wahman Yasn and of the Hordād[40] Yasn and of the Aštād[41] Yasn it is revealed that once the accursed Mazdak son of Bāmdād, the adversary of the religion [i.e. the dēn], appeared. And [his followers] brought detriment to the religion of the yazads.

Then, in ZWY 3:29 (related to the seven-branch version of the cosmic tree):

The one on which iron had been mixed [is the evil dominion of the parted hair[42] dēws of the seed of Xēšm,] when it will be the end of the tenth century of your [millenium], o Spitāmān Zarduxšt.

Again, in ZWY 4:2–4:

2. Ohrmazd said, 'O Spitāmān Zarduxšt, I will make it clear. The sign of the end of your millenium will be [that] 3. the least of periods will arrive. One hundred kinds, one thousand kinds, a myriad kinds of parted hair dēws of the seed of Xēšm,[43] 4. those of very mean stock.'

And, finally, in ZWY 6:10:

10. And the third one [i.e. the third great escathlogical battle] [will take place] at the end of your millenium, O Spitāmān Zarduxšt, when all those three, the Turk,[44] the Tāzīg[45] and the Hrōmāyīg,[46] [together], will arrive at this place … And there will be such a flow of those of the seed of Xesm into these Ērānian lands which I, Ohrmazd, have created.

So, concrete men and whole peoples not only help us date some passages but also reinforce the same idea in all of them: the material world has a moral purpose.

On that note, it is fair to say that men and matter have a particular moral purpose which is attacked not only by Ahriman – whose capacity is, after all, limited – but also by whole peoples and nations. Moreover, regardless of the contemporary division of

---

[40] One of the *Amesa Spentas*. This name is the Pahlavi form of the Av. 'Hauruuatāt-' and means that this spirit is the one related to 'wholeness' or perfection.
[41] From the Av. 'Arštāt-', the goddess of rectitude or justice. Yt. 18 is dedicated to this spirit but does not mention her name.
[42] 'Parted hair', equivalent to 'dishevelled hair'; cf. *CPD*, 'wizārd-wars', with parted hair (also 'wizārdan', 'wizār': 'separate', 'explain', 'interpret', 'perform', 'fulfil', 'redeem').
[43] Ibid.
[44] *CPD*, 'Turk': 'Turk' (i.e. of Turkish stock).
[45] *CPD*, 'Tāzīg': 'Arab'.
[46] *CPD*, 'Hrōm-āyīg': 'Greek', 'Byzantine', 'Roman'.

apocalypses as 'historical' or 'other-worldly', the questions surrounding the purpose and development of men remain the same. Indeed, if one were to compare the only two remaining texts of each subgenre in Zoroastrian apocalypse – the ZWY and the AWN – that difference, as well as the common background theme, would become much more conspicuous.

§7 Dishevelled hair, heirs of Wrath and other enemies of Ohrmazd

At this point, a few other questions line up: how do human foes compare to the other 'wicked' creations of Ahriman? How do the enemies of the *dēn* phisically appear in 'historical' events to Persians who strive to keep their faith? And are these 'good' peoples and events at all present?[47]

The answers to these questions entail a good deal of apocalyptic material, for they would explain not just how the world came into being and what will be the ultimate destiny of Creation, but also – and perhaps more importantly given the dating we do have for MP texts, that is, after the Arab conquest – what was going on in-between these events. Also, it is not clear why that particular moment was made so difficult to endure, especially given the extensive promises of deliverance, common to apocalypses of the 'historical' type.[48] All those enquiries fall into the same category of problems rendered more difficult because of the dating of the mss, for internal evidence shows multiple layers of redaction which are, as expected, 'out of sequence'.[49]

One solution for this matter is circumventing the dead end of mss dating and concentrating on the contents themselves. By doing so, it might be possible to deal with the issues of peoples and places just as they appear in a given ms.[50] However, this would pose some weird questions about the role of the Chinese, for example, for they were the last fierce allies of the Sasanians, and yet they appear in a quite inimical position in ZWY 4:[51]

---

[47] Cf. Matthew P. Canepa. 'Unceasing Embassies' in: Matthew P. Canepa (ed.). *The Two Eyes of the Earth: Art and Ritual of Kingship between Rome and Sasanian Iran*. Berkeley: University of California Press, 2009. The Byzantine historian Theophylakt Simocatta mentions foreign peoples, friend or foe to the Persians, with some detail; cf. his work in a modern edition, Michael Whitby and Mary Whitby (eds). *The History of Theophylact Simocatta*. Oxford: Oxford University Press, 1986 (he wrote a 'History' in eight volumes, generally considered trustworthy, during the reign of Emperor Maurice (582–602 CE)).

[48] As Max Weber pointed out long ago but which continues to be true, every need for imminent salvation is a reply for current needs of a given social group.

[49] Bailey. *Zoroastrian Problems*. Bailey does so examining at length the MP term 'farrah' (loosely translated as 'glory', and with several important consequences for dating of Av. and even OP texts, with some difficulty. *CPD* refers 'farr-' to 'xwarrah', het. GDE, as 'fortune', 'glory' or 'splendour'). Any definite translation, however, is far from being a settled issue.

[50] On the matter, cf. the following articles by Carlo G. Cereti. '*Padīriftan ī dēn* and the turn of the millennium' in: *East and West* 45.1/4 (1995); 'Sconfiggere il demone della menzogna: Guerra santa, guerra giusta nell'Iran preislamico' in: *Studi Storici* 43.3 (2002); and *Guerra santa e guerra giusta dal mondo antico alla prima età moderna*. 2002. For the role of the Chinese in that specific apocalypse, the ZWY, cf. Matteo Compareti. 'The Last Sasanians in China' in: *Eurasian Studies* 2.2 (2003).

[51] Chapter 6 of this book will go back to the soteriological schemes in the ZWY in more detail.

57. The earth, Spandarmad, will open [her] mouth and all gems and metals, like gold, copper, tin and lead,⁵² will be revealed. 58. And lordship and sovereignty will go to those of non-Ērāniān origins, such as the Hyōn, the Turk, the Xadur, the Tōbīd, such as the Hindūg, the Kōfyār, the Činīg,⁵³ the Kābulīg.

In the end, all of these matters look very similar to Daniel, but a fundamental distinction remains: Second Temple Jewish apocalyptic, or for that matter, the NT, allows the practice of evil and still *predicts* a 'happy ending' in the final combat. That is quite different from knowing beforehand the result of such combat, as is the case of Zoroastrianism, but then why are there complaints about Ohrmazd in ZWY 3:29 after nights of dreams of omniscience by Zaraθuštra?⁵⁴

19. And I saw a tree on which were seven branches, one of gold, one of silver, one of copper, one of brass, one of lead, one of steel and one on [which] iron had been mixed. 20. Ohrmazd⁵⁵ said, 'O Spitāmān Zarduxšt,⁵⁶ this what I foretell. 21. The trunk of the tree that you saw, that is the material world that I, Ohrmazd, have created.⁵⁷

As in all apocalypses of the sort, it is the final era, the last branch, the last animal or the feet of the statue that matter, the others being either completely good or at least partially blessed:

29. The one on which iron had been mixed [is the evil dominion of the parted hair dēws of the seed of Xēšm,⁵⁸] when it will be the end of the tenth century of your [millennium], o Spitāmān Zarduxšt.

---

⁵² A very strange component in a very strange sequence, where not only we have five metals instead of the usual four or, less frequently, seven but also there is only one truly precious metal in the sequence, gold. Cereti suggests that we have a gloss here: *CPD*, 'arzīz': 'tin', 'lead', but also 'srub'. Ms K43 of ZWY omits this altogether. Cereti suggests a better reading, 'surb'. Cf. the transliteration in Cereti's ZWY, p. 101. The reconstitution by Cereti goes like this, in MP: 'ud arzīz ud *surb' in the transcription; Cereti suggests (correctly, in my view) that this might be a gloss – '*like gold, copper, tin and lead*'. *CPD* does not have any entry, in any of its parts, for 'surb', however, only 'srub' in the 'English-Pahlavi Index'. Cf. *CPD*, p. 121.
⁵³ Cereti himself refers this theme to the article by Harold W. Bailey. 'Iranian Studies' in: *BSOAS* 6.4 (1932): 945–55, but with special regard to p. 948: here Bailey uses the alternative 'Čēnīk', referring to an embassy sent by the Chinese to the Sasanians at the time of Khusraw I (509–571 CE). They appear in other parts of the ZWY and, fully described, in the ZN.
⁵⁴ Another parallel to Danielic lore: Zaraθuštra is also a dreamer to whom the gift of forethought and omniscience are given; however, he is better compared to the bewildered Daniel from Dan 7–12 than to the extremely clever and sure-of-himself Daniel of Dan 2.
⁵⁵ A later form of 'Ahuramazdā' in MP, kept in other's translations for the sake of coherence.
⁵⁶ That is, from the family of the Spitamids. Their common ancestor, *Spitāma*, appears in many verses in the Gāθās Y 46.13; 51.12; 53.1; and in Zoroastrian literature at large.
⁵⁷ Again, an interesting feature, since we have references to the main part of a plant (the vine) in another Danielic-related apocalypse, 2 Baruch (29:5–6).
⁵⁸ Already mentioned in ZWY 1.11; these may be Macedonians or, more likely, later enemies of Central Asian origin. Cf. Mary Boyce. 'The Poems of the Persian Sybil' in: *Études Irano-aryennes offertes à Gilbert Lazard. Studia Iranica*, Cahier 7. Paris: Association pour l'avancement des études iraniennes, 1989, p. 73; Hans G. Kippenberg. 'Die Geschichte der Mittelpersischen apokalytischen Traditionen' in: *SIr* 7 (1978): 60; and Behramgore T. Anklesaria. *Zand ī Vohûman Yasn and two Pahlavi Fragments*

Zaraθuštra asked Ohrmazd for immortality, arguing that if he is made immortal, more people will believe in the true religion, but his demand is negated. Ohrmazd denies him this, alleging that if he did so, the Resurrection of the Dead in the Final Body would be impossible. In these passages lies yet another example of the need for enemies to be defeated and the importance given to the material world within Zoroastrianism, which sparks another meaningful question: if the twin enemy gods must face each other – and only one of them has the gift of omniscience – then what is the role of matter?

Well, matter is not a privilege of Ohrmazd. In fact, Ahriman's attack on the whole of Creation is remarkable for its relentless speed and disastrous damage. However, in Zoroastrianism, since there is no periodical fight to be re-enacted as in all previous cults in the Near East, a permanent victory needs to be visible, tangible for most men. That is the main reason why matter is not merely a burden to be carried aimlessly by men while a purely spiritual life awaits the good and just. The desirable ending is the opposite: like an engraving in stone, the final victory of Ohrmazd must take place in a concrete, intelligible shape with direct consequences, as proposed in Dan 12:2. The Resurrection of the Dead and the Final Judgement are, both in Daniel and in Zoroastrianism, proof of a godly power that is able to create matter not only once, but twice. It is fair to conclude that Ohrmazd was a God that put 'order' to the world, rather than one who created things *ex nihilo*.[59]

§8 If the universe has a Creator, nature has a moral purpose

The moral implications of all that should by now be clear – if matter is a battlefield between Good and Evil, then each one of us must take a stance, the 'correct' one, and 'help' Ohrmazd win for the sake of our spirits. Now, there is a unique aspect to that: perhaps for the first time in the history of religious thought, free will had to be somehow reconciled with predestination.[60] Ohrmazd plotted against Ahriman by means of a ruse, fully aware that they both could fight on a material world and that would present the only possibility for a decisive defeat of Evil, as described in the GrBd 1a.6. The conflict itself, on the other hand, is vividly described in Bd 1.21–23:

---

with *Text, Transliteration and Translation in English*. Bombay: K.R. Cama Oriental Institute, 1957. This is perhaps the most important identifier – if the riddle can be solved – in the ZWY in order to place it definitely just before Daniel or at any other, later time.

[59] Antonio Panaino. 'Cosmologies and Astrology', in: *WBCZ*, p. 235. The expression means, literally, 'out of nothing'.

[60] As we have seen, Zoroastrianism gives a solution to this dilemma that may not be perfect but solves some of the more thorny issues: victory is final (i.e. not cyclical, not a ritual that needs to be reset every year, cosmic year or similar terms) and, secondarily, each person is needed for this victory to be assured. This turns us back to the old question: if it is assured, why the need to collaborate? For the examination of the DSS in the next chapter, this will be a central issue. It is not incompatible with free will but requires some rhetorical contortions to fit in the idea of a destiny established beforehand (in the case of Zoroastrianism, as seen, even before matter was created).

21. The Evil Spirit snarled:[61] 'I will not help your creatures and I will not offer praise! No, I will destroy you and your creatures for ever and ever! I will incite all your creatures to hate you and to love me.' 22. The explanation is that he believed that Ohrmazd had offered peace because he was helpless against him.[62] He did not accept it, and made his vow. 23. Ohrmazd said: 'You are not omnipotent, Evil Spirit. You cannot destroy me nor can you prevent my creatures from returning to my possession.'

This is most interesting: although plentiful in brute force but lacking in omniscience, Ahriman is, nonetheless, capable of thinking. It is precisely his 'thinking' that leads to his downfall: while Ahriman is considering the best way to cause the most harm to Ohrmazd, the latter answers proudly that Ahriman is deficient and cannot permanently harm him. That exchange points to some sort of later repair in the future, most likely in the Final Judgement.

24. Then Ohrmazd in his omniscience[63] realized: If I do not set a time for our battle, he will be able to do to my creation as he vowed, and the strife and Mixture will be forever. During the Mixture, he will be able to mislead the creatures and make them his own. Just so, now during the Mixture, there are many people who commit more sins than good deeds; that is, they always do as the Evil Spirit desires. 25. Ohrmazd said to the Evil Spirit: 'Let us set a time, so that by this pact our battle will be limited to nine thousand years.'

Ahriman's lack of foresight, if not of intelligence, is astonishing: he had been warned of the conflict but does not measure the consequences. Ohrmazd is so absolutely sure of the outcome of the combat that he does, in an amazing and reckless sequence, offend Ahriman, summons him to a duel and even fixes the time allotted for that. By comparison, millenarist tendencies in Second Temple Judaism are far vaguer and less informative.[64]

Much later on, the main tendencies of millenarism will arise among Christians (who were an offspring of Judaism): the wish that Jesus will come very soon[65] and the calculations for the exact time of his Passion, in a reverse counting from the Creation

---

[61] An important point to be made here is that what follows are not speech acts (as is the case in the God of Abrahamic faiths) but sounds more like a 'report' of what was and what will become; the promise of destruction still lies ahead: it is guaranteed but that does not take effect by any device connected to what Ohrmazd says. It is a promise and sounds, in a way, like the mutual threatenings and lists of awesome feats in singular combat, both in Iranian and Homeric facings. The stupidity of *Ahriman*, imagining (wrongly) that Ohrmazd is looking for peace due to lack of strength is remarkable in another sense too: whereas in the Homeric world the feats of each hero are comparable – if not equal – in 'quality' (i.e. there is no distinction between good and evil between, say, Glauco and Diomedes), here this distinction is made clear from the start, showing the faithful that there is only one side worthy of our efforts.

[62] The same idea in note 61 but in a slightly different fashion.

[63] *CPD*, 'ōšyār', 'ōš(īh)': 'consciousness', 'conscious'.

[64] These are, in fact, updated: Daniel's last kingdom was at first the heritage of Alexander, then Rome – in 4 Ezra and in AJ 10.276.

[65] Matt 24:21; Mark 13:26–15:31; 15:39; Luke 21:32; Rev 1:13–15; and 1 John 2:18, among the most prominent. The technical term for that second coming is, in Greek, παρουσία – a term that had long

of the world.⁶⁶ In Zoroastrianism, both the event itself and its outcome are known in comfortable advance, which once again brings us to the discussion regarding free will and predestination.

> 28. Ohrmazd knew this too, by means of omniscience: Within these nine thousand years, three thousand years will pass all according to the will of Ohrmazd; three thousand years [will pass] in the mingled state, according to the will of [both] Ohrmazd and Ahriman; and, in the final contest [He ought to render] the Evil Spirit useless, and He will withhold adversity from the creatures.
> 29. Then, Ohrmazd chanted forth the 'Ahunwar', that is, He uttered a 'Yatha ahu-vairyo' of twenty-one words;⁶⁷ He showed to the Evil Spirit His own final victory, the inability of the Evil Spirit, the perishing of the Devs, the rising of the dead, the final material life, and the unopposed condition of the creatures, upto eternity and eternal progress.
> 30. When the Evil Spirit saw his own inability, and the perishing of all the Devs,⁶⁸ he fell back into darkness, having become stupefied [and unconscious⁶⁹].

Finally, because he can feel and think, albeit in an awkward and cumbersome manner, Ahriman realizes that he had fallen into a trap when Ohrmazd recklessly shows him a 'spoiler' of the outcome of their fight. Therefore, in this scheme, the whole Creation, material and non-material, will last twelve thousand years – three thousand years of latency and another nine thousand years of conflict, with alternating advantage between the duellers.

Now, regarding the choosing of sides, one fairly simple explanation would be that Zaraθuštra, as Ohrmazd's prophet, widely announced the better destiny of the souls of the good in many texts. Thus, the idea of a reward *for deeds and not according to grace* can be considered a good enough motivation for most believers to choose the 'right side' in the fight. This is justice by retribution on its own right, a common feature in the HB (e.g. Exod 20:5) which was targeted in the New Testament (John 9:2). It does appear as a typical example of Talion's law: no good deed gets unrewarded and no bad deed gets forgotten.

§9 And how does it all end for Zoroastrians compared to Second Temple expectations?

The most widespread idea for Zoroastrians regarding Creation is that it will all end up in a big conflagration, probably by fire. An alternative view is that of the *Činwad* bridge

---

before Jesus's Passion been used to describe the visit of a king or important officer or, even simpler, that we have someone present to assist us (LSJ).

[66] On that subject, the best work so far is Georges Declercq. *Anno Domini. The Origins of the Christian Era*. Turnhout: Brepols, 2000, especially his first chapter, 'Between Gospel and Tradition'.

[67] Again, a display of power rather than a speech act.

[68] CPD, 'dēw', 'dēwēsnīh': 'devil', 'devil-worshipper'.

[69] CPD, 'abēōš', 'abēōšīh': 'unconscious', 'unconsciousness'.

or 'Bridge of the Separator', a replication of an idea common to many religions: basically the soul must cross an abyss by means of a bridge, which becomes larger and larger for the just and narrower and narrower for the impious until they fall into the pit. For reference, Y 46.10–11:

> 10. Whoso, man or woman, doeth what thou, Mazda Ahura, knowest as best in life, as destiny for what is Right (give him) the Dominion through Good Thought. And those whom I impel to your adoration, with all these will I cross the Bridge of the Separator.
> 11. By their dominion the Karapans and the Kavis accustomed mankind to evil actions, so as to destroy Life. Their own soul and their own self shall torment them when they come where the Bridge of the Separator is, to all time dwellers in the House of the Lie.

For Zoroastrians, the end will only come when the resurrected body finally meets the soul, as described in Bd 35.4–5:

> 4. It also says: Zoroaster asked Ohrmazd: 'How will you restore the body after the wind has wasted it and the water carried it away? How can the Resurrection be?'
> 5. Ohrmazd replied: 'When I created the unpillared sky fastened on a spiritual foundation, broad and light, from the substance of shining metal; when I created the earth that bears all corporeal existence but has no material support; when I loosed the sun, moon and stars in the atmosphere, moving as bodies of light; when I created the grain that is sown in the earth and returns growing forth in abundance; when I gave colors to the plants of every kind, and I placed in them and other things a burnless fire; when I created the child in its mother's womb and protected him, creating individually hair and skin, nails and blood, sinews and eyes, ears, and other limbs; when I gave feet to the water to flow; when I created the spiritual clouds that bear material water and rain where they will; when I created the visible air that by the power of the wind blows above and below as it wills, and hands cannot grasp it: creating each one of these was more difficult than the Resurrection. For, at the Resurrection, I will have the aid of those I did not have when I made them; it will be as it was. Consider this:[70] If I could create what was not, how could it be that I will not be able to re- create what was? For at that time I will ask the spirit of the earth for the bones,[71] the water for the blood, the plants

---

[70] The whole passage, which reads 'rīst-ākhēzisnih' (in Anklesaria's rendering) is astonishing to anyone comparing it to Second Temple texts dealing with the same issue: here again the huge effort involved in material creation (*CPD*, 'rist': 'dead', + 'kešīdan', 'keš-': 'pull', 'draw') sounds incompatible with the ease with which God creates the world (as in Genesis) and also with the lack of detail present in the ressurrection (as in Dan 12:2). In the Gospels many impressive passages deal with Jesus presenting himself resurrecting the dead, not to mention his own ascension and katabasis.

[71] *CPD*, 'ast': 'bone'; 'dam': 'creature'. 'Dami ast' in Anklesaria's rendition. Cf. also Philippe Gignoux. '"Corps osseux et âme osseusse": Essai sur le chamanisme dans l'Iran ancient' in: *JA* 267.1–2 (1979): 41–79; also Meuli. 'Scythica', pp. 128–51.

for the hair, and the wind for the vital breath, just as they received them at the primal creation.'

The original state of the world is the work of Ohrmazd, and there is a very clearly defined order on what will be redone. Gayōmard rightfully takes first place in the resurrection line, and the remembrance of the bones is crucial in that process. It is a simpler solution (in the GrBd) that the *saošyant*, the most important Zoroastrian redeemer, shall raise the dead later himself – just as they died. Furthermore, the meeting of a son with his father can only happen simultaneously: a father, grandfather and so on need to take precedence, otherwise their descendants will have nobody to recognize.

6. First, the bones of Gayōmard will rise up, then those of Mašyā and Mašyāne, and finally the bones of all others will stir. 7. Sōšāns[72] will raise the dead and raise up all people in fifty- seven years, the righteous and the wicked; every person will stir again from the place where his vital breath left him or near the place where he fell to earth. 8. Then when all corporeal existence, body, and form[73] are again restored, then they will give them their individuality. They will give half of the light of the sun to Gayōmard and half to other people. 9. Then people will begin to recognize each other, soul to soul and body to body. They will know this: that is my father; that is my brother; that is my wife; that is one of my closest relatives.

Nowhere in the HB can something of the sort be found, except for a particular apocalyptic text where the setting is partly in Babylonia and partly, not by coincidence, in Persia. That text is Dan 12:2, which belongs to, roughly, the Maccabean period and conveys remarkably similar ideas:

2. 'Many of those who sleep in the dust of the earth shall awake, some to everlasting life, and some to shame and everlasting contempt. 3. Those who are wise shall shine like the brightness of the sky, and those who lead many to righteousness, like the stars forever and ever. 4. But you, Daniel, keep the words secret and the book sealed until the time of the end. Many shall be running back and forth, and evil shall increase.' 5. Then I, Daniel, looked, and two others appeared, one standing on this bank of the stream and one on the other. 6. One of them said to the man clothed in linen, who was upstream, 'How long shall it be until the end of these wonders?' 7. The man clothed in linen, who was upstream, raised his right hand and his left hand toward heaven. And I heard him swear by the one who lives forever that it would be for a time, two times, and half a time, and that when the shattering of the power of the holy people comes to an end, all these things would be accomplished.

---

[72] That is, the *Saošyant*.
[73] *CPD*, 'mādišt': 'matter', 'protoplast'.

As seen previously, it is tricky to posit 'unquestionable traits of Persian influence' in Daniel or in Jewish apocalyptic in general, for all these concepts – finitude of time, ordeal of body and soul and final rewards, and so on – are strange to the whole Semitic setting of the HB or, as Christians call it, the OT. Given the problems of the redaction layers and the poor preservation of the texts, it is impossible to hard-proof the anteriority of Persian ideas against Jewish ones. Still, it seems reasonable to assume that the influence is indeed there, which most scholars agree with.

A superficial look at the *Gāθās* will show the reader a world that resembles much more the warrior-like pastures of the *Iliad* (i.e. the second-millenium BCE IE world) than anything else. I concede that a big 'official' ambience could have been 'retrospectively' set for Zoroastrianism during the Sasanid Period[74] – but it would take a lot of imagination to build from scratch the entirety of, say, hunting and pastoral scenes of now long-lost worlds such as those described by Zaraθuštra in the *Gāθās*.

§10 Lawful deaths in the Maccabean Revolt: Cause or consequence of a rethinking of the world beyond?

A turmoil shook the Semitic world following the meeting with the Romans. Chaos arrived in the person of ambassador Gaius Popilius Laenas, who began to mess around with Seleucid affairs after Antiochus IV Epiphanes's manipulation of the Lagids' kingship.[75] In simple terms: the Seleucids won the war but, since that made them too powerful in the eyes of Rome, they had to give up their gains and still pay an indemnization.

Therefore, Antiochus IV had another serious issue to contend with: a great sum of unpaid money, owed by his predecessor Antiochus III to the Romans after the Peace of Apamaea (187 BCE).[76] As per usual, Antiochus left to his *filobasilei* (i.e. lit. 'the king's friends') the role of getting him what he needed, since Hellenistic states did not have the elaborate legislative and fiscal apparatus that characterized Roman affairs, in this case, regarding tax-paying.[77] Clearly, matters such as the debt with Rome was just another case of decision making in the heat of the moment.[78]

That scenario seems quite peculiar when we take into account that even among the Jews, with the treasure-rich Temple in Jerusalem, there were many in favour of

---

[74] Cf. Maria Macuch. 'Pahlavi Literature' in: Ronald E. Emmerick and Maria Macuch (eds). *A History of Persian Literature*. London: I.B. Tauris, 2009, vol. 17, p.116. By 'retrospectively', I mean that the settings, stories, chronologies and feats described could not be exactly what appear in the sources, given (again) the problems of dating the mss.

[75] Polybius. *History* 29.27.

[76] Paul J. Kosmin. *The Land of the Elephant Kings: Space, Territory, and Ideology in the Seleucid Empire*. Cambridge, MA: Harvard University Press, 2014, pp. 21, 121.

[77] Mikhail Rostovtzeff. *The Social & Economic History of the Hellenistic World*. New York: Oxford, 1941, vol. 2, p. 1053.

[78] Martin Goodman. *The Ruling Class of Judaea: The Origins of the Jewish Revolt against Rome A.D. 66–70*. Cambridge: Cambridge University Press, 1987, p. 10.

'Hellenization' – a word that had a very different meaning in the second century BCE (mostly because of Droysen's efforts).[79] Even so, despite this semantic shift, the text of 1 and 2Maccabees – not to mention other sources such as Josephus or Philo – are unanimous regarding the outcome of Palestinian Jews. They were the ones directly affected by the dispute between Antiochus Epiphanes and the partisans of 'Hellenization'. Those Jews and the others who wished to make no concessions to the Romans had a common problem.

From that point onwards, a strong relationship was established between martyrdom and hopes of a fine afterlife. In those cases, it would not suffice to say that religion was, as in many others after, the pretext for action: the historian was the one, after all, who stood at the end of the complete process and was thus in a privileged position to assess events, characters and modes of thinking, and to deal with death and the sacred.

Now, for the Jews who were on the receiving end of the revolt against Antiochus Epiphanes and his followers, a new sub-problem arose: in a religion very much matter-of-factly regarding duties to God and corresponding rewards (e.g. Gen 49:10; Mic 3:11; 1 Sam 10:11; Ezra 16:34; Eccl 4:9; and Isa 3:11, among countless examples), what about those who were 'martyred', who died unnaturally not in war but executed out of 'stubbornness' due to unwavering religious ways and religious practices? It appeared that this matter – among other issues – shed light on the idea that maybe *šeol*, or ᾅδης ('Hades' in the LXX translation for the term e.g. Job 17:16), was just not enough anymore for an afterlife worth the kind of persecution the Jews were enduring.

Too much suffering was involved and, what is more, rebels were publicly and shamefully humiliated. That formed the ideal background for a new idea to find strength within the killings happening during the Revolt: the righteous dead may, after all, get a 'different' *šeol* or, to put it in a more sophisticated way, they deserved a better world beyond. Indeed, the whole scenario became so preposterous that even those in need of atonement felt that they could no longer do so in this life (2 Macc 12:43–44).

Nonetheless, the text goes beyond that and suggests atonement for the dead, and, what seems all the more incredible, repeats the idea that Judas Maccabeus would not have made any of this; he did not believe that the dead were to rise again (εἰ μὴ γὰρ τοὺς προπεπτωκότας ἀναστῆναι προσεδόκα, περισσὸν καὶ ληρῶδες ὑπὲρ νεκρῶν εὔχεσθαι).[80] That was a whole new feature in both the Jewish religion and, given the recent events, in their political expectations. The dead, pious or otherwise (v. 45), could expect something good even in the gruelling circumstances of the war – or, perhaps, in the event of it.

---

[79] Plutarch. *De fortuna aut virtute Alexandri Magni*. Cited in Martin Hengel. *Jews, Greeks and Barbarians*. Philadelphia: Fortress Press, 1980, p. 52.
[80] 'For if he were not expecting that those who had fallen would rise again, it would have been superfluous and foolish to pray for the dead.'

§11 Daniel and the Maccabean Revolt: Two converging other-worldly perspectives

It is more than interesting that the main texts in the OT (or Greek Jewish Bible) that deal with real expectations for a world beyond, Daniel and 2 Maccabees, should be dated to approximately the same time lapse. Daniel, for one, is generally accepted as a second-century BCE book, and, in the shape that it came down to us, it is also generally accepted that chs 1–6 contain a somewhat motley array of material whose origins in time can be indeed very late.[81]

In any event, both Dan 12:1–3 and 2 Macc 12:39–45 are key texts in the introduction to what may have been a very attractive idea at the time: *šeol* is not necessarily the sombre and unpleasant abode of all dead, for they would rise once again. Moreover, at least in Daniel, different rewards and punishments were clearly in store for those souls according to the nature of the deeds each person has accomplished in life:

> 1. At that time shall arise Michael, the great prince[82] who has charge of your people. And there shall be a time of trouble, such as never has been since there was a nation[83] till that time; but at that time your people shall be delivered, every one whose name shall be found written in the book. 2. And many of those who sleep in the dust of the earth shall awake, some to everlasting life, and some to shame and everlasting contempt. 3. And those who are wise shall shine like the brightness of the firmament; and those who turn many to righteousness, like the stars for ever and ever.

Or in the HB:

¹ וּבָעֵת הַהִיא יַעֲמֹד מִיכָאֵל הַשַּׂר הַגָּדוֹל הָעֹמֵד עַל־בְּנֵי עַמֶּךָ וְהָיְתָה עֵת צָרָה אֲשֶׁר לֹא־נִהְיְתָה מִהְיוֹת גּוֹי עַד הָעֵת הַהִיא וּבָעֵת הַהִיא יִמָּלֵט עַמְּךָ כָּל־הַנִּמְצָא כָּתוּב בַּסֵּפֶר׃
² וְרַבִּים מִיְּשֵׁנֵי אַדְמַת־עָפָר יָקִיצוּ אֵלֶּה לְחַיֵּי עוֹלָם וְאֵלֶּה לַחֲרָפוֹת לְדִרְאוֹן עוֹלָם׃ ס
³ וְהַמַּשְׂכִּלִים יַזְהִרוּ כְּזֹהַר הָרָקִיעַ וּמַצְדִּיקֵי הָרַבִּים כַּכּוֹכָבִים לְעוֹלָם וָעֶד׃

The novelty here is v. 12 since now those who have ever since their demise slept in the netherworld will come to life again and, more importantly, will receive rewards accordingly.[84] That was the most important contribution of Zoroastrianism to other

---

[81] Cf. W. Lee Humphreys. 'A Life-Style for the Diaspora: A Study of the Tales of Esther and Daniel' in: *JBL* 92 (1973): 211–15; also John J. Collins. 'The Court-Tales in Daniel and the Development of Apocalyptic' in: *JBL* 94.2 (1975): 218.

[82] Also in Dan 10:21; here as BDB שַׂר but with interesting variations in the Greek text: in the LXX, Μιχαηλ ὁ ἄγγελος, but in TH, Μιχαηλ ὁ ἄρχων ὑμῶν – in the LXX lit. 'angel', although in the later context of the NT it had already become synonym with 'messenger' (e.g. Matt 1:24), but in TH the recension follows LSJ 'ruler', 'commander'.

[83] Comparable to the distress described in Jer 30:7; Exod 9:24; Mark 13:19; Matt 24:21; and Rev 16:18.

[84] John J. Collins. *Daniel: A Commentary on the Book of Daniel*. Hermeneia. Minneapolis: Fortress Press, 1993. It should also be remembered that Collins related the doctrine of retribution after death to 1QS 2; 4:7–8; and 1QH 6:34 in the DSS (although he firmly supports the link between the DSS and the Essenes, something I remark as untenable. Cf. ibid., p. 398).

faiths: a new theological solution to a concomitant political problem, namely the unconceivable punishment of souls who did no more than stand firm to their faiths in times of great oppression.⁸⁵ I shall not judge the merits of this arrangement, for that is not the historian's task, but I must concede that it was a clever decision, one that had the deepest effects in Second Temple Judaism for some centuries to come and, by domino effect, in Christianism.⁸⁶

The same issue of the contact between Persian and Jews having a more than casual affinity has also been underlined by Martin Goodman's analysis of Judaea's occupation between 40 BCE and 37 BCE. That has highlighted the similarities between 'combat myths' in the Ancient Near East and the Jewish concept of 'Holy War', and that parallel was used as the Maccabean propaganda during the revolt.⁸⁷

§12 Contemporary Persian possibilities on the resurrection of the dead acceptable to Jews during the second century BCE

The 'apparent' feature in that distinction must be stressed for, in practice, both religions frequently share the same sources, and it would be too far-fetched to think that Persians or Jews of the second century BCE would raise the exact same objections to their mutual problem. For starters, there is no certainty about the identity of Zaraθuštra⁸⁸ or, if he

---

⁸⁵ Hengel. *Jews, Greeks and Barbarians*, pp. 2, 9; Martin Hengel. 'Judaism and Hellenism Revisited' in: John J. Collins and Gregory E. Sterling (eds). *Hellenism in the Land of Israel*. Christianity and Judaism in Antiquity Series 13. Notre Dame: University of Notre Dame, 2001. Hengel points out, in his pioneering work as well as in his chapter devoted to re-examining his ideas, that Greek civilization has became vital to all Jews, including Palestinian ones – that kind of need is not the 'anti-theocracy' tried by Antiochus Epiphanes and/or Menelaus (p. 19).

⁸⁶ Here it seems useful to remind the reader that the work on Cohn (*Cosmos, Chaos and the World to Come*), generalizing as it has been accused of being, points rightly to many issues on the subject of the relations between Persian and Jewish ideas after the Exile; nor does Cohn make any proposition without taking into consideration the specialized secondary literature involved. What can be (rightly) said about this work of his is that he takes on the 'majority point of view' and does not argue enough on other possibilities regarding the issue in question. Cf. especially the following passage:

> At the heart of *Zaraθuštra*'s teaching is a sense of cosmic war: a conviction that a mighty spiritual power intent on maintaining and furthering life in an ordered world is locked in struggle with a spiritual power, scarcely less mighty, intent on destroying life and reducing the ordered world to chaos. Had this worldview a prehistory amongst the Iranians? Is it perhaps a novel version – thoroughly intellectualised and spiritualised – of the combat myth? Unfortunately, no god comparable with Indra figures in the Avesta, nor any combat comparable with Indra's fight with Vritra; and this silence has led even very eminent scholars to dismiss the possibility. But the matter is of such importance to the argument of this book that it cannot be left there: one must look further afield. (Kindle locs 2437–43)

⁸⁷ John J. Collins. 'The Mythology of Holy War in Daniel and the Qumran War Scroll: A Point of Transition in Jewish Apocalyptic' in: *VT* 25.3 (1975): 596–612, 597.

⁸⁸ Although in more recent times this issue seems more settled:

> Certain modern scholars have maintained that *Zaraθuštra* was not the name of a historical but of a mythical personage, a mere construct. This view can only be called perverse. A single, distinct personality speaks to us out of the poems, and in several places the poet names himself

existed, about the time of his activities.[89] Even so, it is generally accepted that by the time of Darius the Great (550–486 BCE), Ohrmazd[90] was at least accorded a special place in the pantheon of Persian gods. Whether Cyrus, Darius and the Achaemenids were strictly Zoroastrians is an altogether different matter.[91]

The scriptures ascribed to Zaraθuštra the Prophet, such as the 'Old Avesta' containing the *Gāθās* and the 'Young Avesta' containing the *Yašts*, the *Visperad* and the *Vendidad*, constitute an important but altogether different set of sources, which poses different problems. The Khordeh Avesta is still newer than both and contains merely some fragmentary materials which, regardless of the time of the final redaction, are in themselves full of clues related to the world at the end of the second millennium BCE. These scriptures were kept in oral tradition long before being put into written form[92] and may have, indeed, been kept in that way until the time of the Maccabees.

These poems resemble closely the world of Homeric poetry and Vedic literature,[93] from a different angle, in the discussion of the *Činwad* bridge, but we do not know how

> as *Zaraθuštra*, or rather (in his own language) Zarathushtra. In the one poem that is not by him, *Yasna* 53, he is named again as a real person, either still living or of recent memory. In the later parts of the Avesta as well as in other Zoroastrian literature he is frequently spoken of, with never a doubt as to his historical reality. His existence is as well authenticated as that of most people in antiquity. (Cf. West. *The Hymns of Zaraθuštra*, Kindle locs 116–27)

[89] This is especially important for the general public, given the widespread fascination that the idea of Achsenzeit arose; it would be more correct, in my view, to read Jaspers's opinions regarding Zaraθuštra and his birth date more carefully – or, rather, to take more care with the whole concept as it appears in *Vom Ursprung und Ziel der Geschichte* (Frankfurt am Main: Fischer, 1955. The English edition was given in the introduction of this book). A scholarly antidote to such enthusiasm can be found in Jan Assmann. 'Cultural Memory and the Myth of the Axial Age' in: Robert N. Bellah and Hans Joas (eds). *The Axial Age and Its Consequences*. Cambridge, MA: Harvard University Press, 2012, pp. 366–408.

[90] *CPD*, <'whrmzd>, later as *Ohrmazd*, following the common contraction of names that came from Av. and acquiring shorter forms in MP. David MacKenzie gives the full explanation in the entry: '['whrmzd / M 'whrm(y)zd, N Hōrmuzd] *Ahura Mazda*: astr. Jupiter.'

[91] Alireza S. Shahbazi. 'The Achaemenid Persian Empire (550–330 BCE)' in: Touraj Daryaee (ed.). *The Oxford Handbook of Iranian History*. Oxford: Oxford University Press, 2012, Kindle loc. 1845; also Maneckji N. Dhalla. *History of Zoroastrianism*. New York: Oxford University Press, 1938, pp. 115–288; and Jean Kellens. 'Avesta' in: *Encyclopaedia Iranica*. New York: Routledge and Kegan Paul, 1987, vol. 3, pp. 35–44.

[92] Boyce. *Textual Sources*, pp. 104–8; Carlo G. Cereti. *La letteratura pahlavi*. Milano: Mimesis, 2001, pp. 13–40. It should be noted that the idea that Alexander was responsible for the destruction of the sacred writings of Zoroastrianism is currently held as part of the process of 'demonization' of his public persona, and not as historical fact.

[93] In this matter, too, I follow West's reasoning – that the world depicted in Zoroastrianism sacred scriptures is very much like that of other late second-millenium BCE Bronze Age pastoral cultures. Cf. West. *The Hymns of Zaraθuštra*, Kindle locs 193–206:

> The society reflected in the *Gāthās* is loosely structured. There is no sense of a central imperial authority. Zaraθuštra speaks in several places of a hierarchy of social units, starting with the (family, clan) and rising to the (local community) and aryaman- (a wider network or alliance, perhaps something like a tribe). He has a separate scale for the domains within which personal authority may be exercised, from the individual household through the (manor) to the (settlement) and the (region). The last corresponds to the word later used by Darius and his successors for the provinces into which their empire was divided. It is the largest political unit in Zaraθuštra's world. He speaks critically of the 'rulers of the region' or 'of the regions'. But they appear as rather dim and distant figures. It is a pastoral society in which the cow and its products have an important place. But the dairy-farmer's peaceful

much of that had survived – or was even composed – by 167 BCE. Some of the relevant Persian ideas we have gathered so far regarding the fate of the dead during and after the Maccabean Revolt can thus be summarized as such (always considering the dating problems):

1. The world beyond life is 'egalitarian', in the sense that rich and poor, powerful and humble will be tried and saved or damned in the same way. Literal evidence for that is plentiful (albeit sometimes difficult to date with precision) and can be found within the Avesta in Y 31:20; 43:4; and 51:9.[94]

> Y 31:20 (Av. *Tā.və̄.uruuātā Hāiti*): If anyone attacks the guardian of Harmony, his final lot will be lamentations, the unending darkness and bad food [Av. *duš.x ᵛarəθəm*[95]], despair in [his] voice. May [your] conscience, o supporters of the Lie, take yourselves to that existence [Av. *ahūm*] because of your own very deeds!
>
> Y 43:4 (Av. *Uštauuaitī Hāiti*): If the dominion of the divine Thought comes to me, I would think, o Mazdā, that you [state of mind] and [Man] unmovable are two hands; by means of each one you ask about the grants given to the guardian of the Lie and to the guardian of Harmony by means of the fire [Av. *āθrō*] that keeps the power of Harmony.
>
> Y 51:9 (*Vohuxšaθrā Hāiti*): The satisfaction you give to both … by your raging fire, o Mazdā, to pose an obstacle to … by means of molten metal [Av. *aiiaŋhā*], when … So that the defender of the Lie may perish, [and] that of the Harmony never ceases to be opulent!

In all three examples of the Avestan text, evidence of concrete and material exhibits of what the world beyond should be like are thoroughly present. The issue of the 'molten metal' in Y 51 comes, admittedly, in a very fragmentary state but remains of utmost importance for final judgements in Zoroastrianism. The theme of Zaraθuštra's vision of both rich and poor alike (i.e. pairs of opposites during life on earth) in the netherworld is even more explicitly clear in this passage, ZWY 3.15–18:

> 15. Zarduxšt said, *Ohrmazd, bountiful spirit, Creator of the world of material beings,[96] I have seen a rich man of much property who was honoured in the body and thin [weak] in the soul and was in hell, and it did not seem praiseworthy to me. 16. And I saw a poor man lacking everything and needy, his soul was fat [and was] in paradise, and it seemed praiseworthy[97] to me. 17. And I saw a powerful

---

existence is threatened by violent intrusions. In one of his most striking poems (*Yasna* 29), Zaraθuštra represents the cow's soul as complaining to the powers above of the cruel *aggression* to which she is subject. It is not her righteous-living herdsman that is to blame, but others who, guided by priests of a false religion, drive her off and condemn her to be sacrificed.

[94] *Yasna* passages and commentary taken from the three-volume set: Kellens and Pirart, *Les textes vieil-avestiques*, vol. 1.
[95] CPD, 'dosōx' has a cognate, 'dō-saxwan': 'two-tongued', 'deceitful' and, by extension, 'liar'.
[96] CPD, 'astwand' = 'astōmānd': 'corporeal', 'material'; ZWY 3:15; 4:1; 5:1; 6:1; 7:1 (also in the variant plural form 'astōmandān').
[97] CPD, 'burzišnīg', 'stāyišnīg'.

man without offspring, and it did not seem praiseworthy to me. 18. And I saw a poor man endowed with much offspring, and it seemed praiseworthy to me.[98]

The example above is very clear – although the antiquity of the text of the ZWY is disputed, or posited in different compositional levels – regarding a couple of important matters related to the world beyond: first, there is something similar to the physical world we live in, and that similarity is such that it was visually approached by Zaraθuštra; second, some desirable social standards also apply to that world,[99] such as 'property'[100] and 'offspring', to name a few examples of common vocabulary used to depict the world beyond, its blessings and its curses.

That post-mortem judgement has two versions, which, like what is proposed in the Maccabean Revolt, are not mutually exclusive: we have, on the one hand, the individual's own judgement and, on the other, that of the whole ensemble or community of men. The few examples above, both in Y and in the ZWY, should suffice to demonstrate how the two kinds coexist.

On that note, it is pretty much clear from Zoroastrian earliest sources (i.e. from the second millennium BCE in terms of the content of the Avesta,[101] but in Western historical records those appear only in the sixth century BCE, with Herodotus) that it pays off to do good deeds and it is very unsafe, to say the least, to be wicked.[102] Two varieties of trial for those accused of treachery stand out: one by fire or molten metal,[103] to ordeal the material body, and the other by the crossing of the spiritual Činwad bridge,[104] to ordeal the soul. The first one was more effective in causing a lasting impact amongst Jews, and the popularity of this trial by fire[105] would later migrate to Christian apocalypses.

---

[98] Cf. Cereti's ZWY, p. 151.
[99] *CPD*, 'driyōš': 'poor', 'needy'. By analogy, someone in such a condition would be unable to raise an offsring; also 'nēst-frazand', that is, not plus child, son, offspring.
[100] *CPD*, 'was' + 'xwastag': 'wealthy', 'rich', 'one who has property'.
[101] Foltz. *Spirituality in the Land of the Noble*, pp. 4–6.
[102] That is, we are dealing with a 'give-and-take' theological reasoning, absolutely devoid of the notion of Grace. One can only be saved by means of the triad of Zoroastrian virtues – 'Good Thoughts, Good Words, Good Deeds'.
[103] Cf. above Y 31:20; 43:4; 51:9.
[104] This would be a bridge over an abyss that the departed should cross (individually, so it seems), and that would become broader for the just and ever narrower for the unrighteous; cf. Y 71, Vd 19.27–30 (especially 27: 'O Maker of the material world, thou Holy One! Where are the rewards given? Where does the rewarding take place? Where is the rewarding fulfilled? Whereto do men come to take the reward that, during their life in the material world, they have won for their souls?'). Literature concerning the universal theme of a bridge between the world of the dead and of the living is immense and the different – albeit of an encyclopedic nature – should not be dismissed.
[105] The theme of the destruction of the world by fire, that is, εκπυρόσις, appears in a variety of guises in Antiquity, in religious or even secular thinking: see e.g. Seneca, *Quaestiones Naturales* 3.29 (here the issue has to do with a certain alignment of 'planets' i.e. αστερες πλανετες, 'moving stars'); among the Stoics, according to Diogenes Laertius, *Lives of the Eminent Philosophers* 7.137–156; 9.7–11; Clement of Alexandria, *Stromateis* 5.104; and, more than any other, perhaps, Berossos, whose explanations on the matter came mostly down to us in Seneca's passage cited above. On the whole theme, cf. Charles Penglase. 'Foundations' in: *Greek Myths and Mesopotamia: parallels and influence in the Homeric hymns and Hesiod*. London: Routledge, 1994.

Bearing those concepts in mind, it is safe to move ahead and analyse *how* they could have made such an impact on Judaism at the time of the Maccabean Revolt. It is almost consensual that, eccentricities aside,[106] the radical dualism that necessarily accompanies the idea of a final judgement and of a world beyond is not to be found before the beginning of the second century BCE within Jewish texts. The grand problem here is, like most big problems in the history of ideas, *how* that concept spread. Perhaps these ideas originated in Judaism and 'travelled' eastwards towards the Iranian plateau, or perhaps they have Babylonian[107] origins or even Vedic roots, which is much more plausible.[108] Nonetheless, the possibilities are manyfold and complex in nature, so they shall be discussed in a separate paper.

§13 Persian *Yahud*: Possible influences and mutual contacts in Asia Minor and its social environment

As we have seen thus far, any scholar dealing with Zoroastrianism and Second Temple Judaism is faced with a set of noticeably clear propositions to be explained. The controversial issue of the dating of Zoroastrianism and the mainstream conception of Zaraθuštra as a Late Bronze Age prophet from what is today the northern part of Iran are some of the trickiest ones. In order to present fulfilling answers for those, we would need other manuscripts at least as old as the DSS. It would be equally ideal if those manuscripts were from, say, the beginning of the Sasanian Period or if we had an efficient cross-checking process in the absence of pre-CE mss.

However, even if we had all those resources, there would remain a problem: *how* to posit concrete influences having this amazingly imaginary set of texts We could

---

[106] Some students of mine claimed that this idea was nonsensical on the grounds that 'light and darkness were already a pair of opposites in Genesis, so why look for this in an outlandish source?' Of course, what is meant is 'Light' and 'Darkness' in a very specific context, not just as Divine Creations but much more in terms of opposing and fighting opposites, such as we find in Zoroastrianism – and that would be much later the source of critique by Eastern Christian scholars.

[107] Foremost among the proponents of such ideas are Duchesne-Guillemin. 'Apocalypse juive et apocalypse iranienne'; and Helge S. Kvanvig. *Roots of Apocalyptic: The Mesopotamian Background of the Enoch Figure and of the Son of Man.* Neukirchen-Vluyn: Neukirchen Verlag, 1988.

[108] Alberto Cantera Glera. 'Ethics', in: *WBCZ*, pp. 319–21:

> This journey of the Vedic sacrificer prepares him for the journey of the soul after death, whose success is secured through the sacrifices performed during life. In fact, only those who have performed the most complex and the highest rites in the hierarchy of rituals may reach the highest levels of the sky in the afterlife. ... Similar symbolism is also found in the Zoroastrian ritual. ... The same exact premises apply for the individual crossing of the soul in the Avesta. In order to promote life, the sacrificer shoulders death. With the help of his 'election soul' (*frauuaši*), that has experienced former sacrifices, his 'breath-soul' (*uruuan*-) would be able to encounter his 'vision (-*soul*)' (*daēnā*) and to attend the expected reward: 'best life' (*ahu vahišta*). The sacrifice is thus the model for the well-known and broadly attested travels into the world of the deceased, like the journey to heaven and hell described in the *Ardā Wirāz-Nāmag* or in *Kerdīr*'s inscriptions. ... This travel of the sacrificer is clearly underscored in the *Vīsprad* and *Vīdēvdād* ceremonies, in which before Y 53, the *Yasna Haptaŋhāiti* (the proper Yasna, where the meat offering is performed), is repeated and after Y 53 the description of the journey of the soul after death is included (Vd 19.28; Vyt 8).

move forward only if direct contact and use of Zoroastrian ideas was so obvious as it happens with the Creational myths regarding primeval combats (a literary *topos* from Elam to India). Moreover, this quest would be much easier if we could identify a clear development of a given idea, such as the approximation of the concept of Hades as similar to *Seôl*, a sombre state of existence that is not really worthwhile for Greeks nor for Jews.

The same can be said about the sequence of metals, for even the most sceptical and possibly wrong reasoning would conceive that Hesiod came before Daniel. As for the peculiar tree in the ZWY and the statue in Dan 2, arriving to a conclusion is not easy, since most of the information appears on secondary sources only. In short, some of the issues between Second Temple Judaism and Zoroastrianism beg scholars to posit an order of arbitrary 'priority', which is no scientific method and thus forces us to stick with analysing the undeniable parallels.

Now, as per usual, some other issues fall into discussion: do the questions posed previously refer to Palestinian or Diaspora Jews? The dividing water between those two peoples is the usage of Greek, Hebrew or both languages, but since Hengel's milestone book on this subject, that became somewhat of an empty question. After all, what concerns scholars the most here is the degree of Hellenization rather than 'Palestinian' versus 'Greek' (i.e. from the Diaspora) Judaism.[109] Moreover, regardless of the original composition site, the plot in Daniel is set in the Exilic Diaspora, so we can move forward with the analysis bearing that relative assurance in mind.

To a great part of the scholars involved in this debate, Jewish contact with Zoroastrian ideas began full-scale during the Babylonian Diaspora, the very setting of the Danielic texts. Furthermore, it is of general consensus that if Daniel has some moral lesson to teach (including the apocalypse in Dan 2), it is precisely that one could remain a faithful, kosher-observant Jew and still work for a Pagan patron or for a number of patrons.

Besides the interesting issues raised by Daniel from chs 1–6, which include the fall of Babylon to the non-historical figure 'Darius, the Mede',[110] we also see in other stances in the HB (in not less than in twenty-three different places, at least[111]) confirmation of the temple-renewal policy pursued by Cyrus. The end of the Exile and the gathering of scattered Jews in order to relive their religious traditions might as well have been Cyrus's attempt to partake on the Zoroastrian idea of 'good words, good thought, good deeds'.

The mutual Zoroastrian and Second Temple idea that 'good deeds' form some sort of 'bank account', to be drafted from at the end of this life or of this world, allows us to at least consider that there might be a common source between those two. In the case of Cyrus, however, it seems to be no more than a eulogy to a foreign king who was 'nice' towards the Jews. In fact, considering the terms of social history, *how* and *where* these two religious groups could have interacted posits a much more worthwhile question.

---

[109] Cf. Martin Hengel. *Judaism and Hellenism*. Philadelphia: Fortress Press, 1974, pp. 311–14.
[110] Cf. Rowley. *Darius the Mede and the Four World*.
[111] E.g. Ezra 1:1–8; 3:7; 4:3; etc.

Babylonia appears to be the first choice for the religious common ground, and the setting of Daniel makes that conclusion much more attractive, but the lack of evidence hinders a definite closure to the matter. However, locations in Asia Minor where Persian settlers coexisted with Jews seem to be much more likely, and not because of the old cliché associated to Asia Minor as a 'religious melting-pot'.[112] The answer to this riddle necessarily involves a more precise dating of the texts, at least from the Persian side, as well as full-fledged studies of the circumstances in which these communities first encountered each other. The possibilities are manyfold and entail bounteous auxiliary sources such as material remains, coins, archaeological work and so forth. It is not the scope of this book, yet it is, nonetheless, a fruitful field where speculation plays a bigger role than usual.

§14 And those who left us forever?

Finally, the right idea is presented to us in the proper moment: combined with Danielic and even Enochic apocalyptic, Zoroastrianism provided a reasonable, acceptable and functional solution for the big problem of what to do, so to speak, with the souls of the departed Jewish martyrs. The novelty of the death of Jews, for the sole reason of professing their faith, combined very well with the Zoroastrian theological solution for the souls of the dead in general: rewards as well as punishments, as one can see in the 'stories' of Antiochus Epiphanes's gruesome death legends, could be merely postponed. That idea is clearly, in a sense, a departure from Pentateuchal conceptions of *šeol* and the like, but which could, nonetheless, be harmonized with it.

Thus, the Persian setting of Daniel was more than providential: it not only equips the possibility of a concrete, even positive, Persian-Jewish contact but also puts the revelation that there was more to death than dust to dust in a distant, safe and of 'sacred memory' period (the Exile). The question that has not been answered conclusively thus far, and probably never will, is how the translation of Zoroastrian ideas to Judaism took place or, as some might defend, how the precise opposite happened. As I mentioned before, parallels can be collected, exposed and examined, but there are just too many problems that afflict this field of study, most of them being 'solved' or 'rebuffed' using philological arguments.

This is the *raisonnée* that locks the proper study of 'influences', but at the same time the appearance of such ideas immediately after the beginning of the Exile (Ezekiel), in the middle of the Exile (Deutero-Isaiah; the setting of Daniel) and then in the DSS and definitely during the time of the Maccabean Revolt cannot be ignored. The setting of Zaraθuštra's stories – not all of them specifically related to apocalyptic

---

[112] Clive Foss. 'The Persians in Asia Minor and the End of Antiquity' in: *The English Historical Review* 90.357 (1975): 722-3, gives a good example of that long-standing relation, quoting the events in Caesarea in Cappadocia around 609, as reported by Sebeos (James Howard-Johnston. *The Armenian History Atrributed to Sebeos*. Liverpool: Liverpool University Press, 1999, 63): 'When he [Shahin, a Sasanian general] arrived, the Christians abandoned the city, and the Jews threw the gates open to the invader.'

material or individual eschatology – is also something especially important to be considered. Partial attempts have been made to exemplify such associations, which general common sense indicates have taken place, but for scholars, that common sense is never enough, for only indirect evidence of these contacts in Persian satrapies and their smaller administrative regions, the *pahwas*, can be found.[113]

As a provisional conclusion to that theme, one may speculate that Jews in Persian Babylonia, or elsewhere in the Persian Empire, had contact with other peoples and, most importantly, with Persians themselves. That by the time of the return from the Exile Ohrmazd was already revered is beyond doubt; what remains as a thorny issue is whether he was exclusively revered. If that proves to be true, not only are the ideas of Resurrection, Final Judgement and the like more easily understood but also the urges of Deutero-Isaiah, after praising Cyrus as the Messiah, or 'Anointed'. This word – Messiah – would have a great future ahead.

---

[113] *HZ* 1, Part Three. 'In Non-Iranian Lands of the Former Achaemenian Empire'.

3

Aspects of dualism: Pairs of opposites and the cosmic fight in Zoroastrian texts

§1 Zoroastrian dualism: A fight with a fixed number of rounds

This chapter and the next deal with the issue of dualism as it appears both in Zoroastrian texts and in a particularly interesting branch of Second Temple Judaism, which is usually linked to the enormous batch of biblical and extra-biblical manuscripts found in the caves of Qumran. For the moment, let us simply name those relevant for the discussion in this book: the Dead Sea Scrolls or DSS.

The theme of dualism will be properly examined through the following sub-items: (1) the primeval origin of Zoroastrian dualism, rooted in other *PIE fighting creeds; (2) individual choice (i.e. taking sides in the cosmic struggle); (3) temporal schemes which contain the Zoroastrian struggle; (4) the need for redeemers; and (5) forms of judgement and the nature of the end of times. Both the language and the dating issues will be exposed to the reader in more depth as well.

§2 Persian Exile, Second Isaiah and an original solution for the choosing between Good and Evil plus a glimpse at combat hymns

The ideas mentioned in the heading will be examined together here, even though they may apparently have nothing in common. Besides the role of some important hymns in Zoroastrianism as related to dualism, we are going to encounter a character that may have overlapped with Daniel in his Exilic setting: the sequel of Isaiah (Isa 1–39), which is now almost unanimously considered the work of a separate author who took the liberty, the inspiration or both to write in the name of Isaiah. Yet by no means this allows a hurried conclusion that Isa 40–55 'influenced' Daniel neither in the first part (chs 1–6) nor in the apocalypse proper (chs 7–12). Even so, they do share some interesting issues:

1. Daniel is a proper name, but there is no reason to think that the book of Daniel, as it came down to us, was the work of a single man; it makes more sense to think of a folk-tale character called 'Daniel', who may not even be of Jewish origin.[1] Indeed, it is no accident that Dan 1–6 have a somewhat improvised arrangement; yet, with the exception of the sequence Dan 1–2, one has the impression that the sequence in which the rest (up to ch. 6) is read does not really matter. So much cannot be said about Dan 7-12. Hence, 'Daniel' is most likely a pseudonym for someone else or rather for a group of writers who chose to use this name for their authorship.
2. A similar phenomenon happens with Isa 40–55, which is precisely the reason that it is called 'Deutero-Isaiah' or 'Second Isaiah', and that allows for the conclusion that we have a second writer to Isa 1–39. Moreover, that is an important case of pseudepigraphy, that is, falsely attributed works, one of the most important traces of apocalyptic literature. The third section of Isaiah, from chs 56 to 66, is ever more confusing: it is called 'Trito-Isaiah' or 'Third Isaiah', conveniently, since we do not have here the homogeneity that allows the neat division of First and Second Isaiah. As a matter of fact, more than one person may have meddled with this last section of Isaiah.
3. Both Second Isaiah and Daniel, whomever the real people are behind the texts, share some common grounds: both are a product of the Exile and both share the belief that God is in charge of all history and all affairs, while in more ancient prophecy the *goyim* or 'other nations' are the instrument by which God chastises His people (only to be reconciled afterwards, in Deuteronomic fashion). Things happen slightly differently in Second Isaiah, where God is lavish in praise to other nations and even to a Pagan in particular, Cyrus. God controls everything, all Creation – natural and political, an important change – is subject to His will and no harm can be done to His people without His prior knowledge:

Thus says the LORD to his anointed, to Cyrus, whose right hand I have grasped, to subdue nations before him and ungird the loins of kings, to open doors before him that gates may not be closed: 'I will go before you and level the mountains, I will break in pieces the doors of bronze and cut asunder the bars of iron, I will give you the treasures of darkness and the hoards in secret places, that you may know that it is I, the LORD, the God of Israel, who call you by your name.' (Isa 45:1–3)

---

[1] As John J. Collins points out, Daniel may have been a much earlier and non-Jewish figure at his origin: cf. *Daniel*, p. 1, where attention is caught by a sage-like character called Dn'il, who appears in Ugaritic literature as someone who eagerly prays in order to have a son, Aqhat; the latter is killed by the goddess Anat. His sister avenges him and this Dn'il receives the power to judge and take care of widows and orphans. Ezek 14:14 and 28:3 already present a 'Daniel' who is also a sage-like figure, but to link all this information to the Daniel on the book that bears his name is still too conjectural.

Besides showing in the first section (Dan 1–6) how a good exiled Jew of the Diaspora can peacefully coexist with his Pagan neighbours (and even climb up the stairs of bureaucracy while keeping himself *kosher*), at the end of the book of Daniel,[2] there is a dialogue that borders on the funny, whether that was the actual intention of the writer(s). Daniel is chatting with the angel who protects Israel, but the latter excuses himself and declares he is leaving early because he has some score to settle with the angel of Persia. In Dan 11 the same theme of God-given protection to Pagan rulers (even if by proxy, in this case) is repeated, despite 'Darius, the Mede' remaining an unknown and historically unattested character: 'And as for me, in the first year of Darius the Mede, I stood up to confirm and strengthen him.'[3]

4. Finally, in both Second Isaiah and Daniel there is a smooth demoralization of foreign deities: in Dan 2 our portrayed hero manages not only to keep his head in one piece but also, as a collateral effect, to save the (Pagan) sages of Babylon, nearly killed in Nebuchadnezzar's fit of rage. The last sign of God's goodwill towards the 'nations' – *goyim* – is that in both Second Isaiah and Daniel there are unequivocal statements that other nations are God's instruments, such as Isa 43:8–20, among others that could equally be cited on the matter in Second Isaiah:

Bring forth the people who are blind, yet have eyes, who are deaf, yet have ears!

Let all the nations gather together, and let the peoples assemble. Who among them can declare this, and show us the former things? Let them bring their witnesses to justify them, and let them hear and say, It is true.

'You are my witnesses,' says the LORD, 'and my servant whom I have chosen, that you may know and believe me and understand that I am He. Before me no god was formed, nor shall there be any after me.

I, I am the LORD, and besides me there is no saviour.

I declared and saved and proclaimed, when there was no strange god among you; and you are my witnesses,' says the LORD.

'I am God, and also henceforth I am He; there is none who can deliver from my hand; I work and who can hinder it?'

Thus says the LORD, your Redeemer, the Holy One of Israel: 'For your sake I will send to Babylon and break down all the bars, and the shouting of the Chaldeans will be turned to lamentations.

I am the LORD, your Holy One, the Creator of Israel, your King.'

---

[2] In most Danielic mss in Greek, the end of 10:20 is translated as '*τοῦ στρατηγοῦ βασιλέως τῶν Περσῶν ... καὶ ἰδοὺ στρατηγὸς Ἑλλήνων*', but here as in other places, Theodotion's recension (a version either from other Greek texts or from mss of the HB, around 150 CE – Justin Martyr already quotes his passages) gives us something closer to angelic beings: '*τοῦ πολεμῆσαι μετὰ ἀρχοντος Περσῶν ... καὶ ὁ ἀρχων τῶν Ἑλλήνων*', from Heb. שר (a similar idea to the Greek term ὁ ἀρχων τῶν) and BDB, 'chieftain', 'commander', 'prince', but here in a supernatural context.

[3] It is an interesting point here that both the more common Gr. OT text and Theodotion does not have 'Darius' but 'Cyrus' ('*Κύρου*'; the HB retains המדידריוש, 'Darius the Mede').

Thus says the LORD, who makes a way in the sea,[4] a path in the mighty waters, who brings forth chariot and horse, army and warrior; they lie down, they cannot rise, they are extinguished, quenched like a wick:

'Remember not the former things, nor consider the things of old.

Behold, I am doing a new thing; now it springs forth, do you not perceive it? I will make a way in the wilderness and rivers in the desert.

The wild beasts will honour me, the jackals and the ostriches; for I give water in the wilderness, rivers in the desert, to give drink to my chosen people.[5]

So cosmic order in both these Exilic or post-Exilic books rests on the assumptions that either God has full command of everybody and everything, mostly concerning political matters, or that the dead who did not see justice in their lifetime can expect the decidedly un-Semitic Resurrection, where each will be given their share. How did these emphatically dualistic ideas pop up in both these books? What with God plus all the other nations He controls, the living and the dead, the Diaspora Jews and their Pagan neighbours and Cyrus, his Pagan Anointed?

These pairs of opposites will have a distinct important role in shaping Second Temple Judaism and, thus, it is important to relate them to an Exilic – more specifically, a Late Exilic – context. Again, we should tread carefully, for it would be too easy to talk about 'Zoroastrian' influence in Second Isaiah due to the mention of Cyrus. In fact, assuming that would only raise another difficulty, namely if Cyrus himself was a strict Zoroastrian or if he worshipped Ohrmazd amongst other deities.[6] Looking back

---

[4] A small remembering of the God of Israel as a challenger of the primeval chaos' waters; the same can be said of the references to the chariot and horse (cf. below).

[5] To be fair enough to the idea, First Isaiah already showed this idea in Isa 10:5, when Assyria is called 'the rod' of God's anger. Developments of this idea in Second Isaiah can be found in Isa 41:8–20; 43:1–7, 14–21; 44:18; and finally in 44:24–45:7, with the mention of Cyrus as God's shepherd and, as seen, anointed.

[6] An array of references is available and most show that the issue of Cyrus's exclusive observance of Zoroastrianism does not change the dates posited normally for the existence of Zaraθuštra either as a Late Bronze Age man, I assume, or a relatively recent addition to the Persian religion, such as the 'traditional' date of 258 years before Alexander for the lifetime of Zaraθuštra. Cf. *EIr* online for a good overview on the matter (cf. also Shahbazi. 'The Achaemenid Persian Empire', pp. 25–35)

> that this date was in all probability calculated after the establishment of the Seleucid era in 312/311 B.C.; and if the demonstration is accepted, Zoroaster's traditional date ceases to be relevant for determining the faith of Cyrus. Attention has long been drawn to the testimony of Achaemenid proper names. [Cf. Friedrich Spiegel. *Êrânische Alterthumskunde I*, Leipzig: Wilhelm Engelmann, 1871, p. 700 n. 2; Ferdinand Justi. *Iranisches Namenbuch*. Marburg: N. G. Elwertsche Verlagsbuchhandlung, 1895; Herman Lommel, *Die Religion Zarathustras: Nach den Awesta dargestellt*. Tübingen, Verlag von J. C. B. Mohr-Paul Siebeck, 1930, p.16. For later works, cf. Mayrhofer. *Zum Namengut des Avesta*, p. 10 n. 20]. An older cousin of Cyrus, *Aršāma* [Arsames, fl. *c*.600], called one of his sons *Vištāspa* (Hystaspes), which was the name of Zoroaster's royal patron; and Cyrus himself gave his eldest daughter the name *Hutaosā* (Atossa), which was that of Kavi *Vištāspa*'s queen. Thereafter Darius the Great, son of the Achaemenid *Vištāspa*, again gave one of his sons this name; and this second Achaemenid *Vištāspa* had a son called Pissouthnes, a Greek rendering, it seems[,] of *Pišišyaoθna*. The Avestan *Pišišyaoθna* was a son of Kavi *Vištāspa*. This group of family names, when taken together, thus provides evidence that members of both branches of the Achaemenid royal house had accepted Zoroastrianism at least by the early 6th century B.C. and wished to declare their allegiance to it publicly. For Cyrus further evidence is

to a much more clearly divided literary corpus – one which probably antecedes both Second Isaiah and Daniel – what we have is a repetition of a theme current from the Nile to the Indus, from the northern plains of Central Asia to pre-classical Greece.

Following this reasoning, the hymnary attributed respectively to *Mithra* and *Verethragna*[7] demonstrates that gods related to warfare and primaeval combat myths are commonly associated to the maintenance of daily cosmic order. That is something much less sophisticated than what happens in either Second Isaiah or Danielic schemes, but everything ends in a stable cosmic order nonetheless. This reflects very concretely in daily life, to the extent that we assort a fixed order of hymns in the Zoroastrian calendar. Down below is a useful arrangement for the Yts as a reminder, or perhaps a remnant, of the importance of keeping cosmic maintenance on a daily basis. In terms of Zoroastrian days and months the same order regarding days and months can be observed.[8]

Now, this ordainment – which is quite simple in its form – could not be more different from what will be proposed later by Second Temple texts, with Second Isaiah and Daniel at the forefront or as their precedents. In earlier (older) sections of the HB, *Yahweh* himself fulfils that organizing role in two of the Psalms, and there is also a significant example of the same idea in the first part of the book of Isaiah.[9] So far, no novelties, just a variation of the cosmic fight that puts *Yahweh* in a similar if not identical guise to that of *Marduk*, *Indra* or *Ra*.

It should be noted that, again, there are the issues of redaction layers, place and time: Deutero-Isaiah (i.e. 'Second Isaiah' or Isa 40–55) is a sequel to 'First Isaiah' (Isa 1–39), which is the 'original' prophetic text. The intriguing part here is that we are presented with, arguably, the first monotheistic text where the notion of 'other' gods is questioned in terms of not just cult but also existence.[10] In Isa 45:6, the very idea

provided by verses from Isaiah: 40-48, generally held to have been composed in Babylon by an anonymous poet-prophet of the Jewish captivity, known as Second Isaiah.' (Mary Boyce. 'Achaemenid Religion' (entry originally published 15 December 1983 and last updated 21 July 2011). Available online: http://www.iranicaonline.org/articles/achaemenid-religion (accessed 18 November 2019))

References only partially complete were retained so as not to meddle with the text; complete references can be found in *EIr* online.

[7] A usual companion to Mithra; cf. *MihrYašt* 10.70, among other references.

[8] Zoroastrian calendars are by no means a simple matter; as with other things Zoroastrian, they hint at older Babylonian systems but ultimately can only be traced to medieval Iranian calendars, all of them liturgical. The best authority on the matter was most likely Willy Hartner (d. 1981); cf. his series of articles on the theme: 'Die Störungen der Planeten in Gyldénschen Koordinaten als Funktionen der mittleren Länge' in: *Mitteilungen der Universitäts-Sternwarte Frankfurt am Main*, Stück 5, Arbeiten d. Planeteninstituts 6 (1928): 1–51; 'The Pseudoplanetary Nodes of the Moon's Orbit in Hindu and Islamic Iconographies' in: *Ars Islamica*, 5 (1938): 113–54; 'The Young Avestan and Babylonian Calendars and the Antecedents of Precession' in: *Journal for the History of Astronomy* 10 (1979): 1–22, 144–65; 'Old Iranian Calendars' in: Ilya Gershevitch (ed.). *CHIr Vol. II, The Median and Achaemenian Periods*. Cambridge: Cambridge University Press, 1985, pp. 714–92.

[9] Ps 74:14 ('Thou didst crush the heads of Leviathan; Thou didst give him as food for the creatures of the wilderness'); Isa 27:1 ('In that day the Lord will punish Leviathan the fleeing serpent, With His fierce and great and mighty sword, Even Leviathan the twisted serpent; And He will kill the dragon who *lives* in the sea'). Regarding the primeval combat myth, cf. also Yt 14 to *Verethragna*, a deity with a long story both in Vedic and Persian pantheons.

[10] General bibliography on Second Isaiah comprises the following: Roger N. Wybray. *The Second Isaiah*. Sheffield: JSOT Press, 1983; John Goldingay. *God's Prophet, God's Servant: A Study in*

that there may exist other gods besides the God of Israel is denied: '[So] that men may know, from the rising of the sun and from the west, that there is none besides me; I am the LORD, and there is no other.'

Again, the provenance of the second part of the book of Isaiah, as well as the dating and place, could not be more fitting. Among many distinctive features, the notion that Cyrus is the 'Messiah' (as seen previously, just a term for anyone anointed to be capable of fulfilling a certain function) means that God's control over history is complete and without exception: even a (good) Pagan as Cyrus does what is in accordance with God's plan. That is an important aspect of apocalyptic thinking and will be especially relevant both in the DSS and in the NT. Other passages have less importance regarding this ethical monotheism, and they usually display a number of similarities with other 'combat-myth' cults in the Near East, but the idea proposed in Second Isaiah is far more efficient in shaping monotheistic thought. A key passage in Deutero-Isaiah's study by Joseph Blenkinsopp is worth quoting in full, as it underlines the importance of the novelties brought by Isa 40–55 as well as some provisos:

> It should be neither surprising nor disedifying that the religious language in this important passage [45:23–49:23], expressive of what we call monotheism and universalism, is still closely linked with and dependent on contemporary political circumstances and events and the emotions to which they gave rise. With the passing of time the author and his audience had to come to terms with different situations that, in their turn, precipitated different religious emotions and perceptions. Isaiah 45:20-25 is not the final word. We must also take account of the language of servanthood in these chapters, the mission to establish justice and the rule of law (42:4), the servant as a covenant to the peoples of the world and a light to the nations (42:6-7; 49:6, 8-9; 51:4). Furthermore, since the author of these chapters is only one voice among many, we should also take into account texts that speak of, among other things, Gentiles being attracted to Judaism as a way of life (Isa 2:2-4 = Mic 4:1-4) and of Yahveh's blessing on Egypt, his people, and on Assyria, the work of his hands (Isa 19:24-25).[11]

In sum, Second Isaiah is one of the hallmarks where primeval *PIE dualism takes a sharp turn, not because it is abandoned – it is very much the opposite – but because it is 'perfected'. The combat myth depicted is one-sided in the sense that there is only one 'real' combatant fighting against vice, list or ignorance that lead men either to believe in other deities, as in 1 Sam 26:19, or to worship one true deity, as had happened with Naaman, the Syrian general who wanted to worship Yahweh, 2 Kgs 5:17.[12] Even so, this combat is by no means easy: some men chose to belong to the 'wrong' side even while

---

Jeremiah and Isaiah 40–55. Carlisle: Paternoster Press, 1994; and Blenkinsopp. *Isaiah 40–55*. For a recent overview of (now) traditional ways of dealing with Second Isaiah, cf. Heiser. 'Monotheism, Polytheism, Monolatry, or Henotheism?'.

[11] Blenkinsopp. *Isaiah 40–55*, p. 263.

[12] Ibid., pp. 109, 237. On the role of Yahweh as a warrior God, cf. as a useful introduction Wakeman. *God's Battle with the Monster*; and a newer – if more general – useful introduction in Alberto R.W. Green. *The Storm-God in the Ancient Near East*. Winona Lake: Eisenbrauns, 2003.

living in the Holy Land separated by God for His chosen people, as can be seen in the canonical books of Ezra and Nehemiah.

In any case, this is not a Zoroastrian combat as pictured in texts anymore. In Second Isaiah some non-Semitic ideas took hold of the texts, as they would do in Daniel: the substitution of monolatry by monotheism, the predetermined winning side and the cooperation of at least one Persian figure, Cyrus. Any similar solution for dualistic problems will only be found in much later Zoroastrian texts, especially those called *Zurvanite* (i.e. where *Zurvan*[13] is a proper deity that rises above Ohrmazd and Ahriman).

In order to better apprehend Second Isaiah's proclamation of 'one true God only', let us end this section with another remark by Blenkinsopp: 'Isaiah 1-55, therefore, read as a literary continuum, provides coverage of the three great empires – Assyria, Babylonia, Persia – preceding Alexander from a specifically prophetic point of view.'[14] Nonetheless, from an apocalyptic point of view it seems incorrect to limit the geographical scope of influence, since one of the most remarkable features of apocalyptic literature (especially in what John J. Collins classified as 'historical apocalypses') is the broadening of the geopolitical horizon. Prophets dealt with the world near them, while apocalypticists took on the whole new world exhibited by Alexander's conquests.

§3 From combat myths in the Ancient Near East to Zoroastrian apocalyptic

To discuss the set of writings scholarly classified as 'apocalyptic',[15] the now-classical definition by Collins remains standard:[16] as part of a genre of revelatory literature with a narrative structure in which the revelation is mediated by an angel or divinity to a human recipient, bringing to light some transcendent reality that can be either temporal (as visions of a historical-eschatological salvation) or spatial (involving the revelation of the secrets of the supernatural world).[17] Although there are significant differences within apocalyptic texts regarding these two basic types of content, its

---

[13] CPD, 'zurwan': 'time'; the god of Time, *Zurvan*. That is not a simple answer, although in terms of strict vocabulary David N. MacKenzie is correct; but the implications of having this god together with two deities who really do battle in the material world is too great to be summarized here. Robert C. Zaehner's is still the classical work in the field (and perhaps his best work overall, which is more remarkable considering that he wrote it at the beginning of his career in Oxford): *Zurvan: A Zoroastrian Dilemma*. Oxford: Clarendon Press, 1955. A deeper discussion of this will be done in the last chapters of this book.

[14] Blenkinsopp. *Isaiah 40–55*, p. 43.

[15] I am particularly thankful for discussions on this topic with my former student, Mrs Rafaela Widmer, whom I had the pleasure of supervising in her BA Hons paper.

[16] Collins. *Daniel, with an Introduction to Apocalyptic Literature*, pp. 2–33. It should be noted that, as two colleagues remarked informally to the author, it is the task of a younger generation to perfect this definition or replace it where feasible. One of the reasons given is that Collins's definition puts too much emphasis in the narrative inside each text themselves (instead of, say, visionary processes); another colleague remarked that for all the improvement that this concise and standard definition brought, much ground has been covered since 1979 when it was first proposed – which is also true.

[17] John J. Collins. *The Apocalyptic Imagination*. Grand Rapids: William B. Eerdmans, 1998, p. 5.

forms are generally similar. The shape of an apocalypse involves, according to Collins, 'a narrative structure that describes the manner in which it has the revelation. It also entails visions or journeys in the afterlife; the presence of an angel interpreter or guide the journey; written usually under the guise of pseudonymity[18] using the signature of a venerable figure of the past.'

Clearly, human powerlessness when faced with the supernatural is one of the key elements found in apocalyptic literature, and Zoroastrian apocalypses are no exception.[19] Collins's system, which is still a valid taxonomy for scholars, divides apocalypses into relatively conventional categories. The study of the literary genre (i.e. 'form criticism' or 'form-critical studies'[20]) remains important because it involves conceptual frameworks and connected world views which indicate the functioning of the world to the faithful. These characteristics are shared by all apocalypses, although we do have a considerable higher number of Jewish, Christian or Judaeo-Christian texts.[21]

To better understand the development of apocalyptic beliefs in the Middle East, we must first sketch their emergence, how and where they first appeared, and – as it will prove to be a decisive issue in Zoroastrian scholarship – when the transition of oral belief to written text happens. It is important to observe here that differently from Jewish pre-Exilic prophecy, which embodies an oral tradition put in written form later, apocalypses begin from scratch as written texts. Even so, that does not mean that they were necessarily consumed privately as sacred literature as modern man understands it, which once again renders us limited for we cannot conclude what the reading habits in Antiquity were.[22]

---

[18] Josef A. Sint. *Pseudonymität im Altertum; ihre Formen und ihre Gründe*. Innsbruck: Universitätsverlag Wagner, 1960, is (still) a good starting point to study the subtleties and assorted problems of pseudonymity in ancient literature. It is a common mistake to assume that authorship was not important in Antiquity, or that consumers of texts in Antiquity would be easily and, perhaps, gladly fooled. What happens is pretty much the opposite: authorship was especially important to ancient readers, buyers or hearers, hence the device of pseudonymity. This logic is alien to us but accounts even for ancient literary criticism that already dealt with authorial issues (e.g. in Alexandrian scholars debating subtleties in Homeric verse, Porphyry, Jerome and Augustine, among many). Pseudonymity in Zoroastrian texts is the norm, but this only underlines the importance the Zoroastrian community (then as now) attaches to the right attribution of texts.

[19] For a much more detailed examination of Zoroastrian literature regarding visionary processes, cf. Chapter 5 in this book.

[20] The key names here are Martin Noth (*Überlieferungsgeschichtliche Studien: Die sammelnden und bearbeitenden Geschichtswerke im Alten Testament*. Tübingen: M. Niemeyer, 1957), Gerhard von Rad (*Theologie des Alten Testaments*. Munich: Christian Kaiser Verlag, 1960, especially Band 2, *Die Theologie der prophetischen Überlieferungen Israels*), Rudolf Bultmann (*Die Geschichte der synoptischen Tradition*. Göttingen: Vandenhoeck und Ruprecht. 1921) and Hermann Gunkel (*Die Psalmen*. Göttingen: Vandenhoeck & Ruprecht, 1929). The field of form criticism has greatly expanded since the beginning of the twentieth century, but their works remain as an indispensable introduction in the field. A very quick overview can be found in Kenton L. Sparks. 'Form Criticism' in: Stanley E. Porter (ed.). *Dictionary of Biblical Criticism and Interpretation*. New York: Routledge, 2007, pp. 111–14.

[21] The latter category comprising texts that have a clear or putative Jewish core (like 4 Ezra 3–14) but have been appropriated and/or embezzled by Christians. This group usually can be traced back to the Greek *Urtexte* in general.

[22] A recent approach that discusses both secondary literature on the theme as well as giving an inventory of primary sources in the end is that of Aleksandr K. Gavrilov. 'Techniques of Reading in Classical Antiquity' in: *The Classical Quarterly*, New Series, 47.1 (1997).

§4 Apocalyptic beliefs before Zoroastrianism

The appearance of the organized world in ancient religions – portrayed in broad traces by Norman Cohn in *Cosmos, Chaos and the World to Come*[23] – always presents some common elements. In their cosmogonies, both the world and the gods originate from an earlier chaos that existed before anything else, which is a narrative that can be broadly traced – alongside its gods and goddesses, rituals and texts – from Egypt to Vedic India. A closer analysis of Egyptian ideas is useful here since they arguably provide the oldest of such schemes, which probably had great impact on neighbouring cultures, like that of Ugarit and pre-Exilic Israel.

For ancient Egyptians, chaos is most frequently depicted as a primeval sea that has a latent creative power. At the beginning of time, the gods waged a mythical battle between the representatives of cosmos and those of chaos, and the world as we know it was created thanks to the victory of a certain divinity representative of the cosmos. Yet, this victory is not final for the believers of such ancient religions. More often than not, the combat takes place both in daily customs (e.g. in religious rituals) and in wars against foreign peoples.[24]

The fact remains that the balance of the cosmos was constantly threatened by chaos and its agents, and it was the role of men to combat chaos and defend the cosmos in every ritual and daily attitude. Among the Egyptians, the primordial chaos was called 'nun', and when in a state of somnolence, 'demiurge', which in time became associated with the solar god Ra. In turn, Ra would be responsible for the organization and ordering of the world from the moment he became self-conscious. Tired of floating in the 'nun', the demiurge rose to a knoll, already endowed with human form and ready to begin the creation of the world and the gods. All of that was underpinned by a general principle of order called *Ma'at*.[25]

The Pharaoh himself was an embodiment of Ra, a keeper of *Ma'at* and should thus warrant order in society. Another force, however, was always threatening the cosmos: *Isfet*, which was represented by Apophis – a dragon who personified chaos. All rituals were part of the cyclical theme of constant renewal of cosmos and defeat of chaos.[26] Similarly, the Mesopotamian world view (i.e. Sumerian, Akkadian and Babylonian) understood that in the beginning there was nothing beyond salty and unlimited primordial ocean from which all was formed, including the gods.

The whole of Babylonian cosmogony, derived from the Mesopotamian world, reveals the salty waters as the chaos repository. It was thanks to his victory against *Tiammat* (who dwelt in the depths of the primordial sea) that *Marduk*, the tutelary god

---

[23] On the general theme, besides the cited work of Cohn (*Cosmos, Chaos and The World to Come*), cf. Jan Assmann. *The Price of Monotheism*. Stanford: Stanford University Press, 2009.

[24] Jan Assmann. *Zeit und Ewigkeit im Alten Ägypten: Ein Beitrag zur Geschichte der Ewigkeit.* Heidelberg: Carl Winter, 1975, pp. 21–2, 30; and Erik Hornung. 'Licht und Finstemis in der Vorstellungswelt Altägyptens' in: *Studium Generale* 18 (1965): 73–83, with special regard to pp. 78–9.

[25] Hermann Grapow. 'Die Welt vor der Schöpfung' in: *Zeitschrift für ägyptische Sprache und Altertumskunde* 67 (1931): 34–8.

[26] Cf. another seminal work by Jan Assmann. *The Mind of Egypt: History and Meaning in the Time of the Pharaohs*. New York: Metropolitan Books, 1996, pp. 169, 369–88.

of Babylon, was able to craft the world from the monster's marine body and remained able to keep it in good order. *Tiammat* was, however, still present in the sea and as the supreme personification of chaos. The *Akitu*, or New Year Party in Mesopotamia, was central to the renewal of a cycle, for it ensured the peaceful sorting out of the world. Also, it is an excellent example of how the rituals had the specific function of managing the order of the universe.[27]

Finally, it is useful to take a look at the beliefs and practices of Vedic India, as Indo-Aryans and Iranians probably have a common origin in *PIE-speaking populations who inhabited the steppes of Russia. Perhaps that is the reason that many of the Iranian beliefs present in Zaraθuštra's teachings have great similarities with the Vedic convictions. The RV[28] is the main source for this period, and its relations with our own dualism is sometimes too easily taken for granted by scholars of the *Religionsgeschichtliche Schule*. Nevertheless, their efforts should not be dismissed straight away as parallelomania but just taken with care.[29] As recently as 2006, the discussions on attribution and antiquity of the language were still vivid, with solid defences:

> The oldest documents of Iranian literature are the seventeen hymns of Zarathushtra (Zoroaster, [sic]) known as the Gāthās. They are transmitted as part of the Avesta, the corpus of Parsi sacred books. The three largest components in what has survived of the collection are the Yasna liturgy (Y.), the Yašts or hymns of praise (Yt.), and the Vidēvdāt or Vendidād (Vd.), a book that sets out (in the words of R. C. Zaehner) 'dreary prescriptions concerning ritual purity' and 'impossible punishments for ludicrous crimes'. The Gāthās form chapters 28–34, 43–51, and 53 of the Yasna. Their language is about as archaic in Indo-Iranian terms as that of the Rigveda, and this persuades some scholars to date them to before 1000 B C E; others put them as late as the sixth century. The truth very likely lies between these extremes. Next in age is another section of the Yasna, the 'Gāthā of the Seven Chapters' (Y. 35–41). The remainder of the Avesta, known collectively as the

---

[27] Wilfred G. Lambert. 'Trees, Snakes and Gods in Ancient Syria and Anatolia' in: *BSOAS* 48.3 (1985): p. 447; cf. Wilfred G. Lambert, 'Destiny and Divine Intervention in Babylon and Israel' in: Adam S. Van der Woude (ed.). *The Witness of Tradition*. Leiden: Brill 1972, p. 65.

[28] The text is an epic about the history of humanity. It seems to be from the second century BCE (or even earlier, from the fourth century BCE) but assumes the use of older material, as it shows parallels with the *Skambha* Hymn. These are a collection of over a thousand hymns in Sanskrit, which probably was already in written form around 600 CE. Although it was put in writing later than their composition, these texts were composed in times in the comparatively recent arrival of the Aryans in the Indian subcontinent, around 1200 BCE. They are part of an oral transmission tradition that ran through priestly schools since their organization around the first millennium BCE. They were considered sacred, and no changes are allowed to the recited or written texts, which entail a vision of cyclical world decline and restart. This cyclical view is portrayed in the myth of the Indian *yugas* described in the *Mahabharata*; they are of the utmost importance to our understanding of ancient man's comprehension of the meaning of time, although only a very brief treatment can be given to this issue here when we discuss the cosmological schemes of which Zoroastrians are only a few among many.

[29] They are *krita*, *treta*, *dvapara* and *kali*. While they are part of the divine body, they represent four world ages in order of degradation. Cf. Widengren. 'Les ages du monde selon hésiode', pp. 24–5.

Younger Avesta, dates probably from between the eighth and fourth centuries BCE, the Vidēvdāt being the latest part.[30]

In conclusion, while some peculiar themes in Zoroastrianism are still open to debate – such as oral continuity of the most important theological texts, Zaraθuštra being an historical figure or not and so on – there is plenty of material related to how several peoples in the Ancient Near East dealt with the uncertainties of chaos and sought ways to establish order. The novelty of Zoroastrianism is that it not only proposed a definite timing for this opposition, with a foreseeable finale, but also took individual judgement to a group scale, that is, it proposed a collective final judgement. All those issues are also found in Exilic or post-Exilic texts, mainly in Second Isaiah and Daniel.

§5 Winning the combat in Zoroastrianism: Older forms

After briefly considering the older, Semitic and non-Semitic forms alike of keeping order against chaos, another question is naturally raised: how did Zoroastrians do that, regarding both the order of the world as a whole and the maintenance of order on a personal level? The next paragraphs emphasize the cosmic order schemes, which converge at some point, remarkably so in the last lines of Daniel, where individual resurrection is promised to a whole group. That idea is current in Zoroastrian texts too.

The ideas of a final and total victory over chaos and of the concrete reality of the material world first appear in the teachings of Zaraθuštra, who lived between 1700 and 1500 BCE.[31] He was most likely a priest of a traditional Iranian religion who became a pilgrim at 20 years old, visiting visionaries, ascetics and seers until he was finally graced by the sight of the great Ohrmazd. From then on, he became the prophet of a new faith for the religious, an outcome not that much different from that of Siddhartha Gautama, the traditional founder of Buddhism.

Whether or not we are dealing with the teachings of a historical figure remains a modern and quite heated debate, where the benefit of doubt favours mainstream scholars. The Avesta, particularly the *Gāθās*, display a certain homogeneity of style that would be challenging to create out of nothing. On the other hand, if there is a continuous chain of transmission, then it is highly likely that we are dealing with the works of an individual called Zaraθuštra:[32]

---

[30] West. *Indo-European Poetry and Myth*, p. 14.
[31] Cohn proposes dating from 1200 BCE (*Cosmos, Chaos and The World to Come*, p. 109). This fits in well with the Greek poetry passages seen above – we are facing a Late Bronze Age scenario, one that could hardly have been created out of the blue two thousand years after Zaraθuštra's actual life according to mainstream scholarship on the subject.
[32] If the Avesta had an individual author, as a matter of fact, it should be noted that there is no consensus regarding the etymology of the name 'Zaraθuštra' and its variations, although most scholars agree that part of his name refers to 'camel' or 'to someone who has a camel' (cf. Chapter 2 of this book for part of the discussion that follows below). To start with most viable propositions, '*zarant-*', 'old' (Ved. 'járant-'; cf. Oss. 'zœrond'); this would emphasize the humble origins of the prophet, implying that he had an 'old camel'. But here again evidence becomes confused since the MP cognates could be written and read as the following, according to the *CPD*: 'zard', 'zardih': 'yellow',

The Gāthās, Zarathushtra's own compositions, are not hymns in the Vedic mould but songs or poems that he sang or recited at gatherings of his family and/or his followers, and in which he voiced his devotional and other aspirations. They contain nevertheless some typical hymnic elements. The Younger Avesta, less firmly imprinted with the master's personality, is also less purified of older residues.[33]

Within Zaraθuštra's visions stood the origin of the fight. In the beginning there was Ohrmazd, creator and guardian of the ordered world, material and immaterial. Beside Ohrmazd, Zoroastrian teaching placed Ahriman, a twin spirit of the great creator who, by choosing falsehood and lie (*drōz*), mixed material creation and tarnished its purity. This is a passage worth quoting since it illustrates the shape of dualistic thinking in Zoroastrianism as coexisting schemes. One passage – probably the oldest one – will suffice to exemplify these choices on cosmic and individual levels (Y 30.2–4):

2. Hear with your ears the best things; look upon them with clear-seeing thought, for decision between the two Beliefs, each man for himself before the Great consummation, bethinking you that it be accomplished to our pleasure.
3. Now the two primal Spirits, who reveal themselves in vision as Twins, are the Better and the Bad, in thought and word and action. And between these two the wise ones chose aright, the foolish not so.
4. And when these twain Spirits came together in the beginning, they created Life and Not-Life, and that at the last Worst Existence shall be to the followers of the Lie, but the Best Existence to him that follows Right.[34]

'yellowness' (Zaraθuštra here would be the one who had 'a yellowish camel' – it could be interpreted as a battered or old camel); 'zarmān', 'zarmanīh': 'old', 'old age' (Zaraθuštra here would be the one with 'an old camel'; Y 46 portrays him as a poor man); 'zarr', 'zarrēn' (from the het. ZHBA, DHBA, in *BDB*: Heb., Aram. זהב; 'gold'; here Zaraθuštra would have a 'golden camel', which is unlikely especially. concerning the late MP usage with a het.). 'Old' or 'yellowish' look more likely; consider also *zarant-, 'yellow', parallel to YAv. 'zairi'. Regarding the other half of the name, *CPD* gives 'uštar' [also from het. GMRA, in BDB Heb., Aram. גמל meaning 'camel']. For problems of early attestations and popular etymologies, see the discussion in *EIr* by Rüdiger Schmitt ((entry originally published 20 July 2002 and last updated 20 July 2002). Available online: http://www.iranicaonline.org/articles/achaemenid-religion (accessed 18 November 2019)).

[33] West. *Indo-European Poetry and Myth*, p. 304.
[34] The standard text for this is the old but useful edition by Lawrence H. Mills. '*Yasna XXX* as the Document of Dualism', in: *JRAS* (1912). Helmut Humbach had a very interesting and different rendering in the late fifties. He sustained that the *Gāθās* were hymns originally not intended to be recited by men to gods but by gods among themselves (updated version in Helmut Humbach (in collaboration with Josef Elfenbein and Prods O. Skjærvø). *The Gathas of Zarathushtra and the Other Old Avestan Texts. Part I – Text and Translation*. Heidelberg: Carl Winter, 1991, p. 128. This idea would be carried on until our day by Prods O. Skjærvø, who was once an assistant to Humbach). Cf. also Karl F. Geldner. *Avesta: The Sacred Books of the Parsis*. Stuttgart: W. Kohlhammer, 1896. Unless otherwise noted, the translation of Mills is still easier to read while keeping the flavour of IE poetry of the Avesta and is the one used throughout this book. A recent overview on whether Iranians already had a fully developed eschatological system before Judaism or if there are other possibilities worth analysing can be found in Shaul Shaked. *Dualism in Transformation: Varieties of Religion in Ancient Iran*. London: University of London, 1994, esp. pp. 28–9.

As Ohrmazd and Ahriman made their choices between *ard*[35] and *drōz*,[36] men should also choose between good and evil in their daily struggle and on the final eschatological battle.[37] Zoroastrians believed that after death people would have to cross a bridge that would, in itself, judge if their deeds in life aligned with *ard* or *drōz*. Those who chose *ard* during their lifetime would go to the 'House of Good Thought',[38] while those who chose *drōz* would fatally be directed to the underworld known as 'House of Deceit'.[39]

Death separates the body from the mind; thus, both good and bad are judged in spirit and would only receive their bodies again in the end times for the final judgement. That hope is found in passages such as the one in Bd regarding the comparative ease (for Ohrmazd) of re-creating with the help of other spiritual beings, after creating everything all alone. Also in Y 51.9,

> This retribution which thou shalt set for both parts, O Mazda, through thy bright fire and burning, is a sign for all living beings in order to destroy the wicked and save the just.

Now, although Zoroastrian schemes to judge and separate the righteous from the wicked look universal at first glance, we must consider that Zoroastrianism was never a religion of proselytism and that the idea of *Ērān ud Anērān*[40] remained a very strong factor throughout its development. At the same time, even though some people firmly believed that Zaraθuštra was 'the first universal prophet', it appears that if he was that indeed, it was not by design but rather by the after-effect of his teachings.[41] If the other lands were so starkly independent and separated, what would happen with the teaching of universal consequences and judgement?

One popular practice adopted throughout IE peoples was the 'trial by ordeal'. It is quite possible that at that time the proposed ordeal was universal; yet, originally, it was intended only for those who practised the correct religion (*dēn*). These ordeals were often very harsh and even cruel – from a modern perspective – which is probably the reason for the gradual alleviation on the judgement itself and of the punishments. Nonetheless, when we analyse a comparatively late text such as GrBd,[42] the conclusion

---

[35] The MP form of the older, Av. 'asha'. Not to be confused with 'ārd', 'flour'.
[36] The MP form of the older, Av. 'druj'.
[37] Y 30.3–5. Cf. Boyce. *Zoroastrians, Their Religious Beliefs and Practices*, pp. 20–1.
[38] Y 71.16.
[39] Y 46.11. This is, of course, only *one* among other visions of the end of times among Zoroastrians.
[40] As the privative alpha suggests, this is a stark and sometimes pejorative between the lands of 'Iranians proper' and other lands, where Iranian values were unknown or not observed. (Philippe Gignoux. 'Anērān' (entry originally published 15 December 1985 and last updated 3 August 2011). Available online: http://www.iranicaonline.org/articles/achaemenid-religion (accessed 18 November 2019)).
[41] Here as in other passages, 'Zaraθuštra's teachings' are used for the sake of practicality. It can be argued that there never was a historical V in the same sense that it can be argued that there never was a historical Moses, but we are referring here to the collective teachings placed under his name.
[42] *CPD*, 'bun-dahišn(īh)', 'primal creation'. Besides *CPD*'s definition, Bd and GrBd are books that deal with creation: the longer form ('bun-dahišnīh') probably derives from an Av. cognate now lost. Both books of the Bd (the 'smaller', simply called Bd) and the GrBd (the 'greater' or 'longer' Bd, abbreviated as GrBd here) came to us in Pahlavi (MP). In the strict sense of the word, both are not sacred (i.e. scripture) as the Avesta is, although they comment, expand or develop Avestan themes. The shorter, Indian recension is visibly more corrupted in its text – what we call simply Bd – whence the other,

might be different: perhaps the general dissatisfaction was not due to a hostile religion that sprang from the rough environment of Central Asia and then became more amenable in contact with other cultures, but mostly because the idea of an ordeal, no matter how much cosmic, made less and less sense if only applied to the followers of the *dēn*. The comparative easing of the judgement itself does correspond, or so it seems, to the plurality of religions in the Sasanid Empire as well as to the perceived justness of the way of life of non-Zoroastrians, for they made no distinction between Iran and non-Iran.

Ordeal remained a way of either separating wheat from chaff at the end of time (Bd 30) or, in a much more softened version in GrBd 35, to make sure each human being, no matter their wrong deeds on earth during their lifetime, would come out to the next life – to the world beyond – purified. Comparing the two, we have in Bd 30 the twofold affirmation that the earth will become plain, for mountains were one of many undesirable physical consequences of Ahriman's brief but strong attack on material Creation:

> This, too, it says, that this earth becomes an iceless, slopeless plain; even the mountain, whose summit is the support of the Chinwad bridge, they keep down, and it will not exist.[43]

And in the later, more 'humane' and compassionate form in GrBd 30:

> 16. During the making of the Restoration, fifteen men and fifteen maidens – those righteous people about whom it is written that they are living – will arrive to help Sōšāns.[44] 17. The snake Gōzihr[45] will fall through the firmament from the tip of the

---

the Iranian Bd, or GrBd, derives from a manuscript brought from Iran to India in the 1870s. For the Bd, we have two codices, both from the fourteenth and fifteenth centuries CE, respectively; for the GrBd we have two mss with colophons from 1587 (Codex K43) and 1597 (Codex DH), respectively. The editing and publishing stories of both is truncated: according to MacKenzie,

> In 1933 Bailey presented a complete and annotated transliteration and translation of the *Iranian Bundahišn* as a doctoral thesis in Oxford. Although it has not yet been published, one copy of this work circulated among other scholars for some years, and it is presently being revised for publication by the author [something no longer feasible since Harold Bailey passed away in 1996]. Another transliteration and English translation by B[erahmgore]. T. Anklesaria, begun in 1908, was laboriously set in type in Bombay and, all but the introduction was ready for publication by 1935. A year after the death of the author in 1944, however, the printing press was destroyed by fire and with it almost all the printed copies. The work finally appeared only in 1956, reproduced by photozincography from a surviving copy of the original print, under the title *Zand-ākāsīh*. A complete edition by the late Kaj Barr, long awaited, has never been published. (David N. MacKenzie. '*Bundahišn*' (entry originally published 15 December 1989 and last updated 15 December 1989). Available online: http://www.iranicaonline.org/articles/achaemenid-religion (accessed 18 November 2019)

Bailey's thesis is perhaps the best choice available to scholars and is available informally in its original, typewriter set, and this is the edition of the GrBd used throughout this book.

[43] Edward W. West. SBE, vol. 5. Oxford: Oxford University Press, 1897. On the 'Chinwad' or *Činvāt* bridge, cf. Chapter 4 of this book.
[44] Fifteen men and fifteen women will come to the aid of Sosans, also called Saoshyant.
[45] That is, the 'dragon' Gōzihr: cf. *CPD*, 'Gōzihr': 'astrological Dragon'.

moon to the earth, and the earth will feel as much pain as a sheep whose fleece is torn off by a wolf. 18. Then fire and divine Ērman will melt the metal of the mountains and the hills which will lay on the earth like a river. 19 Every person will pass through that molten metal and will be pure. To the righteous it will feel like walking through warm milk,[46] while to the wicked it will feel like walking through molten metal in the material world. 20. Then all people will come together with great affection, fathers and sons, brothers and friends, and they will ask each other: 'Where have you been these many years? What was the judgment of your soul? Were you righteous or wicked?' 21. First, souls will see their bodies and question them and the bodies will answer. People will join in one voice, loudly declaring praises to Ohrmazd and the Amahraspands.[47]

§6 Taking sides in the cosmic fight: Godly and human obligations

What matters most here has less to do with the difficulties in dating the manuscripts chronologically and more with the fact that, taking Zoroastrian internal evidence at face value (i.e. following the narratives of sacred or otherwise highly esteemed texts), it is during the life and times of Zaraθuštra that a portion of mankind was faced with the distinct possibility of a future that is controllable and, at the same time, reliant on the moral choices of each individual.[48]

Here we are dealing not exactly with a god that protects a given pool of people, that is, an 'ethnical' god, but rather with entities that are responsible for keeping the whole universe, both for the elected and the despised, in shape. The role of Yahweh for a long time rested on monolatry (i.e. before Second Isaiah, the Exile and all that came after that), not just for being the creator of the world but also due to the successive allegiances He made with the few chosen ones.

The covenants forged by Yahweh and these individuals are in a sense understandable only to those who inhabit this inner circle, be them Adam, Abraham, Moses, Noah or whomever.[49] Even so, those decisions affect the whole world,[50] not only the 'special ones'. In the case of Ohrmazd, the ethnical inclination of the choices and promises is

---

[46] The image of 'warm milk' is clearly one of several reminiscences of a pastoral society: one will not find one single agricultural reference in Avestan texts.
[47] That is, Amesha Spentas, the immortal good beings that help Ohrmazd administer his (good) Creation.
[48] In this sense, Second Temple Judaism is again much easier to assess than Zoroastrianism – both in terms of literary history (e.g. AWN, Dk) and of sheer evidence, we have far less in terms of textual volume of quotations. That notwithstanding, it is clear that Zoroastrianism faced the same moral dilemma – maybe for the first time in the history of religions – namely that of the implications between moral choice (free will) and a preordained cosmological order, with a universe created and destined to be destroyed and utterly changed. Cf. in particular the MX besides the GrBd and AWN on the subject.
[49] Gen 17:10; Exod 6:5.
[50] Gen 9:12–13, 17; Exod 19:10.

even more prominent.⁵¹ However, even if these are late formulations regarding the end of the world, they retroactively fit into the same category of a unique, ethnical divinity whose choices, orders, and wishes would maintain and reshape the whole Creation.

Hence, it would be correct to argue that these gods, with such virtually limitless power, chose by their own accord to make allegiances with humanity or with some parts of it. The reason for this theme to appear in the history of religions is unclear, but we do know that there is some sort of relation between the gods that chose to redeem humanity and the need for those redemptions to be performed by intermediates or special individuals, per se. Even so, the possibilities are quite manifold, like in the particular case of Jesus, when God voluntarily transmuted Himself into human flesh in order to intervene with humanity.

The ultimate goal here, nonetheless, is to have the link between the divine, ineffable, unpronounceable things and the sacred sphere of existence, translated in an easier, understandable way for the ordinary man. That idea is very clearly laid down in the Gospels, in all the parables given by Jesus and perhaps even in the theme of the conversion of *Vištasp*, the first patron of Zaraθuštra and his first important political ally. Some of the main variations on this cosmic drama are in Av. and ZA⁵² traditions, among which Yt 13 is of great importance.

§7 A few words on Zoroastrian textual sources: Where the main issues lay

Over and over again throughout this book the reader was informed, or rather warned, about the problems of taking Zoroastrian texts at face value: our earliest sources are from the Middle Ages, from the fouteenth century onwards, with the meagre exception of a colophon in a ZA ms. that credited the copy with an original from the tenth century. The other bit of first-hand written testimony is a fragment of the Psaltery.⁵³

---

⁵¹ However, a Babylonian document entitled 'Verse Account of Nabunaid' tells a very similar story regarding the uplifting of the people's mood in Babylonia after the conquest by the Persians (Cyrus):

[To the inhabitants of] Babylon a heart is given now;
[They are like prisoners when] the prisons are opened;
[Liberty is restored to] those who were surrounded by oppression;
[All rejoice] to look upon him as king. (ext from the edition by James B. Pritchard. *Ancient Near Eastern Texts related to the Old Testament*. Princeton: Princeton University Press, 1969, p. 315)

⁵² *CPD*, 'zand': 'commentary', 'explanation', 'Zend'.

⁵³ This is constituted by a fragmentary sequence of the Psalms in a translation from the Syriac, found among other documents in the Chinese oasis of Turfan by the German expedition led by André von Le Coq in 1904. Since what was found includes the modifications by Mar Abba (Patriarch of the Eastern Church, 520–552), the fragments must be from the sixth or, at the latest, the seventh century CE. Of interest is the fact that it has five more graphemes than the thirteen of Pahlavi script (which has, none the less, far more than twenty-five sounds – making its transliteration, transcription and translation much of a guesswork). Cf. Friedrich Carl Andreas and Kay Barr. *Bruchstücke einer Pehlewi-Übersetzung der Psalmen aus der Sassanidenzeit*. Berlin: Sonderausgabe aus den Sitzungsberichten der Preussischen Akademie der Wissenshaften, 1933.

This means that we do not have textual witnesses to our discussions, which enables us to, say, compare Codex Vaticanus texts with their fragments from the papyri in Oxyrrinchus, if not with the DSS themselves.

We have nothing of the sort when it comes either to texts or to testimonies of the language. Regarding the latter, we have a few inscriptions like SKZ, KIns - a general term for the Kirder inscriptions KKZ, KSM, KNRb and KNRm[54]- and a few inscriptions in OP, a language that not only left very little testimonia - all of which monumental - but also resembles more Sanskrit. In a sense, this similitude may help scholars find their way through the maze.

On the other hand, we have lots of sources and even 'cross-references' to 'Zoroaster', the Hellenized form of the name Zaraθuštra. These go back to Late Antiquity and they were used as spurious oracles, such as the OH or the SibOr, in order to legitimate a fairly new religion like Christianity. Even so, the text itself brings another possibility, namely that the Av. was invented at a much later date. Nonetheless, the similitude with Sanskrit could not be left behind during the golden era of linguistics, roughly the whole nineteenth century and the first half of the twentieth.[55] On that note, the important issues are the following:

1. Given its resemblance to Sanskrit (and by extension to other IE languages), Avestic or Avestan - the language that is sacred and used only in the collection of texts called, again, 'Avesta',[56] whose nature is complex and fragmentary as it happens with most Zoroastrian material, is as old as it purports to be, or is it possible that Av. came after other Iranian languages like MP or Pz.?
2. Do Zoroastrian textual sources *as we have them* represent the transmitted wisdom and lore related to a Late Bronze Age man called Zaraθuštra?[57]

---

[54] For the meaning of these sigla, please check the Abbreviations section at the beginning of the book.
[55] A concise list of works to guide the reader must include the books of Christian Bartholomae (*Altiranisches Wörterbuch*. Berlin: Walter de Gruyter, 1961; original edition from 1904); Bailey's small but still useful tome, *Zoroastrian Problems in the Ninth-Century Books*; and Boyce's *Textual Sources*). It must be said that Boyce's version of how Zoroastrianism came to be and developed is the mainstream position but is not without its faults, which are increasingly explored among the scholars' community. But her positions - besides being usually the first ones that the interested person will find in divulgation works - merit enough credit for being based on solid scholarship and also, it must be said, because they make sense. As one scholar noted informally to this author, 'modern Zoroastrian history is what Mary Boyce told them what it was'. That could well be true, but she would be at the most following a tradition that goes back to the great Iranologists of the end of the nineteenth century: among them, Martin Haug displayed such a connoisseurship of all things Zoroastrian that the Parsee community in India thought in earnest about bestowing him with religious authority.
[56] CPD, 'abestāg', 'Avesta', the Mazdean [i.e. related to the followers of *Ahuramazda*, the older form of our contracted Ohrmazd]. Perhaps related to older forms like the Sans. 'upa-stavaka' or 'praise-song', Lobgesang; in any case it is similar to Sans. (this cannot be denied: what is of interest is if it is a late imitation, a contemporary oral language that was later put into written form or if Av. and Sans. stemmed from the same branch of Indo-Iranian languages). Bartholomae favoured the first option (*Altiranisches Wörterbuch*, pp. 87, 1161, 1237, 1588–90, 1608).
[57] Here again the benefit of doubt belongs to the mainstream scholars: it would take an immense amount of skill, time and craftsmanship to 'forge' a text in, say, the twelfth century CE that matches in detail both the prowess of warrior gods like Indra (seen in a very unfavourable light in the Avesta, since they are, in essence, cattle-raiders) and the world of the Iliad (which is also a composite of Late Bronze Age, Dark Ages and classical ideas). The very theme of cattle (central to a pasturing people)

3. If Av. can be reconstructed in order to prove its age, what is its relation to OP?
4. The linguistic issues all make the theme of this book shift from 'influence' to 'parallels'. Even with the benefit of doubt, it would be very difficult to state without any restrictions that there was, say, an 'original' BY in Av. and that this text shaped the ideas regarding the succession of metals/ages/empires in the book of Daniel.

So, the linguistic problems shaped above define, to a great extent, the limitation of considering Zoroastrianism as a source for Second Isaiah or for Daniel's eschatological themes. Nevertheless, it remains a tenable position since both were Exilic or post-Exilic texts, which means that Zoroastrians probably encountered Iranian ideas and even with Iranian characters, like Cyrus or Darius, 'the Mede'. *Yašt* 13, one of the best surviving examples, is called the *Frawardīn Yašt* (MP *Farvadīn Yašt*),[58] that is, the *Yašt* devoted to the good spirits who assist *AhruaMazdā* in defending Creation.[59]

In that scenario, choosing what other texts than the Avesta (or the ZA) can be useful is a pricky task. *Yašt* 13 is one of the most useful ones.

> 118. We worship the Fravashi[60] of the holy Hugau.
> ...
> 138. We worship the Fravashi of the holy Fradhakhshti, the son of the jar,
> To withstand Aeshma, the fiend of the wounding spear, and the Daevas that grow through Aeshma; to withstand the evil done by Aeshma.[61]

Clearly, the balance between good and evil is a kind of continuous test between both, a contest even. This image of a combat that is at the same time a judgement,

---

appears also in Homer: compare the glory that follows that youthful, successful cattle-raider in the *Iliad* 11.665–675 –

> For my strength is not such as it once was in my supple limbs. I wish that I were as young and my strength were as firm as when strife arose between the Eleans and our people about the stealing of cattle, that time I slew Itymoneus, the mighty son of Hypeirochus, a man who dwelt in Elis, when I was driving off what we had seized in reprisal; and he, while fighting for the cattle, was struck among the foremost by a spear from my hand; and he fell, and the country people about him fled in terror. And very great booty did we drive together out of the plain, fifty herds of cattle.

– and Y 11, where the cow (sacred to the pastoral people depicted in the world of the Avesta) despises those who hurt her. It seems that we are all speaking about the same thing, perhaps with the mark of 'positive' and 'negative' inverted, but nonetheless the same age and usages. As it often happens, one religion's god becomes another religion's demon.

[58] *CPD*, 'yasn': 'adoration', 'worship'; 'yašt': 'prayer', 'worship'. Cf. also *CPD*, 'yaštan', 'yazišn': 'worship', 'celebrate', 'recite'.

[59] *CPD*, 'Frawardīn': 'the first month', the nineteenth day, from 'frawahr', 'fraward': man's immortal soul, guardian angel [sic] during his lifetime. Cf. Chapter 5 of this book for more detailed analysis of the word and its meaning regarding final judgement of the individual soul.

[60] From the Av. form 'fravaši', ibid.

[61] James Darmesteter. *Sacred Books of the East*, vol. 23. Oxford: Oxford University Press, 1897 (*SBE*). This is an old but still very readable translation, which can be supplemented with more recent studies. Cf. also Jean Kellens. *Fravardin Yast (1-70)*. Wiesbaden: Reichert, 1975; and Johanna Narten. 'Avestisch frauuaši-' in: *IIJ* 28 (1985).

although a quite long-lasting one until the final judgement, has no correlations with dispute-solving practices in a given society, be it Av. or any other.

§8 Temporal schemes: The format of the Zoroastrian struggle and their resemblance to Dan 2 and 7

While the idea of dividing the world into four phases of degradation was nothing new (or at least such an idea had its parallels in the Vd. RV), Zoroastrian apocalyptic brings the novelty that after the last stage, which is always the worst of all, the cycle would not be renewed nor relived. Zoroastrian thinking is linear and provides for one-on-one occurrences of events, either of individual or cosmic significance.[62] The closest scheme to Daniel is that of the ZWY, although there is still no agreement on the precedence of the seven- or four-branched tree. Even if other different schemes appear scattered throughout Zoroastrian scriptures, at large they are all linked to the fundamental idea that time itself is divided into distinct periods, and these periods are each filled with a particular character or a peculiar quality.[63]

At some point, Zoroastrian soteriology became enmeshed with that periodization regarding world order (e.g. ZWY 1.3; 3.15), which made it possible for the relationship between Zoroastrian saviours accorded to each period of time to be fit into distinctive time frames. Now, whether this was done before or after the reforms of the early Sasanid period (i.e. by *Tansar* or *Kirdēr* by the middle to the end of the third century CE) cannot be defined with precision.

My personal opinion is that such schemes are a late elaboration, for two reasons: first, the 'end-of-time enemies' are as usual the way to determine the *terminus post quem* of the text; and, second, the whole schemes are too nicely shaped, including the end-of-time combats, to attribute them to an earlier date such as, say, the mid-fifth century BCE. Some of them – possibly the later ones – appear in the four world ages concept, such as in ZWY 1 and 3. Others, however, will fit into categories that are in a sense also fourfold, but these are divided into larger units of three thousand years each.[64]

Similar to the four world empires myth, there is the sequence of four world ages, which might be understood as only three from a purely human point of view, discounting the time when Creation existed only as a possibility – as seen, *mēnōg*. That sequence represents one of the stages throughout the cosmological drama which

---

[62] The myth of the Indian *yugas* will have a wide impact in the old world. The parallel degeneration of the human race with Hesiod's WD is clear, beyond the relationship between the *yugas* and the tree with metal branches represented in the Zoroastrian text BY 1. To a deepening in the subject of the cosmic tree and the four ages cf. Anders Hultgård. 'Persian Apocalypticism' in: John J. Collins (ed.). *The Encyclopedia of Apocalypticism*. New York: Continuum, 1998, vol. 1, pp. 39–83; Gerhard Hasel. 'The Four World Empires of Daniel 2 against its Near Eastern Environment' in: *JSOT* 12 (1972): 17–29.

[63] It is interesting to note that both in Jewish and Zoroastrian apocalyptic the 'obsession' with numbers is the same, as is the idea of a different quality, permeating each period. It is, however, debatable whether that concept arose from the theme of successive empires or is in itself a variation of the myth of the ages (such as in WD) or if it can be considered a stand-alone complex.

[64] Bd 1.44; 3.10, 23; Y 23.1; Yt. 13.22, 13.28; *Visperad* 7.4, among other stances.

unfolds according to the plans of Ohrmazd.[65] Those concepts are, arguably, the biggest point of contact between Daniel and Zoroastrian literature, for in both literary corpora there is some sort of divine final judgement marking the end of a purposeful human existence as well as the periodization of history up to its conclusion.

§9 Historical development schemes and saviour figures

The timing and historicity of Sasanian religious reforms will be dealt with in Chapter 7 and the conclusion to this book. A brief sketch starts from the earliest historical dating point regarding standardization of Zoroastrian texts (above all the Avesta) throughout Iran. This may well do to the reforms of Kirdēr and, perhaps even more, with the canonization of Av. texts (or else we must take into account the role of Tosan in that process) and, sequentially, of their MP counterparts.

The schemes proposed in ZWY are by no means the only ones in Zoroastrianism. Whether they are old or comparatively late relies, again, on internal textual evidence and on discussions. Some of the most important apocalyptic themes found in the Av. corpus itself appear in Yt. 13 and 19, Y 26 and 43, Vd 19 and chs 34 and 35 of GrBd and Dk,[66] which in chronological terms include the *Saošyant*, one of the Iranian redeemers. These issues, coupled with eschatology, include judgement of ideas and deeds performed by each man in the cosmic struggle, for Paradise is a place of reward for the righteous who chose the right side, and Hell, of punishment. A redeeming figure will thus defeat the forces of chaos and forever guide the righteous towards a new era of perfection. This scenario will, in fact, happen more than once.

According to Almut Hintze, the relevant passages in Pahlavi eschatology have a common normative basis, the Av. tradition, regarding not only the linguistic character as presented by Anders Hultgård and others but also the doctrinal system found within the Avesta.[67] References such as Y 37.1, portraying Ohrmazd as the Creator of both the spiritual and material worlds, are of fundamental importance to Zoroastrian eschatological development, as it is in the material world that Ohrmazd will battle and overthrow Ahriman. Yet, remembering Y 30.2–4, both men and spirits must take sides in the Zoroastrian cosmic struggle, regardless of its outcome.

Men should choose which side they will follow in the war, a key point in the development of the dualistic religion of Zaraθuštra. Even so, in the redemptive and eschatological Y 26, he is announced and hailed as the victor, so we have here a protoform of the problems related to freewill versus Providence. If the result of the combat is known beforehand and even declared to the faithful, why do men have

---

[65] In the manual called *Pand-Nāmag* it is thus written in MP: 'azmēnōg mad hēm, nē pad gētīg būd hēm,' that is, a person, to be considered truly righteous, must declare to be divorced from *gētīg*. It is in this context – a late theological development in Zoroastrian thought – identified with the realm of demons.
[66] Just as a reminder, the Vd text containing ceremonial rites and formulas, is part of the Avesta; the *Denkard*, an encyclopaedia of sorts containing beliefs and customs common to Zoroastrianism, and the *Bundahišn*, the book about Creation, are MP texts that received written form in the Sasanid era.
[67] Hintze. 'Avestan Literature', p. 11.

to help win a battle that is won? In other words, what difference will that make – especially in the older, milder forms of final individual judgement where everyone is purified, regardless of their moral alignment? This question – of whether the doctrine of grace is a late, important development that will be key to Christianity (especially in Pauline thought) – is one that can also be found in a number of texts among the DSS. By comparison, both Second Isaiah and Daniel give little attention to this aspect of conflict between Good and Evil.

Y 26.6 speaks of Creation and of its renewal depending on the *Saošyant*'s later prophecies, which again brought up the whole issue of the need for choosing sides in a battle that is decided beforehand:

> We praise the life, intelligence and soul of Fravashis
> the next generation of male and female saints who
> They struggled as a true ritual, which are those
> of the living and dead saints, and those who are also of
> men unborn, future prophets,
> along with all of them helped in the renovation and
> completeness of human progress.[68]

Further on, another Y shows some of the human features that will lead the saints to housing Ohrmazd. The same idea can be seen more clearly in Yt. 19:

> It is Astvat-ərəta, and this symbolism has an identification
> clear with this description:
> Can you pay attention to that which is better than the good,
> that teach us the right ways of bliss
> this life here and that body of thought –
> true paths that lead to the world where Ahura
> Mazda dwells – a reliable man, known and holy
> like you, oh Mazda.[69]

These passages, among others, clearly show that the apocalyptic ideas were already present in initial texts of Zoroastrianism and formed the basis for all beliefs that came next with the later MP texts. Even so, for some reason these eschatological ideas in apocalyptic garb are not found in Jewish texts prior to their closer contact with the Persians in the Exile.[70] Although the Hebrew idea of a 'Messiah' is nothing new in the Exilic period, the growing supernatural abilities of the 'Anointed One' move remarkably fast after the Exile. In fact, the Jewish Messiah of Second Temple literature that would become the Christian Messiah may have earned some of its supernatural abilities from Zoroastrian sources.

---

[68] Y 26.6.
[69] Y 43.3.
[70] Cohn. *Cosmos, Chaos and The World to Come*, pp. 289–90.

§10 Why does Creation need defenders on earth?

The roles of opposites are much more important in Zoroastrianism than in Judaism, as we have seen beforehand. It should be clear by now that Zoroastrianism had – from its core founding texts within the Av. to other texts of admittedly less importance – to deal with the theme of battling antagonistic twins, or forces, in every single aspect of the believer's life. However, differently from other Eastern religions that had a cyclical rhythm for everything, Zoroastrianism was the first religion to propose a scheme where this fight of opposites will come to an end once and for all.

That being the case, who is going to fight against whom? The solution for that comes in the shape of a future redeemer, who will see the battle to its end. Second Temple Judaism will also have several soteriological figures who also grow in power and importance. The historian Josephus names many of them, the NT quotes a few others apart from Jesus Christ, and even in the middle of the second century CE there were Jews who found in Simon Bar-Kochba, leader of the 132–5 CE revolt, a Messiah.

This issue, related as it is to apocalyptic thinking, implies very specific questions. Zoroastrian teachings bring the promise of a spiritual war that will forever remove disorder from the world, in order for existence to never again be threatened by chaos. The transformation of the world and their *drōz* release has a redemptive function, and this is clear in the very role of the *Saošyant* ('future benefactor'),[71] who would lead the *ard* armies against Ahriman and its allies. The period that will precede His coming will be marked by an apparent victory of *drōz* over *ard*, and the signs of the end of times, as described in ZWY 4, will become more prominent.[72] Some of the themes related to Zoroastrian redeemers have already been examined in apocalypses such as the ZWY.[73] The general role of saviours in these situations is to act on behalf of a deity who is subject to the rules of justice and courtesy common to all and to bring justice to men.[74]

§11 Central issues in Zoroastrian versions of the final combat

It should be clear by now that all Zoroastrian soteriological schemes rely on a few core issues. The idea that a universal cosmic ordeal, the *Frašagird*, will take place may have varying degrees of harshness depending on the dating of the texts, but the general schemes in Zoroastrian thought usually follow a pattern already found in Jewish apocalyptic. Likewise, the obsession of Jewish apocalypticists with numbers is similar to that already found in Zoroastrian apocalypses; thus, for the mere organization of such schemes, dating is not important.

---

[71] *CPD*, 'Sōšyans': 'adoration', 'worship' (the MP form).
[72] It can be seen that before the absolute end, the world situation is worse than at any other time. There is a clear parallel with the myth of the present world ages in ZWY 1–3, wherein the last age is the greatest degeneration of both man and nature.
[73] ZWY 3:3; 11.
[74] Cf. Chapters 4 and 6 of this book.

However, it should be noted that all Zoroastrian schemes of salvation depend, in one way or another, on the presence of a saviour who becomes more universal as the Zoroastrian faithful situation becomes more desperate. Furthermore, the saviours are not chosen randomly, yet they share some common traits. Hence, they differ fundamentally from the Jewish Messiah, who is yet to come, and from the Christian one, who has already come and left but will return. There are no such parallels in Zoroastrian redeeming figures.

§12 Ordeal as a definite solution, as in the combat myth

One way of looking into the role of Zoroastrian saviours is to see them as part of the outcome of law in the steppes. In this sense, we must make an effort to see salvation, in Zoroastrian terms, as an answer to a previous offence (Bd 1.3). Also, there is more than a hint of arbitrary choosing of the souls entering the material world in order to improve efforts against Ahriman, for example, Bd 3.27:

> With their all-knowing wisdom, the frawahrs of men saw the evil that would befall them in the material world from the demons and Ahriman. But because in the end the Adversary would be vanquished and they would become whole again and immortal forever in the Final Body, they agreed to go to the material world.[75]

That gives a whole different meaning to the fight of the Av. *fravašis* (MP *frawahr*) seen in the previous section, Yt. 13. Even the conduction of the fight against evil must be done according to 'correct' rules: see the ninth-century DD by Manuščhir:

> To go to a preemptive battle against the Lie [MP *drōz*], when the other one is not fighting against the lights, to smite him when he has not smitten the lights, to demand expiation before the damage to demand revenge before an act of vengefulness has taken place – this he [Ohrmazd] did not consider to be right and lawful.[76]

Thus, we have here two basic approaches to the fight for the redemption of Creation: it can be either predetermined, with all the secondary problems that this entails, or it can be a matter of free will, which poses even more historical and theological problems. Additionally, there is yet another interpretation, namely to look at the problem as a matter of *dād* instead of as the developments of the primary combat myth.

Hence, it is more about a judgement in the common sense of the term (i.e. *dād*, or what can be ordinarily considered right or wrong according to judicial practices that go way back to *PIE practices, ordnance and vocabulary[77]) than about a cosmic, gigantic

---

[75] Cf. also Anklesaria. *Zand-Ākāsīh*, p. 45; Cereti. '"And the *frawahrs* of the men"', pp. 21–37.
[76] DD 36.13. Cf. also Maria Macuch on the application of the concept of *dād* (roughly, 'law') on early Zoroastrianism (Macuch. 'Law in Pre-Modern Zoroastrianism').
[77] *Dād* means, even in NP, 'law', 'lawful', 'right' and the entirety of issues related to legality.

combat myth. This last aspect has been, for better or for worse, duly emphasized by several scholars since the nineteenth century.[78] I am not denying that the combat between Ohrmazd and Ahriman is indeed cosmic; what I am questioning is whether it would be more appropriate to consider the hypothesis that the whole concept of such a combat might have originated in the steppes and ordinary affairs solved by means of ordeals and not the other way round.

Even Ohrmazd is not exempt from cosmological and moral order, which brings about a late but rather different moral consequence for Creation itself: whereas the Jewish God is someone different and apart from Creation, Ohrmazd is also submitted to the principles, the righteous norms he made together with the material world.[79] In an ordeal, innocence or guilt of a given subject is proven not as is usual in modern, post-Renaissance societies, by means of proof and counterproof. In fact, in an ordeal it is less important to set the subject free or have him killed than to establish, before the gods, guilt or innocence by means of tests that can roughly be called 'endurance' tests.

Ordeals can take many forms, most of which would appear as utterly irrational to us. Although they may seem like some sort of transitional ceremony, they should not be taken for rites of passage: those are intended to mark the making of an adult individual in a given society and in that sense can be found even in our days. An ordeal is a trial that, in essence, puts the suspected individual before a test – usually by fire, water or molten metal – after which they will be sentenced either innocent or guilty.

The outcome is *not* necessarily the survival of the subject; rather, it is some other sort of confirmation. In an ordeal by water, the subject is thrown into the water in some fashion where they cannot get free and there are usually two possible outcomes: either they are found guilty and float, meaning not even nature itself, the divinities that preside the rite or the river want the subject; or else they drown, which means, in that case, that they were innocent after all. That sounds absurd to the modern frame of thought: law represents, after all, an attempt to establish, or re-establish, a modicum of balance in an uneven situation. It is also unconceivable to the Western mind, even before Justinian's codification of Roman Law, that an innocent should be punished in case of doubt[80] (with the remarkable exception of completely authoritarian regimes).

In another set of examples, the typical ordeal practices in the steppe are fully represented in many Av. passages – even Zaraθuštra himself is sometimes referred to as having undergone such tribulations. Thus, we are facing, from what is left of these millennia-old practices, a world where divine favour ultimately defines guilt or innocence.

---

[78] In modern times, it would be correct to ascribe its diffusion and popularity in academic circles to, first, Boyce and, next, Cohn to a broader public.
[79] *WBCZ*, p. 217; also MX 1.49 and Y 31.7.
[80] The best example can be found on Justinian's codification of Roman Law, the *Digesta* (23.3 in our case): *Ei incumbit probatio qui dicit, non qui negat* ('It is the duty of the accuser to prove, not [of the accused] to prove his innocence', in a quite free translation just to convey the meaning).

§13 Ordeal and political resistance

How and when the notion of ordeals in a cosmic scale became fully developed in Zoroastrianism is a matter, like many others, related to myth and history: we simply cannot postulate a definite time or place for the spread of the theme. A public execution carried out by Mithridates VI of Pontus in 88 BCE, that of the Roman consul Manus Aquilius, presents a fine earlier example of such practices. However, it is by no means certain that this was an 'ordeal' in the exact sense of the term. It could be simply a way of killing a convicted individual by means of torture or it could be the traditional fashion of ordeals: evaluating guilt while simultaneously punishing/acquitting the subject.[81]

The amplification of the individual scope to that of common judgement or ordeal seems to me rather one of scale than of content. Alternatively, the idea of a 'cosmic' ordeal may be related to natural phenomena such as volcanoes, earthquakes, comets and the like. Pompeius Trogus notes such phenomena associated with pro-Mithridates propaganda:

> Again, heavenly prodigies predicted his future greatness. In the year that he [Mithridates] was begotten, and again when he first began to rule, a comet blazed in such a way, on both occasions for seventy days, that the whole sky seemed to be on fire.[82]

---

[81] Mithridates VI of Pontus, the fearsome enemy of the Romans for three decades, is a case in point. There will probably never be evidence that he belonged to one and only one cult (as it so often was the case in ancient Asia Minor), but he had close relations with Zoroastrianism throughout his life. There was even a Zoroastrian magus (see below Chapter 7) called Hermaeus who accompanied him on his war with the Roman Lucullus. On the end of Lucullus – in a Pergamene theatre, forced to swallow molten gold in front of a multitude – cf. Vi(n)cente Dobroruka [sic]. 'Mithridates and the *Oracle of Hystaspes*: Some Dating Issues' in: *JRAS*, forthcoming; by the same author, 'Zoroastrian Apocalyptic and Hellenistic Political Propaganda' in: *ARAM Periodical* 26.1–2 (2014): 110–12. As a useful introduction to the life and times of Mithridates, the work of Adrienne Mayor is very useful (*The Poison King: The Life and Legend of Mithradates, Rome's Deadliest Enemy*. Princeton: Princeton University Press, 2010). As a curiosity that does not impair the book, Mayor is one of several authors that (still) take for granted that 'another prophecy, the Zoroastrian apocalyptic scripture of the third century BC called the Bahman Yasht, envisioned an avenging savior-prince who would be born under a shooting star: this prince would drive foreign tyrants out of Asia' (ibid., p. 61). Much, if not all, of Mayor's passage quoted is composed not by proven ideas but by common lore. The choice by Mayor of 'Mithradates' and not the more usual 'Mithridates' is justified by the fact that the king was a devotee of solar deities – and Mithra was one of the most important of those. His name would then mean 'The gift of Mithra'; throughout this book the more common form Mithridates is kept for the sake of practicality.

[82] Justin. *Epitome of Pompeius Trogus*, 37.2: *Huius futuram magnitudinem etiam caelestia ostenta praedixerant. Nam et eo quo genitus est anno et eo quo regnare primum coepit stella cometes per utrumque tempus septuagenis diebus ita luxit, ut caelum omne conflagrare uideretur* (cf. John C. Yardley. *Justin and Pompeius Trogus: A Study of the Language of Justin's Epitome of Trogus*. Toronto: University of Toronto Press, 2003, p. 126). On the matter – that is reminiscent of the Star of Bethlehem – cf. Deniz B. Erciyas. *Wealth, Aristocracy and Royal Propaganda under the Hellenistic Kingdom of the Mithradatids in the Central Black Sea Region of Turkey*. Leiden: Brill, 2006, pp. 139–41.

Finally, as a curiosity among final judgement lore, an interesting question rose some years ago in 1 Enoch. In modern translation there are some problems in the Ethiopic text of 1En that may be enlightened by similar Persian passages. Here, the confusion between 'fire' and 'water' may appear as some sort of modern adjusting of translation, especially if we consider the few mss of 1En available. But reading more carefully the *Rasn Yašt*, another kind of water ordeal is involved – and this time we may not be dealing with mere confusion but with a permanence or even a distant echo of the idea that 'sulphurous water' could be used in such trials.

It should also be noted that in the case of Daniel we have some sort of third way of carrying out justice: whereas Nebuchadnezzar is the one who actually has the vision, it is others that he is wishing to put to trial. That includes Daniel, but in the narrative itself this idea appears almost incidentally. The writer is at pains to make the audience believe that something is about to change in the way that Daniel is regarded in Nebuchadnezzar's court, which is probably the reason why they decided not to include him among the many soothsayers and diviners at the beginning of ch. 2. That is not only showing that he is different by means of his own faith from the other professionals of soothsaying, but also providing a clue about why he is asked by the chief of the king's guard when anyone can see that Daniel is in no way linked to the revelation made to Nebuchadnezzar.

Everything happens exactly as intended by the writer of this section: when Daniel is mixed in with the rest of all the Pagan soothsayers, he can state the case for the Jewish God in a much clearer way than any of the other characters might have devised. He is chosen unjustly but he passes the ordeal, nonetheless, presenting Nebuchadnezzar with the full depiction of the course of world history according to God's plans (almost the whole of Dan 2).

Justice is supplied not by means of proof and counterproof but by supernatural means, just as Nebuchadnezzar's dream was a supernatural device chosen by God himself to display his plans for the whole of human history. One must be aware that what Daniel explains has parallels with a well-developed Persian theme, namely the one presented in ZWY 1, about the tree with several branches representing different world empires. This will be seen in detail in the last chapter of this book.

4

GŠR, or crossing the bridge: A similarity with *Činwad*?

§1 A bridge to the world beyond: The plot

The previous chapter dealt with what can be considered the end of earthly life for men/women: in the form of schemes (better developed in Chapter 6) or with dualistic aspects of Zoroastrianism and of the DSS.[1] The Bd also has a whole chapter devoted to the *Činwad* bridge.[2] The travels and inscriptions of Kirdēr were also mentioned, and it is never sufficient to underscore the importance of his reports on the world beyond. He is the only actual named character known to have done this (at least in Eurasia, and in other continents there will be similar shamanistic reports, only many centuries later).

It is reasonable to say that Kirdēr was the only apocalyptic writer who had a katabatic experience and had the will to register it in such a fashion that his audience could read forever what he did. This audience was supposedly composed of Persian nobles, but since Kirdēr's inscriptions are found in unusual places – together with royal inscriptions – it may well have been the opposite, that the early Sasanids wanted all this recorded in order to reinforce Zoroastrian beliefs. This is an actual possibility that does not hang upon dating: Kirdēr could simply be 'restoring' or 'standardizing' the complex of beliefs found in the Avesta.[3]

---

[1] This chapter is divided in sections as didactic as possible since the theme is an evident similarity of form (and perhaps of plot, too, in its DSS fragment), but, again, talking about 'influence' poses every single problem other issues had in their relation between Zoroastrianism and Second Temple Judaism.

[2] The 'Peak of Dāitī' is also mentioned in the chapter devoted to the mountains in Bd 9.9: 'The Peak of Dāitī is in the middle of the world, as tall as one thousand men, on which stands the Činwad Bridge where souls are judged.' But in the sequence another mountain is linked to the gate of Hell, in the Ridge of Arzūr: '10. The Ridge of Arzūr is a peak at the gate of hell from which the demons all scurry – that is, they all do their fiendishness here. 11. As it says: "Which is the most sorrowful place on earth? They say: The Ridge of Arzūr, at the gate of hell, where the demons scurry."' It appears also in Bd 26.28, 48, as a joyous place when the souls of the righteous cross it. Bundahišn 26.53 enphazises the role of Srōš in accompanying the souls of the departed.

[3] All matters related to the role of Kirdēr in reforming or instituting Zoroastrianism are still subject to debate; what is sure is that he existed, possibly continued reforms undertaken before him by a priest called 'Tonsar' or 'Tansar' (in this case his existence is less certain) and left many, if not all, of his deeds in four rock-relief texts. For a general view of Kirdēr, the man, cf. Philippe Gignoux. 'The Private Inscriptions of Kirdir' in: *CHIr* III.2 (1985); Martin Sprengling. 'Kartīr, Founder of Sasanian

One crucial distinction should be made between Zoroastrian passages on *Činwad* and 4Q521: the 'anointed one' (i.e. the 'Messiah') announced in Fr. 2 Col. II of 4Q521 is not a priestly messiah but a Davidic one. The things he will produce resemble very much the perfected material world that Kirdēr and Wiraz saw. But the context is entirely different as we shall see at the end of this chapter using a Sasanid source – state and religion could not be more separated in Persia then they were.[4]

§2 Kirdēr, priest and shamanic traveller

The life and times of Kirdēr[5] – a figure briefly mentioned before in this book, who flourished during Narseh I's reign (i.e. 293 CE), is worth comparing to the wealth of information provided by 4 Ezra because, while the aforementioned text is loaded with information regarding ASC-inducing processes that resemble very much Persian texts as seen above, the dating of the latter remains problematic and, thus, we can only go so far in ascribing Persian influence of any sort in Second Temple Jewish apocalyptic literature.

On the other hand, we have four inscriptions and other reliefs displaying lots of information regarding trance, voyages to the world beyond and what is more important: they are all written in first person and can be safely dated compared to anything else we have regarding written sources. Important as they are, sources in MP (like, say, AWN) are relatively late, and the same goes for Arab-Persian authors. This is valid even when we can compare them safely with Western or Eastern Christian authors.[6]

Zoroastrianism' in: *The American Journal of Semitic Languages and Literatures* 57.2 (1940); and James R. Russell. *Zoroastrianism as the State Religion of Ancient Iran*. Bombay: K.R. Cama Oriental Institute, 1984. Another contribution to be examined is that of Alberto Cantera Glera. 'Los viajes al más allá en la tradición irania preislámica' in: *Cicle de Conferències sobre Religions del Món Antic (4º. 2003. Palma de Mallorca)*. Salamanca: Gredos, 2004.

[4] On kingly messianism in 4Q521, cf. Stephen Hultgren. '4Q521, the Second Benediction of the "Tefilla", the "Ḥasîdîm"', and the Development of Royal Messianism' in: *Revue de Qumrân* 23.3(91) (2008): 315–17. Hultgren's many arguments shift the attention from the DSS to second-century BCE synagogues in Palestine (which is not a convincing argument) and underline the Davidic character (thus, royal or kingly) of the promised messiah in 4Q521. Hultgren's discussion goes, however, too far away from the boundaries of this book, taking us to the Cairo genizah fragments and much of the discussion around it.

[5] The reader may well ask at this point why the name of the priest in question is transcribed as 'Kirdēr' and not as 'Karter', 'Kirdir' and so on. This is so because of the variety in which the inscriptions are found themselves: in MP we only have 'kltyl', 'kltyly', 'kryr' and 'kltyr'; in Parthian 'krtyr' or 'qyrdyr'; in Greek *KARTEIR*; and in Coptic *Kardel*; Manichean MP has 'kyrdyr', Sogdian (phonetically Parthian) 'kyyr'δyyr'. As noted by Prods O. Skjaervø, these various spellings suggest a protoform with a vocalic 'r', that is, '*kr̥t' (Prods O. Skjærvø. 'Kartir' (entry originally published 15 December 2011 and last updated 24 April 2014). Available online: http://www.iranicaonline.org/articles/kartir (accessed 18 November 2019)).

[6] Philippe Gignoux. 'Middle Persian Inscriptions' in: E. Yarshater (ed.). *CHIr, Vol. 3: The Selucid, Parthian and Sasanid Periods, Part 2*. Cambridge: Cambridge University Press, 1983, p. 1205:

> Few as they are, these documents constitute a remarkable inheritance; they represent the only strictly Iranian source of Sasanian history, inasmuch as the Graeco-Latin, Armenian or Syriac historical literature is foreign in origin, while the Arab-Persian authors, although they provided useful evidence by drawing on Sasanian writings of which nothing has survived, were much later in date than the events which they record; their perspective may have been

As Philippe Gignoux[7] points out, 'the earliest of these inscriptions, that of Ardashir at Naqsh-i Rustam, mentions only the titles of the king. The majority of the others were executed on the instructions of Shapur I (240-272 CE), to whom is due also the great inscription of the Ka'ba-yi Zardusht, as well as several short inscriptions.'[8] The attribution of inscriptions in KKZ makes sense when one thinks that the later the kingdom in question, the more titles would be put together with the king mentioned. It was discovered relatively late, in an expedition from 1936.[9]

It is of the utmost importance to note the fact that we can find repetition of the same inscriptions far away in several places of the Sasanid Empire, which means that the precaution to preserve his own memory and version of the facts was not something randomly done by Kirdēr but that he was following royal usage.

The plot of Kirdēr's relevance as an apocalyptic traveller is not new. It appears already in Dk 4.7, when Zaraθuštra's first patron, Vištasp, is hesitant to accept the 'new' religion and also travels to the other world; Zaraθuštra himself undergoes a similar experience in ZWY 3.7-8.[10] The AWN ('The Book of Arda Wiraz') also has something of the sort, and in the same way that ZWY represents the prototype of a Zoroastrian 'historical' apocalypse following the definition of John J. Collins, the AWN is very much the same regarding 'other-worldly' travels. Given the importance of the AWN it will be dealt with at the end of this chapter in greater detail.

Consequently, there are two other undisputed Persian (or Iranian, in a broader sense considering the tale in the Dk) parallels to what Kirdēr does: the visionary episodes of Vištasp and Wīrāz.[11] This time, however, the mainstream scholars who

> open to question and their memory fallible. Thus there is good reason for regarding the Sasanian inscriptions as a cultural heritage of first importance. Moreover they are of especial interest on the linguistic level, for they provide the earliest examples of Sasanian Middle Persian, which otherwise, apart from the Manichaean documents of Turfan, occurs in quantity only in Mazdaean works, which gradually came to be written in a scholarly language at the last stage of its development, into which neologisms and persianisms were intruding. The fact that the inscriptions are bilingual or trilingual makes the study of them even more rewarding for the philologist. The connoisseur of *belles-lettres*, on the other hand, is likely to be disappointed, for the style of royal proclamations by official writers avoids neither rhetoric nor redundancies, and is often flat and devoid of all literary merit. Exceptions are the highly individual texts of Kirdir and the great inscription of Shapur I, which may be reckoned among the finest examples of Iranian epigraphic material.

[7] Of special value here are not only Skjærvø's analysis of the inscriptions but also Gignoux's work on text and reliefs. Cf. Philippe Gignoux. *Les quatre inscriptions du mage Kirdir: Textes et concordances, Collection des sources pour l'histoire de l'Asie centrale pré-islamique II/I*. Studia Iranica 9. Leuven: Association pour l'avancement des études iraniennes, 1991.

[8] Gignoux. 'Middle Persian Inscriptions', p. 1206.

[9] The decipherment and publication of that inscription is perhaps the greatest accomplishment of Walter B. Henning. Cf. Henning. 'The Great Inscription of Šāpūr I' in: *BSOAS* 9.4 (1939). In the same year (1939), Henning sent to Bombay for the *Jackson Memorial Volume* his 'Notes on the Great Inscription of Sapur I', but the volume, with that article on pp. 40–54, reached publication only in 1954. See Mary Boyce and Ilya Gershevitch (eds). *W. B. Henning Memorial Volume*. London, 1970, p. viii. Gignoux. 'Middle Persian Inscriptions', p. 1206.

[10] In both cases their experiences are evaluated in a closer fashion in Chapter 6 of this book.

[11] For a general exposition on the theme, cf. Philippe Gignoux. 'Les voyages chamaniques dans le monde iranien' in: Acta Iranica 21 (1981). Obviously, Kirdēr's narrative has all the advantages of being told by someone who claims to have done that trip while alive; we know his name and his deeds. By comparison, Vištasp and Wīrāz are legendary characters.

posit the reality of Avestan lore in Late Bronze Age pastoral, Central Asian societies have a decisive advantage: while the Dk and the ZWY have all the problems Harold Bailey already tackled (cf. Chapter 3), and the AWN in all likelihood falls into the same category. Kirdēr's inscriptions are unanimously accepted as third-century sources. What was the effective role of Kirdēr in the Sasanid court? Was he the one to protect, standardize or enforce Avestan teachings even if he persecuted religious minorities with the violence he alleges to have done? What is of interest here is the travel of Kirdēr to the other world and also what he told after coming back (very much a shamanistic feature[12]). Even Jesus, who went to the mansion of the dead and came back in the flesh, has nothing to tell in the canonical Gospel narratives: in the Gospels, a non-exaustive list contains Matt 3:2.; 4:17; 5:3, 10; 10:7; 13:24–52; 16:19; 18:3, 21–35; 19:14, 23–24; 20:1–16; 22:1–14; 25:1–30; Mark 4:26–34; 10:14, 23; Luke 8:10; 18:29–30; and John 3:3. Moving to the Apostles' Creed (*crucifixus, mortuus, et sepultus, descendit ad inferos, tertia die resurrexit a mortuis, ascendit ad caelos*; note how quickly the transition from a katabatic experiences shifts to an anabasis), Jesus confirms to have gone there and come back, but there is no detail of how this underworld is. There are several promises in the Gospels regarding the Heavenly Kingdom and many hints by whom and how it is likely to be achieved in many of the verses quoted above: if taken as a whole, they convey much less detail than Kirdēr's voyage.

The outstanding difference here (even if Kirdēr knew some sort of Christianity, otherwise he would not boast of having persecuted Christians), besides the authorial and detailed description of the world of the dead, is that Kirdēr has to confront a kind of ordeal that relates more to individual soteriology than to meta-historical schemes of succeeding ages, metals, empires and saviours: he has to cross a bridge to enter the abode of the good or else fall into a disgusting pit full of noxious animals to Zoroastrians.[13] The theme of a frontier between the living and the dead is nothing

---

[12] James Russell. 'Kartīr and Mānī: A Shamanistic Model of Their Conflict' in: Dina Amin and Manuchehr Kasheff (eds). *Iranica Varia: Papers in Honor of Professor Ehsan Yarshater*. Acta Iranica 30. Leiden: Brill, 1990. Apparently the first scholars to note this connection were Grigoriĭ M. Bongard-Levin and Ėdvin A. Grantovskiĭ. *Ot Skifii do Indii: Zagadki istorii drev. ariev* ('From Scythia to India: Mysteries of the History of the Ancient Aryans', in Russian). Moscow: Academy of Sciences, 1974, but with a later French translation from 1981 (*De la Scythie à l'Inde: Énigmes de l'histoire des anciens Aryens*. Paris: Klincksieck, 1981); and Philippe Gignoux, too, in an important article relating shamanism, bones and Kirdēr: '"Corps osseux et âme osseuse"'. Especially important is Gignoux's translation and commentary of KKZ 18-19: 'Et celui qui verra et récitera ce texte, qu'il soit généreux et droit envers les dieux, les souverains et sa propre âme, de la même façon que moi je [l']ai été, en sorte qu'à cette âme osseuse, la sienne, échoiera l'état de sauvé.' Gignoux pays special attention to the het. YḤMTWNt, which may be in the present or past perfect: 'to come', 'to arrive' (Aram. 'to bring'), 'to reach', 'to arrive'. This poses a relation between the good remembering the name of the deceased regarding his bones and his soul. Cf. Philippe Gignoux. 'YḤMTWN' in: Nyberg, *Frahang i Pahlavik*, p. 97; another interesting instance of the use of this verb is in the colophon of ms. P, also in the *Frahand i Pahlavik* edition quoted above. 'Bony' appears as opposed or complementary to 'spiritual' in the *Gāθās* as well: cf. Y 28.2; 31.11; 34.14; 43.3; and 43.16. This is no insignificant discussion: Stanley Insler (*The Gāthās of Zarathustra*. Iranica 8. Leiden: Brill, 1975, p. 25) translates quite freely 'of matter as well of mind' when it comes to bones, for example, in Y 34.14, and he is not the only one to do this. Gignoux is quite right when emphasizing that 'il n'est pas admissible de remplacer un adjectif par un substantive. On voit bien l'embarras des traducteurs.' Cf. Gignoux. '"Corps osseux et âme osseusse"', p. 54.

[13] Av. Y 71 has an identical description of the bridge; so does Vd.

new; usually it takes the form of a river.[14] Here the bridge itself is the limit between these two worlds.[15]

The plot of Kirdēr's voyage is simple (and has been exposed briefly in Chapter 3[16]): like everybody else after dying, Kirdēr (while alive) is in front of an abyss, where there is a bridge. On the other shore lies the house of the good, the pious and the just. If he fits

---

[14] For a general overview on the subject, cf. Eileen Gardiner (ed.). *Greek & Roman Hell. Visions, Tours and Descriptions of the Infernal Otherworld*. New York: Italica Press, 2019, p. xiv, on rivers, waters and creatures of the other world: 'The rivers of the otherworld can vary from text to text, but consistently the Styx and the Acheron seemingly form a border between this world and the other.'

[15] Another important detail is that usually such passages between living and dead are guarded by dogs: in the case of the *Čīnwad* bridge, there are two dogs with four eyes each – just like in Vedic Hell, where the ruler of the underworld, Yama, also has two four-eyed hounds as sentries.

[16] Following the translation by Darmesteter. *SBE*, in Vd Fargard 19.5, there is also a detailed description of the bridge motif:

> 26. Zarathushtra asked Ahura Mazda: 'O thou all-knowing Ahura Mazda: Should I urge upon the godly man, should I urge upon the godly woman, should I urge upon the wicked Daeva-worshipper who lives in sin, to give the earth made by Ahura, the water that runs, the corn that grows, and all the rest of their wealth?'
> Ahura Mazda answered: 'Thou shouldst, O holy Zarathushtra.'
> 27. O Maker of the material world, thou Holy One! Where are the rewards given? Where does the rewarding take place? Where is the rewarding fulfilled? Whereto do men come to take the reward that, during their life in the material world, they have won for their souls?
> 28. Ahura Mazda answered: 'When the man is dead, when his time is over, then the wicked, evil-doing Daevas cut off his eyesight. On the third night, when the dawn appears and brightens up, when Mithra, the god with beautiful weapons, reaches the all-happy mountains, and the sun is rising:
> 29. Then the fiend, named Vizaresha, O Spitama Zarathushtra, carries off in bonds the souls of the wicked Daeva-worshippers who live in sin. The soul enters the way made by Time, and open both to the wicked and to the righteous. At the head of the Chinwad bridge, the holy bridge made by Mazda, they ask for their spirits and souls the reward for the worldly goods which they gave away here below. 30. Then comes the beautiful, well-shapen, strong and well-formed maid, with the dogs at her sides, one who can distinguish, who has many children, happy, and of high understanding.
> 'She makes the soul of the righteous one go up above the Hara-berezaiti; above the Chinwad bridge she places it in the presence of the heavenly gods themselves.
> The soul of the dead, on the fourth day, finds itself in the presence of a maid, of divine beauty or fiendish ugliness, according as he himself was good or bad, and she leads him into heaven or hell: this maid is his own Daena, his Religion [i.e. *dēn*], that is the sum of his religious deeds, good or evil.' [Cf. also HN 2.9 and DD 21]. … Brief explanation on characters (most in older, Av. forms): 'Vizaresha': a devil that carries the soul of the wicked to Hell; Hara-berezaiti: in Av., the highest mountain from which other mountains spring; cf. Y 19. Perhaps 'High watcher' from *PIE 'Harā Bṛzatī'; 'Garo-nmanem', 'Garothman', 'garōdmān': lit. 'the abode of songs' or Zoroastrian Paradise (CPD: 'gar', mountain + 'niwāg', music, song, melody; 'Barashnum': in the Vd, a purifying ritual for the (living) person that is impure; CPD (MP): 'baršnūm', the major purification ritual; 'Nairyo-sangha': one of the Amesha Spentas, a messenger of Ohrmazd; from Av. 'nairyo', male + 'sangha', word. MP CPD: 'nar', (from het. ZKL, male) + 'čegamāg', 'niwāg', 'srōd', song). Most common form, Neryosang, an yazad who elevates love and ideals. Also a proper noun for the priest who translated the Yasna about 1,100 CE.
> 32. 'Gladly pass the souls of the righteous to the golden seat of Ahura Mazda, to the golden seat of the Amesha-Spentas, to the Garo-nmanem, the abode of Ahura Mazda, the abode of the Amesha-Spentas, the abode of all the other holy beings.' The Garothman of the Parsis; literally, 'the house of songs;' it is the highest Paradise.
> 33. 'As to the godly man that has been cleansed, the wicked evil-doing Daevas tremble at the perfume of his soul after death, as doth a sheep on which a wolf is pouncing. That has performed the Barashnum. Ohrmazd is all perfume, Ahriman is infection and stench;

this description, as he crosses the bridge it becomes wider and wider (i.e. safer), and at some point – but only for those like him, pious and just – he sees his den in the form of a beautiful woman who comes to meet him.[17] Having seen this, Kirdēr returns and spreads his message regarding what awaits the just. This story is repeated with small variations in Kirdēr inscriptions: the whole, edited, inscription is mostly about Kirdēr's boasting about his feats regarding visions about what shall happen in the afterlife.[18] The reconstituted text by Gignoux appears to be the more readable so far, and it is the Činwad bridge that concerns most in the comparison to 4Q521; this is a translation full of lacunae and MP words that are not clear: the final part of Kirdēr's trip to the world beyond proper begins thus:

> They told [me] so: 'we see the commander[19] of the horsemen and the horsemen, and the fast horses on which they sit, and the master-guard[20] ... but ... and about ... [him who has] the same form as Kirdēr [is] visible in ... and now a woman appears from the East side, and I have never seen a woman prettier than this one, and the road by which [came this woman] [was] lightened, and then, [this woman] and this man who has the same form as [Kirdēr] are placed face to face, [and now] ... [this] woman and this man who has the same form as Kirdēr, they hold their hands[21] together and [Kirdēr's doublet and that woman] walk in direction ... of the most enlightened path ... and there ... appears the goldsmith, and a golden

---

> the souls of their followers partake of the same qualities; and by the performance of the Barashnum both the body and the soul are perfumed and sweetened.'
> 34. 'The souls of the righteous are gathered together there: Nairyo-sangha is with them; a messenger of Ahura Mazda is Nairyo-sangha.'

[17] Perhaps a reminiscence of the primeval twins' myth, or of the fourfold creatures that Apollo split.

[18] A scholarly and readable edition of Kirdēr's voyage is that of Gignoux ('Les voyages chamaniques dans le monde iranien', n. 23:

> Le texte que je donne ici, appelé dans mon ed. de KNRm le texte II, est une reconstruction encore inedité, à paraître das mon edition definitive des quatre inscriptions de Kirdīr. Il est base sur un texte concordant don't je ne peux fournir ici la justification et que j'ai établi dans mes editions successive et pu améliorer grâce à des verifications sur le terrain faites en 1972 ... Mais le texte présenté ici, est une reconstruction basée soit notamment pour KNRb, soit sur des parallèles internes à KSM / KNRm, soit éventuellement sur d'autres passages. En raison des oppositions continuelles dans ce texte, entre l'enfer et le paradis, le sauvé et le condamné, etc. ..., beaucoup de ces reconstructions 'pures' me paraissent évidentes. Cela permet une meilleure comprehension du texte, mais non basée sur l'imagination.

There are several other pieces by Gignoux that will interest those willing to go further on Zoroastrian trips to the world beyond: 'L'inscription de Kirdīr a Naqš-i Rustam' in: *SIr* 2 (1972); 'La signification du voyage extra-terrestre dans l'eschatologie mazdéene' in: Suzanne Lassier (ed.). *Mélanges d'histoire des religions offerts a Henri-Charles Puech*. Paris: P.U.F., 1974; 'Les voyages chamaniques dans le monde iranien'; and *Le mage Kirdīr et ses quatre inscriptions*. Our translation follows the transcription of Gignoux, but for the sake of brevity some parts are omitted.

[19] This character may well be a *fravashi* as in FY 37. Cf. Jean Kellens. ,Les frauuashis dans l'art sassanide' in: *IrAnt* 10 (1972).

[20] Besides the dogs, the military references are obvious: the door to the world beyond is always guarded. Cavalry has a very important role in Kirdēr's vision, with parallels in Oss. themes and perhaps in Herodotus's description of the Scythians' funeral rites.

[21] The inscription says literally that they hold their hands, but as Gignoux mentions, it would be very difficult to walk with hands held by both of them (MP text).

throne, [there is a ?] celebration and a scale is found in front of him;[22] the one [which has] the same [form as Kirdēr] takes (it), and now this woman and this man who has the same form as Kirdēr [march via the luminous path] towards the East; [and on the golden throne] where there is the celebration, which [is] like the Xwarrah[23] and better than what saw at the beginning, and their [fire?] ...

The rest of the episode is dedicated to the *Činwad* bridge itself:

[They] will say this: the guilty[24] is equally visible than ... illuminated and ... they find themselves full of owls and other plagues[25] [and they], when they see the forms of Hell and snakes ... now they have no light[26] ... and they will say thus: 'This [horse] groom also ... there, this woman and the man who doubles Kirdēr in front' ... they leave, and there ... and [for] this man [the bridge] becomes larger, and now it is obviously larger than longer, and this woman and man who doubles Kirdēr ... take each other and they say this: 'another ... showing of the luck of the Just ... They were seen, on the other side, ahead of the bridge, and now they arrive at the bridge,[27] ... This woman and the man who doubles Kirdēr

---

[22] While the scale to weigh the good and evil deeds of the dead is an almost universal theme, it does not make any sense in this part of the inscription. Gignoux suggests that it was placed there merely due to Kirdēr's curiosity.

[23] CPD, 'xwarrah': 'fortune', 'glory', 'splendour' (from het. GDE). However, 'xwarrah' may have had many more meanings related to 'glory' but not necessarily 'glorious'.

[24] Here too the text can diverge in transliteration and, thus, transcription: CPD, 'dēn' + 'ēranj' (= 'ēraxtan', 'to blame', 'condemn', 'damn') or the transliteration DYN'ylndy, (condemned in a law court). In both cases in is worth noting that Kirdēr's vision of Hell begins almost immediately with terms associated with judgement.

[25] Literally 'vermin' or 'noxious creatures' (according to Zoroastrian taxonomy, some creatures are good and should be protected, while others are evil and should be destroyed as an obligation of Zoroastrians).

[26] CPD, perhaps 'abē': 'without doubt', 'certain', + 'rōšn', 'rōšnīh': 'light', 'bright'. A viable proposition (but not so readable) is 'doubtless with no light'.

[27] All these movements are – like the scales – difficult to understand, even for a seasoned scholar like Gignoux. In this case, if Kirdēr's likeness and his 'dēn', the woman, cross a bridge (*Činwad*) that becomes wider than longer because Kirdēr is just, then why in the next line are they again ahead of the bridge? The very incomplete state of the inscriptions does not help, either. Cf. Gignoux, 'Les voyages chamaniques dans le monde iranien', p. 257. The woman, or girl, is depicted in very graphical detail in Bd 30.17-19:

> 17. If the soul is wicked, then the form of a parched cow, lean and frightful, approaches him, bringing drought and leanness to the soul. 18. Then comes the form of a frightful and ugly girl, cloaked in perversity, in every way frightful, causing terror and fear in the soul. 19. Then comes the form of a waterless, treeless, and joyless garden that causes bad thoughts in the soul. Some say it is the infernal land.

On the brighter side, a bright description of the girl of the just is also given in Bd 30.26:

> 26. It says this: 'Whoever has been righteous in his generosity, when the wind approaches him, sees the form of a girl in the wind. He asks the questions. The girl, guiding him, brings him to a street on which he takes three steps, and reaches heaven in three steps on this road – which are good thoughts, good words, and good deeds. The first step is to the star station, the second to the moon station, and the third to the sun station, that is bright heaven. These are the signs the soul sees before the reckoning.'

take each other hands, and the commander[28] [and the woman and the man who doubles Kirdēr] advance over the bridge[29] ...

The end of the inscription is replete with gaps: in one inscription (KSM 45) the cavalry commander is in front of the man who acts as Kirdēr's double but the woman follows behind the commander (implying that although linked, they no longer hold their hands together). A bit further, in KSM 47 the 'golden throne' appears again, and in KSM 50 there is, apparently, some paradisiac food. The end is very lacunar as well and is devoted to Kirdēr's departure back.

Kirdēr's voyage, faulty as the inscriptions may be, provides some unequivocal elements to the plot of an other-worldly journey. He does it (or the man in his likeness – it is still an open discussion whether they are the same), sees his *dēn* in the bridge and crosses it (with ease, since he is just and the bridge becomes extremely wide), and also sees what lies in the abyss for the unjust. These three elements are the most important to have a complete overview of the plot, even with parts of the text missing, and it must be remembered that there are older mentions to the Činwad Bridge, as seen in Vd Fargard 19.5 above.

This is a theme that also appears, in pseudepigraphic form, in Second Temple literature[30] (e.g. in Enochic literature). Some themes look similar: Ezekiel hints at some sort of living bones too (Ezek 37);[31] Second Isaiah mentions what God can do in a messianic future (e.g. Isa 41, 42; Isa 49:6); Daniel, at the very end of his book, mentions the resurrection of the dead in some detail (Dan 12:1–4). None of them, however, gives much detail on how the dead will be raised again, much less what their world looks like. Daniel, in typical HB fashion, even says that they were lying in the dust (i.e. under the earth in a kind of Šeol); some will be chosen to eternal glory, some to eternal doom, but he does not venture into what these two categories look like (in Dan 12:10 the angel mentions that the Elect will come out 'white', but this cannot be taken, in the context, as a description of clothing). It is fair to say that no canonical HB text mentions crossings between the world of the living and the dead. Even in a desperate

---

[28] The same cavalry commander at the beginning of Kirdēr's adventure over the bridge.
[29] Extremely difficult to make sense of; it looks like a back-and-forth movement since this is the third time they cross the bridge or stand over it. The presence of the mounted commander is also redundant, since he had them pass the bridge before, at the beginning of Kirdēr's description of Hell.
[30] Yet there are scholars who deal with 4Q521 only in a 'Qumranic-prophetic tradition' that is ultimately linked to Christology – and this without even mentioning the 'bridge'. Michael Becker's article is, in a sense, very useful since it connects – and even tables – aspects of messiahship in 4Q521 as related both to OT and NT traditions (Michael Becker. '"4Q521" und die Gesalbten' in: *Revue de Qumrân* 18.1(69) (1997): especially 93–4). This book takes a very different approach, considering 4Q521 in a context wider than Qumran or even wider than Second Temple texts alone. This is not a mistake in itself, but the focus of this book's discussion is on the bridge, not so much on parallels regarding Christology (although these are also of interest inasmuch as they provide parallels to Zoroastrian saviours).
[31] There is another, often overlooked, character in Zoroastrianism explicitly related to the bones theme – world of the dead: the demon of death, Astō.viδōtu, who harms the soul of the dead and whose name is probably linked to the idea of 'separating bones', a dangerous enterprise in shamanistic terms. Cf. Gignoux, 'Corps osseux et âme osseuse', pp. 56–7.

moment such as when Saul summons the witch of Endor, she was lying in Šeol (1 Sam 18); Jacob, in despair for the loss of Joseph, wants to die as a means to be together with his son, but the text does not imply in the least that this reuniting will be like living again, as on earth (Gen 37:34).

However, there is one small fragment from the DSS that tells a very different story. This piece, organized and numbered as 4Q521 (or 4Q Messianic Apocalypse) has, indeed, many similar features to the bridge-crossing of Kirdēr and other features of this kind of Zoroastrian soteriological hope. It is an educated guess that if there is so much in such a tiny fragment, there was arguably more in the bigger, full text to which it once belonged. 4Q521 is outside the curve, so to speak, of Second Temple other-worldly canonical writings: there are others (1 Enoch is perhaps the most important), and in the NT, frequent allusions to the world beyond are made as seen above. But nothing as exotic and peculiar as 4Q521. For a proper examination of this fragment in a possible cultural-borrowing context, it is better to go step by step on each side, Second Temple DSS on one and other Zoroastrian texts on the other (among these underscoring the relevance of Kirdēr and the AWN).

§3 The wording: Semitic

BDB, Heb. גשר. This word, as far as scholars have investigated, does appear only once in Scond Temple Hebrew (i.e before the Mishnah, Talmudim, etc.) and it is precisely in the fragment dealt with in this chapter, 4Q521.[32] *BDB* marks it as an unattested form in the HB but gives cognates with the same root in other Semitic languages: in As., 'gašāru', 'strengthen', 'make firm' (this can be related to a bridge: it must be firm and 'strengthen' any kind of crossing, mundane or otherwise); Ar.جَسَر,, 'be bold', but it can also mean the arch of a bridge (associated ideas: to cross a bridge, one must be bold or at least sure the bridge will not fall apart while crossing)[33]; modern Hebrew has the word גשר in use. Aram., which in *BDB* is usually Syr., has ܓܫܪܐ.

And yet there are two passages in the HB where closely related words are used, but *BDB* shows the readers that the meaning is somewhat clouded: הגשורי in Josh 13, 1 Chr 2; נושר מלך in 2 Sam 3, 13 (*BDB* alerts that the text in not in good order); and גשורה in Josh 13 and 2 Sam 14, a territory not clearly defined east of the upper Jordan. In any case, this second possible meaning in a corrupted text has nothing to do with bridges.

---

[32] Although in later (Targumim, Midrashim and Talmud) Hebrew it does appear. MJ has גשר in several correlated meanings: 'bridge', 'ferry', even one related to bridges on the outskirts of towns that lead to graves. It can also mean to fell trees in order to build bridges. The term is also used to refer to those who built not only one, but several, bridges. It can also mean to take persons from one shore to the other (in any case that is what most bridges do). Similar forms also appear in Aram.: גשרא, גישרא can mean more precisely a ferry in the Euphrates connecting Babylon. It can also mean 'to proceed' (reminding of the Aram. form above, 'to be bold').

[33] Also in Aram., HW gives جبر, with several meanings but not very far from *BDB*: to span, cross, traverse; to venture, risk, have the courage; to build a dam or dike (in a sense, a related meaning: dams and dikes can usually be used as bridges at their top); to embolden, encourage; to dare, venture, risk, have the audacity; to be bold, forward, insolent, impudent. No word of that sort is found in the Qur'an.

So it is fair to say that HB does not have the root גשר. And yet it appears in one of the tiniest fragments of the DSS.

Now, let us examine how the same ideas work in *PIE, IE and Iranian languages.

CPD provides a very concise definition for the word in MP: 'činwad' + 'puhl': the 'divider bridge' which separates the souls of the righteous dead, who cross, from those of the wicked, who fall off.

That is accurate, but it accounts for late usages and meanings (as is the proposal of *CPD*). 'Puhl', however, can acquire two meanings, very similar because of the context of the unique *Činwad* bridge: (1) 'puhl': bridge; and (2) 'puhl': expiation/atonement, punishment. This second meaning (without contradiction to the first) supposes already some sort of judgement. 'Expiation' and 'punishment' are both forms of paying for bad or questionable deeds; in our contexts, to pay or atone in the world to come.

What are the other passages where this bridge can be seen? And why it is also called 'The Bridge of the Selector'? Who selects what?

CPD translates 'Činwad' as the 'divider bridge', perhaps from two possible meanings for the beginning of the word (1) 'čīdan', 'čīn' as gather, pile up, gathering; or (2) 'čīdan', 'čēh' as mourn, lament, grieve and cognates related to 'widār', 'widarag', 'widardan', 'wider', all meaning passage, crossing, and in 'widarišnīh', passage, crossing death. A gathering (of souls) that shall pass or cross. In Av. is činuuatū pərətu-, again meaning a bridge of the selector, defining the ultimate place of rest for the souls of the just and the wicked.[34]

§4 The dead crossing the path to another world: A Zoroastrian novelty?

In almost every culture in the Mediterranean world, the theme of the dead having to cross a river, a stream or an abyss is fairly common, so much that it can be found even in comedy, for example, Aristophanes's *Frogs* (where a comical Dionysus is forced to row his way on the River Styx – depicted as a lake – which separates the world of the dead from that of the living[35]). We have seen before the role that the *Činwad* bridge plays regarding the resurrection in the world to come; yet the peculiarity of Zoroastrianism is, perhaps, that we do not have merely the souls or just the bodies but rather a meeting of them both in order that one, facing the other, may have a fair judgement regarding his/her share in the world to come.

But this is under no circumstances a novelty (perhaps in chronological terms, but there is no way of proving that in favour of Zoroastrianism), not even a novelty brought about by Zaraθuštra's revelation; the scales (found completely out of place in Kirdēr's voyage as seen above) appear in other religions (most remarkably among Egyptians, who had the heart of the deceased weighted against a pen in the netherworld, and Greeks – Homer uses this in regard to Achilles in the *Iliad* 22.208–213). In Second

---

[34] Schwartz. 'Dimensions of the *Gāthās*', pp. 52–4.
[35] Arist., *Frogs* 142–3. A similar theme can be found in Seneca, *Mad Hercules*, with particular reference to Hercules having subdued Hell.

Temple Judaism it is attested in a number of pseudepigrapha and is a known belief of Early Christianity although not attested in the NT.[36]

§5 Flesh and bones

The idea of bones coming together with the flesh makes sense in that both together will make a complete human being once again; another idea to be taken into account here is that the importance of the body as an instrument of what the soul thinks – and therefore plans – is drafted.[37] Thus far, we have seen this operating in a world of hunters and cattle raisers, to whom the idea of resurrecting deceased animals would be a prelude to an ordeal where the same rebirth could be reasonably expected after the death of human beings.[38]

Now, we have also seen that the equivalent concept does not appear in Semitic texts or in the Semitic world at large. Neither in the Hebrew Bible, nor in Mesopotamian myths, do

---

[36] Cf. the recent article by Llewellyn Howes. '"Who will put my soul on the scale?" Psychostasia in Second Temple Judaism' in: *Old Testament Essays* 27.1 (2014); and Samuel G. F. Brandon. 'The Weighing of the Soul' in: Joseph M. Kitagawa and Charles H. Long (eds). *Myths and Symbols: Studies in Honor of Mircea Eliade*. Chicago: University of Chicago Press, 1969.

[37] Cf. Mladen Popović. 'Bones, Bodies and Resurrection in the Dead Sea Scrolls' in: Tobias Nicklas, Friedrich V. Reiterer and Joseph Verheyden (in collaboration with Heike Braun) (eds). *The Human Body in Death and Resurrection*. Berlin: de Gruyter, 2009, pp. 221–42; and Manfred Hutter. 'The Impurity of the Corpse (*nasā*) and the Future Body (*tan ï pasēn*): Death and Afterlife in Zoroastrianism' in: Nicklas, Reiterer and Verheyden. *The Human Body in Death and Resurrection*, pp. 13–26.

[38] As seen in Chapter 3 of this book, this ordeal could essentially take one of two forms: that of the bridge in the river or that of trial by fire. The first one, although more common in religions at large, as seen at the beginning of this chapter, would not have a big future in Christianity; the second one, on the other hand, would be developed into other varieties that can, ultimately, refer to the theme of ordeal by molten metal or by the role of the bridge in final judgement (e.g. Rev 20:1–2; 4 Ezra 16:15). It is important to note that in both cases we are dealing with mythical material that is non-Semitic, that is, material constructed by mythical themes popular among *PIE but not so among Arameans, Hebrews or Punic peoples:

> Several daughter traditions believed that the soul journeyed after death across a body of water to an afterlife. The journey undertaken could be arduous, and required prayers and offerings of food on the part of the soul's living kin, at least for a period of time. ... A Hittite ritual calls for pouring honey and oil onto the ground to 'smooth out' the path for the soul. The journey on land culminated in reaching a body of water across which the soul had to be ferried, probably by an old man; the Greek myth of Charon and the river Styx is the most familiar descendant of this, but comparable myths are found in Celtic, Old Norse, and – with some modification – Indic and Slavic. There is no particular agreement across the different daughter traditions on what the underworld was like (according to one theory, it was originally conceived as a meadow, but this is disputed). In Greek, Germanic, and Celtic myth, a dog guards the entrance to the underworld (the 'hellhound'), and dogs are choosers of the dead in Indic and Celtic. In several traditions, underworld bodies of water are associated with memory, either taking it away (as the river Lethe in the Greek underworld) or imparting great wisdom (as the wellspring of Mímir in Old Norse myth). (Fortson IV, *Indo-European Languages and Culture*, pp. 37–8)

Most important among such passages would be Ezek 37:1–14; but here again the mixing between national redemption and resurrection of individuals per se is unclear. As Popović makes clear, the Pseudo-Ezekiel fragments from Qumran Cave 4 are more important in that regard, especially because of the treatment given to v. 11.

we have such a 'hereafter' that is, in a sense, worth waiting for – except for a few texts from the DSS. Of those, one, 4Q521, must be examined apart from others given its odd nature.

The same problem that haunts most of scholarly issues related to 'influence' when speaking about Persian ideas and Second Temple Judaism surfaces here, namely that the discussion of dating Zoroastrian texts makes more sense than ever in this regard; we ought to speak about influence on the matter of afterlife or any related issue only if those ideas were already circulating, whether in written (very unlikely) or oral forms. Besides that, one of the problems that haunt DSS scholars who deal with death and resurrection is the fact that these are 'reticent', as one modern scholar put it, regarding these matters. Therefore, broadly speaking, we are dealing with a very sparsely distributed theme, besides the fragmentary nature of the physical remains themselves.[39]

Thus, the reader should be warned that a variety of materials will be used here in a 'non-sequential' fashion, more so than in any other chapter in this book; the 'Book of a Thousand Judgments' (*Mādigān ī Hazār Dādistān*), which 'has reached us in a single, defective, and relatively late manuscript copied in Iran in the XVIIth century',[40] also called the 'Sasanian Law Book', for obvious reasons contains Sasanid material, but, as it happens so often in this field of inquiry, entire passages are better understood in the context of a pastoral society many centuries older. This alone justifies the use of such previous material, as well as apocalypses that one way or another have reached us in their present form via quite late reductions, such as the ZWY and the AWN.

DSS material regarding the afterlife is considerably varied and, frustratingly, also very fragmentary in content and form as stated above. However, 4Q521 stands out in the uniqueness of its promises.

§6 A weird variety of crossing, an unusual root and what it can tell us about the destiny of the soul

Among the world-renowned DSS[41] found in Cave 4 (4Q) is a fascinating document, albeit as fragmentary as the rest found in that cave (it is notorious that from the caves

---

[39] Popovič. 'Bones, Bodies and Resurrection', p. 242.
[40] Anon. *Mādigān ī Hazār Dādistān* (The Book of a Thousand Judgements; A Sasanian Law Book. Introduction, transcription and translation of the Pahlavi text, notes, glossary and indexes by Anahit Perikhanian; translated from Russian by Nina Garsoïan), ed. Anahit Perikhanian. New York: St. Petersburg Branch of the Institute of Oriental Studies, Russian Academy of Sciences, Center for Iranian Studies, Columbia University, 1997, p. 6 (reprint in facsimile by Mazda Publishers).
[41] Here, as in other parts of the text, I am most grateful for the help of Eibert Tigchelaar, who allowed the following private correspondence to be quoted and which sums up quite well a good deal of what has been done so far regarding DSS and afterlife:

> [Cf.] Jean Duhaime, *The War Texts: 1QM and Related Manuscripts*, Companion to the Qumran Scrolls 6 (London: T&T Clark, 2004). The series is intended to give an indepth introduction to and survey of the scholarship of core texts of the Dead Sea Scrolls. Duhaime's book is the best general introduction to matters of content, structure, possible relations to Hellenistic war treatises, etc. He points at previous attempts to connect the (eschatological) dualism of 1QM to that of some of the other scrolls, in particular the so-called Treatise of the Two Spirits in 1QS, but never even mentions the suggestion that this might be connected to Zoroastrian material. Ellie Marie Louw-Kritzinger, *Die Eskatologiese/Apokaliptiese Oorlog Tussen Goeden Kwaad in*

involved in the discovery of the scrolls, it was ironically in Cave 4 that the greatest variety came out, but, as if destiny wanted to play a bad joke on us, they are also the worst preserved as a whole, sometimes amounting to very small pieces).

The document in this case is known internationally among scholars by the name we have already seen: 4Q521 or 4QMessianic Apocalypse.[42] Among the several notes that would interest only the specialist in Hebrew writing, or else in dating the fragment according to the style of the letters, there are very few noted by Émile Puech that could be useful to us, in any sense.

However, there are a number of comments related to the content that cannot be left behind. Consequently, an overview of the document is in good order.[43]

---

die Zoroastrisme, die Judaïsme (Qumran) en'n Vroeg-Christelike Geskrif (Die Apokalyps) (PhD 2009, Stellenbosch). Little known PhD thesis, written in South African (Afrikaans) with a one-page English abstract, which compares war themes in the Gathas/Bahman Yasht, the War Scroll, and the NT Apocalypse. The author sees correspondences, and possible areas of influence, but clearly does not commit herself to the thesis of influence; on this, cf. Brian Schultz. *Conquering the World: The War Scroll (1QM) Reconsidered*, STDJ 76 (Leiden: Brill, 2009). [Another diss.] Argues for an original Hellenistic period work comprising of 1QM cols. 1–9, to which in the Roman period later the text that now is 1QM cols. 10–19 was added. I have not read the book integrally, but I do not believe that he deals with any Zoroastrian background at all. Géza G. Xeravits and Peter Porzig, *Einführung in die Qumranliteratur: Die Handschriften vom Toten Meer*. Berlin: de Gruyter, 2015, pp. 276–82. This is a thorough German introduction, with listing of literature, manuscripts, literary structure, content, with discussion of time of provenance, relation between liturgy and eschatology, etc. Here we have another discussion of dualism without any reference to Zoroastrianism: Kipp Davis and others, *The War Scroll, Violence, War and Peace in the Dead Sea Scrolls and Related Literature*, STDJ 115. Leiden: Brill, 2015. A *Festschrift for Martin Abegg* with a series of topical and thematic articles on the War Scroll. I cannot find the book (I think I lent it to someone, [sic]), but as far as I can judge from authors and titles, there is no-one who would deal with the Zoroastrian issue. Basically, it seems that ever since the 1970s very few scrolls scholars were interested at all in a possible Zoroastrian influence. James Barr's article seems to reflect the turn. Only Florentino García Martínez (very cautiously), John J. Collins (in general thematic terms), Klaus Koch (specifically with regard to the Ten Weeks' Apocalypse), and Emile Puech (with regard to the afterlife) have suggested some kind of influence. Personally, I am very much attracted to the ideas of Shaul Shaked and Albert de Jong, who see both systemic correlations and occasional correspondences of detail. I also prompted my PhD student, Arjen Bakker, who defended in December [sic], to deal (cautiously) with specific Zoroastrian concepts as a heuristic key for understanding better some phenomena in the scrolls (note how we dodge the question of influence).

[42] Much of the following discussion owes, again, to the collaboration of Tigchelaar. In personal communication, both in person and also via email, he pointed out several fine points on the subject to me, where he exhorted the excellence of the commentary by Émile Puech: 'As I told you, the evidence is from a very fragmentary context, but is interpreted maximally by Émile Puech, in his edition, and probably also in this previous *La croyance des Esséniens*.' It should be noted, however, that there is a *parti-pris* involved in the whole discussion inasmuch as Puech, like so many other scholars – I must confess that I do not include myself among them – especially coming from the earlier generations who dealt with the scrolls, takes for granted the link between Essenism and the Dead Sea findings. That aside, our main instruments to deal with the fragment are precisely Puech's own analysis and an old but rather underestimated book from the forties of the last century. This is David Cohen (in collaboration with François Bron and Antoine Lonnet). *Dictionnaire de Racines Sémitiques ou attestées dans les langues sémitiques. Comprenant um fichier comparatif de Jean Cantineau*. Brussels: Peeters, 1993 (Fascicule 3 of 10, 'GLD – DHMLKR'). The entry on GŠR is comparatively small and is to be found on p. 197 of the aforementioned fascicule.

[43] As mentioned before, Puech's analysis is thorough enough to be followed throughout my own commentaries. For those interested in a full-fledged discussion of the text, cf. Émile Puech.

The fragment is composed by an ensemble made of four successive columns, obviously incomplete as most things are in Cave 4 of Qumran. Although the integral piece is composed by eleven parts of a well-prepared leather surface, fragments numbered 2 to 7 are the ones that interest us here.

Relevant content of 4Q521, edited

Fr. 7 + 5 col. II[44]

1   [...] see th[at has made]
2   [Lord: the ear]th and all that is in it, *Blank* the seas [and all]
3   [they contain,] and all the reservoirs of waters and torrents. *Blank*
4   [...] those who do the good [deeds] before the Lor[d]
5   [...] like these, the accursed. And [they] shall b[e] for death, [...]
6   [...] he who gives life to the dead of his people. *Blank*
7   And we shall [gi]ve thanks and announce to you [...] of the Lord, wh[o ...]
8   [...] ... and [he] opens [...]
9   and [...]
10 and [...]
11 he reveals them ... [...]
12 and the/a **bridge** of the abys[ses...]
13 the accur[sed] have coagulated [...]
14 and the heavens have met [...]
15 [and] all the angels [...]
16 [...] ... [...]

4Q521, Heb. Text

Fr. 7 + 5 col. II

1 [...]ראו [א]ת כל א[שר עשה]
2 [אדני האר]ץ וכל אשר בה vacat ימים [וכל]
3 אשר בם [וכל מקוה מים ונחלים] vacat
4 [...].[...]העושים את הטוב לפני אדנ[י]
5 [...]א כאלה מקלל[י]ם [ולמות יה]יו[...]
6 [...]ם המחיה את מתי עמו vacat
7 ונ[ו]דה ונגידה לכם צ[...].[...] אדני אש[ר...]

Discoveries in the Judaean Desert. Textes Hébreux (4Q521-4Q528, 4Q576-4Q579). Qumrân Grotte 4. Vol. XXV [continued in XXVII]. Oxford: Clarendon Press, 1998, p.1. Also by Puech is the slightly dated but still useful article (with special regard to the composition of the fragment in a material sense and in palaeographical dating) 'Une apocalypse messianique (4Q521)' in: *Revue de Qumrân* 15.4(60) (1992). According to him, the fragment as a whole is nicely written and its style is the formal Hasmonean type, following Frank M. Cross in this reasoning ('The Development of the Jewish Scripts' in: George E. Wright (ed.). *The Bible and the Ancient Near East: Essays in Honor of W. F. Albright*. New York: Doubleday, 1961, pp. 133–202).

[44] The original text, that is, the one found in the DSS fragment, follows the edition of Florentino García-Martínez and Eibert J. C. Tigchelaar, DSS, pp. 1044-7.

8 [...ותה ופתח]...[
9 ופ]...[
10 ו]...[
11 יגלם...[...]
12 וגשר תה]ומות...[
13 קפאו ארור]ים...[
14 וקדמו שמים]...[
15 [וכ]ל מלאכים]...[
16 [...]ל[...]

Analysing the key passages of 4Q521, in Fragment 1 there is the promise of 'an eternal kingdom, [of] freeing prisoners, giving sight to the blind, straightening out the twis[ted], which is of utmost importance because it is one of the very few passages in the DSS or even Second Temple Judaism literature as a whole to relate to an afterlife that is remarkably similar to life as we know it, if not the same: health woes (i.e. bodily issues, problems related to the flesh) will be cured in the world to come.[45] That only makes sense if the bodies in the afterlife are similar or identical to the human ones as they were in this one. All those bodily issues make sense in the context of the whole fragment that speaks for judgement of the dead in a similar way to Zoroastrianism.[46]

As we shall see, even more outspoken texts regarding the selection (i.e. the fragments of Pseudo-Ezekiel – 4Q385, 386, 388, discussed below) are by no means so clear concerning health – something that only makes sense when considering its counterpart, that is, disease and death. Messianic themes in 4Q521 resemble those found in Zoroastrian lore: they are worth quoting again.

1 [For the heav]ens and the earth will listen to his anointed one,
2 [and all th]at is in them will not turn away from the precepts of the holy ones.
3 Strengthen yourselves, you who are seeking the Lord, in his service!

Like the three Zoroastrian saviours, the 'anointed one' (coherent with Second Temple Judaism and its derivatives) is in charge of heavens (note the plural, typical in 'other-worldly-type' apocalypses).[47]

Again, in the following fragment, resurrection is described in lively terms that make the afterlife look like a continuation of life as we know it (Frag.1 col. I, 4Q386, edited):

---

[45] Becker. '"4Q521" und die Gesalbten', p. 93: deeds similar to the works of Jesus in Matt 11:2–5 and Luke 7:22.
[46] In Bd 34.24:

> 24. It also says this: 'Those who had reached their middle years will be restored at the age of forty. Those who were small and immature will be returned at the age of fifteen.' Every person will be given his wife and children, and he will copulate with his wife just as in the material world, but no children will be born.

[47] Common usage here as just a few examples: 1 En. 1:2; 11:1; 18:10; 39:3; 42:1; 47:2; 54:7–8; 55:2; 60:1; 61:9; 71:1–5; 84:2–4; 93:12; 98:6; 2 Enoch in many passages but with special regard to chs 1–68; 3 En. 5:11; 12:4; 17:1–3; 18:1–2, 25; 19:1; 22:3–4; 26:5–6, 10; 38:1; 44:7 (twice); 46:13 (twice), 14; 48:1; 3 Bar. 2:1; 3:1; 7:2; 10:1; 11:1; and Ascen. Isa. 6–11, among many.

1 'YHWH, I have seen many in Israel who lov]e your name
2 [and walk on the paths of justice. When will these things happen? And] how will they be rewarded for their loyalty?'
3 [And YHWH said to me: 'I will make] the children of Israel [see] and they will know
4 [that I am YHWH'. *Blank* And he said: 'Son of man, proph]esy over the bones
5 [and say: 'May a bone connect with its bone and] a joint with its joint'. And it Happened
6 [thus. And he said a second time: 'Prophesy, and sinew]s [will grow on them] and they will be covered with skin
7 [all over'. And so it happened. <And he said a second time: 'Prophesy,] and sinews [will grow] on them
8 [and they will be covered with skin all over. And so it happened.> And again he said: 'Prophesy] over the four winds
9 [of the sky and the winds of the sky will blow upon them and they will live, and] a large [cro]wd of men [will rise]
10 [and bless YHWH Sebaoth who caused them to live.' *Blank*] *Blank*

The same themes reappear in Fr. 7 + 5 col. II, where a promise similar to Dan 12:2 is made – that some were reborn to eternal damnation and others to eternal bliss.

Currently, the novelty here is that we have both passages referring to resurrection in the flesh together with bones *and* a bridge to be crossed.[48] The question is that the presence of this bridge is unique – the Lord announces something missing from the fragment, yet undoubtedly related to resurrection, and then mentions the bridge which crosses abysses; in my opinion, the parallel link with the *Činwad* bridge is unavoidable not so much because of the resurrection theme (which could after all be traced back, with some degree of force, returning exclusively to Hebrew sources such as 1 Sam 28:3–25 – אֵשֶׁת בַּעֲלַת־אוֹב בְּעֵין דּוֹר, lit. 'a woman who has a family spirit at Endor', the well-known 'Witch of Endor') but because of the resurrection in the flesh.

After all, the questions simply and accurately put down by a colleague are: 'What are those people waiting to cross? What lies on the other side? Will everyone get through?' The fragmentary nature of 4Q521 and the absence of counterparts in biblical or pseudepigraphical literature forbids definite responses.

The idea of following into an abyss, which is why it is mentioned in connection to the bridge (otherwise the interpretation of the 'bridge theme' could be completely different[49]), acts as a separator of the eternally damned and the eternally blessed. It

---

[48] Cf. Johannes Tromp. 'Can These Bones Live? Ezekiel 37:1-14 and Eschatological Resurrection' in: Henk J. de Jonge and Johannes Tromp (eds). *The Book of Ezekiel and its Influence*. Aldershot: Routledge, 2007, pp. 61–78; and Beate Ego. 'Death and Burial in the Tobit Narration in the Context of the Old Testament Tradition' in: Nicklas, Reiterer and Verheyden. *The Human Body in Death and Resurrection*, pp. 87–103. The bridge, of course, only appears in 4Q521.

[49] Vladimir I. Propp. *Morphology of the Folktale*. Austin: University of Texas Press, 2009, Kindle edition. Propp may be especially useful here while describing the typology of the dramatis personae in the folktale, following his usual Afanasiev's numbering – in this case, the hero can be understood simply as the soul moving on after death:

would be fair, then, to assume that the גשר theme is the perfecting of an idea that would have been, arguably, first presented in Daniel: a selection between good and bad in the world to come.

In terms of dating, Puech is uncontested in his reasoning that 4Q521 should be dated to the Hasmonean period on palaeographic grounds:

> A défaut d'indicationclaire ou de critères internes pour une datation de La composition, l'étude paléographique a permis au moins de situer la date de la copie du manuscrit, qui n'est pas l'original. Même si le critère paléographique doit être manié avec souplesse, il donne un repère dans le temps. Cette belle écriture n'appartient pás à La période hérodienne mais au type d'écriture formelle hasmonéenne d'après la classification habituellement acceptée.[50]

This line of reasoning would mean then that, from the fragments we have of the DSS, together with Daniel, we can draw a picture of progression (not in the sense of improvement but rather of the adding of detail) from Daniel to the 'bridge theme', if the fragment is indeed post-Danielic.

§7 The 'Bridge of the Selector' again: What could wait a Zoroastrian in this particular type of eschatology?

This chapter began with the etymology and the episode of Kirdēr crossing the bridge and returning to tell the living what happens after death were examined. Now, what could this particular kind of final judgement mean to the faithful as a whole?

In Zoroastrian texts, notwithstanding the dating problems which should be left aside for a while, the 'Bridge of the Selector' (Av. *činuuatōpərətu-*, 'bridge of the selector'

XV. The Hero is Transferred, Delivered, or Led to the Whereabouts of an Object of Search. (Definition: spatial transference between two kingdoms, guidance. Designation: G.) Generally the object of search is located in 'another' or 'different' kingdom. This kingdom may lie far away horizontally, or else very high up or deep down vertically. The means of unification may be identical in all cases, but specific forms do exist for great heights and depths. 1. The hero flies through the air (G1): on a steed (171); on a bird (219); in the form of a bird (162); on board a flying ship (138); on a flying carpet (192); on the back of a giant or a spirit (212); ad in the carriage of a devil (154); and so forth. Flight on a bird is sometimes accompanied by a detail: it is necessary to feed the bird on the journey, so the hero brings along an ox, etc. 2. He travels on the ground or on water (G2): on the back of a horse or wolf (168); on board a ship (247); a handless person carries a legless one (198); a cat swims a river on the back of a dog (190). 3. He is led (G3). A ball of thread shows the way (234); a fox leads the hero to the princess (163). 4. The route is shown to him (G4). A hedgehog points out the way to a kidnapped brother (113). 5. He makes use of stationary means of communication (G5). He climbs a stairway (156); he finds an underground passageway and makes use of it (141); he walks across the back of an enormous pike, as across a bridge (156); he descends by means of leather straps, etc.

Note that the hedgehog is also pointed out by Ahuramazda in Vd together with the watchdog of the bridge (Vd 13.10).

[50] Puech. *Discoveries in the Judaean Desert*, p. 3. A dating proposed by Puech following Cross is on pp. 133–202.

or, perhaps, more accurately the 'bridge of the accumulator/collector', according to Jean Kellens[51]) appears in many passages, all of them unequivocally connected to the final judgement of the soul. It is accurate that the very term גשר appears only once in a Hebrew fragment, and only in that fragment which in turn has a strong Danielic flavour. The important Zoroastrian passages are then to be found and briefly discussed further on, but it is worth taking a look at least at some of them now.

A brief report on common themes that appear regarding the *Činwad* bridge is in order here. Some of them are shared by other cultures, for example, the two watchdogs that guard the bridge (Vd 13.1–9; 19.30).

> Which [is] the creature belonging to the Beneficient Spirit, among these creatures that are the creation created by the Beneficient Spirit, [that] comes during the whole dawn until sunrise killing a thousand of [those of the] Evil Spirit? [Av.] / Which [is] the Creature of the Beneficient Spirit [his creature], among those creatures that exist, that is, the created creation of the Beneficient Spirit, [that] comes during the whole dawn [it comes up at midnight] until sunrise against the Evil Spirit for the killing of a thousand? [MP] ... No other soul will help his soul in death, when shouting and being chased [in his way] to [the next] life; nor will the two dogs guarding the pass help him in death, when shouting and being chased [in his way] to [the next] life [Av.] / No other soul [different soul] will defend his own soul when passing away [that is, will not be able to provide assistance to him] owing to the shouting and chasing [which he may have done] in life, nor the dog guarding the pass [the Dog of dogs[52]] [there is a commentator who says: 'the bountiful bridge protector' *yaiiā. asti. aniiō. rašnuš. razištō*] will defend him when passing away [that is, it will not be able to provide assistance to him] owing to the shouting and chasing [which he may have done] in life.[53]

Mary Boyce makes a point on that,[54] and it should be noted that in the passages above, the Pahlavi expanded version in Vd 13.9 offers two interesting terms that

---

[51] Aḥmad Taffazolī. 'Činwad Puhl' (entry originally published 15 December 1991 and last updated 11 October 2011). Available online: http://www.iranicaonline.org/articles/cinwad-puhl-av (accessed 25 November 2019); Jean Kellens. 'Yima et la mort' in: Mohammad Ali Jazayery and Werner Winter (eds). *Languages and Cultures. Studies in Honor of Edgar C. Polomé*. Berlin: Mouton de Gruyter, 1988, pp. 329–34.

[52] Arist., *Frogs* 114–15: ΔΙΟΝΥΣΟΣ: ἀλλ' ὧνπερ ἕνεκα τήνδε τὴν σκευὴν ἔχων ἦλθον κατὰ σὴν μίμησιν, ἵνα μοι τοὺς ξένους τοὺς σοὺς φράσειας, εἰ δεοίμην, οἷσι σὺ ἐχρῶ τόθ', ἡνίκ' ἦλθες ἐπὶ τὸν Κέρβερον, τούτους φράσονμοι, λιμένας, ἀρτοπώλια, πορνεῖ', ἀναπαύλας, ἐκτροπάς, κρήνας, ὁδούς, πόλεις, διαίτας, πανδοκευτρίας, ὅπου κόρεις ὀλίγιστοι.

[53] Miguel A. Andrés-Toledo. *The Zoroastrian Law to Expel the Demons: Widewdad 10-15. Critical Edition, Translation and Glossary of the Avestan and Pahlavi Texts*. Iranica 23. Wiesbaden: Harrassowitz, 2016. For the Pahlavi version of the text, cf. Darab D. P. Sanjana. *The Zand i Javīt Shēda Dād or the Pahlavi Version of the Avesta Vendidād the Text Prescribed for the B.A. and M.A. Examinations of the University of Bombay. Edited, with an Introduction, Critical and Philological Notes, and Appendices on the History of Avestan Literature*. Bombay: Education Society's Steam Press, 1895.

[54] Mary Boyce. *A Persian Stronghold of Zoroastrianism. Based on the Ratanbai Katrak Lectures, 1975*. Oxford: Oxford University Press, 1977, p. 145.

deserve a more attentive look: 'the Dog of dogs'[55] that 'guards the pass' (i.e. the bridge, 'sharp as a razor'[56] for the unjust), [...] *sag <ī> puhl-bān* [...] and its apparent relation to the 'commentator' who says that it is different from 'which (two) is *Rašnu* the Most Righteous'.[57]

In the passage above, it is clear that the bridge was created by Ahuramazda (Vd 19.29-36); even more so, it is referred to as *mazda-δāta* (Av. *δāta*, NP *dād* meaning 'law'). This means, personally, that no matter how harsh the judgement may be, it is still lawful and correct according to the plans of the good divinity in Zoroastrianism (the other version of afterlife judgement, that is the river, would come to have a more benevolent version in later times, as we shall see). It is a 'righteous' bridge, too, or rather 'protected by righteousness' (*ašapāta-*, Wištāsp Yt 42[58]).

It is to be noted that the adjective *aša* always means rightfulness as opposed to *druj*, the attribute of the evil god and his minions. That bunch of demons menaces the soul that is going to be tried by the crossing of the bridge; that notwithstanding, it is escorted by good deities, with particular regard to Srōš ('the good [or right] way') and Wahram (Av. *Vərəθragna*, 'the hypostasis of victory') – as depicted in MX 2.115:

> [after the body is dilacerated by birds and dogs] And on the fourth day at down, with the company of the Righteous Sros, the Good Way, the Powerful Wahram, and the opposition of Ashtwihad, the Bad Way, the Demon Frazesht, the Demon Nizesht, and the evil will of evil doing Xeshm of the Bloody Banner, shall go to

---

[55] Here again are some good references to the presence of the underworld dog myth in other cultures, in the cases above with particular detail concerning the head(s) and jaw(s) and other peculiar features of the head: Arist., *Frogs* 110, and many others in Graeco-Roman literature – some of the best-known passages would be Hesiod, *Theogony*, 300-14; Acusilaus, fragment 6; Hyginus, *Fabulae*, Preface, 151; and Quintus Smyrnaeus, *Posthomerica* (or *Fall of Troy*) 6.260-268, which all have Cerberus as the offspring of Typhon and Echidna, while Bacchylides, *Ode* 5.56-62; Sophocles, *Women of Trachis*, 1097-9; Callimachus, fragment 515 Pfeiffer; and Ovid, *Metamorphoses* 4.500-501, 7.406-409, all have Cerberus as the offspring of Echidna without naming a father. In Hesiod, *Theogony*, 309-24 (although it is not certain whom Hesiod meant as the mother of the Chimera: Echidna, the Hydra or Ceto); Apollodorus, 2.5.10, 2.3.1; Pindar, fragment F249a/b SM, from a lost Pindar poem on Heracles in the underworld, according to a scholia on the *Iliad*; Sophocles, *Women of Trachis*, 22-5 ('three-bodied'), 1097-9; Euripides, *Heracles*, 610-11, 1276-8; Virgil, *Aeneid* 6.417-421 ('triple-throated', 'three fierce mouths'); *Georgics* 4.483 ('triple jaws'); Ovid, *Metamorphoses* 4.449-451 ('three-visaged mouths', 'triple-barking'), 9.185 ('triple form'), 10.21-22 ('three necks'), 10.65-66 ('triple necks'); Heroides 9.93-94 ('three-fold'); Seneca, *Agamemnon*, 859-62 ('triple chains'); *Hercules Furens*, 60-2 ('triple necks'), 782-4; Statius, *Silvae* 2.1.183-184 ('triple jaws'), 3.3.27 ('threefold') and *Thebaid* 2.31 ('threefold'), 2.53 ('tri-formed'); Propertius, *Elegies* 3.5.44 ('three throats'), 3.18.23 ('three heads'); and Apollodorus, 2.5.12 ('three heads of dogs'). *CPD*, 'sag': 'dog'. The rest of the phrase is merely a superlative, with 'sagan' in the plural and ''' as a connective.

[56] *CPD*, 'dār-ēw', 'dār': 'keeper', 'holder' ('guardian' would be an educated guess); 'ēw-', 'one' (but an interesting connection to the theme of monosandalism and the world of the dead may be found in 'e(w)-mog', 'wearing only one shoe'). The razor is, according to *CPD*, 'awestarag', which is related to shaving one's face. It was also created by Ahuramazda (*mazda-δāta*, Vd 1929-36) and is very high (*buland*, meaning 'big' in NP as well as MP; MX 2.115), and, finally, *sahmgen* ('fearful', MX 2.115). The 'razor-blade' nature of the Činwad puhl also appears in the voyage of Kirdēr (KNRm 65, KSM 41); in DD 1.21.3 it is also a 'many-sided' blade – dār-kirb ī was pahlūg – *CPD*, 'a many-sided body').

[57] Andrés-Toledo. *The Zoroastrian Law to Expel the Demons*, pp. 286-7.

[58] Only found in two corrupt mss K4 and L5, edited by Niels L. Westergaard. *Zendavesta or The Religious Books of the Zoroastrians. Vol.I: The Zend Texts*. Wiesbaden: Reichert, 1993, pp. 302-12.

the terrible Chinvat Bridge, which every (one of the) righteous and the wicked are comers to there.[59]

Or else in GrBd 30.4–17, where it is principally Srōš,[60] who accompanies the soul (as in the AWN):

> 4. After Soshyant comes they prepare the raising of the dead, as it says, that Zartosht asked of Ohrmazd thus: 'Whence does a body form again, which the wind has carried and the water conveyed [vazhid][61]? and how does the resurrection occur?' 5. Ohrmazd answered thus:

The following lengthy description of the deeds of Ohrmazd is important because it emphasizes the relevance of the material world for the outcome of the combat, no matter how pre-defined it was.

> 'When through me the sky arose from the substance of the ruby, without columns, on the spiritual support of far-compassed light; when through me the earth arose, which bore the material life, and there is no maintainer of the worldly creation but it; when by me the sun and moon and stars are conducted in the firmament [andarvai[62]] of luminous bodies; when by me corn was created so that, scattered about in the earth, it grew again and returned with increase; when by me color of various kinds was created in plants; when by me fire was created in plants and other things without combustion; when by me a son was created and fashioned in the womb of a mother, and the structure [pishak[63]] severally of the skin, nails, blood, feet, eyes, ears, and other things was produced; when by me legs were created for the water, so that it flows away, and the cloud was created which carries the water of the world and rains there where it has a purpose; when by me the air was created which conveys in one's eyesight, through the strength of the wind, the lowermost upwards according to its will, and one is not able to grasp it with the hand outstretched; each one of them, when created by me, was herein more difficult than causing the resurrection, for it is an assistance to me in the resurrection that they exist, but when they were formed it was not forming the future out of the past. 6. Observe that when that which was not was then produced, why is it not possible

---

[59] ud rōz ī čahārom andar ōšbām pad abāgīh ī srōšahlā ud way ī weh ud wahrām ī amāwand ud hamēstrīhī astwihād ud way ī wattar ud frazēšt dēw ud nizēšt dēw ud duškām-kardārīh ī xešm ī anāg kardār ī xurdruš tā ō *činwadpuhl ī buland ī sahmgen, kē harw ahlaw ud druwand awiš madār in: TITUS Project. Available online: http://titus.uni-frankfurt.de/texte/etcs/iran/miran/mpers/mx/mx.htm (accessed 15 April 2017). Data entry by David N. MacKenzie, Göttingen 1993; corrections by Thomas Jügel, Frankfurt 2007–2008; TITUS version by Jost Gippert, Frankfurt a/M, 28.2.1998 / 22.6.1998 / 26.9.1999 / 1.6.2000 / 23.11.2002 / 24.11.2007 /17.8.2008. Translation in Zeke Kassock. *Dādestān ī Mēnōg ī Xrad. A Pahlavi Student's 2013 Guide*. Fredericksburg: Author's edition, 2013. Cf. esp. 'xešm' or 'xeshm', an important feature in ZWY.
[60] CPD, 'Srōš', 'srōšīg': 'the god Obedience', 'obedient'.
[61] CPD, 'wāzīdan', 'wāzišn': 'move', 'carry', 'fly'.
[62] CPD, 'andarwāy': 'air', 'atmosphere'.
[63] CPD, 'puštag', 'puštībānīh': 'load carried on the back'; 'supporter', 'bodyguard', 'support', 'protection'.

to produce again that which was?[64] for at that time one will demand the bone from the spirit of earth, the blood from the water, the hair from the plants, and the life from fire, since they were delivered to them in the original creation.'

7. First, the bones of Gayomard are roused up, then those of Mashye and Mashyane,[65] then those of the rest of mankind; in the fifty-seven years of Soshyant they prepare all the dead, and all men stand up; whoever is righteous and whoever is wicked, every human creature, they rouse up from the spot where its life departs. 8. Afterwards, when all material living beings assume again their bodies and forms, then they assign [bara yehabund] them a single class. 9. Of the light accompanying [levatman] the sun, one half will be for Gayomard, and one half will give enlightenment among the rest of men, so that the soul and body will know that this is my father, and this is my mother, and this is my brother, and this is my wife, and these are some other of my nearest relations.

From 7 to 9 a number of crucial family-related issues are explained: there is after all a kind of 'priority order' in the Ressurrection. Mashy and Mashyane are resurrected after Gayomard in a sort of 'reverse' order in regard to the first Creation. Another similar theme is found in 7: the reunion of families disbanded, or lost, or even more surprising, across generations (this presents the problem of how people from several generations can coexist at the same time and place, even if these are out of bounds from Earth). In the beginning of stanza 7 the reference to the bones of Gayomard being raised has a parallel to the dead in Dan 12:2–6, for they also lie reposing in the dust, although their destiny is not the same once risen. This 'inter-dimensional' character is to a certain extent shared by Second Temple Judaism and Zoroastrianism but in less-examined texts.[66]

10. Then is the assembly of the Sadvastaran,[67] where all mankind will stand at this time; in that assembly every one sees his own good deeds and his own evil deeds; and then, in that assembly, a wicked man becomes as conspicuous as a white sheep among those which are black. 11. In that assembly whatever righteous man was friend of a wicked one in the world, and the wicked man complains of him who is righteous, thus: 'Why did he not make me acquainted, when in the world, with

---

[64] This is a very important saying by Ohrmazd: the second Creation will equal the first, but the text suggests that this second time it would be even easier (perhaps because by then the cosmic struggle would have been overcome, while in the first Creation the attack of Ahriman was immediate).

[65] The primordial couple in Zoroastrian cosmogony. Spelling can vary somewhat according to the text used but the story is basically the same: Ohrmazd created Gayomard, a kind of primeval, original beast that was androgynous and killed by the demoness Jeh in the attack of Ahriman; before Gayomard died, Mah (the moon) caught his seed. From Gayomard's body grew all vegetal life including a tree, from which the primordial couple, Mashya and Masshyane, were born.

[66] Cf. Daria Pezzoli-Ogliati. 'Approaching Afterlife Imagery: A Contemporary Glance at Ancient Concepts of Otherworldly Dimensions' in: Tobias Nicklas, Joseph Verheyden, Erik M. M. Eynikel and Florentino García-Martínez (eds). *Other Worlds and Their Relation to This World: Early Jewish and Ancient Christian Traditions*. Leiden: Brill, 2010; and Stefan Beyerle. 'The "God in Heaven" in Persian and Hellenistic Times' in: Nicklas, Verheyden, Eynikel and García-Martínez. *Other Worlds and Their Relation to This World*.

[67] Av. 'Righteous judges'.

> the good deeds which he practiced himself?' if he who is righteous did not inform him, then it is necessary for him to suffer shame accordingly in that assembly.

Clearly in this passage, more than in any other, Zoroastrianism manages to reconcile the idea of predestination (after all the outcome of this combat was decided in the beginning of material Creation) with that of rewards according to each man's deeds: these deeds are of course related to the correct observation of the *dēn*.

> 12. Afterwards, they set the righteous man apart from the wicked; and then the righteous is for heaven [garothman or Garodman],[68] and they cast the wicked back to hell. 13. Three days and nights they inflict punishment bodily in hell, and then he beholds bodily those three days' happiness in heaven. 14. As it says that, on the day when the righteous man is parted from the wicked, the tears of every one, thereupon, run down unto his legs.

The tears here can be seen as a variation of an other-worldly river to be crossed, given their depth.

> 15. When, after they set apart a father from his consort [hambaz],[69] a brother from his brother, and a friend from his friend, they suffer, every one for his own deeds, and weep, the righteous for the wicked, and the wicked about himself; for there may be a father who is righteous and a son wicked, and there may be one brother who is righteous and one wicked. 16. Those for whose peculiar deeds it is appointed, such *as* Dahak [Zohak] and Frasiyav of Tur, and others of this sort, as those deserving death [marg-arjanan[70]], undergo a punishment no other men undergo; they call it 'the punishment of the three nights.'

Here the idea of the world of the dead linked to triads appears again.

> 17. Among his producers of the renovation of the universe, those righteous men of whom it is written that they are living, fifteen men and fifteen damsels, will come to the assistance of Soshyant. 18. As Gochihr falls in the celestial sphere from a moon-beam on to the earth, the distress of the earth becomes such-like as that of a sheep when a wolf falls upon it.

---

[68] 'Pardes' may have developed to our notion of Paradise as a perfect and joyful place (and this is definitely an Iranian idea in our context), and linguistically has a career as a Semitic root in late As.: pardisu, Arab.: فردوس, NP: چالیز, Aram.: פרדס but in Gk.: παράδεισος and, as *BDB* notes, is a 'loan-word from Zend [sic] *pairi-daêza*' (this is Av. or perhaps even older, Indo-Iranian); however, there is no such word in 'Zend' (understood here as MP) but the common 'garōdman' and derivatives (CPD). The Semitic meaning is always related to 'closure with trees', 'garden', 'garden with costly fruits' and mostly 'park', 'preserve'. That is precisely what it meant in Persia – and still holds true to this day – a garden that shelters from the excessive heat. Its size and varieties of plants inside depend on the material means of the owner.

[69] CPD, 'hambāz', NP *anbāz*: 'partner' (similar to 'hambāy': 'companion', but also 'adversary', depending on the text).

[70] CPD, 'marg': 'death', and 'arzān', 'arzānīgīh': 'worth', 'worthy of'.

Gochir is – surprisingly – another agent of chaos who was left to be defeated at the final judgement. The same idea appears in Rev 13–17 and is likely to have the same origin, but in Revelation the two dragons,[71] prostitutes and the like fulfil a political role symbolizing Rome – as the four world empires had done before regarding Daniel, and would be 'recycled' many times over according to the political climate of each historical timing.

> 19. Afterwards, the fire and halo melt the metal of Shahrewar,[72] in the hills and mountains, and it remains on this earth like a river. 20. Then all men will pass into that melted metal and will become pure; when one is righteous, then it seems to him just as though he walks continually in warm milk; but when wicked, then it seems to him in such manner as though, in the world, he walks continually in melted metal.[73]

A variety of similar themes develops here because it is not only a test for the just to cross the bridge in safety but also a moment to be judged before that (one may suspect here that every variety that deals with that theme may be a later addition; if the soul is judged *before* trying to cross the bridge, we would not have an ordeal anymore but rather a straight reward or punishment). An important detail here, to which I shall return by the end of this chapter, is that although the dog may be interpreted as a common feature in Greek mythology as an intermediary between the world of the living in that of the dead, it is altogether missing in Indian tradition.[74] This may have something to do with the special role dogs should play in a pastoral society, as well as the way the dog was created by Ahuramazda.[75]

---

[71] The first dragon or beast, between Rev 15 and 17, resembles the 'political' beasts found in the apocalypse proper in Daniel (7–12) but is much more of a primeval beast seen in Chapters 2 and 3 of this book: it is a sea animal and thus linked to the primordial chaos that sea always represents from Ugaritic to Vedic peoples. The other one, which appears in Rev 13, is more mysterious, but as chief characteristics, one could say that the two horns (much like 'duqarnain' in the Qur'an, probably Alexander), the demand for being idolized (Roman emperors did this but Alexander had a lot of trouble among his fellow Greeks for the same reason); he is able to kill but those who died for not letting themselves be deceived by him will have their part in Heaven secured. For a balance of reasonable scholarly speculations on the identity of the dragon, cf. Craig R. Koester. *Revelation: A New Translation with Introduction and Commentary*. New Haven: Yale University Press, 2014. On p. 526, Koester makes an important remark on a medieval scheme of interpretation by Joachim of Fiore: in Chapter 6 of this book and in its conclusion we will return to the theme. An interesting article relating artistic representations of dragon-fighting and dragon-slayers in between Christian and Zoroastrian themes is that of Sara Kuehn. 'The Dragon-Fighter: The Influence of Zoroastrianism Ideas on Judaeo-Christian and Islamic Iconography' in: *ARAM Periodical* 26.1-2 (2014). Kuehn is not the only one to refer to this theme as related to the 'melting-pot of Near Eastern religions' (cf. pp. 65–7).

[72] *CPD*, 'Šahrewar': 'Best Rule', the third Amahraspand (one of the good spirits that help Ohrmazd), guardian of metals.

[73] Cf. Chapter 3 in this book for more on that theme.

[74] Kellens, 'Yima et la mort', p. 330, discussing the two dogs in RV 10.14,11.

[75] 'No house would stand *firmly founded* for me on the Ahura-created earth were there not my herd dog or house dog ... (Vd 13.49)' (Mahmoud Omidsalar, Teresa P. Omidsalar, Mary Boyce and Jean-Pierre Digard (entry originally published 15 December 1995 and last updated 29 November 2011). Available online: http://www.iranicaonline.org/articles/dog#pt2 (accessed 20 November 2019)).

Finally, the bridge in itself can be understood as a kind of ordeal – for the righteous will see their own *dēn* as a beautiful maiden, who assists the soul of the just in the crossing (MX 2.124; Vd 19.30), something that will be nonetheless 'well-wishingly and free of sorrow', *appār-čēh*[76] (DD 1.21.6).

Hence, in a sense, we have here the same qualitative problem turned into a quantitative one much as we have it in apocalyptic – take 4 Ezra as an example: it is the one apocalypse where, as will be seen in Chapter 6 of this book, mention to chemical induction is made; in contrast, a number of examples follow in Zoroastrian apocalypses or other texts with apocalyptic passages where ASC inducers are used.

The same reasoning prevails in here, but now in a sort of reversed sense: while we have plenty of examples of the 'bridge theme' in Zoroastrian literature, the גשר appears only once. It would seem cynical to attribute this absence to the whole mess of the fragments found in Cave 4, but it seems only logical to me that we could have more examples of the same word appearing in other fragments, now lost.

What we have, though, is enough to go on tracing the trajectory of the idea of resurrection in this peculiar time and place of Second Temple Judaism, both in its early and late periods (from the third century BCE to the second century CE). It should also be noted that, in a sense, it was a dead-end idea: all the resurrection in the flesh passages after that one failed to mention any sort of bridge to be crossed, and abysses would be relegated to other functions, the most famous of which would appear in Revelation,[77] yet not as a means of selecting the elect from the damned. The importance this fragment might have had in the Qumran community remains unknown, but from this lonely reference to the גשר together with resurrection of the flesh, it is fair to relate both. In this sense, the idea of an afterlife fleshly similar to ours and involving a final judgement to discriminate the good from the bad had come to stay and would have a very fruitful future in Christianism, Manichaeism and Islamism.

§8 Can the formation of the canon and the bridge be related?

A fundamental issue to be taken into account when dealing with anything related to Kirdēr is that his life and deeds were punctuated by two very important processes that cannot be understood separately but should rather be taken as a whole: the consolidation of the Sasanid dynasty and the definition of – or at least the earliest organization we can be certain of – the Zoroastrian canon, as well as secondary literature that is religious in nature but not necessarily sacred (e.g. MX, DD). In this sense, Kirdēr may not have been the precursor he claims to have been: although this is

---

[76] CPD: compound of 'appār': 'taken away', 'removed', and 'čēh', 'čīdan': 'mourn', 'lament', 'grieve'. Thus, 'free of grief', 'free of sorrow'.
[77] Cf. among the many works related to the topic one that stood the test of time: Adela Y. Collins. *The Combat Myth in the Book of Revelation*. Missoula: Scholars Press, 1976; and the more recent work by Koester. *Revelation*.

still disputed, he may have had a predecessor who tried not to merely organize some sort of canon but even more to paint Arsacid[78] rulers as depraved and unfaithful. The name of this character is 'Tansar' or 'Tonsar' and he may have written a letter that survived by very indirect means to our day.[79] No dating argument for or against Tansar or the Arsacids is possible given the material we now have, but in any case, if Tansar existed, he must have been immediately prior to Kirdēr. We know something about his existence not only through the 'letter' but also by a truncated passage in the Dk 1.12 – he had gathered authoritative texts at the service of Ardašir-i Pāpagan, the first Sasanian ruler (*pad rāst-dastwarīh i Tansar*). Another passage in the Dk mentions again that he managed to arrange the (right) scattered works (*Tansar abar mad ud han i ewag fraz padirift ud abarig az dastwarih hist*).

From what we know of the life of his successor (Kirdēr), he had a very successful career up to the highest point of religious authority in Sasanid Persia.[80] This might have been accomplished against the backdrop of persecution of other minorities, and especially against the condemnation of Mani (for whom there are several versions[81]). That this was a success can hardly be doubted – see, e.g. ZWY 3:20–26, already examined before in this book and again in Chapter 7.

Here more than one golden age is depicted – as a matter of fact, six of them. Furthermore, the same can be said in the opening lines of the AWN:

---

[78] That is, Parthian. The Parthian empire lasted from 247 BCE to 224 CE, and written information on that Empire is even more scarce than on the Sasanians who succeeded them.

[79] The way his 'letter' survived is the following: a Zoroastrian convert to Islam (whose true beliefs are hard to ascertain now), Ibn al-Muqaffa (d. *c.* 760 CE) left a translation of the 'letter' that must have been fluent and elegant, like the rest of his work. But this has not survived and what we have is a third-hand account by another Central Asian scholar, Ibn Isfandiyār (thirteenth century CE), who found (by chance) a copy of the 'Letter of Tansar' (from al-Muqaffa) in Xwārezm. We depend largely on him (in his *History of Ṭabaristān*) and on a few scarce quotations by al-Mas'ūdī and al-Bīrūnī to imagine what this letter may have looked like. To understand the 'letter', its context and consequences, cf. Mary Boyce. *The Letter of Tansar (translation)*. Roma: Istituto Italiano per il Medio ed Estremo Oriente, 1968.

[80] The life of Kirdēr is puzzling in many ways. Besides his inscriptions (the only first-hand account of a travel to the world beyond and back, at least in Antiquity) sharing space with royal inscription (a remarkable exception that was never explained), we know that he is said to have persecuted Christians, Buddhists and even conspired to have Mani killed – but there is no primary source by Christian or Jewish groups complaining about any kind of persecution in the period (cf. Payne. *A State of Mixture*, pp. 23–4). Kirdēr also 'vanishes' after his own death – no other Persian sources mention him. Conversely, it is only natural that modern scholars are so radically divided in their opinions about who he was; here, too, Skjærvø is correct while affirming that modern scholars have the advantage of hindsight. Most important scholars who claim that Kirdēr was authoritarian, fanatical, intolerant and zealotic are Richard Foltz. 'Buddhism in the Iranian World' in: *Muslim World* 100 (2010): 206; Russell. 'Kartīr and Mānī'; and Zaehner. *Zurvan*, pp. 11–24. Scholars showing Kirdēr under a favourable light are Walther Hinz. 'Mani and Kardēr' in: VVAA. *La Persia nel Medioevo. Atti del Convegno Internazionale sul Tema*. Roma: Accademia Nazionale dei Lincei, 1971, p. 492; and Jacob Neusner. *A History of the Jews in Babylonia II: The Early Sasanian Period, III: From Shapur I to Shapur II*. Leiden: Brill, 1999.

[81] A useful introduction to Mani's life and the several versions for his end can be found in Michel Tardieu. *Manichaeism*. Urbana: University of Illinois Press, 2008. It is perhaps significant that Mani dates his own birth with precision (in a MP text named the *Shabuhragan* i.e. written in honour of Shapur I) in 216 CE, during the reign of the last Asrsacid king, Artavan V (in Hellenized or Latinized form, 'Artabanus').

1. They say that at one time, the righteous Zoroaster received the religion and spread it in this world. 2. And until the completion of 300 years, the religion was in a state of purity, of which the people were without doubt. 3. And after the accursedly wicked Gannag Menog [Ahriman?], casting doubt to the peoples in this religion, deceived the accursed Alexander of Rome, who was staying in Egypt, sending him to the land of Ērān with heavy struggles and warfare. 4. And he killed: Bran's ruler, and destroyed the palace and empire, and made it desolate. 5. And this religion, namely all of the Avesta and Zend was arranged upon cow hides with golden lettering, and was laid to rest in a fortress [vault] in Stakhir Papagan. 6. And the ill fated, heretical and wicked adversary brought over Alexander the Roman, who was staying in Egypt, and he burned them.[82]

So much, then, for hatred past or in a given eschatological future; it is not my task to date those two apocalypses, but their resemblance to Danielic material in the case of the ZWY cannot pass unnoticed, just as the tour to the world beyond done by Enoch pseudepigraphically resembles that of Wiraz – and, it must be said, that of Kirdēr as well.

In short, for all the usual shortcomings in its transmission (including Isfandiyār's lack of style and stature, according to Boyce[83]), there is no reason to doubt (according to internal criticism alone, regardless of the verborrage and lack of taste by our main witness, Isfandiyār) that we are dealing with two very plausible situations.

1. The lack of uniformity in the cult and understanding of Zoroastrianism in Parthian times: this can be true or false but it does refer to Zoroastrianism after the Seleucid period. That it needed correction only adds credibility to the 'letter': he had to build it (and, Kirdēr, reform and standardize it) according to existing traditions. Whether these were written or oral cannot be proved – but Tansar takes us very close to the 'Hasmonean lettering', that is, the Hasmonean period to which Puech attributes the fragment on palaeographical ground of 4Q521. This, together with the linguistic evidence of the term 'Činwad' (older than Kirdēr, even older than the AWN but perhaps from the time of the Vištāsp legend examined in next chapter i.e. coming from the old Av. form 'Cinvatô', which in turn may lead to Vedic forms, as seen above). Tansar's letter may perhaps be too harsh on the Parthians but testifies to Zoroastrian teaching very possibly simultaneous to 4Q521: again, what we have is a third-hand account,

---

[82] 6. *Udōy petyārag ī wad baxt ī ahlomōy ī druwand ī anāgkardār Alaksakdar Hrōmāyīg Muzrāyīg mānishn abarā wurdud bēsōxt.* 'Aleksandar i-Hrōmāyīg' or 'Akandar', 'Skandar' (*CPD*, 'Aleksandar': 'Alexander' [of Macedon]; 'Sakandar' = 'Aleksandar'), are ways of referring to Alexander the Great as 'the Roman', not because Persians had been clear to them that this was an anachronism and an impossibility but because he ruled, in their mentality, across the Euphrates in Asia Minor: enough for the area to get the nickname 'Rome' (*CPD*, 'Hrōm', 'Hrōmāyīg': 'Byzantium', 'Rome'; 'Greek', 'Byzantine', 'Roman'). This would happen in later times with other conquerors: the Turks successfully captured a large chunk of the Byzantine Empire after the Battle of Manzikert (1071). Other names derive from this, most importantly that of the Persian poet Rūmi (he came from Central Asia but settled in that part of Asia Minor still very young).

[83] Boyce. *Letter of Tansar*, pp. 3–5; Darmesteter. *SBE*, pp. xxxi, 414.

but what reason would Isfandiyār have to concoct it as a whole? And the references to Tansar in the Dk are also arguments supporting the authenticity of the letter.

2. Given the possibility above – and the absence of the root GŠR in biblical or extra-biblical texts – 4Q521 may not have been (like so much of the scattered and destroyed material from Qumran Cave 4) a one-off but part of a peculiar vision of the other world by some sort of Second Temple Judaism (Essenes, for those who believe there is a clear relation between the DSS and that sect – a discussion too old, too lengthy and that does not concern us here, as the bridge itself did not matter in Michael Becker's analysis of the fragment). To quote a friend who is a very fine scholar, 'if one DSS fragment testifies something, one Jew must have had contact with it. One Jew would lead to two, three, four and as many as now we cannot imagine.' 4Q521, as it is, stands alone: but the 'Letter of Tansar' is perhaps our best bet on the parallel (it is too tempting to call it 'influence' again – but would be an educated guess since references to the 'bridge' are much easier to find in Zoroastrianism than in the DSS, where there is only one).

And here lies, perhaps, the biggest asset inscriptions attributed to Tonsar, whose historical existence is beyond doubt. They are not pseudepigrapha, and they are not even to be confused with the activity of Tonsar, another *mowbed* who might have paved the way for Kirdēr's action in reforming Zoroastrianism.[84] It is also my personal opinion, as well as that of other scholars (most remarkably Gignoux), that his travels to the world beyond have a strong shamanic flavour, something which should not surprise us – the same scent can be found in many Second Temple Jewish apocalypses and even in Islamic eschatology,[85] both of historical and other-worldly nature. This kind of literature would have a promising future in Christianity, beginning with the Revelation of John and having as one of its most frightful examples the Vision of Tundal.[86]

§9 Who are those people waiting to cross this abyss in 4Q521?

One vital question remains among the fragments that compose what came to be called 4Q521:[87] it is the Lord who 'announces', 'opens' and 'reveals' something to 'them' – who

---

[84] One of the last academic works on the theme is almost two decades old by now: cf. Franz Grenet. 'Pour une nouvelle visite à la "Vision de Kerdir"' in: *Studia Asiatica* 3 (2002).
[85] For a general introduction to the theme cf. David Cook. *Studies in Muslim Apocalyptic*. Princeton: Darwin Press, 2002, pp. 77, 87 and 94-5 are especially interesting, on the relations with Zoroastrian apocalyptic, although the author touches this point only slightly.
[86] This is perhaps the most graphic, detailed and horrifying description of Hell among Christian medieval traditions: the standard edition remains that of Wagner Albrecht. *Tundale: Das Mittelenglische Gedicht über die Vision des Tundalus*. Halle: Max Niemeyer, 1893, although there are also works on Middle English traditions (among these stand the doctoral thesis of Eileen Gardiner. 'An Edition of the Middle English "Vision of Tundale"'. PhD diss., Fordham University, 1980; and Rodney Mearns. *The Vision of Tundale, Edited from the B.L. MS Cotton Caligula A II*. (text in Middle English). Heidelberg: Carl Winter, 1985).
[87] For the sake of fluidity the reconstructed parts are written here as a continuum; the reader can always go back to the fragment and the way it was scholarly reconstructed, in an earlier part of this chapter.

are are we talking about? There is something missing in the text but this gap is followed immediately by a 'bridge of the abyss' (or perhaps 'abysses' in a reconstructed form) in the text. Before that, there is the separation of those who do 'good before the Lord' and a similar but inverted group, the 'accursed' – like Dan 12:2, these are destined to death – but this has to be understood in a supernatural death, since on earth (at least until the Final Judgement, again present in Dan 2) all shall die.[88]

The mention of 'abysses' in the plural is also puzzling (even if in a reconstructed form), but if GŠR is a bridge for the few, for the chosen, for the elect, it makes all the more sense that it has a void on one side as well as on the other (Kirdēr's 'report' does not contradict this, nor does any other version of the Činwad bridge, including two important episodes in the Gāθās that link Zaraθuštra explicitly to Činwad – Y 45.10–11; 51.13). After GŠR is 'opened' and 'revealed', there is a strange reference to the accursed being 'coagulated' (coagulated blood means lack of movement – in this context, death in the sense of not partaking in all the good things promised to the good).

And in the sketchy ending of this fragment, what else can be inferred?

That 'the heavens have met', and then, after more missing bits, it ends with a reference to 'all the angels'. It clearly is a promise (one that is neither strange to Second Temple Judaism nor to other mss of the DSS or even the NT) of being with the angels. Strangely for the passage, the heavens 'meet' before the angels: in any case, Heaven is the abode of angels, and of the good ones. What is striking in this reading of God's promises is that apparently many will be waiting before a bridge, GŠR: that God will 'open' it can mean that the bridge will become larger (although this is admittedly very speculative), but in any case there is no mention in the fragment, as we have it, of a counter act by God where the bridge will be closed or may become so narrow that the accursed will fall.

It is more than an educated guess that the abyss is the abode of the accursed, who are not alone in the fragment – there is also reference to others 'like these' (whom?), the 'accursed'. This may be just hyperbolic language – what could be worse than being 'accursed' at the moment of trial?

There is a possibility of another group, which would bring 4Q521 even closer to Činwad. The enemies of God (like the enemies of Ohrmazd) have the noxious abyss as their abode. The bad will only share what is already impure, fatal and dirty in all senses to the bad spirits (in Zoroastrianism, the devils of Ahriman;[89] in 4Q521, some other category that may either be just a stylistic feature to enhance how bad is the fate of the accursed or, taken literally, may imply another group of condemned). Since there is mention of angels

---

[88] A reminder on Danielic material is in order here: Peter Flint. 'The Daniel Tradition at Qumran' in: John J. Collins and Peter W. Flint (with the assistance of Cameron Van Epps) (eds). *The Book of Daniel: Composition and Reception*. Leiden: Brill, 2001 (2 vols), vol. 2, pp. 329–32. Flint reminds us that in the eight canonical Daniel mss found in Qumran, only one passage is missing, Dan 12:10, but even that can be supplemented by 4QFlorilegium (4Q174). Although the eight mss present scattered parts of Daniel, they are 'much like that found in the received Masoretic text, not the longer form as found in the Septuagint'. For the resurrection theme in Daniel, as related to other Qumranic texts, cf. John F. Hobbins. 'Resurrection in the Daniel Tradition and Other Writings at Qumran' in: Collins and Flint. *The Book of Daniel*.

[89] CPD, 'dēw': 'demon', 'devil'.

at the other side of the bridge, the 'abysses' may well be reserved for those supernatural creatures who oppose God – bad angels. They are unmentioned in the text but, as stated above, either there is a hyperbole for the 'accursed' or there was a (now missing) part of 4Q521 that dealt with the 'other' angels. This is speculative but not impossible, given the judgement context of the whole of 4Q521. It has been stated many times, bordering on the obvious, that the context of most DSS is eschatological (but not necessarily apocalyptic) in nature. 4Q521, for at its unique aspect related to the bridge, is in alignment with that, even if in a modified form. Furthermore, the 'Letter of Tansar' places some sort of Zoroastrianism roughly in the same dating of 4Q521, at least as a possibility.[90]

And here again, the parallels are striking – but it would be very unwise to speak of 'influence'. Tansar makes this possibility very real; Kirdēr informs on the bridge and on the good things awaiting the (Zoroastrian) faithful; and other Zoroastrian tales – these, too, much distanced from 4Q521 to allow even for parallels – give us a template of other-worldly voyages. It is correct to say that the Enochic cycle, not to mention 3 Baruch and other Second Temple texts, are also reports on voyages to the world beyond – other-worldly apocalypses, in Collins's taxonomy. However, the similarity of another trip to the world beyond by a Zoroastrian character, Wiraz the Just (in this case, unlike Tansar or Kirdēr, the text is pseudepigraphical), to later, Middle Age apocalypses, is even more striking.[91]

---

[90] Boyce. *Letter of Tansar*, p. 12.
[91] There are two issues that no matter how better the shape of 4Q521 were would still be in doubt. In the KIns, we saw a cavalry commander, or a knight. There are four of them (called 'Šahryār'); there is no possibility of four simultaneous messiahs in any Second Temple texts (although the general reference to the angels could, in theory, relate to a definite number of them). The Šahryār also has in his hands something whose meaning is still doubtful, and even its transliteration is not established. It is the MP word 'cydyn' – that is in the hands of the Šahryār. All kinds of proposals have been made regarding 'cydyn': the text appears in KSM 38–40 and KNRm 63–64, in two places: once referring to something that the Šahryār has in his hands, a 'cydyn', and in the other as a word qualifying the abyss – both Kirder's image and the maiden looked at 'a terrible "cydyn", that had no bottom etc.' (it could be, according to Skjærvø, an abyss (?), or a small bucket, perhaps a miniature of Hell – cf. 'Kirdir's Vision',p. 298). Gignoux, who devoted so much time to the study of the Kirdēr inscriptions, proposes that 'cydyn' be related to the Parthian 'cydyg' or Sogdian Manichaen 'cytyy', both meaning 'demon' or 'spirit' (Gignoux. *Les quatre inscriptions du Mage Kidir*, pp. 76–96). Gignoux handles well this possibility (after all, the voyages of Kirdēr, Wiraz and Zarathustra himself have very strong Central Asian shamanistic features, as already discussed) but goes perhaps too far in suggesting a relation between 'cydyn' and the specific demons Xēšm (*CPD*: anger, the demon Wrath) and Astwihād (*CPD*: the demon of Death) that are circling round *Činwad* together with the benevolent spirits Mihr (*CPD*: Mithra, or the sun itself), Srōš (*CPD*: the god Obedience) and Rašn (*CPD*: the god of Justice). It is difficult to imagine a knight holding two demons (even less being two but with different names). These demons or (lost) spirits – if indeed 'cydyn' refers to them – can as a matter of fact lie in the abyss but not be the abyss themselves. Grenet goes further suggesting that 'cydyn' could be a kind of shell used to add wood to a bonfire in Central Asia; shells are also prominent in ossuaries in that area (Frantz Grenet. 'Crise et sortie de crise em Bactriane-Sogdiane aus IVe-Ve siècles: De l'heritage antique à l'adoption de modèles sassanides' in: VVAA. *La Persia e L'Asia centrale da Alessandro al X secolo*. Roma, 1996, p. 385, pics 13–14). The maiden meeting Kirdēr or his image is also unthinkable in a DSS text and, if present, would never have the same role as she has in the final destination of the soul in Zoroastrianism: women appear (if at all) in perverted roles in the DSS (e.g. 4Q184 or 'The wiles of the wicked woman' – cf., inter alia, Magen Broshi. 'Beware the Wiles of the Wicked Woman' in: *Biblical Archaeological Review* 9.4 (1983): 54–5; it is even less likely that women were full members of the Qumran community, given that they are not allowed to take the 'oath of the covenant' (CD xv.6; regulations regarding them are strict (1Q28a). On the other hand,

The text in question is the AWN (Ardā Wirāz Nāmag, or cognates – 'The Book of Wiraz, the Just'). As part of the bigger heritage of Zoroastrianism, it will be dealt with in its ASC-inducing aspects in Chapter 5, as well as regarding its plot and derivatives.

---

a number of texts shed a different light upon them: they are not excluded from the assembly (again 1Q28, CD xv.15–17 and 4Q266 8). But most of the Qumran texts, when dealing with women, seem to ascribe them one of these three roles: eventual members of the community but with limited rights, perverted women like the one in 4Q184 or, more generally, they appear in all sorts of texts regarding marriage laws and usages. There is also the case of the feminine representation of wisdom, but this occurs in the HB as well (Ps 122).

5

Visionary experiences: Striking parallels, first-hand accounts and pseudepigrapha

§1 Text-dating and ecstasies: Some remarks

Among the numerous visionary experiences referred to in Jewish apocalyptic literature in the Second Temple period, a small group of episodes is striking because they involve unusual visionary preparatory practices when the whole of the literary corpus is considered. In the text examined in this part of the chapter,[1] 4 Ezra, more usual means of visionary preparation are present – fasting, mourning, praying – but chemical episodes stand out in their uniqueness. Such practices are altogether absent in other apocalypses, but there are many parallels in Persian texts, which may imply influence of the latter on the Jewish text. From another point of view, we must take in consideration whatever scientific information on the nature of such inducers there is, as well as to try to identify the plants in question in Jewish and Persian sources alike. Some work on links between Persian and Jewish apocalyptic visionary episodes has been done but not on the same scale as proposed here: among the research previously done, the work of Anders Hultgård is in my opinion the most significant one, and this chapter came about from some of the issues that he raises.[2]

It is also expected that some of the problems related to dating of texts and precedence of Persian lore over Jewish apocalyptic themes may be seen under a different light when examined from the point of view of chemically induced visionary practices. On another front, attention is given to the actual scientific information conveyed on the effects of hallucinogenic drugs such as those that may lie behind the visionary experiences described in 4 Ezra and in Persian sources. This may clarify some of the most difficult issues at stake by allowing or forbidding some inducers as the

---

[1] An earlier version of this chapter was first drafted as an article in *Jewish Studies Quarterly* (2006) with the title 'Chemically-Induced Visions in the *Fourth Book of Ezra* in Light of Comparative Persian Material'. It is reworked here and quoted to a very great extent with the kind permission of the editors of *Jewish Studies Quarterly*, whose personnel (especially Dr Elizabeth Wener) I would like to thank warmly.
[2] 'Ecstasy and Vision' in: Nils Holm (ed.). *Religious Ecstasy: Based on Papers read at the Symposium on Religious Ecstasy held at Åbo, Finland, on the 26th-28th of August 1981*. Stockholm: Almqvist and Wiksell, 1982.

hallucinogenics eventually responsible for the episodes described – in other words, the discussion on the nature of the species involved in the processes may help date texts considered and thus clarify the issue of the precedence of Persian material over Jewish apocalyptic. This discussion has moved from an almost unanimous position in the *Religionsgeschichte* scholars from the beginning of the twentieth century, a position that takes for granted that those apocalyptic elements in late Judaism are the result of IE (i.e. Persian) influx and not the other way round. These assumptions have been recently challenged by scholars such as Philippe Gignoux, and I hope that discussion on the particular items raised in this chapter may contribute to the debate.

The term 'chemical inducement' should first be defined while dealing with the proposed theme, since ambiguity might arise. By this I understand the textual passages where it is clear that the vision described by the seer is a consequence of the ingestion of some substance that, although not always described with the precision the scholar wants, has a mind-altering character in the story subsequently told. Unorthodox dietary practices such as vegetarianism might as well cause a mind-altering effect (this is in fact described in Dan 1:8–15 and, surprisingly, in some modern case studies as well), but since in Jewish texts they are more likely related to plain *kashrut* laws, they shall not be discussed here; fasting can have much the same preparatory effect in the stories told about visions but likewise shall not be dealt with here.[3]

§2 ASC in Daniel and other Second Temple material

In this chapter I am concerned with apocalyptic passages in which it is clear that the vision described by the seer is a consequence of the ingestion of some mind-altering substance, which allows us to speak about 'chemical inducement' as a cause-effect relation between that substance and a following visionary experience.

This leaves us with four passages in the corpus of Second Temple Jewish literature where the ingestion of some substance appears to be related to mystical experience: 4 Ezra 9:23–29; 12:51; 14:38–48 and Mart. Isa. 2:7–11. Of those, the last one cannot be properly established as portraying a cause-and-effect relation in terms of chemical inducement and the seer's vision, and it shall be left out of this analysis. The three passages of 4 Ezra, on the other hand, provide clear links between the ingestion of substances and experiences undergone thereafter. It should be noted that no significant variations in the passages examined were found in the different readings of the manuscripts, according to the textual discussion by Michael E. Stone.[4]

---

[3] The text of 4 Ezra used has been Metzger's translation in OTP 1. 'ASC' stands, from now on, for 'altered state of consciousness'. The transliteration of Persian sources was left as they stand in the original editions, thus accounting for differences in spelling of the same word.

[4] The mss of 4 Ezra can be divided in two main groups, the first comprising the Latin and Syriac versions, and the second the Georgian, Ethiopic and Coptic. Some differences in detail are sometimes found and shall be noted. Cf. Michael E. Stone. *Fourth Ezra: A Commentary on the Book of Fourth Ezra*. Hermeneia. Minneapolis: Fortress Press, 1990, pp. 1–3.

§3 4 Ezra or the metamorphosis of a visionary

The Fourth Book of Ezra is an apocalyptic text of Jewish origin (with the exception of what came to be known in the Vulgate as chs 1-2 and 15-16 of II Esdras, which are Christian interpolations) that was probably written between 70 CE – because of the importance that the author attached to the fall of the Temple – and the end of the second century CE (where the first clear mention of it is to be found in Clement of Alexandria[5]). The text of 4 Ezra is structured around seven sequencial visions, of which the fourth (explanation for the weeping woman) and the seventh (the command to write the ninety-four books) are the most important for this chapter. Also of importance and attached to the context of the fifth vision (the eagle), although it in fact introduces the sixth, is 4 Ezra 12:41, for after 12:51 the seer sleeps seven days and then gets a vision.

In the first passage, 4 Ezra 9:23-29, we have a dialogue between God and Ezra where the seer is still perplexed about the fate of the wicked in relation to the righteous. For God to explain in further detail to Ezra why so many will perish while He is only concerned about the fate of the just, He orders Ezra to go to a field without any human construction and not fast[6] but instead eat only the flowers of the field and abstain from meat or wine (4 Ezra 9:23-25).

> But if you will let seven days more pass – do not fast during them, however; but go into a field of flowers where no house has been built, and eat only of the flowers of the field, and taste no meat and drink no wine, but eat only flowers, and pray to the Most High continually – then I will come and talk with you.

Here, once more, the theme of vegetarianism is present (maybe as a reminder of the pre-Diluvian diet that man enjoyed once, closer to Edenic times), but the reference to the eating of the flowers alone is striking and even absent from some versions of the text;[7] since the Latin and Syriac texts provide the best mss of 4 Ezra, it looks more plausible that the reference to the flowers was already in the Greek or Hebrew original and eliminated in the less important versions than the other way round – it would make little sense to think of them as later insertions. It should be noted that Nebuchadnezzar also abstains from wine and meat in his madness (in the account of the *Vitae Prophetarum* 79:3-5).[8]

After this, Ezra goes to a field called Ardat (4 Ezra 9:26). This poses a few problems, since there are so many variant readings for the name of the field as to dishearten the

---

[5] Ibid., p. 9. Cf. *Stromateis* 3.16.
[6] Stone. *Fourth Ezra*, p. 302. Variant readings in the Ethiopic text and in the first Arabic version give a positive command, 'do fast'; however, a witness as ancient as Tertullian already dismissed Ezra's practice in the episode as full fasting (*De ieiunio*. 9.1) and called it a 'partial' one as in Daniel. Cf. Stone. *Fourth Ezra*, p. 36.
[7] The reference to the flowers appears only in the Latin, Syriac and Armenian versions. Cf. Stone. *Fourth Ezra*, p. 302.
[8] David Satran. 'Daniel: Seer, Philosopher, Holy Man' in: George W. E. Nickelsburg and John J. Collins (eds). *Ideal Figures in Ancient Judaism: Profiles and Paradigms*. Chico: Scholars Press, 1980, p. 39.

search for an actual place; but it is anyway clearly stated that the seer is commanded to go out of his house in Babylon (as we can see from the very beginning of the Jewish section of the apocalypse, 4 Ezra 3:1), and the writer pays great attention to location details in the text, such as the name given to the field.[9] However, Ezra apparently does not obey the command strictly, for he admits having eaten flowers *and* the plants of the field (the well-being described by Ezra after eating them echoes Daniel). It would look from this passage that Ezra is undergoing a vegetarian diet rather than ingesting the flowers for their own sake. However, the reference to vegetables other than the flowers may be casual and Ezra's visions are apparently attached to the eating of the flowers indeed, because the command and the story themselves are odd (i.e. a command to avoid meat or to observe *kashrut* would not seem strange in the context). After seven days, Ezra lies on the grass and finally begins to enquire God about His justice, then he gets the vision of the weeping woman who, in time, turns out to be heavenly Jerusalem (4 Ezra 9:38).

In the whole complex of preparation for the vision described in the last passages, it must be noted that the seer possibly did not perceive vegetarianism and the eventual inducement by the flowers as separate processes. In this respect, too, we may have another parallel between Daniel and 4 Ezra – both are men whose action takes place in Babylon, one Danielic vision finds its way explicitly in 4 Ezra and both men undergo a diet of vegetables.

The field without any human construction ('in campum florum ubi domus non est aedificata') echoes the stone cut out 'not by human hands' of Dan 2:34.

Besides the flowers, God commands Ezra to pray 'continually', also a means of ecstatic inducement present in many other texts (1 En. 13:6–10; 39:9–14; Dan 9:3; 3 Bar. 1:1–3; T. 12 Patr. 2:3–6, etc.). However, Ezra himself does not mention praying after God's command but just states that he went to the field, ate the flowers and the plants, and 'the nourishment they afforded satisfied me' (4 Ezra 9:26); then he speaks to God (this can be understood as a prayer, in the terms it is formulated, but it comes as an effect of having sat in the field and eaten the flowers; this is what makes Ezra's heart troubled and is the cause of his mouth being opened).[10]

Regarding the theme that interests us here, it should be noted that the eating of the flowers, far from casual, is a strict command of God to the seer; while it is not stated that the vision arises as a consequence of eating them (rather, the seer tells us that he was nourished after eating – this could be a metaphor for spiritual fulfilment), it is reasonable to link them both because of the first command. The following points sum up the story told in 4 Ezra:

---

[9] The name has so many variants in the versions as to turn actual identification almost impossible: 'Arpad' in the Syriac version, 'Araab' in the Ethiopic, some Latin texts with 'Ardad', 'Ardas', 'Ardaf' or 'Ardaph'. Cf. Stone. *Fourth Ezra*, p. 304. The location of the field shows that the author is willing to give detail about the experience, and it is another element to be taken into consideration in order to consider it authentic (compare the huge amount of detail offered by Paul on his mystical experience, which gives a more real outlook to it).

[10] The Ethiopic and the first Arabic versions have it in an active meaning, that is, Ezra opens his mouth by himself. Cf. Stone. *Fourth Ezra*, p. 304.

1. The command comes together with other features (like the need of the flowers to be in a field with no human constructions).
2. God commands Ezra to pray as preparation (which he does, not before as ordered, but rather as a result of 'being nourished').
3. Complete fasting is altogether absent.
4. Vegetarianism is commanded both in the form of abstinence from meat and in the eating of the flowers but may be related to purity worries and not to health issues (i.e. not to be related to gaining more concentration or mental accuracy).
5. Wine is also forbidden to Ezra, and this is somewhat peculiar when the reader already knows he may take it in the seventh vision.
6. Having consumed other unspecified plants together with the flowers, the case for holding the latter responsible for the whole process of preparation in ch. 9 is somewhat weakened, although the reference may well have been casual (i.e. flowers = plants).
7. Nevertheless, whether it is the effect of a proper diet or of chemical inducement, from the seer's point of view it arrives as a consequence of God's command.

§4 4 Ezra after the ASC-induced experience

The key preparatory themes of ch. 9 are resumed in 4 Ezra 12:51: here Ezra consoles the people for his prolonged absence due to the fifth vision (the eagle, explicitly related to Dan 7).

> So the people went into the city, as I told them to do. But I sat in the field for seven days, as the angel had commanded me; and I ate only of the flowers of the field, and my food was of plants during those days.

The opposition between city and field location for the visions of the text is present again in Ezra's statement that he would remain seven days more (as the angel commanded him in 12:39) in the field, only eating the flowers (here the text of 4 Ezra has 'flowers' and 'plants' as equivalent terms). While the visionary episodes in 4 Ezra 9 most likely describe experiences while awake, the sixth vision in ch. 13 is described by Ezra as a dream. It should be noted, in addition, that the relation between flowers and the visionary episode is far less clear in ch. 12: the angel simply pleads Ezra to wait seven days more to discover whatever more God would tell him besides the interpretation of the eagle vision (4 Ezra 12:38–39). The cause-effect relation here, if at all present, is less clear than in ch. 9.

Finally, the last passage of 4 Ezra describing possible inducement for visions by means of mind-altering substances comes in ch. 14. There, in 14:38–48, Ezra is again in the field (it seems quite clear that it is referring to Ardat or to the field named in a similar way in the versions). Ezra shall not be disturbed for forty days (echoing Moses's experience[11] and possibly also that of Abraham, although in Apoc. Ab. 9:7 the

---

[11] Ibid., p. 303.

command is not exactly to fast but 'to abstain from every kind of food cooked by fire, and from drinking of wine and from anointing [yourself] with oil'[12]); and contrary to most visionary experiences described in apocalyptic texts, Ezra is not alone but has taken five scribes with him.[13]

What happens next is not a vision in the strict sense of the term but an auditive experience: Ezra hears a voice that commands him to drink from a cup, thus marking the beginning of the visual part of the experience proper (4 Ezra 14:38).

> So I took five men, as he commanded me, and we proceeded to the field, and remained there. And on the next day, behold, a voice called me, saying, 'Ezra, open your mouth and drink what I give you to drink.' Then I opened my mouth, and behold, a cup was offered to me; it was full of something like water, but its color was like fire. And I took it and drank; and when I had drunk it, my heart poured forth understanding, and wisdom increased in my breast, for my spirit retained its memory; and my mouth was opened, and was no longer closed. And the Most High gave understanding to the five men, and by turns they wrote what was dictated, in characters which they did not know. They sat forty days, and wrote during the daytime, and ate their bread at night. As for me, I spoke in the daytime and was not silent at night. So during the forty days ninety-four books were written.

After having taken it, Ezra undergoes a transformation, and three things happen to what we would call Ezra's 'mind': his heart pours from understanding, his wisdom increases in his breast and his spirit retains his memory.[14] His mouth was opened and did not close; Ezra's companions were also given the gift of understanding by God (the means of which are not stated), so that they might write down what Ezra was saying in 'characters that they did not know' (rather than describing some ecstatic phenomenon like glossolalia, speaking in unknown tongues, this reference probably implies the use of the square Aramaic script by the scribes[15]). We are not told that Ezra ate anything after he drank from the cup (contrary to the scribes who, we are told, ate at night); he does this for forty days, with the final output of ninety-four books, of which twenty-four should be made public and the remaining seventy not. This marks the end not only of the visions of ch. 14 but also of the chapter itself and, thus, of the Jewish core of the book besides the last two chapters, of Christian origin. The Syriac text includes two more verses that say that Ezra was 'caught up and taken to the place of those who are like him, after he had written all these things', but this reference alone does little to consider

---

[12] Cf. also Ithamar Gruenwald. *Apocalyptic and Merkavah Mysticism*. Leiden: Brill, 1980, p. 52.

[13] Gunnel André. 'Ecstatic Prophesy in the Old Testament' in: Holm. *Religious Ecstasy*, p. 190, for the idea of the relative 'loneliness' of the classical prophet as related to the pagan prophets, going together in groups.

[14] In Jewish apocalyptic writings, 'heart' can, among other things, represent the intellectual function; 'breast' is possibly related to it. Cf. David S. Russell. *The Method and Message of Jewish Apocalyptic*. Philadelphia: Westminster Press, 1964, pp. 142–4.

[15] Stone. *Fourth Ezra*, p. 439. The use of Aramaic, also important in Daniel and in the Persian world at large, reinforces this idea on the part of the author of 4 Ezra.

the revelatory experiences described by the author as being essentially concerned with heavenly journeys as, for example, 1 Enoch or 3 Enoch. In the passage from ch. 14 there is the clearest cause-and-effect relation in the chemical practices discussed: the seer states clearly that *when* he drank the liquid his heart poured understanding and so forth. The command, the action and the vision are very clearly linked.

As a final balance of the ecstatic experiences described in 4 Ezra 14:38-48 we could state the following:

1. The experience described involves other people than the apocalyptic seer (the scribes).
2. The ingested substance resembles something hitherto forbidden (wine).
3. The subsequent experience is not exactly a vision but a prodigious deed (the writing of the books).
4. The scribes, although performing a secondary role and although we do not have the same amount of information about them, end up inspired in a similar way to Ezra, albeit with less impressive means and less intensity (for they must stop to eat at night, while Ezra needs not stop).[16]

§5 A brief typology of the apparatus involved in the experience of 4 Ezra

The chemically induced experiences described by the apocalyptic seer disguised under the name of Ezra can be roughly divided in two groups: 4 Ezra 9:23-29 and 12:51 on one side and 4 Ezra 14:38-48 on the other. The first group involves certain foods and abstinence from alcohol, together with prayer which, however, may be playing only a conventional role in the visions described (i.e. while being a major ASC inducer in other texts, it is clearly less underlined than the ingestion of substances in 4 Ezra, and not only from the modern scholar's point of view; it looks so stereotyped in 4 Ezra that prayer appears *after* the eating of the flowers, thus not being a cause of inducement).

On the other hand, the second group, 4 Ezra 14:38-48, involves a more fantastic and elaborate experience. Before trying to find out what the drink was, we should bear in mind that the theme of something 'like fire' that gives inspiration may be connected to the Holy Spirit.[17] Besides, the mere idea that Ezra was 'dictating' sacred books probably implies that the Sinaitic revelation still had room to be enlarged,[18] an idea

---

[16] All the considerations above are subject to one major difficulty permeating the whole issue, namely the pseudepigraphic nature of authorship; thus, we cannot discuss properly who had the experience (if there is any indeed), but nevertheless we can analyse the practices described in the passages. For possibilities regarding the relationship between the presumed and actual authors, see Michael E. Stone. 'Apocalyptic – Vision or Hallucination?' in: *Selected Studies in Pseudepigrapha and Apocrypha with Special Reference to the Armenian Tradition*. Leiden: Brill, 1991; and Frederik Torm. 'Die Psychologie der Pseudonymität im Hinblick auf die Literatur des Urchristentums' in: Norbert Brox (ed.). *Pseudepigraphie in der Heidnischen und Jüdisch-Christlichen Antike*. Darmstadt: Wissenschaftliche Buchgesellschaft, 1977 (original chapter from 1932).

[17] An association made by many and well developed by Russell. Cf. *Method*, pp. 171-2.

[18] Stone. 'Apocalyptic', p. 424.

that may reinforce the presence of the Holy Spirit in Ezra as he drank from the cup. The episode has parallels in the scroll eaten by Ezekiel (Ezek 2:8–3:3) and thus to the author of Revelation (Rev 10:9–10), who also claims to have had sensory experiences related to ingestion.

The cup may also have a negative connotation as the means for God to madden peoples or nations (Jer 25:15–16); it may also be a symbol of vocation (Mart. Isa. 5:14; Mark 10:38; 14:36). There are also many parallels for describing mystical experience in terms of drunkenness, the best known perhaps being Philo's *De ebrietate* 146–148:

> To many of the unenlightened it may seem to be drunken, crazy and beside itself … indeed, it is true that these sober ones are drunk in a sense … and they receive the loving cup from perfect virtue.

Even if several different authors are not the case, the spirit of both groups of visions analysed is a bit diverse from each other. The theme will be resumed in the conclusion to this chapter.

§6 ASC-induced experienced in Persian texts

The material used in this next section is mainly composed of Persian texts. Persian influence in the theme of preparation for visions in 4 Ezra is a reasonable supposition; however, it should be noted that the dating of all the Persian texts listed below is considerably later than those possible for 4 Ezra. This is the greatest single reason that renders impossible any definite conclusion about the influence of Persian sources on the apocalypse text we are examining; it may indeed pose a definite barrier.[19] A different matter is presented by the dating of the mythical themes contained in them, which will be addressed at the end of this section.[20]

The sources quoted here derive basically from eight Persian texts, the JN, the WD, the ZN, the 'Conversion of Vištasp', the ZWY, the experience of Vištasp referred to in the Dk, a reference in the AWN and passages of the Vd.[21]

In the JN (also a pseudepigraphic text, written in the name of an old sage), Jāmāsp receives from Zaraθuštra the gift of knowledge by means of a flower. This is also the theme of the Pahlavi text WD 19 (this text should be from the twelfth century – there

---

[19] John J. Collins. 'Apocalypse: The Morphology of a Genre' in: *Semeia* 14 (1979): 207. As the issue stands, Persian material is more recent than Jewish sources, although the mythical cores of the first most likely antecede the latter. But this cannot be hard-proofed as investigation stands.

[20] Examination of Mesopotamian relations to Jewish apocalyptic ecstatic practices showed no similar means of preparation but rather similar contents of the visions, not to be dealt with here. Cf. Wifred G. Lambert. *The Background of Jewish Apocalyptic*. London: Athlone Press, 1978; and Helmer Ringgren. 'Akkadian Apocalypses' in: *AMWNE*, pp. 379–86.

[21] For a brief overview of the place of these books in relation to the output of Zoroastrian texts, cf. Geo Widengren. *Die Religionen Irans*. Stuttgart: W. Kohlhammer, 1965; and Sven Hartman. 'Datierung der jungavestischen Apokalyptik' in: Daniel Hellholm (ed.). *Apocalypticism in the Mediterranean World and the Near East: Proceedings of the International Colloquium on Apocalypticism, Uppsala, August 12-17, 1979*. Tübingen: Mohr, 1983, pp. 61–76.

is a dated manuscript from 1123 CE, referring to another one from 609 CE, whose existence is far from sure – written in Persian and 'disguised' as MP);[22] indeed, the tradition that described the acquisition of mystical knowledge by Jāmāsp resembles very much that of Ezra regarding the flowers, as the drinking of the blessed wine looks like the experience of 4 Ezra 14 – the main difference in the passage being the fact that here we have two different seers:

> 19. And behold: One day King Vištâsp, king of kings, [willing] to challenge his [Zaraθuštra's] prophetic achievements, asked Zaraθuštra that he gives him what he would ask: 'That I may be immortal and exempt from old age, that swords and spears be incapable of hurting my body, that I may know all the secrets of heaven, present, past and future and that I may see, in this life, the better existence of the just!' Zaraθuštra said: 'Ask any of these four things for yourself, and the other three for three other people; the Creator will grant them more easily.' So King Vištâsp wanted to see in this life the better existence of the just. With the help of Lord Ohrmazd, just Zaraθuštra [performed a sacrifice rite] and laid down milk, a flower, wine and a grenade. After having exalted and invoked the Well-doing Creator, he gave the blessed wine to Vištâsp so that he would fall asleep and see the better existence; he gave the flower to Jamâsp, the best of men and he was taught, by means of visions, about all events present, past and future; he gave the grenade to Spanddât whose body became sacred and invulnerable to pointed swords; he gave the blessed milk to Pêšôtan son of King Vištâsp who obtained immortality in the field and eternal youth.[23]

In the ZN (after the ninth century, for it quotes the earlier Dk and is written in Pahlavi[24]) it is said that Jāmāsp acquired his gift by smelling the flower consecrated by Zaraθuštra in a ceremony:

> He gave to Jāmāsp a bit of the consecrated perfume, and all sciences became understandable to him. He knew about all things to happen and that would happen until the day of resurrection.[25]

The form of the text also resembles 4 Ezra because of the question-answer form as introduced by Vištasp (e.g. 'This pure religion, how long will it last?'). In terms of the visionary process itself, it is remarkable that Jāmāsp interprets for King Vištasp a

---

[22] Tord Olsson. 'The Apocalyptic Activity: The Case of Jāmāsp Nāmag' in: Hellholm. *Apocalypticism in the Mediterranean World and the Near East*, p. 32. For the dating, cf. Marijan Molé. *La légende de Zoroastre: Selon les textes Pehlevis*. Paris: Klincksieck, 1967, p. 9.
[23] Molé. *La légende de Zoroastre*, p. 133.
[24] Yamauchi. *Persia and the Bible*, p. 410. It was probably written in the thirteenth century.
[25] Olsson. 'The Apocalyptic Activity', p. 32. In Mary Boyce's translation ('On the Antiquity of Zoroastrian Apocalyptic' in: *BSOAS* 47 (1984): 60), the flower is rendered as 'incense': the mixture of the latter with wine has a maddening effect not on visionaries but on the elephants of 3 Macc 5:45: 'Now when the animals had been brought virtually to a state of madness, so to speak, by the very fragrant draughts of wine mixed with frankincense.'

dream in much the same fashion that Daniel did it for Nebuchadnezzar.[26] Drinking is alluded to also in the PahRiv 47 ('Conversion of Vishtaspa', the *rivayats* were composed between the fifteenth and eighteenth centuries, in MP[27]), when Vištasp receives the perception on the ways of religion after a visit by a divine messenger who makes him drink a cup full of wine or haoma[28] mixed again with a narcotic, *mang* (whose significance will be discussed shortly):

> 27. Ormazd sent Nêrôsang: 'Go to Artvahišt and tell him: Put mang in the wine and give it for Vištâsp to drink.' 28. Artvahišt did so. 29. Having drunk it, he evaporated into the field. 30. His soul was taken to Garôtmân [Paradise] to show him what he could gain if he accepted the Religion. 31. When he woke up from the sleep, he cried to Hutôs: 'Where is Zaraθuštra so that I may accept the Religion?' 32. Zaraθuštra heard his voice, came and Vištâsp accepted the Religion.[29]

Zaraθuštra drinks the water that Ahura Mazda gives to him and acquires his wisdom, in a similar fashion to the cup episode in 4 Ezra 14. In the ZWY (the text is in MP and a *zand* intends to be an interpretation of a (putative) lost book of the Avesta, the BY;[30] it is quite similar in themes to the *Oracles of Hystaspes*, something which may suggest its antiquity) 3:4–8:

> 4. Zarduxšt, in thought, was displeased. 5. Ohrmazd, through the wisdom of omniscience, knew that he, Spitāmān Zarduxšt of the righteous frawahr, thought. 6. He took the hand of Zarduxšt, he Ohrmazd, the bountiful spirit, the Creator of the world of material beings, holy ... put his wisdom of omniscience, in the form of water, on the hand of Zarduxšt and said 'Drink'. 7. And Zarduxšt drank of it. He blended the wisdom of omniscience in Zarduxšt. 8. Seven days and nights was Zarduxšt in the wisdom of Ohrmazd.[31]

In Dk 7.4.84–86, Vištasp drinks a mixture of wine or haoma with some narcotic, possibly henbane. The same episode in the ZWY, a later redaction, has this potation replaced by water as we saw above, possible evidence of the practice being rejected in later times.[32]

---

[26] Anders Hultgård. 'Forms and Origins of Iranian Apocalypticism' in: Hellholm. *Apocalypticism in the Mediterranean World and the Near East*, p. 401.
[27] Boyce. *Textual Sources*, p. 5.
[28] An intoxicating mythical drink whose exact nature has yet to be explained; it is generally identified with soma, or even with other hallucinogenic plants, as we will see below.
[29] Molé. *La légende de Zoroastre*, p. 121.
[30] However, efforts to reconstruct an Avestic *Bahman Yasht* from the late commentaries we have remain problematic: for a full discussion of the many problems involved, cf. Cereti. ZWY, p. 14.
[31] Cereti. ZWY, pp. 150–1. The author suggests the passage implies a reference to psychotropic drugs and refers to the parallel in AWN 3.15 (cf. the commentary on the *Bahman Yasht* by Cereti, op.cit. p. 179). Ezra also sits in the field for seven days in 4 Ezra 12:51, as seen above.
[32] Hultgård. 'Ecstasy and Vision', p. 222. The *Dinkard* is not earlier than the ninth century.

Ohrmazd the creator sent ... to the residence of Wishtāsp the divinity Nērōsang ... to cause Wishtāsp to consume the illuminating nourishment which would give his soul eye vision over the spiritual existence, by reason of which Wishtāsp saw great mystery and glory. As it says in the Avesta, 'Ohrmazd the creator said to the divinity Nērōsang: "Go, fly on ... to the residence of Wishtāsp ... and say this to Ashawahisht: 'Powerful Ashawahisht, take the excellent bowl, more excellent than the other bowls which are well made ... for conveying for our own sake hōm and mang [maybe henbane, see the conclusion of this chapter] to Wishtāsp and cause the lofty ruler Kay Wishtāsp to drink it.'"'[33]

The AWN (a late text, possibly late Sasanian, in Pahlavi[34]) also talks about preparation of the seer by means of taking wine with narcotic, in 2.25-31:

The priests of the religion filled three golden cups with wine and with henbane of Vištāsp and presented to Vīrāz one cup for the Good Thought, one second for the Good Word and a third for the Good Deed.[35]

It must be noted that in the passage above, no ascetic practice similar to the ones of 4 Ezra occurs (much on the contrary, Viraz prepares himself by eating – not fasting – and nothing of the ascetic practices of the seer in 4 Ezra seems present).

Finally, in Vd 4.14 (the text may have been started during Vologeses IV (r. 148-191 CE) and completed under the Sasanian Khosraw I (r. 531-579 CE), in Pahlavi[36]), old women bring henbane to cause abortion:

Thus this who [is] a girl [looks] for an old woman; these girl-injurers consulted together; this who [is] an old woman brings mang or šēt [one is called that of Vištāsp, one that of Zartušt]; [it is something] that kills [i.e. kills (the fetus) in the womb], or [it is a means to] throwing off [i.e. (the fetus) comes, afterwards dies], or whatever plant which is aborfacient [a sort of drug]; [and she says] thus 'with this [drug] the son is killed.'[37]

---

[33] David S. Flattery and Martin Schwartz. *Haoma and Hermaline: The Botanical Identity of the Indo-Iranian Sacred Hallucinogen 'Soma' and Its Legacy in Religion, Language, and Middle Eastern Folklore.* Ann Arbor: University of Michigan Press, 1989, p. 18. An older and slightly different translation can be found at Molé. *La légende de Zoroastre*, p. 59.

[34] Walter Belardi. *The Pahlavi Book of the Righteous Viraz.* Rome: University Department of Linguistics and Italo-Iranian Cultural Centre, 1979, p. 10.

[35] Gignoux considers these three cups are merely symbolic of the fact that Vīrāz observes those three virtues better than anybody else; besides, he translates *mang* for henbane (*jusquiame* in the French translation). Cf. translation and notes in 'Apocalypses et voyages extra-terrestres dans l'Iran mazdéen' in: Claude Kappler (ed.). *Apocalypses et voyages dans l'au-delà.* Paris: CERF, 1987, p. 367. An older version and commentary can be found in Belardi. *Pahlavi Book*, p. 92; cf. also from Philippe Gignoux. 'Notes sur la rédaction de l'Ardāy Vīrāz Nāmag' in: *Zeitschrift der Deutschen Morgenländischen Gesellschaft*, Supplementa 1 (1969).

[36] Yamauchi. *Persia and the Bible*, p. 407.

[37] Belardi. *Pahlavi Book*, p. 114.

In the passage above we apparently have two different drugs, which may be vision-inducing or abortifacient.[38]

It should be noted that the passages above, important as they may be, do not suggest that chemical inducement was the unique means by which Persian seers might prepare themselves for ecstatic experiences: Persian references are also comparatively rare, although outnumbering by far the ones in Jewish apocalyptic, and do not replace more traditional forms of preparation such as prayer or fasting in Zoroastrian texts.[39] But the insistent mentioning both of wine and plants as means of getting inspired deserves closer attention.

§7 Varieties of ASC inducers

Evidence from 4 Ezra checked against Persian data gives us the following items as being possibly chemical stimulants for the visionaries: wine (in 4 Ezra 14:38-48; ZWY 3:7-8; WD 19), wine or haoma with narcotics (Dk 7.4.84-86; AVN 2.25-28; Y 10.17; CV 47), henbane (as abortive in Vd 4.14), unspecified flowers that could be henbane (4 Ezra 9:23-29; 12:51; again Jāmāsp in WD 19; ZN) and a further reference to haoma/soma in utterly unfavourable terms, which shall be examined below. Since in these references we are generally not guessing what the substance is, but the sources tell us in a much clearer way than in 4 Ezra, we should take a look at the possibilities of these ASC-inducing substances being available to the visionary of 4 Ezra in the conclusion to this chapter.

The fact that the Persian texts that relate to practices similar to 4 Ezra are, without exception, later than the Jewish texts does not mean their mythical cores cannot be older. To begin with, the figure of Vishtaspa (or, in its Greek form, Hystaspes) is much older than the earliest Jewish apocalypses themselves (i.e. earlier than the third century BCE) and came to be known in a variety of syncretistic guises throughout the Mediterranean.[40] This is no proof of the anteriority of the Persian texts (after all, we also have an 'earlier' Ezra) but at least assures that the figure of Vishtaspa cannot be later than that of Ezra. Besides that, there are a number of other mythical themes portrayed in late Persian texts (like the ZWY) that are known through earlier sources (like the

---

[38] Ibid., p. 115.
[39] Hultgård. 'Ecstasy and Vision', p. 224. The voyages described here have a non-historical flavour, that is, they were supposedly performed by mythical characters. This does not exclude allusions to historical practices, but these should be taken with care – while the visionary is taken to an otherworldly voyage in the *Arday Vīrāz* passage, by contrast to the historical and earthly explanations given in 4 Ezra. Real mystical experiences similar to those described above can be found in ancient Iran and will be discussed below. Cf. Gignoux. 'La signification du voyage extra-terrestre dans l'eschatologie mazdéenne', pp. 64–8; and Shaked. *Dualism in Transformation*, p. 49.
[40] We have in fact two different characters that sometimes get mixed up in later tradition – one being the king that protects Zaraθuštra and the other being the father of Darius I. In the texts here discussed, we are referring to the first. Cf. Hans Windisch. *Die Orakel des Hystaspes*. Amsterdam: Koninklijke Akademie van Wetenschappen te Amsterdam, 1929, p. 10; cf. also Vicente Dobroruka and Robert A. Kraft. 'Oracles of Hystaspes: A New Translation and Introduction' in: James Davila, Richard Bauckham and Alexander Panoyatov (eds). *Old Testament Pseudepigrapha: More Noncanonical Scriptures*. Vol. 2. Grand Rapids: Eerdmans, forthcoming.

four ages associated to metals and monarchies, already quoted in Theopompus – fourth century BCE – or in the fragments collectively known as the *Oracles of Hystaspes*). This is indirect evidence that late Persian texts contain cores that can be of an earlier date even if not of Persian origin. The theme of the cup that gives wisdom, being already present in the Y 10.17, is quite older: the Y preserves material from the *Gāthās* (sacred texts traditionally attributed to Zaraθuštra himself), including Y 10.17, which deals with the theme of the wisdom cup, in this case related to haoma:

> Thereupon spake Zarathushtra: Praise to Haoma, Mazda-made. Good is Haoma, Mazda-made. All the plants of Haoma praise I, on the heights of lofty mountains, in the gorges of the valleys, in the clefts [of sundered hillsides] cut for the bundles bound by women. From the silver cup I pour Thee to the golden chalice over. Let me not thy [sacred] liquor spill to earth, of precious cost.

The dating of the Y depends on the dating attributed to Zaraθuštra, but even supposing the prophet to be a figure living as late as the sixth century BCE (unlikely, because of the many parallels of Gathic material to the RV), the Y is much earlier than 4 Ezra.[41]

For the relation between the flowers and disclosure, however, no earlier parallel than that of the JN was found (there is one reference to flowers in a similar context in Y 42.4, related to haoma, but not exactly the same as older texts). It should be noted that, while if the *mang* put in the wine is henbane, we would be deprived of long-duration links were it to be translated as hemp, the latter being present in Scythian rituals reported by Herodotus; this would give us an earlier dating for shared Indo-Iranian ecstatic practices.

As a conclusion to this part of the chapter I should begin by pointing out that the difficulties in establishing a definite conclusion are overwhelming and that, unless dramatic new evidence changes the current picture, we will be left forever with no certainties on the matter of the relation between 4 Ezra and eventual Persian sources.

That being said, I am inclined to accept a relation other than casual between them, for many reasons. First of all, the themes of the flower and the drink that beget knowledge are striking parallels: it is important to notice that, contrary to other quotations of 'cups' playing an important part in stories both in the OT and the NT, in 4 Ezra the cup is part of a revelatory process: the seer becomes enlightened after taking it (or rather does an amazing feat which is in itself some revelation, the writing of the ninety-four books).

These parallels leave us, as always, with three possibilities: they can be genealogically related, structurally related or simply a coincidence that these themes are shared by our sources. And to say with certainty that there is any kind of genealogical link is out of question, for reasons already stated.[42]

---

[41] Boyce. *Textual Sources*, p. 2.
[42] A possible exception would be the shamanistic traces present in the *Testament of Abraham*, according to Gignoux – the whole episode resembling, in fact, the voyage of Arda Viraz. Cf. Gignoux. 'Les voyages chamaniques dans le monde iranien', pp. 263–5. By the same reasoning, the

§8 Cultures and chemistry

Structurally, it has already been said that different societies attain a similar level of organization by means of different institutions;[43] this would imply that the role of Persian seers and the author of 4 Ezra might be analogous and independently achieved. While we know very little about who wrote, read and/or consumed Jewish apocalyptic literature, and even less about its Hellenistic counterparts (i.e. Persian, Egyptian and Babylonian apocalypses), it should be noted that both Persian and Jewish visionaries were subject to similar conditions as related to foreign rule and oppression. In this sense, dating of the Persian sources may be less important than in a direct genealogical approach, for even being late redactions, their updating shows anomic conditions similar to those experienced by the author of 4 Ezra (e.g. the four kingdoms in the ZWY, taken to mean Greek, Byzantine, Muslim and Turkish rules).[44] It must be stated that we know almost nothing about the seers themselves, both in Jewish as in Persian apocalyptic – while we have much information about *magoi* and Zoroastrians at large, it is unwise to just identify those groups with the seers of the texts examined.

Finally, the Persian seers and the visionary of 4 Ezra may have gone through similar experiences by pure chance: taking the same ASC inducers, they had similar frames of visions, although these were developed in fairly different ways due to the cultural differences between their two worlds; after all, it is culture that changes, not chemistry.[45] I do not think this should be the case; similarities between hallucinogenic cults both in the Old and in the New World point to a common shared heritage that may go back to the Palaeolithic.[46]

In terms of the experiences described in 4 Ezra (alas, in Persian sources, too), we have the additional difficulty of pseudepigraphy. Thus, even while using Elmer O'Brien's categories to understand our object (i.e. if the object confronted by the mystic is definite, if the confrontation is direct and if the experience goes contrary to his/her own cultural frame of mind, we should be facing evidence of an authentic experience),[47] we are still left with very little; however, if these criteria are applied to the text we have, we must bear in mind the unique character of the preparatory practices described, in terms of Second Temple Jewish literature.

The effects of one candidate plant described (henbane) and its spread would make it quite possible that we are referring to an actual preparatory process here.[48] Other possibilities, such as hallucinogenic mushrooms, have been discussed in the

---

use of hallucinogens in Zoroastrian mystical experiences is considered by Gignoux as having a key role to establish a link with Siberian shamanism (ibid., p. 244).

[43] Ioan M. Lewis. *Ecstatic Religion: An Anthropological Study of Spirit Possession and Shamanism*. Harmondsworth: Penguin, 1971, p. 2.

[44] Samuel K. Eddy. *The King Is Dead: Studies in the Near Eastern Resistance to Hellenism 334–31 B.C.* Lincoln: University of Nebraska Press, 1961, p. 17; Collins. *Apocalypse*, p. 209.

[45] Peter Furst. *Hallucinogens and Culture*. San Francisco: Chandler & Sharp, 1976, p. 17.

[46] Ibid., p. 2.

[47] Elmer O'Brien. *Varieties of Mystic Experience: an Anthology and Interpretation*. New York: Holt, Rinehart and Winston, 1964, pp. 4–6.

[48] In opposition to the effects of hemp.

past with controversial methods and results.[49] However, the use of the term *mang* has been recently proved to refer not particularly to henbane or to hemp, at least in the time of the writing of the older sources, but it appears to be rather a generic term for 'psychoactive drug'.[50]

Discussing the substances quoted in the sources, I think that wine should be left out of this analysis as a stand-alone ASC inducer for the simple reason that its diffusion, availability and use were nearly universal to Eurasian peoples at the time of the writing of 4 Ezra (wine with narcotics is an altogether different matter and shall be examined below); this universality renders it useless as proof. Even if we were dealing with plain wine in 4 Ezra 14:38-48, scholars consider it a comparatively weak ASC inducer.[51]

Regarding the other agents cited, hallucinogenic drugs in general have the power to induce visual or other kinds of hallucinations and of divorcing the subject from objective reality.[52] Most of these substances derive from plants, hemp being one of the most common; its effects are disputed among modern scholars, but ancient testimony gives credit to it as a powerful ASC inducer.[53] It looks possible (but unlikely) at first sight that the experience described by the Persian seers in the passages listed above is real, and even that Zaraθuštra's ecstatic experiences have been aided by hemp.[54] It should be noted, however, that the Persian terms *bang*, *banj* and *mang* only came to be used as a reference including hemp after the Arab conquest, possibly in the twelfth century: according to Walter Belardi, in the AVN this virtually excludes the possibility that the seer is mixing wine with hemp but rather with henbane.[55]

Wine mixed with hemp has its use well attested in ancient sources: Galen attests to its use mixed with wine after meals as a digestive aid (*De facultatibus alimentarum* 100.49). Pliny says a lot about hemp in the *Natural History* (20.97) but mostly in therapeutic terms. However, the best reference on the issue for our purposes comes

---

[49] It is a pity that this specific theme lacks more bibliography; the only major work devoted to the theme is John Allegro's highly and understandably controversial *The Sacred Mushroom and the Cross; a Study of the Nature and Origins of Christianity within the Fertility Cults of the Ancient Near East* (London: Hodder & Stoughton, 1970). In his book Allegro says nothing about 4 Ezra, Persian visionary processes or even henbane at large.

[50] We cannot know what the earlier use of the term was, but it should be noted that the Arabic *banj* refers to henbane, to datura and to intoxicating plants in general (al-Bīrūnī used the term in the eleventh century to refer to datura). In thirteenth-century Persia *mang* meant both henbane and hashish. Cf. Flattery and Schwartz. *Haoma and Hermaline*, pp. 16-17, 127. Hultgård is also vague on the interchangeable use of hemp and henbane regarding Persian texts; cf. 'Ecstasy and Vision', p. 223.

[51] Furst. *Hallucinogens*, p. 17.

[52] Norman R. Farnsworth. 'Hallucinogenic Plants' in: *Science*, New Series, 162.3858 (1968): 1086.

[53] Ibid., p. 1087; cf. William A. Emboder Jr. 'Ritual Use of the *Cannabis Sativa* L.: A Historical-Ethnographic Survey' in: Peter Furst (ed.). *Flesh of the Gods: The Ritual Use of Hallucinogens*. London: Allen & Unwin, 1972, pp. 219-20.

[54] H. Leuner. 'Die toxische Ekstase' in: Theodor Spoerri (ed.). *Beiträge zur Ekstase*. Bibliotheca psychiatrica et neurologica. Basel: Karger, 1968, pp. 87-8. For the textual reasons given below, I find this not to be clear as Leuner puts it; I find even less convincing Mircea Eliade's explanation, which simply accepts *bangha* and its derivation *mang* to mean 'hemp' already in Sasanian times. Cf. 'Ancient Scythia and Iran' in: George Andrews and Simon Vinkenoog (eds). *The Book of Grass; an Anthology of Indian Hemp*. Harmondsworth: Penguin Books, 1972.

[55] Cf. Belardi. *Pahlavi Book*, p. 114. See also a newer translation by Fereydun Vahman. *Arda Wiraz Nāmag: The Iranian 'Divina Commedia'*. London: Curzon Press, 1986, p. 9.

from Homer (*Odyssey* 4.220). Being received by Menelaus, Telemachus is having a banquet and there Helen mixes something in the wine which deserves our attention:

> Then Helen, daughter of Zeus, took other counsel. At once she cast into the wine of which they were drinking a drug [νηπενθές] to quiet all pain and strife, and bring forgetfulness of every ill.[56]

In the sequence of the text it is also stated that this drug, *nepenthes*, had been given to Helen by Polydamna, a woman from Egypt – a land abundant to these drugs and where, according to Homer, every man is a doctor. The nature of *nepenthes* is far from clear; the reference to Egypt is especially obscure if it is to be understood as hemp, thus matching the effects described by the poet.[57]

But the most important hallucinogenic plant in our context is henbane. It was present in Palestine of the time of 4 Ezra (*Datura*, the genus of henbane, has existed for many millennia all over the world, with the exception of South America)[58] but is not quoted in the authoritative work on biblical flora by Grace Crowfoot and Louise Baldensperger.[59] In this work extensive reference is made to the mandrake, a plant surrounded by bigger folklore. Mandrake is also used as a narcotic,[60] and ancient reference points to its use mixed with henbane and poppy capsules in Diodorus Siculus and with wine in Homer.[61]

§9 The most popular ASC inducer

Henbane, besides being available throughout the Near East, is often related to the *Atropa belladonna* (nightshade) and, more importantly, gives us many instances of its uses and effects in first-person experiences, old and recent. We should now take a closer look at these.

Hyosciamus niger is the scientific name of henbane and it belongs to the family of the *Solanacae*, which includes common plants like potato and tobacco, and that comprises the most important group of plants used to establish contact with the other

---

[56] Shaul Shaked makes the point that in Zoroastrian myth *mang* was also given to *Gayomart*, the primordial ox, to soothe the pains of death; cf. *Dualism in Transformation*, p. 45.
[57] I shall return to this issue of the effects described in the passage; however, the interpretation given by Pascal Brotteaux to the whole text is worth mentioning, being so original. He claims that the drug used should be either henbane, datura or belladonna (all of which effectively cause a loss to the mnemonic faculties, according to the author); it should not be hemp, which according to him is incapable of causing the described effects. This is surprising when the effects on memory caused by hemp is almost commonsensical lore. Cf. 'The Ancient Greeks' in: Andrews and Vinkenoog. *The Book of Grass*, pp. 27–8.
[58] Richard E. Schultes and Albert Hoffman. *Plants of the Gods: Origins of Hallucinogenic Use*. New York: McGraw-Hill, 1979, pp. 27–8.
[59] Grace M. H. Crowfoot and Louise Baldensperger. *From Cedar to Hyssop: a Study in the Folklore of Plants in Palestine*. London: Sheldon Press, 1932.
[60] Ibid., p. 118.
[61] Emboder Jr. 'Ritual Use', pp. 218–19. In Diodorus, it appears in his *History* 1.97 and in Homer in the *Odyssey* passage, if we should understand *nepenthes* to be identical to it.

world, in terms of diffusion.⁶² All plants similar to henbane contain toxic substances in great quantity, one of which may be absorbed via the skin (atropine); there have been many reports of its use in medieval and modern times in witchcraft trials⁶³. The use of henbane and the practice of vegetarianism is even combined in some reports;⁶⁴ this is remarkably similar to the pattern of the first group of visions in 4 Ezra (9:23-29; 12:51) and may be a technical issue related to enhancing the effects of henbane.

Modern experiences with the use of henbane include those of Kiesewetter (1907) and of Prof. Will-Erich Peukert from Göttingen (1966). Both prepared ointments as Porta suggested in the seventeenth century and claimed to have had ecstatic experiences similar to those described by witches; Schenk breathed the smoke of burning henbane, said he felt his body separated from his soul, and had visions of rivers of molten metal (remarkably similar to the Persian experience regarding the Final Judgment e.g. in JN 17.14).⁶⁵ It should be noted that the experiences described are notably similar even taking into account that medieval reports - but not contemporary - have been informed via inquisitorial processes; there is also a difference in pattern regarding witchcraft/shamanism, for while both practices purport encounters with the other world, witches, contrary to shamans, would not manipulate spirits while in trance.⁶⁶

§10 Dead ends regarding ASCs

Apart from hemp and henbane, there is a third group of ASC-inducing plants that must be dealt with here, namely fly agaric (*Ammanita muscaria*). This must be done - even if briefly - for the reference in 4 Ezra 9:23-25 to the flowers in the field could relate to the agaric. We should remember that 4 Ezra 12:51 takes 'flowers' to be synonymous to 'plants'.

---

⁶² Michael Harner. 'The Role of Hallucinogenic Plants in European Witchcraft' in: Michael Harner (ed.). *Hallucinogens and Shamanism*. New York: Oxford University Press, 1970, p. 128.
⁶³ Ibid., 135-7. This explains the connection of witches with the broom, something that may have phallic connotations because of its use in applying the henbane ointment in the vagina. There are also accounts like the one by Nider (1692) and Laguna (1545), which tell of the use of henbane by suspects who claimed to travel to Sabbaths. Fray Diego Durán, an early witness of Spanish rule in Mexico (*Book of the Gods and Rites and the Ancient Calendar*), establishes a link in terms of the effects between henbane and the magical agaric of the Mexicans, *teotlacuali* ('flesh of the gods). Cf. Furst. *Hallucinogens*, pp. 13-14.
⁶⁴ See the reports by Porta, colleague of Galilei, in Harner. 'The Role of Hallucinogenic Plants', p. 138.
⁶⁵ Ibid., p. 139. On this issue it should be noted that, while not everybody has the same experiences with the same drugs (people who took LSD in controlled experiments in the fifties claimed to have had no experience at all, in contrast to the then fashionable accounts by Huxley; cf. Ernst Arbman. *Ecstasy or Religious Trance: In the Experience of the Ecstatics and from the Psychological Point of View*. Stockholm: Bokförlaget, 1963-70 (3 vols), vol. 1, Vision and Ecstasy, p. 196). The visions described are seldom - if ever - much different from the cultural environment of the seer. This means that, knowing exactly why they were taking henbane, modern scholars were consciously or unconsciously bound to have visions similar to the medieval witches. This accounts at the same time for the stereotyped visions of apocalyptic literature in general, and specifically of 4 Ezra, and gives an explanation to the same stereotype - the ancient seer, like the modern, could only 'see' what his cultural environment allowed him to.
⁶⁶ Harner. 'The Role of Hallucinogenic Plants', p. 146.

There are a number of references in Persian literature that also point to the mushroom, namely the parallel between the Indian passage in RV 8.4–10 and Y 48.10 – both suggesting the ingestion of urine, a practice known from Chinese Manichaeans.[67] It basically consists of the ingestion of the urine of people who had taken the fly agaric previously, and it is attested in Siberian shamans; the Persian passage in Y condemns it while the RV states that Indra was urinating soma. It is known that Indians have for long used mushrooms for hallucinogenic purposes, and it is possible then that both Persian and Indian passages relate to this usage.[68]

We have seen that cross-cultural parallels offer pictures where inductive processes similar to the ones reportedly undergone by the seer in 4 Ezra are abundant. The question remains, however, if these help explain something of the nature of the story told about the quoted vision episodes in 4 Ezra.

All these parallels in themselves do not prove direct borrowing by Jewish apocalypticists from external sources. When it comes to Persian issues, some specific points of disagreement arise.

The sharpest criticism of the idea of a Persian origin for Judaeo-Christian apocalyptic is laid out in the famous article by Gignoux.[69] In the text, Gignoux points out the greatest obstacles in tracing a direct, that is, genealogical, line from Persian to other apocalyptic forms. The major issues raised in the chapter are that on one hand the content of the so-called Persian apocalypses is composite, and, on the other, the dating offered even by the defendants of the influence theory is problematic.[70] Besides, Gignoux raises the always relevant issue about apocalyptic as a genre, something unheard of in Antiquity. This gets worse when it comes to Persian apocalyptic visionary passages, due to their lateness, with Gignoux suggesting even that the trajectory of the common *topoi* may have been quite the reverse, that is, Jewish-Christian ideas influencing Persian texts.[71]

Taken seriously, Gignoux's objections apparently make no distinction between the text as manuscript and taken as meaningful, cultural artefact – no matter how late the manuscripts of a given tradition may be, the ideas therein may be quite older. Homeric epic may be the most famous stance of oral tradition put down in writing centuries after its composition, although Gignoux has some right in claiming that a continuity between 1400 BCE (an eventual early date given for Zaraθuštra) and 900 CE (when a big part of the Zoroastrian texts had already been put down in writing), as proposed by Boyce, may be an exaggeration.[72] Even as we consider the latest evidence in the texts here dealt with, we would only end up with a second-century reference for the

---

[67] Robert G. Wasson. 'What Was the Soma of the Aryans?' in: Furst. *Flesh*, pp. 204–6. So in the Y passage, 'When, O Mazda, will the nobles understand the message? When will thou smite the filthiness of this intoxicant, through which the Karapans evilly deceive, and the wicked lords of the lands with purpose fell?'
[68] Farnsworth. 'Hallucinogenic Plants', p. 1089. The chapter also points to the possible identification of soma with *Ammanita muscaria*.
[69] 'L'apocalyptique iranienne est-elle vraiment la source d'autres apocalypses?'.
[70] Ibid., p. 71.
[71] Ibid. This is also the theme of Duchesne-Guillemin's 'Apocalypse juive et apocalypse iranienne', p. 759.
[72] Ibid., p. 76.

Vd – more likely to be from the fourth century – which is very little to speak with certainty about Persian influence on the preparatory processes of 4 Ezra, a first- or, at latest, second-century text.

§11 How seriously should the experiences described in the Persian sources be taken?

Another issue which we just hinted at above is that of the non-historical character of the experiences described, both for 4 Ezra and for the Persian sources. A different and important source altogether is provided by four inscriptions, dated between 290 and 293 CE, which describe in detail the other-worldly journey undergone by a priest called Kirdēr.[73] He asks for a visionary experience to reinforce his beliefs and is granted a tour of Heaven and Hell; stereotyped as the theme is in ancient literature, here we have dated evidence for people who claim to have undergone similar experiences.[74] The inscription is in a poor state so we cannot know exactly what preparations Kirdēr underwent before his voyage,[75] but we can at least hint that they should not be dismissed, as a whole, as late additions to Persian apocalyptic.

As has been pointed out, the change from fasting to the eating of flowers marks a decisive stage in Ezra's acquisition of understanding.[76] This leads us to the process described in 4 Ezra itself, which is surprisingly overlooked in Gignoux's chapter – we have a description of practices that lead to visions, something quite important when it comes to the use of the cup in 4 Ezra 14:38–42.

The cup, in every significant stance where it appears in the OT and also in the NT, has all kinds of meanings – but never the revelatory role ascribed to it in the passage above.

Vegetarianism as cleansing practice or as *kashrut* prescription also is not related to the ingestion of flowers, as in 4 Ezra 9 and 12. And resuming the issue of wine mixed with *nepenthes*, the main character in 4 Ezra is at pains to make it very clear that whatever the supposed experience was that he went through (or claims to have been through), *he retained the memory of it*. This can be understood as a negative conclusion regarding the use of hemp, whose physiological effects, regardless of other opinions seen above, include partial loss of memory.[77] The passage may be a clue to the idea that the experience described is real and involves actual ASC-inducing substances, whose nature the author tries to disclose. In some of the medieval cases quoted by Harner,[78]

---

[73] This was dealt with in other aspects in Chapter 4, especially in n. 82.
[74] Gignoux. 'La signification du voyage extra-terrestre', p. 65.
[75] Shaul Shaked. 'Jewish and Iranian Visions in the Talmudic Period' in: Isaiah M. Gafni et al. (eds). *The Jews in the Hellenistic-Roman World: Studies in Memory of Menahem Stern*. Jerusalem: The Zalman Shazar Center for Jewish History, 1996 (in Hebrew), p. 481; for the inscription itself, cf. Skjaervø. 'Kirdēr's Vision: Translation and Analysis', pp. 296–306.
[76] Earle Breech. 'These Fragments I Have Shored against My Ruins: The Form and Function of 4 Ezra' in: *JBL* 92 (1973): 272.
[77] Cf. above and the discussion on the mixed wine taken by Helen in the *Odyssey*.
[78] Harner. 'The Role of Hallucinogenic Plants', pp. 135–7.

the 'witch' claimed to have gone to orgies while intoxicated with henbane ointment, but since there were sober witnesses around, they could ascertain tha the 'witch' did not go anywhere but, in fact, stayed all the time still and unconscious. The 'witches' claimed to 'remember' being away on the Sabbath and not staying in the actual place where they sat; this would be a quite weird use of memory. But bearing in mind that henbane – if it is indeed the flower of chs 9 and 12 and the mixer at ch. 14 of 4 Ezra – is effectively hallucinogenic and not a mere memory eraser, the emphasis of the author to tell us about the persistence of memory could have a different meaning, showing he regarded the visionary experience as so real that he could not forget it. In any case, in 4 Ezra we have a very direct experience and claim from Helen in Homer, which suggests that we are dealing with different mixtures (wine with hemp in Homer, wine with henbane in 4 Ezra).

Taking the hypothesis seriously that there is no relation whatsoever between 4 Ezra and Persian sources is rendered even more difficult due to the fact that practices like the ones examined above seem out of place and rare in both the OT and NT – by comparison, much more common in Persian texts. A derivation of the idea, namely that it could have been the practices described in 4 Ezra that influenced Persian texts, looks even less likely and leaves us with the question of how such dim references to these preparatory practices would have made their way to the Zoroastrian world, and why the all-conquering Persians would be so interested in Jewish practices and not the other way round. In this sense, it is symptomatic that the pseudepigraphic author of the apocalypse that bears most resemblances to Persian practices should be someone so closely related to Persia as Ezra; and while every location has been suggested as a birthplace of the text – including Rome itself – due to the insistent reference to wisdom and its granting, it could well be that 4 Ezra was originally composed in the sapiential milieu of Palestine or Babylon.[79] This would be another way of focusing on the issue of the relations between Persian religion and Jewish apocalyptic in 4 Ezra, but it may in fact be the same – the appropriation of the pseudepigraphic authorship, the echoes of actual ecstatic practices and the writing in an environment familiar with Persian thinking making sense when taken together, although this is far from constituting definitive proof of Persian influence on 4 Ezra.

The whole theme of the possible relationship between the practices described in 4 Ezra and similar ones in Persian sources depends, of course, on the nature of actual contact between Jews and Persians (if we are not to assume structural similarities, which, by their own nature, are independent of direct borrowing or mere coincidence). Such contacts are more than guesses and in fact pose a number of possibilities. Jews lived beyond the Euphrates at least since the large-scale deportations of Assyrians and Babylonians, and after the Persian conquest came in direct contact with Iranian culture. Jewish communities also knew Persian neighbours in Asia Minor during the greatest extent of the Persian Empire and even before;[80] in later times, the community

---

[79] Hultgård. 'Figures messianiques', p. 743.
[80] This being another possible way of explaining the meeting and exchanging of ideas between Persians, Jews and Greeks early on. Cf. Eddy. *The King Is Dead*, pp. 13, 65.

that lived in Parthia was large enough to deserve the attention of leading characters in the Jewish Revolt such as Titus and Josephus. Before that, for a short time (40–37 BCE), Judaea was even occupied by the Parthians.[81]

The idea that we may have here a reverse process, that is, that the practices described in fact travelled from West to East (originally part of Jewish or Greek religion appropriated by Persians), I find rather improbable; we should find more instances of the practices described in 4 Ezra to see them make way for another religious system as complex and old as Zoroastrianism (although this is by no means obligatory). Additionally, we have noticed that, even if the texts which have come down to us are quite recent, the mythical complexes herein contained are not. All this tends to support the idea that the two mythical themes examined that find way in 4 Ezra (namely that of the cup and that of the flower, both of which bestow wisdom) were, both by their antiquity and their frequency, primarily Persian ecstatic practices that found themselves echoed in a Jewish apocalypse.

§12 Final considerations on ASC inducers in Jewish and Persian apocalyptic texts

As final considerations, I would like to summarize the arguments for and against Persian influence on the theme of chemical induction in 4 Ezra. Supporting the idea, the following must be pointed out:

1. The preparation procedures in 4 Ezra are quite odd in the general picture of Second Temple Jewish literature.
2. The choice of Ezra as pseudepigraphed, a character well acquainted with Persian things, may point to intentional absorbing of Persian lore.
3. The parallels occur, in Persian sources, both for the flower and the drink.
4. Evidence for chemical induction, as we have in 4 Ezra, is just what was left over in the course of time in terms of survival of texts (i.e. in theory there could have been many more apocalypses with the same practices, but only 4 Ezra came down to us). However, we cannot deal with 'ifs' here, and the same criteria should apply (even more so) to Persian texts – where the references are more usual. It makes sense to think that, if this practice were common in Second Temple Jewish literature, we could perhaps have more examples of it.

Against the influence between them, we must bear in mind the following:

---

[81] For the issues above, see, among others, Emil Schürer. *The History of the Jewish People in the Age of Jesus Christ (175 B.C – A.D. 135)*. Rev. by Geza Vermes, Fergus Millar, Martin Goodman and Matthew Black. Edinburgh: T&T Clark, 1979 (3 vols), vol. 3a, p. 5. The diffusion of Jews throughout the Mediterranean world is well attested in many ancient sources, sufficing it to quote Philo (*In Flaccum* 7) and Acts 2:9–11, which specifically speak about Jews in Media.

1. The dating of the Persian texts poses a formidable barrier; even when there are parallels in earlier myths, to posit the existence of, for example, a pre-CE BY does nothing to prove conclusively that Persian texts anteceded 4 Ezra.
2. There is no direct mentioning of the relation between those sets of texts, either in 4 Ezra or in commentators (like the citing of Daniel, which makes it clear that 4 Ezra must be later).
3. Strange as the idea of Jewish influence may initially seem (a very odd Jewish preparation practice finding its way to become popular in Persian circles), the episode of the conversion of the royal house of Adiabene (a Parthian buffer state) shows that the West–East adoption of Judaism, in part or whole, was a real possibility in a period roughly corresponding to that of the redaction of 4 Ezra.

Even with the limitations above stated, I tend to favour the idea of Persian influence on 4 Ezra and not the other way round: the theme appears with much greater frequency in Persian texts than in Second Temple Jewish literature (remembering that in both cases we have but a sample of a larger output), the mentioning of the cup in the Y passages puts the myth of the enlightening drink way back from 4 Ezra (and it is not present in the OT at all) and the name of the pseudepigraphic writer (even more if 4 Ezra was indeed written in Babylon) suggests the link with Persia being a clear one. The dating of most texts, however, forbids any definite conclusion.

6

Meta-historical schemes

§1 Zoroastrian and Danielic age periodizations: An overview

Zoroastrians[1] were the first[2] to offer a teleological conception of time, that is, the first to assert one *telos*, a definitive and not rhythmic or 'seasonal' order to historical events (actively avoiding the term 'cyclical' for it can lead to confusion regarding the repetition of identical events, which does not always imply other periodizations. Periods are similar but do not repeat the same events in every single detail).

The basis for this question, that is, how the question of time as a blessing or a menace (both periodical) was dealt with by other peoples – was examined in Chapter 3. It is now time to emphasize how different and groundbreaking Zoroastrian thought was in this regard.[3] This is probably the area in which lies Zoroastrianism's greatest contribution

---

[1] A great extent of this part of text was developed in Vicente Dobroruka. 'The Order of Metals in Daniel 2 and in Persian Apocalyptic' in: *ARAM Periodical* 26.1 (2014).

[2] Here we have a discrepancy that is not unusual, especially when dealing with very old texts: external criticism gives us Hesiod as the oldest source for the three mythical complexes discussed (or at least for two of them combined, the ages of the world associated to metals in decaying order). However, it seems unwise to ascribe to Hesiod the creation of these myths, even less that it was from him that the themes travelled to the rest of the Near East and 'influenced' Daniel, Tobit, Herodotus and Zoroastrian material. In the latter, the myths appear developed in a cruder manner, but as we will see, the ZWY, the best Zoroastrian source for this study, has so many redactional levels that it is also difficult to define which is the older. As a final note on the subject, the interloping of the 'Age of Heroes' in Hesiod also looks like a crude mixing of two mythical complexes – the ages of the world in decaying sequence (and, importantly, with one technological doublet, the ages of bronze and then iron) and, between the bronze and the iron ages, the presence of the heroes. This is due to the relatively recent presence of Homeric poetry and also to the fact that the Greeks were not willing to abandon the tales related to heroic cycles (the Trojan being the most popular and complete, but others are important as well – the Thebaid, for instance). Where to place the 'heroic age' in Hesiod in one of the facts that betray the non-original source of the ages plus metals sequence in Hesiod. Cf. the next section for Hesiod's text.

[3] One book that shares this opinion and dwells further is Sharokh Raei. *Die Endzeitvorstellungen der Zoroastrier in iranischen Quellen*. Wiesbaden: Harrasowitz, 2010. Especially important is the section 'Die apokalyptischen Ereignisse in den letzten Jahrhunderte'. Right at the beginning, Raei affirms the relevance of Zoroastrianism in shaping posterior ideas of future, perfection and related themes:

> Der Glauben an jemanden, der in der Zukunft kommen und die Welt zur Vollkommenheit führen wird sowie der Glauben an die Entstehung einer Gesellschaft, in der jede Spur von

to the development of modern notions of history as a process. This applies to our own times universally, given globalization and the post-colonial world. However, by the tenth century it was already the only notion of time as process (the term 'meta-history' or 'meta-historical' will be used with some freedom from this point on) from Scotland to Central Asia. Its modern developments – such as Marxism – made this phenomenon even more universal. But what are the parallels between the organization of history in Zoroastrianism and in Daniel (in both cases we are dealing with two specific texts: the ZWY and the canonical book of Daniel[4])?

Around 167 BCE, as Antiochus IV Epiphanes made his infamous move on the internal quarrels of the Jews of Palestine regarding who should have highest authority – namely their High Priest – the splitting of the Near East between the remnants of Alexander's political heirs in the region, that is, the Lagids and Seleucids, had undergone a recent change, one that would cause the most profound effect in the historical development of the region.

Summing up the factual history of the time immediately prior to the Maccabean Revolt, we may see in Dan 2:43 an allusion to the marriage between Antiochus II and Berenice (252 BCE, in order to seal a treaty to end the Second Syrian War from 260 BCE to 253 BCE and make peace with Ptolemy II of Egypt) and, as a consequence, to the Laodicean War (246 BCE – possible reference in Dan 11:7–11 to Laodice I coming back and forcing Antiochus II Theos to leave Berenice); however, we could also see v. 43 as an allusion to 193 BCE, with the intromission of the Romans against Antiochus III in his attempt to conquer Greece.

Now Daniel is a remarkably awkward source for factual history (let us just remember the figure of 'Darius, the Mede' – Dan 5:31); nonetheless, both its final redaction and its *ex-eventu* prophecy in ch. 2 allude, unequivocally, to political events happening at that time in Judaea. The author of that section in Daniel 2 is in charge of both telling Nebuchadnezzar, the Babylonian king, what he has dreamed and also provide an explanation to that very same dream.

The metals are put in Hesiod in a clearly decaying sequence and, in my opinion, with the 'heroes' age' as an 'intruding mythical complex' that had to be coped with somehow. However, this is a theme too complex to be dealt with here, as we would digress from the initial proposal of this book.

As such, the Persian sequence equals roughly the Danielic and the Hesiodic forms of the myth: the iron age means that humankind has reached rock bottom and thus,

---

Schlechtigkeit und Übel fehlt und alles Gute und Schöne in ihr gegenwärtig ist, stellt sich uns im Grunde als eine der Ideen dar, die seit frühester Zeit, genauer gesagt seit uns schriftliche Überlieferungen erhalten sind, existierte. (P. 15)

However, a full-fledged work on the meta-historical themes dealt with in this chapter remains to be done – by now it will need to be the job of a team and not of one scholar alone.

[4] Parallels in Para-Danielic literature in the DSS and Jewish apocalyptic literature in the Second Temple period can be found in Vicente Dobroruka. 'On Trees and Visionaries: The Role of the Cosmic Tree and Related Material in Baruch, Daniel and Pseudo-Danielic Literature' in: Jonathan Knight and Kevin Sullivan (eds). *The Open Mind: Essays in Honour of Christopher Rowland*. London / New York: Bloomsbury, 2015. This will be used to some extent below in this chapter.

in MP parlance, is called the age of the *dēws*, who are particularly mean and share a number of peculiar attributes.

The ZWY contains many layers of redaction, but in the following passages, it seems understandable that the dwelling of the *dēws* is clearly identified with that of the Greeks (ZWY 6.5; *yōnān ī asūrestān-*manišn*[5]); variations on that would be *Yonan* (OP), *Yauna* (Sans.), *Yavana* (Aram.) and *Yavan* (Heb.).[6]

As explained before, this could represent a very old text layer in the ZWY and then be identified with Greeks in Anatolia and/or Mesopotamia.[7] Alternatively, we may be witnessing a reference to earlier Greeks settled in Central Asia, although their presence (and massacre by Alexander, who dealt with them as if they were traitors) is still disputed; they could be the *branchidae*, descendants of the deported population of Miletus.[8]

§2 Zoroastrian patterns in meta-historical terms

Broadly speaking, the meta-historical systems known in Antiquity – and, for many people, well beyond the Middle Ages – were developed according to a fourfold scheme. This may be due to the observation of the seasons. It is hinted in sapiential works like Hesiod's WD (roughly from the eighth century BCE):[9]

> 106. ... Golden was the race of speech-endowed human beings which the immortals, who have their mansions on Olympus, made first of all. They lived at the time of Cronus, when he was king in the sky; just like gods they spent their lives, with a spirit free from care, entirely apart from toil and distress. ...

---

[5] Cf. Rowley. *Darius the Mede*, pp. 76–7, for some amusing possibilities of the mixtures alluded; for a more detailed discussion on the 'mixture', cf. André LaCoque. *Daniel in His Time*. Columbia: University of South Carolina Press, 1996, pp. 65–6.
[6] Fabrizio A. Pennacchietti. 'Gli Acta Archelai ed il viaggio di Mani nel Bēt 'Arbāyē' in: *Rivista di Storia e Letteratura Religiosa* 24.3 (1988): 503–14.
[7] Cereti. ZWY, p. 200.
[8] Frank L. Holt. *Into the Land of Bones: Alexander the Great in Afghanistan*. Berkeley: University of California Press, 2005, pp. 393–6:

> They happily welcomed Alexander within the walls of their town, expecting nothing like the so-called liberation they were about to receive. On this sesquicentennial of their exile, the Branchidae learned just how long their fellow Greeks could hold a grudge. Alexander's army decided that the Branchidae were traitors living under the protective custody of the Persians, to whom they had once betrayed a famous temple in Miletus. The Branchidae remained, therefore, enemies rather than friends, criminals rather than compatriots. Alexander and his soldiers plundered the town and butchered every single person. No mercy was shown to the defenseless citizens, not even those begging as suppliants.

For the primary source of the episode, cf. Quintus C. Rufus. *History of Alexander*, 5.7.11.
[9] The best critical edition for Hesiod's WD remains that of Martin L. West. *Works and Days*. Oxford: Oxford University Press, 1977. It is recommended for a deeper study of the matter, but most of its information is not needed for the purposes of this book; the suggestion remains for those who wish to deepen the study of the Hesiodic text.

127. Afterward those who have their mansions on Olympus made a second race, much worse, of silver, like the golden one neither in body nor in mind. A boy would be nurtured for a hundred years at the side of his cherished mother, playing in his own house, a great fool. But when they reached adolescence and arrived at the full measure of puberty, they would live for a short time only, suffering pains because of their acts of folly. …

143. Zeus the father made another race of speech-endowed human beings, a third one, of bronze, not similar to the silver one at all, out of ash trees. … Their weapons were of bronze, bronze were their houses, with bronze they worked; there was not any black iron. And these, overpowered by one another's hands, went down nameless into the dank house of chilly Hades: black death seized them, frightful though they were, and they left behind the bright light of the sun. …

156. When the earth covered up this race too, Zeus, Cronus' son, made another one in turn upon the bounteous earth, a fourth one, more just and superior. …

174. If only then I did not have to live among the fifth men, but could have either died first or been born afterward![10] For now the race is indeed one of iron. And they will not cease from toil and distress by day, nor from being worn out by suffering at night, and the gods will give them grievous cares.[11]

---

[10] This part of Hesiod's text remains a bit mysterious – if the iron age is that bad and is the last one in the cycle, what sense would it make to wish and to be born after that, unless the cycle started over again in the golden era or, less likely, went on with a better race than the iron one?

[11] Gk. original:

εἰ δ' ἐθέλεις, ἕτερόν τοι ἐγὼ λόγον ἐκκορυφώσω, εὖ καὶ ἐπισταμένως, σὺ δ' ἐνὶ φρεσὶ βάλλεο σῇσιν, ὡς ὁμόθεν γεγάασι θεοὶ θνητοί τ' ἄνθρωποι. χρύσεον μὲν πρώτιστα γένος μερόπων ἀνθρώπων ὀαθάνατοι ποίησαν Ὀλύμπια δώματ' ἔχοντες. οἱ μὲν ἐπὶ Κρόνου ἦσαν, ὅτ' οὐρανῷ ἐμβασίλευεν ὥστε θεοὶ δ' ἔζωον ἀκηδέα θυμὸν ἔχοντες, νόσφιν ἄτερ τε πόνου καὶ ὀιζύος· οὐδέ τι δειλὸν γῆρας ἐπῆν, αἰεὶ δὲ πόδας καὶ χεῖρας ὁμοῖοι τέρποντ' ἐν θαλίῃσι κακῶν ἔκτοσθεν ἁπάντων· θνῆσκον δ' ὥσθ' ὕπνῳ δεδμημένοι· ἐσθλὰ δὲ πάντα τοῖσιν ἔην· καρπὸν δ' ἔφερε ζείδωρος ἄρουρα αὐτομάτη πολλόν τε καὶ ἄφθονον. οἱ δ' ἐθελημοὶ ἥσυχοι ἔργ' ἐνέμοντο σὺν ἐσθλοῖσιν πολέεσσιν. ἀφνειοὶ μήλοισι, φίλοι μακάρεσσι θεοῖσιν. αὐτὰρ ἐπεὶ δὴ τοῦτο γένος κατὰ γαῖα κάλυψε, τοὶ μὲν δαίμονές εἰσι Διὸς μεγάλου διὰ βουλὰς ἐσθλοί, ἐπιχθόνιοι, φύλακες θνητῶν ἀνθρώπων, οἵ ῥα φυλάσσουσίν τε δίκας καὶ σχέτλια ἔργα ἠέρα ἑσσάμενοι, πάντη φοιτῶντες ἐπ' αἶαν, πλουτοδόται· καὶ τοῦτο γέρας βασιλήιον ἔσχον. δεύτερον αὖτε γένος πολὺ χειρότερον μετόπισθεν ἀργύρεον ποίησαν Ὀλύμπια δώματ' ἔχοντες, χρυσέῳ οὔτε φυὴν ἐναλίγκιον οὔτε νόημα. ἀλλ' ἑκατὸν μὲν παῖς ἔτεα παρὰ μητέρι κεδνῇ ἐτρέφετ' ἀτάλλων μέγα νήπιος ᾧ ἐνὶ οἴκῳ· ἀλλ' ὅτ' ἄρ' ἡβήσαι τε καὶ ἥβης μέτρον ἵκοιτο, παυρίδιον ζώεσκον ἐπὶ χρόνον, ἄλγε' ἔχοντες ἀφραδίῃς· ὕβριν γὰρ ἀτάσθαλον οὐκ ἐδύναντο ἀλλήλων ἀπέχειν, οὐδ' ἀθανάτους θεραπεύειν ἤθελον οὐδ' ἔρδειν μακάρων ἱεροῖς ἐπὶ βωμοῖς, ἣ θέμις ἀνθρώποισι κατ' ἤθεα. τοὺς μὲν ἔπειτα Ζεὺς Κρονίδης ἔκρυψε χολούμενος, οὕνεκα τιμὰς οὐκ ἔδιδον μακάρεσσι θεοῖς οἳ Ὄλυμπον ἔχουσιν. αὐτὰρ ἐπεὶ καὶ τοῦτο γένος κατὰ γαῖα κάλυψεν, τοὶ μὲν ὑποχθόνιοι μάκαρες θνητοὶ καλέονται, δεύτεροι, ἀλλ' ἔμπης τιμὴ καὶ τοῖσιν ὀπηδεῖ. Ζεὺς δὲ πατὴρ τρίτον ἄλλο γένος μερόπων ἀνθρώπων χάλκειον ποίησ', οὐκ ἀργυρέῳ οὐδὲν ὁμοῖον, ἐκ μελιᾶν, δεινόν τε καὶ ὄβριμον, οἷσιν Ἄρηος ἔργ' ἔμελε στονόεντα καὶ ὕβριες· οὐδέ τι σῖτον ἤσθιον, ἀλλ' ἀδάμαντος ἔχον κρατερόφρονα θυμόν· ἄπλαστοι, μεγάλη δὲ βίη καὶ χεῖρες ἄαπτοι ἐξ ὤμων ἐπέφυκον ἐπὶ στιβαροῖσι μέλεσσιν. τῶν δ' ἦν χάλκεα μὲν τεύχεα, χάλκεοι δέ τε οἶκοι, χαλκῷ δ' εἰργάζοντο· μέλας δ' οὐκ ἔσκε σίδηρος. καὶ τοὶ μὲν χείρεσσιν ὑπὸ σφετέρῃσι δαμέντες βῆσαν ἐς εὐρώεντα δόμον κρυεροῦ Ἀίδαο, νώνυμνοι· θάνατος δὲ καὶ ἐκπάγλους περ ἐόντας εἷλε μέλας, λαμπρὸν δ' ἔλιπον φάος ἠελίοιο. αὐτὰρ ἐπεὶ καὶ τοῦτο γένος κατὰ γαῖα κάλυψεν, αὖτις ἔτ' ἄλλο τέταρτον ἐπὶ χθονὶ πουλυβοτείρῃ Ζεὺς Κρονίδης ποίησε, δικαιότερον καὶ ἄρειον, ἀνδρῶν ἡρώων θεῖον γένος, οἳ καλέονται ἡμίθεοι, προτέρη

The first pattern is the most familiar one because it lies in other ancient texts (Sib. Or. 4:88–101, Dan 2, among others) and presents the sequence of four units, that is, four empires is equivalent to other sequences of four, including those of four ages and four metals.

One argument is that the ordering of empires and metals in ZWY 1 is simpler and coarser (i.e. includes fewer elements in the plot, either 'historical' or 'mythical') than in ZWY 3. This can be considered an important element when arguing that the fourfold sequence could be a 'simplification' of the 'original' sevenfold in ZWY 3. To this we can add another argument: sevenfold empires' orderings, ages or metals are much less common – the best-known surviving example can be found in Sib. Or. 3.156–195. However, the series with four elements (with an older sequence of three, apparently) are much more frequent, either in religious or secular texts.[12]

Another important factor to consider is that the later examples (like, say, Daniel 2 or even Daniel 7) convey, in fantastic language, zoomorphic and anthropomorphic images of successive empires incorporating grades of metals: this means that there are several mythical complexes at work simultaneously, with Daniel 2's statue being one possible outcome.[13]

> γενεὴ κατ' ἀπείρονα γαῖαν. καὶ τοὺς μὲν πόλεμός τε κακὸς καὶ φύλοπις αἰνὴ τοὺς μὲν ὑφ' ἑπταπύλῳ Θήβῃ, Καδμηίδι γαίῃ, ὤλεσε μαρναμένους μήλων ἕνεκ' Οἰδιπόδαο, τοὺς δὲ καὶ ἐν νήεσσιν ὑπὲρ μέγα λαῖτμα θαλάσσης ἐς Τροίην ἀγαγὼν Ἑλένης ἕνεκ' ἠυκόμοιο. ἔνθ' ἤ τοι τοὺς μὲν θανάτου τέλος ἀμφεκάλυψεν, τοῖς δὲ δίχ' ἀνθρώπων βίοτον καὶ ἤθε' ὀπάσσας Ζεὺς Κρονίδης κατένασσε πατὴρ ἐς πείρατα γαίης, καὶ τοὶ μὲν ναίουσιν ἀκηδέα θυμὸν ἔχοντες ἐν μακάρων νήσοισι παρ' Ὠκεανὸν βαθυδίνην· ὄλβιοι ἥρωες, τοῖσιν μελιηδέα καρπὸν τρὶς ἔτεος θάλλοντα φέρει ζείδωρος ἄρουρα. μηκέτ' ἔπειτ' ὤφελλον ἐγὼ πέμπτοισι μετεῖναι ἀνδράσιν, ἀλλ' ἢ πρόσθε θανεῖν ἢ ἔπειτα γενέσθαι. νῦν γὰρ δὴ γένος ἐστὶ σιδήρεον· οὐδέ ποτ' ἦμαρ παύσονται καμάτου καὶ ὀιζύος οὐδέ τι νύκτωρ τειρόμενοι· χαλεπὰς δὲ θεοὶ δώσουσι μερίμνας. ἀλλ' ἔμπης καὶ τοῖσι μεμείξεται ἐσθλὰ κακοῖσιν. Ζεὺς δ' ὀλέσει καὶ τοῦτο γένος μερόπων ἀνθρώπων, εὖτ' ἂν γεινόμενοι πολιοκρόταφοι τελέθωσιν. οὐδὲ πατὴρ παίδεσσιν ὁμοίιος οὐδέ τι παῖδες, οὐδὲ ξεῖνος ξεινοδόκῳ καὶ ἑταῖρος ἑταίρῳ, οὐδὲ κασίγνητος φίλος ἔσσεται, ὡς τὸ πάρος περ. αἶψα δὲ γηράσκοντας ἀτιμήσουσι τοκῆας· μέμψονται δ' ἄρα τοὺς χαλεποῖς βάζοντες ἔπεσσιν, σχέτλιοι, οὐδὲ θεῶν ὄπιν εἰδότες· οὐδὲ μὲν οἵ γε γηράντεσσι τοκεῦσιν ἀπὸ θρεπτήρια δοῖεν. χειροδίκαι· ἕτερος δ' ἑτέρου πόλιν ἐξαλαπάξει· οὐδέ τις εὐόρκου χάρις ἔσσεται οὐδὲ δικαίου οὔτ' ἀγαθοῦ, μᾶλλον δὲ κακῶν ῥεκτῆρα καὶ ὕβριν ἀνέρα τιμήσουσι. δίκη δ' ἐν χερσί καὶ αἰδὼς οὐκ ἔσται· βλάψει δ' ὁ κακὸς τὸν ἀρείονα φῶτα μύθοισι σκολιοῖς ἐνέπων, ἐπὶ δ' ὅρκον ὀμεῖται. Ζῆλος δ' ἀνθρώποισιν ὀιζυροῖσιν ἅπασιν δυσκέλαδος κακόχαρτος ὁμαρτήσει, στυγερώπης. καὶ τότε δὴ πρὸς Ὄλυμπον ἀπὸ χθονὸς εὐρυοδείης λευκοῖσιν φάρεσσι καλυψαμένω χρόα καλὸν ἀθανάτων μετὰ φῦλον ἴτον προλιπόντ' ἀνθρώπους Αἰδὼς καὶ Νέμεσις· τὰ δὲ λείψεται ἄλγεα λυγρὰ θνητοῖς ἀνθρώποισι, κακοῦ δ' οὐκ ἔσσεται ἀλκή.

---

[12] For the empires' theme, order and sequence, José Alonso-Nuñez's articles are still relevant and the best start: 'Die Abfolge der Weltreiche bei Polybios und Dionysios von Halikarnassos' in: *Historia* 32 (1983): 411–426; 'Appian and the World Empires' in: *Athenaeum* 62 (1984): 640–4; 'Die Weltreichsukzession bei Strabo' in: *Zeitschrift für Religions- und Geistesgeschichte* 36 (1984): 53–4; and 'The Emergence of Universal Historiography from the 4th to the 2nd Centuries B.C.' in: Herman Verdin, Guido Schepens and Els de Keyser (eds). *Purposes of History: Studies in Greek Historiography From the 4th to the 2nd Centuries B.C.* Leuven: Orientaliste, 1990.

[13] There is a clear similarity with a Vedic myth here: The statue may be more important than it appears at first sight. In the second century CE the gnostic Bardesanes described, from a report by Indian envoys, that in the centre of the earth was a statue of the primeval man, a representation of the whole world and of what is contained therein. Cf. Stobeaus 2.2, quoted by Widengren. 'Les ages du monde selon hésiode', p. 26.

In ZWY 1 and ZWY 3 we also have a mix of legendary and historical empires, as also happens in a plethora of authors up to the Middle Ages and beyond. This happens because the writers or compilers were still in a stage where meta-historical reasoning was very much attached to mythological thought in the strict sense of the term, unless one considers the canonical book of Daniel as historiography. It is not and does not intend to be even though the picture that unfolds to the reader regards only temporal empires (with the possibility that the Median Empire did not exist as a separate entity[14]). Hence, much of the controversy both in Antiquity and in contemporaneity related to the nature of world powers in Daniel can already be found in Josephus and in 4 Ezra.[15] The eschatological aspects in politically oriented apocalyptic literature needs to be continuously updated, leading sometimes to exquisite outcomes such as the many apocalypses under the name of Daniel with their own plot and text listed by Lorenzo DiTommaso.[16]

One critical point is that from the narrator's point of view, these ages are either to come or have already taken place, and, therefore, they exclude partially the times presented by Ohrmazd in his conversation with Zaraθuštra, except for the brief introduction to the golden age, 'in which I and you converse' (ZWY 1.8). This inversion is very important: from one golden age in the past, lost forever as it looks in Hesiod's WD, in apocalyptic thinking we have the opposite reasoning: the golden era is yet to come.

Therefore, the main question presented to scholars relates to the dating of the sequences, be they metals, ages and empires. As a rule, mention to known politically organized societies (empires, kingdoms, etc.) is the best way to date an apocalypse: but when dealing with the ZWY, this only adds one more layer to our problems. The enemies of the *dēn* are either anachronistically placed or simply do not match accurate historical data (this happens with many of Ēran's enemies in ZWY 1.8-11; 2; 3; 4;[17]

---

[14] In the eighth century BCE it was a vassal state to the Assyrians; the geographical extent of the Median kingdom is still unknown but it hardly qualifies on a par with Babylonians, Persians and Greeks. Cf. *CHIr* II, p. 75.

[15] AJ 10.280-1; 4 Ezra 12:10-12.

[16] DiTommaso. *The Book of Daniel*.

[17] In ZWY 4:57-9 there are two interesting features: a different sequence of five metals (gold, silver, copper, tin and lead). The latter could be a gloss, according to Cereti. *ZWY*, p. 157 (the reading 'arzīz' *surb* is omitted in mss DH and K43; it is transliterated as *slp*; Cereti suggests *swlp*); *CPD*, 'arzīz' can be either tin or lead, hence the gloss; *CPD*, 'srub' is also a possible synonym but is more likely a typo from the MP translation *slp*. There is also the fullest description of Ēran's enemies, ranging from the Hyōn (MP Huns?) to the Spēd Hyōn (White Huns), in a total of twelve peoples (again a suggestive number, a multiple of four; of the twelve mentioned are also another two, the Tāzig and the Hrōmāyīg. All of these are historically attested, but the sequence is very difficult to get correctly: 'Hrōmāyīg', 'those from Rome', is the usual term for the Eastern Roman Empire and even to Alexander the Great; but in this context, as Cereti points out, it is difficult to equate them to the Indo-Greeks of Bactria). Complete discussions on these names and their etymologies can be found in Bailey. 'Iranian Studies', pp. 945-55; Harold W. Bailey. 'Hārabhunā' in: Johannes Schubert and Ulrich Schneider (hrgs). *Asiatica. Festschrift Friedrich Weller. Zum 65 Geburtstag gewindet von seinen Freunde, Kollegen und Schülern*. Leipzig: Harrasowitz, 1954, pp. 12-21. Of those listed, the ones with the leather girdle were once easily identified with the the Greeks due to a kind of Egyptian apocalypse, 'The Oracle of the Potter': it is in a very fragmentary state, but summing up what it is about, this one is definitely against the Greeks; among the fragments that constitute the text as we have it, in $P_3 49$ ff. we have a mention to 'those who wear a leather girdle, who are followers of Seth, will lacerate themselves'. Other references point to Syria (i.e. to the

a catalogue of eschatological enemies). In this incoherence or lack of interest for historical accuracy, what we have as Zoroastrian sources resemble SibOr, especially the last four ones – conceding that Zoroastrian mss are, in any case, far better in their language than the awful Greek of late Sibyllina.[18]

§3 Which series is the best candidate as the earliest matrix?

The sequence of four stages (regardless of being metals, ages or empires) seems to be more homogeneous than that of seven (perhaps because the latter is rarer), though from the perspective of numerological symbolism both have good parallels in the natural world ('four' representing the number of seasons, 'seven' the number of days of a lunar week). But to emphasize the fact that in the sequence of seven the mixture of mythical and historical realms (in the ZWY at least) presents itself embroiled would implicate that it is later rather than earlier than the fourfold one.

That could mean the sequence of four eras would by force be older, merely taking into account the antiquity of the Indian myth of the *yugas*, which have also been preserved orally for a very long time, as long as that of the Avestan tradition, if not longer. The fact that Hesiod is the first traceable, identifiable author using that sequence does not mean he created it: to claim this is a major mistake, confusing internal and external criticism. Hesiod has it finely developed but the whole sequence of verses seems out of place in WD – it is more of a guide regarding what is wise and what is foolish to do or to avoid according to the seasons, and it has a background of judicial intrigue against his brother Perses.[19]

Since this book deals primarily with Zoroastrian sources and their parallels in Second Temple literature (with emphasis on Daniel and to some extent on the DSS), there are more Zoroastrian meta-historical structures than those two examined above in the ZWY. The Bd has another way of organizing cosmological sequences, which are not opposite to the ZWY but just different. Both the Bd and the GrBd propose time frames, more concerned with Creation and its final meaning than with the schemes of the ZWY. Nor are the four and seven age schemes of ZWY 1 and ZWY 3 the only possibilities available in Zoroastrian eschatology. Kirdēr's experience has nothing to do with numeral sequences. The millennial sequence

---

Seleucids), and these are just some references to make it very clear that this text ('The Oracle of the Potter') is definitely a cultural-resistance text in the form exemplified by Eddy. However, since we have two scary enemies in both Egyptian and Zoroastrian apocalyptics, for a long time these were equalled – which would fit very well into Eddy's time frame. This theory, however, has long been discredited. For the text of the 'Oracle', cf. Ludwig Koenen. *Die Prophezeiungen des 'Töpfers'*. Bonn: Habelt, 1968, esp. pp. 187–8. Koenen has a number of useful articles on Egyptian apocalyptic. The reader should bear in mind that there are three different recensions of this oracle.

[18] Johannes Geffcken. *Komposition und Entstehungszeit der Oracula Sybillina*. Leipzig: C.H. Hinrichs, 1902, p. 66.
[19] Hesiod, WD 8–10.

related to the number of saviours – three – is also not related to anything remotely related to the fourfold schemes reminiscent of Hesiod but most likely far earlier than him.[20]

The other passages that evoke the same theme of the 'tenth millennium' of Zaraθuštra can be found, among other texts, in ZWY 5.6: 'Ohrmazd said, "O Spitāman Zarduxšt, these nine thousand years I, Ohrmazd, created, men these <last> hard times will be most upset."' Other important developments are to be found in GrBd 1.14; 27; 28; 32; Bd 30.20; 34; Y 44.15). Twelve-thousand-year schemes, or as some prefer, schemes of nine thousand years (i.e. excluding the period in which matter was in a latent but not yet born state), are parallel with the four and sevenfold structures, and also deal with history having a soteriological nature, that is, the schemes found in the ZWY look more concerned with historical happenings though interpolating them among mythical events. We could also speak of two types of meta-historical organization of time frames, one dealing with years and the other with time blocks. Each part of three thousand has a different saviour: in this respect the difference in Second Temple Judaism and the two Messiahs, one Davidic and one of priestly descent, is unparalled. All Zoroastrian saviours are of sacred, other-worldly nature – a Zoroastrian kingly support is implied since the story of Vištasp being convinced by Zaraθuštra (Y 51.16; 53.2, among others, but all placing both Zaraθuštra and Vištasp in a semi-legendary context).

Finally, the battle between the two stallions is the most usual ending in cosmic combats: two forces, one good and representing cosmos, the other ugly and representing chaos; again the theme of Tištriia (the star Sirius), the white and wonderful stallion, against the demon Apaoša, a black, ugly and hairless stallion who tries to block Tištriia's access to the sea Vorukuša, the mythical place from which flows all rivers and rain.[21]

---

[20] Vicente Dobroruka and Khodadad Rezakhani. 'apocalyptic and eschatology, Zoroastrian' in: *ODLA* 1:

> The Zoroastrian ideas of the apocalypse emerged fully formed in the early Islamic period under the influence of Judaism, Christianity, and Islam, though they are ultimately based on narratives present in the Av. texts. Apocalyptic legends, which appear in different variations in different texts, focus on the final battle between the cosmic forces of good and evil and the struggle to bring about the Frashgird, the 'Renovation' of the earth. Middle Persian texts describe three millennial ages that cumulatively bring about the final battle. At the end of each age a saviour defeats the forces of evil, though eventually the forces of evil return. The first two saviours, Ushedar and Ushedarmah, are born from the seed of Zarathushtra (Zoroaster) preserved in Lake Kayansih at the end of the first two millennia. The third millennium arrives with the birth of *Soshans [Saošyant], the final saviour, in the same circumstances, from a virgin who has been impregnated by the preserved seed of Zoroaster. Ahriman's minions ravage the world and after epic battles the armies of Soshans, which include the hero Karasaspa and the immortal Pishyotan, as well as the legendary king Kay Khosrow, defeat the forces of evil. The perfect state is then restored and all souls are purified by molten metal that cleanses and unites all beings. Ahriman and his works are destroyed and ritual cleansing performed by Soshans restores the world to its perfect and eternal state.

A recent article that deals mostly with numismatic sources but is very useful for different viws on the Arab conquest is Touraj Daryaee. 'From Zoroastrian to Islamic Iran: A Note on the Christian Intermezzo' in: *Vicino Oriente* 23 (2019): esp. 120–2.

[21] Antonio Panaino. 'Cosmologies and Astrology' in: *WBCZ*, p. 243. This is an interesting variation on the theme of the sea as usually seen as evil, or the result of evil actions by demons, or still the result

Tištriia is defeated in the first combat because he was not worshipped with enough strength; this changes in the second one, where he defeats Apaoša:

> 1. We worship the star Tishtrya, the splendid, the glorious, of water-nature, strong, lofty, powerful, shining afar ...; 5. for whom yearn sheep and cattle and men, ... (saying): 'When shall Tishtrya the splendid, the glorious, rise for us, when shall the springs of water flow anew ... ?' 20. Then Tishtrya, the splendid, the glorious, goes down ... to the sea Vourukasha, in the shape of a horse, white, beautiful, with golden ears and golden muzzle. 21. There rushes against him the demon Dearth [Apaoša], in the shape of a horse, black, hairless, ... horrifying. 22. Together the two fight, Tishtrya the splendid, the glorious, and the demon Dearth ... For three days and three nights the two fight. The demon Dearth overcomes him, he conquers him, Tishtrya the splendid, the glorious. 23. He drives him back ... from the sea Vourukasha. Tishtrya the splendid, the glorious calls down woe and misery on himself: 'Woe to me ! ..., misery, O waters and plants! ... Men do not worship me now with worship with spoken name, as other gods are worshipped ... 24. If men should worship me ..., I should take to myself the strength of ten horses. 25. ... I worship Tishtrya, the splendid, the glorious, with worship with spoken name. I procure for him the strength of ten horses. 26. Then Tishtrya the splendid, the glorious. ... goes down to the sea Vourukasha Those two fight at noon tide. Tishtrya the splendid, the glorious, overcomes him, he conquers him, the demon Dearth ... 29. ... He calls down prosperity on himself: 'Well is me! Well, O waters and plants! ... well shall it be, O lands! The courses of the waters shall surge out unhindered for the large-seeded corn, for the small-seeded grasses, and for the material world.' ... 31. He makes ... the sea surge, he makes the sea surge over ... 32. Then Tishtrya rises again from the sea Vourukasha ... Then at that time mists gather on Mount Ush-hendava, which stands in the middle of the sea Vourukasha. 33. Then the bold ... Wind drives the rain and cloud and hail upon places, upon dwellings, upon the seven regions.[22]

Summing these meta-historical schemes briefly, it can be said that three essential types of time frames can be found in pre-Islamic Persian texts, which refer to three numerals: 4, 7 and 12 and their multiples. The numeral 4 reflects the number of seasons, 7 the number of days of the lunar week (to a Christian or Jewish reader or listener, the number of days of Creation) and 12 and its derivatives, the number of months of the year.[23]

---

of the earliest cosmic fights to establish and differentiate order from chaos (as seen above, a common theme throughout Near Eastern religions, including the Yahweh cult). The combat between these two stallions has a strong sexual content, as the sea Vorukuša stands like a mare to be owned by the victorious horse.

[22] Text as exposed in Boyce. *Textual Sources*, p. 32. Cf. also Bernard Forsmann. 'Apaosha, der Gegner des Tishtriia' in: *Zeitschrift für vergleichende Sprachforschung* 82 (1968): 42–9.

[23] There are many such sequences in the Sib. Or., and here are some examples only: 1.387–400; 3.156–161; 8.9.

All these sequences differ from the yearly festivals of neighbouring peoples – these were staged periodically by the divine nature of the monarchs in these regions, themselves proxies of the gods or, in the case of the Hebrew people, of one god.[24]

Briefly, the sequences that appear in the GrBd and the Bd reflect Zoroastrian beliefs in the succession of millennia, in which Zaraθuštra presents 'pseudepigraphically derived' texts.

Let us examine first the unhappy period, quite similar to the Hesiodic last age,[25] as it displays a world turned completely upside down, with perverted values. This can be seen clearly in ZWY 3:29; the subject is repeated in other passages, that is, ZWY 4.1–4:

> Zarduxšt said, 'Creator of the world of material beings, full spirit, which is the sign of the tenth millennium?' Ohrmazd said, 'O Spitāman Zarduxšt, I'll leave this clear. The sign of the end of thy millennium will <that> the worst of times will come. One hundred kinds, a thousand kinds, a myriad of types of parted hair dews[26] of Xēšm seed, those in the worst race will arise in Xwarāsān[27] side of Iran. They will raise their standards, will wear black armor and have their hair parted behind, will be small and the worst race and powerful strokes and urinate poison.'

Alongside the usual demonization of the enemy, the text above gives us some interesting clues for dating the last millennium according to the creational

---

[24] Cohn. *Cosmos, Chaos and The World to Come*, pp. 3, 31, 34–5, 38, 59–60 (regrettably Cohn affirms that the HB and the OT are the same thing; by 'Old Testament' we are referring to a corpus of texts that contains the ones in the HB plus a few more but follows their arrangement in Greek. This was the Bible of the Jews in the Greek Diaspora, but when using the term *Old* Testament we are borrowing Christian usage too – it makes no sense of talking about an Old Testament if there is not a New Testament as its complement), but he is absolutely correct in the late dating of the HB as we know it – it is a post-Exilic concoction of earlier traditions and new ideas, and this helps explain the discrepancies in several passages of the Pentateuch (for an introduction to the subject, cf. Alexander Rofé. *Introduction to the Composition of the Pentateuch*. Sheffield: Sheffield Academic Press, 1999). For issues related to the pre-Exilic monarchy in Israel and its aspects related to cosmos and chaos, the following titles will be of good use: Sigmund Mowinckel. *Psalmen Studien II, Das Thronbesleigungsfest Jääwäs*. Kristiania: SNVAO, 1922; Hans H. Schmid. *Gerechtigkeit als Weltordnung: Hintergrund und Geschichte des alttestamentlicher Theologie*. Zurich: NZN Burchverlag, 1974; Susan Niditch. *Chaos to Cosmos: Studies in Biblical Patterns of Creation*. Missoula: Scholars Press, 1985. More recent titles include a rare approach linking the words of Amos 5:18 to the ritual enthronement of Yahweh (Daniel E. Fleming. 'The Day of Yahweh in the Book of Amos: A Rhetorical Response to Ritual Expectation' in: *RB* 110 (2010)); Thomas C. Römer. 'Du Temple au Livre: L'idéologie de la centralisation dans l'historiographie deutéronomiste' in: Steven L. McKenzie and Thomas Römer, in collaboration with Hans Heinrich Schmid (eds). *Rethinking the Foundations. Historiography in the Ancient World and in the Bivle. Essays in Honour of John Van Seeters*. Berlin: Walter de Gruyter, 2000.

[25] Cf. Vicente Dobroruka. 'Hesiodic Reminiscences in Zoroastrian-Hellenistic Apocalypses' in: *BSOAS* 75 (2012).

[26] Several attempts have been made to identify this people, which appears in several places in the ZWY as the eschatological enemy by definition: some relate them to Egyptian apocalyptic literature inconclusively, and on the other extreme some scholars link them to the Turkic peoples of the steppe – a better but non-conclusive guess.

[27] Khodadad Rezakhani. *Re-Orienting the Sasanians: East Iran in Late Antiquity*. Edinburgh: Edinburgh University Press, 2017, reminds us of how important the Eastern frontier of the Sasanian Empire was, although there is plenty more information on the Western one, with Rome and then the Byzantines.

structure: it matches the chronology adopted in the GrBd with the arrival of invaders from Khorasan, or the East in general.[28] That they urinate poison is a clearly magical allusion – even the dreaded usual suspects for the race of wrath – the Greeks, the Arabs and the Turks – obviously cannot do that.

In short, these several examples show the same theme: we find them in a considerably wide range of texts exposing the Zoroastrian thought, at least as far as the Sassanid period, and usually in a confusing and contradictory manner, as will be examined below.

§4 Mixtures: Zoroastrian and Jewish

An important and often overlooked element that appears both in Daniel and in the ZWY is the presence of some 'mixture' between metals or of a metal with something else incompatible, as in Daniel 2: the passage is too widely known to be repeated *in toto*, so the important ending is Dan 2:41: 'As you saw the feet and toes partly of potter's clay and partly of iron, it shall be a divided kingdom; but some of the strength of iron shall be in it, as you saw the iron mixed with the clay.'

The Aramaic text reads, with Masoretic pointing,

וְדִי־חֲזַיְתָה רַגְלַיָּא וְאֶצְבְּעָתָא מִנְּהוֹן חֲסַף דִּי־פֶחָר וּמִנְּהוֹן פַּרְזֶל מַלְכוּ פְלִיגָה תֶּהֱוֵה וּמִן־נִצְבְּתָא דִי פַרְזְלָא לֶהֱוֵא־בַהּ כָּל־קֳבֵל דִּי חֲזַיְתָה פַּרְזְלָא[29] מְעָרַב בַּחֲסַף טִינָא׃

The Greek has one variation between the LXX and Theodotion's recension; so, taking only the very end, we have in the LXX 'ἐν αὐτῇ καθάπερ εἶδες τὸν σίδηρον ἀναμεμειγμένον ἅμα τῷ πηλίνῳ ὀστράκῳ'[30] but in Theodotion's 'ἐν αὐτῇ ὃν τρόπον εἶδες τὸν σίδηρον ἀναμεμειγμένον τῷ ὀστράκῳ'.

This means that only in the LXX text, as we have it, the translator considered it important to state that the mixture of the elements was simultaneous (provided by the term 'ἅμα', 'at the same time'). This reinforces the idea of intermarriages since a marriage, by definition, is a union between two parts at one given moment.

The elements here are both mineral, fitting to the sequence, one of them being iron. Now, the other element seems misplaced, both in terms of its intrinsic value and of its nature: clay is not a metal and is by far more common and vulgar than any of the previous elements in the statue. It must be said that the composer or compiler of this section of Daniel does not establish any distinction between the Lagids or Seleucids representing either iron or clay; this may mean that both are of the same

---

[28] Carlo G. Cereti. 'Central Asian and Eastern Iranian Peoples in Zoroastrian Apocalyptic Literature' in: Csánad Bálint (hrg.). *Kontakte zwischen Iran, Byzanz und der Steppe in 6.-7. Jh.* Budapest: Archäologisches Institut der UAW, 2000, p. 193 – Bd 33 remembers Yazdgerd III's flight to Khorasan and Turkestan, where he sought help but was killed, as seen above (in any case this is quite different from an invasion by these same peoples).
[29] BDB, 'parzel': 'iron'.
[30] LSJ, 'out of clay for potsherd', keeping the dative; Theodotion's use is simpler and mentions only the potsherd (and, by inference, clay).

value, or simply that he was not interested in their dynastic arrangements – it would not matter to him which was 'more prized', since according to God's plan, both are doomed.

Daniel 2:42 is of little interest here, since it only provides a very naïve explanation of the unsuitability of iron mixing with an uncongenial element, clay. All versions state the same.

In v. 43 we find the point stated in a finer manner: 'As you saw the iron mixed with clay, so will they mix with one another in marriage, but they will not hold together, just as iron does not mix with clay.' The terms to refer to the intermarriage are the following, both in Biblical Aram. (the end of v. 43) and Gk.:

מְעָרַב בַּחֲסַף טִינָא מִתְעָרְבִין לֶהֱוֹן לְזַרְעַ אֲנָשָׁא וְלָא־לֶהֱוֹן דָּבְקִין דְּנָה עִם־דְּנָה הֵא־כְדִי פַרְזְלָא לָא מִתְעָרַב עִם־חַסְפָּא׃

More simply, in Gk., συγκραθῆναι (LSL: to blend or unite), and in TH, again a slight variation, ἀναμείγνυται (LSJ: to mix together or have intercourse). The next question is, can the 'mixture' of iron and clay be proved to be contemporary to the theme to which it refers?

In the ZWY there is no statue but rather a tree: it will play the same role, as will be seen in the DSS Para-Danielic fragments and in 2 Baruch: so, in the very beginning of the ZWY as we have it,

1. As is revealed in the Stūdgar,[31] Zarduxšt sought immortality from Ohrmazd.
2. Then Ohrmazd showed the wisdom of omniscience to Zarduxšt.
3. And therewith he saw the trunk of a tree on which there were four branches, one of gold, one of silver, one of steel[32] and one on <which> iron had been mixed.
4. Then he considered[33] that he had seen it in a dream.
5. Once woken from sleep, Zarduxšt said, 'O Lord of spiritual and material beings, it seems that I have seen the trunk of a tree on which there were four branches.'

Here we have some parallels and at the same time some differences from Dan 2: in the Danielic passage, strangely it is a Pagan who gets the vision first, Nebuchadnezzar; he gets troubled with it and demands not only the meaning of his dream but also

---

[31] According to the 'Doxology' of Cereti in his edition of the ZWY, it is

probably a corruption of *Sūdgar*. According to the *Dēnkard* it was the first nask [a division] of the Avesta while according to the apocryphal *Wizīrgard ī Dēnīg* and to the *Rivāyats* [some kind of exchange between the Indian Parsees and what remained of the Zoroastrian community in Iran], where it is called *Stūdgar* or *Istūdgar*, it was the second nask. In the *Dēnkard* we find a short description of it in book eight and a long and detailed summary in book nine.

Cf. also Andreas and Barr. *Bruhstücke einer Pehlevi-Übersetzung der Psalmen*.

[32] This is one of the sections of the world empires in the ZWY where we depart from the Danielic sequence. CPD, 'almās(t)', 'pōlāwad', as adj., 'pōlāwaden', all mean steel. In the ZWY is of course the adj. 'pōlāwaden' with no remarks on Cereti's edition regarding eventual differences in the mss.

[33] In the mss, 'pad ēd dāšt'; CPD, 'pad ēd dāštan', 'to consider'.

the dream itself from the diviners in the court. After threatening all of them – who were, like Daniel, a sort of 'servants' of the crown, he gets what he wants. But strictly speaking, Daniel has a 'replay' of the king's vision:

> Dan 2:1. In the second year of the reign of Nebuchadnezzar, Nebuchadnezzar had dreams; and his spirit was troubled, and his sleep left him. 2. Then the king commanded that the magicians, the enchanters, the sorcerers, and the Chaldeans be summoned, to tell the king his dreams. So they came in and stood before the king. 3. And the king said unto them, I have dreamed a dream, and my spirit was troubled to know the dream. 4. Then the Chaldeans said to the king, 'O king, live for ever! Tell your servants the dream, and we will show the interpretation' 5. The king answered the Chaldeans, 'The word from me is sure: if you do not make known to me the dream and its interpretation, you shall be torn limb from limb, and your houses shall be laid in ruins.' ... 13. So the decree went forth that the wise men were to be slain, and they sought Daniel and his companions, to slay them. 14. Then Daniel replied with prudence and discretion to Arioch, the captain of the king's guard, who had gone out to slay the wise men of Babylon; Then was the secret revealed unto Daniel in a night vision. Then Daniel blessed the God of heaven. 16. And Daniel went in and besought the king to appoint him a time, that he might show to the king the interpretation. 17. Then Daniel went to his house and made the matter known to Hananiah, Mishael, and Azariah, his companions, 18. and told them to seek mercy of the God of heaven concerning this mystery, so that Daniel and his companions might not perish with the rest of the wise men of Babylon. 19. Then was the secret revealed unto Daniel in a night vision. Then Daniel blessed the God of heaven.

And the tale ends with the passage seen above, where Daniel tells the king both the dream and its meaning. Noteworthy here are the facts that it is a Pagan who is a visionary in the first place, as already stated, and that Daniel requests both the auxiliary prayers of his friends and some time to Arioch, the king's guard in charge of the slaughter.

In the ZWY, Zarduxšt does not request time in the strict sense of a request but needs to sleep to get the vision, that is, like Daniel, he does not get the information he desires instantly. But the exchange of data is quite different: Zarduxšt was seeking immortality, not any kind of prospective dream (in a sense Daniel was also looking for 'life', not as living eternally but as the survival of himself and the other sages, since Nebuchadnezzar was so mad with all of them, regardless of specialties, origins or religion, that his orders were to kill all of them). The metals in Zarduxšt's vision are also different (in this sequence and in the one in chapter 3 of the ZWY). So far these are items that can be considered parallels with some minor differences, but the context in which each vision is given is quite different. Differences are, so far, the presence of steel, the fact that Zarduxšt sees a tree trunk and not a statue, and that he directly requests Ohrmazd the meaning of his dream (Daniel has the king's dream a second time, it is never enough to bear that in mind). Zarduxšt also takes some time to ponder and recollects his dream, before asking Ohrmazd anything. Daniel prays and only afterward gets the whole story sought by Nebuchadnezzar.[34]

This can immediately be related to the ZWY: 'Ohrmazd said to Spitaman Zarduxšt, "The tree trunk that you have seen, <that is the material world which I, Ohrmazd, have created>."'[35]

Now, in ZWY 1 and ZWY 3 we are still on the same mythical ground as that of Daniel (the earliest documented one to join ages, metals and empires – in Herodotus, Tobit and even Polybius, the sequence of empires, three or more, is featured, but no ages or metals; Hesiod has the ages and metals but no empires). From ZWY 4 onwards there is the distinct disadvantage of a confusing sequence of metals (five in ZWY 4.57–59, with a total of twelve peoples or empires, as seen); not just that, some of these peoples have not even been enemies of the Persians, much less in that sequence.[36] But the peoples described, in the haphazard order in which they appear, may reflect either a lack of interest for historical accurate data on the part of the apocalypticist in that section (it would not be the first time, Zoroastrian or other kinds of apocalyptic in this case) or else they reflect several redactional levels. The latter would be difficult to prove (except for the weird presence of lead composing a strange sequence of five ages/metals/empires). But this sequence is abruptly interrupted without any explanation into the sequence of twelve enemies in the next verse, v. 58: 'And lordship and sovereignty will go to those of non-Ērānian origins.'

Now this lack of agreement between Zoroastrian apocalyptic and 'historiographical' sources (of several kinds, not just Persian but also Arabic and Chinese) does not

---

[34] Besides all the bibliography already quoted on Daniel, a few more titles might be useful regarding the statue and the vision: Raymond Hammer. *The Book of Daniel*. Cambridge: Cambridge University Press, 1976; Reinhard Kratz. 'The Visions of Daniel' in: Collins and Flint, *The Book of Daniel*; a very interesting and different approach lies in Paul Niskanen. *The Human and the Divine in History: Herodotus and the Book of Daniel*. London: Continuum, 2004. The now battered thesis of Eddy, important as it is, gets a new clothing in Anathea E. Portier-Young. *Apocalypse against Empire: Theologies of Resistance in Early Judaism*. Grand Rapids: Eerdmans, 2013; Shaul Bar. *A Letter That Has Not Been Read: Dreams in the Hebrew Bible*. Cincinnati: Hebrew Union College Press, 2001.

[35] Mss K20 and K20b offer different readings of this passage, but the meaning is that established by Cereti.

[36] Cereti. *Guerra Santa*, pp. 700–1, where the first year of the Sasanids and their successes are remembered both in AiP and in the KIns; cf. also Cereti. 'Central Asian and Eastern Iranian Peoples', in Bálint. *Kontakte zwischen Iran*, p. 193: Cereti affirms correctly in n. 3 that 'the events narrated ZWY, taken from different chapters, need not be understood in chronological order'. Just as one of many examples, Bd 33 recalls that in the end of the tenth millennium of Zaraθuštra, Yazdgard (III) lost the battle to the Arabs and went to the East – his son went to 'Hindugān' (India) to regroup and reform his army but lost like his father and was killed (India here features correctly as an ally, not as an enemy). The same goes for the warm reception given by the Chinese to the last Sasanians – cf. Compareti. 'Chinese-Iranian Relations. On that matter, compare Cereti's 'Guerra santa' with Collins's 'The Mythology of Holy War in Daniel' (especially pp. 600–1) where the relevance of Persian apocalyptic is stressed in the formation of Danielic thought, but on very different grounds from this book: 'In fact Dan vii and viii draw particular motifs from very many sources The pattern of four kingdoms derives from a Persian schematisation of history,' justified by the presence of Media among the world empires: it appears to be the opposite, since this poses a problem rather than a solution, given that Media never formed a 'world empire' neither in extension nor in power (this is acknowledged by Collins too (p. 601 n. 24).

happen to the apocalypse proper in Dan 7–12: metaphorical and exaggerated as the language may seem, nonetheless the events described by the author of this section (with the exception of the eschatological outcome) are reasonably precise. First, the combat between Alexander and Darius III, in Dan 8:[37]

> 8:1. In the third year of the reign of King Belshaz'zar a vision appeared to me, Daniel, after that which appeared to me at the first.[38] 2. And I saw in the vision; and when I saw, I was in Susa the capital, which is in the province of Elam; and I saw in the vision, and I was at the river U'lai. 3. I raised my eyes and saw, and behold, a ram standing on the bank of the river. It had two horns; and both horns were high, but one was higher than the other, and the higher one came up last. 4. I saw the ram charging westward and northward and southward; no beast could stand before him, and there was no one who could rescue from his power; he did as he pleased and magnified himself. 5. As I was considering, behold, a he-goat came from the west across the face of the whole earth, without touching the ground; and the goat had a conspicuous horn between his eyes.[39] 6. He came to the ram with the two horns, which I had seen standing on the bank of the river, and he ran at him in his mighty wrath. 7. I saw him come close to the ram, and he was enraged against him and struck the ram and broke his two horns; and the ram had no power to stand before him, but he cast him down to the ground and trampled upon him; and there was no one who could rescue the ram from his power.[40] 8. Then the he-goat magnified himself exceedingly; but when he was strong, the great horn was broken, and instead of it there came up four conspicuous horns toward the four winds of heaven.[41] ... 15. When I, Daniel, had seen the vision, I sought to

---

[37] Here three of John J. Collins works will be followed closely: his article 'Daniel, Book of' in: David N. Freedman (ed.). *The Anchor Bible Dictionary*. Yale: Yale University Press, 1992; *Daniel: A Commentary on the Book of Daniel* [in the Hermeneia series]. Philadelphia: Fortress Press, 1994; and specific chapters from John J. Collins and Peter W. Flint (with the assistance of Cameron VanEpps). *The Book of Daniel: Composition and Reception*. Leiden: Brill, 2001 (2 vols).

[38] In Dan 7.

[39] *BDB*, 'conspicuous' is unclear here: חזות, perhaps conspicuous in appearance as in Dan 8, example given in *BDB*.

[40] Some commentators see, in this passage, parallels in Ezek 34:17 and Zech 10:3; however, in these two cases God is willing to make clear who is worth His grace and who is not – in our text there is nothing even remotely of the kind: both the ram and the goat are Pagans (although, in the usual apocalyptic tradition, instruments of God's will, as the angel Gabriel will explain to Daniel from v. 15 onwards), and their struggle is just a preliminary of God's judgement.

[41] This passage still presents some difficulties – the 'four' horns can be the Diadochi, but in v. 7 the text jumps directly to the Seleucid Empire, of whom Antiochus Epiphanes was part king. However, the sudden death of Alexander in v. 8 has interesting similarities with the first lines of the AWN, although here the hatred for Alexander is expanded:

> Thus it is said that once the righteous Zoroaster had spread in the world the religion he (had) received. Until the completion of three hundred years the religion was in purity and men were free from doubts. Then the accursed Evil Spirit, the sinful, in order to make men doubtful of this religion, misled the accursed Alexander the Roman, resident of Egypt [a reference of Alexandria] and sent him to the land of Iran with great brutality ['fight' in K20] and fear [unclear]. He killed the Iranian ruler and destroyed and ruined the court and the sovereignty. That wicked, wretched, heretic, sinful, maleficent Alexander the Roman, resident of Egypt [emphasis again] took away and burnt those scriptures, namely all the

understand it; and behold, there stood before me one having the appearance of a man. 16. And I heard a man's voice between the banks of the U'lai, and it called, 'Gabriel, make this man understand the vision.' 17. So he came near where I stood; and when he came, I was frightened and fell upon my face. But he said to me, 'Understand, O son of man, that the vision is for the time of the end.' 18. As he was speaking to me, I fell into a deep sleep with my face to the ground; but he touched me and set me on my feet. ... [He said] 20. As for the ram which you saw with the two horns, these are the kings of Media and Persia. 21. And the he-goat is the king of Greece; and the great horn between his eyes is the first king. 22. As for the horn that was broken, in place of which four others arose, four kingdoms shall arise from his nation, but not with his power. 23. And at the latter end of their rule, when the transgressors have reached their full measure, a king of bold countenance, one who understands riddles, shall arise.

Then follows another description, more symbolic than colourful, of the evils perpetrated by Antiochus Epiphanes.[42]

Next, the wars and intermarriages between the Diadochi in Dan 11: there is no second guessing here, as in the feet of the statue on Dan 2; apocalyptic imagery is preserved, as well as anachronistic references to the powers of the time of redaction (e.g. 'Edom'), but otherwise the text is very clear in what is at stake and in the development of political issues, including the meddling of Rome in Seleucid affairs – something that would have far-reaching consequences.

Dan 11:1. And as for me, in the first year of Darius the Mede, I stood up to confirm and strengthen him. 2. And now I will show you the truth. Behold, three more kings shall arise in Persia; and a fourth shall be far richer than all of them; and when he has become strong through his riches, he shall stir up all against the kingdom of Greece. 3. Then a mighty king shall arise, who shall rule with great dominion and do according to his will. 4. And when he has arisen, his kingdom shall be

> Avesta and Zand which had been written with gold water on prepared cowhide ... And he threw hatred and enmity among the dignitaries and lords of Iran, one against another, and he himself was defeated <and> ran off to Hell.

Cf. Vahman. *Ardā Wirāz Nāmag*. The legend of the Avesta written still BCE in purple hide is well spread, though the idea that there was a 'Semitic' written Avesta is mere speculation. Tansar, Kirdēr and other Sasanid priests must have had a written Avesta with whatever material, oral or written, that was available. On the other hand, Alexander barely touched Judaea in his campaigns; the fanciful and sometimes (involuntarily?) comical report of Josephus on this can be found in AJ 11.302–47. For a deeper analysis of Josephus, cf. Shaye D. J. Cohen. 'Alexander the Great and Jaddus the High Priest according to Josephus' in: *AJSR* 7.8 (1982–3).

[42] Two remarks made by Collins (*Daniel*, p. 377) regarding this whole passage are that the portrait of Hellenistic history down to Antiochus Epiphanes's times is very accurate, but 'the quality of the Hebrew in this chapter is exceptionally poor'. A full examination is found in Collins's *Daniel*, but these remarks are widely accepted and leave little in terms of discussion. Examinations in terms of different approaches to Daniel and world empires are by Christopher Rowland. 'The Book of Daniel and the Radical Critique of Empire: An Essay in Apocalyptic'; and Uwe Glessner. 'Die "vier Reiche" aus Daniel in targumischen Literatur' (this one away from Second Temple literature, naturally), both in Collins and Flint, *The Book of Daniel*, vol. 2.

broken and divided toward the four winds of heaven, but not to his posterity, nor according to the dominion with which he ruled; for his kingdom shall be plucked up and go to others besides these [Alexander the Great]. ... 15. Then the king of the north [general term for the Seleucid Empire, or what remained of it] shall come and throw up siegeworks, and take a well-fortified city. And the forces of the south [the Lagids] shall not stand, or even his picked troops, for there shall be no strength to stand. 16. But he who comes against him shall do according to his own will, and none shall stand before him; and he shall stand in the glorious land [Judaea], and all of it shall be in his power. 17. He [Antiochus III] shall set his face to come with the strength of his whole kingdom, and he shall bring terms of peace and perform them. He shall give him the daughter of women to destroy the kingdom; but it shall not stand or be to his advantage. 18. Afterward he shall turn his face to the coastlands, and shall take many of them; but a commander[43] shall put an end to his insolence; indeed he shall turn his insolence back upon him. ... 30. For ships of Kittim[44] shall come against him, and he shall be afraid and withdraw, and shall turn back and be enraged and take action against the holy covenant. He shall turn back and give heed to those who forsake the holy covenant. ... 36. And the king shall do according to his will; he shall exalt himself and magnify himself above every god, and shall speak astonishing things against the God of gods. He shall prosper till the indignation is accomplished; for what is determined shall be done. 37. He shall give no heed to the gods of his fathers, or to the one beloved by women; he shall not give heed to any other god, for he shall magnify himself above all. ... 41. He shall come into the glorious land. And tens of thousands shall fall, but these shall be delivered out of his hand: Edom and Moab and the main part of the Ammonites.

Finally, the description of the four beasts (again, a sequence matching the one in Daniel 2) is information that can be always updated (indeed, it is updated until that time, with the beasts representing several recent powers, such as the Soviet Union); the horns of the last beast, confusing in its appearance as it may seem, fits the role of Antiochus Epiphanes very well and is the decisive clue to date this section of Daniel:

> Dan 7:1. In the first year of Belshazzar king of Babylon, Daniel had a dream and visions of his head as he lay in his bed. Then he wrote down the dream, and told the sum of the matter. 2. Daniel said, 'I saw in my vision by night, and behold, the four winds of heaven were stirring up the great sea. 3. And four great beasts came up out of the sea, different from one another. 4. The first was like a lion and had eagles' wings. Then as I looked its wings were plucked off, and it was lifted up from

---

[43] Not quite – a 'magistrate' with commanding powers would be a better description for Lucius Cornelius Scipio, who will impose the immense war debt to the Seleucids, since their victory against the Lagids was not in the best interests of Rome. Heb., קצין, BDB, 'chief', 'ruler'; Theodotion's Greek text has ἄρχοντας.

[44] A general term already found in Genesis meaning first Cyprus, then Greece, then Rome and finally anyone coming to battle from the West.

the ground and made to stand upon two feet like a man; and the mind of a man was given to it. 5. And behold, another beast, a second one, like a bear. It was raised up on one side; it had three ribs in its mouth between its teeth; and it was told, "Arise, devour much flesh." 6. After this I looked, and lo, another, like a leopard, with four wings of a bird on its back; and the beast had four heads; and dominion was given to it. 7. After this I kept looking in the night visions, and behold, a fourth beast, dreadful and terrifying and extremely strong; and it had large iron teeth. It devoured and crushed, and trampled down the remainder with its feet; and it was different from all the beasts that were before it, and it had ten horns. 8. I considered the horns, and behold, there came up among them another horn, a little one, before which three of the first horns were plucked up by the roots; and behold, in this horn were eyes like the eyes of a man, and a mouth speaking great things.[45] ... 12. As for the rest of the beasts, their dominion was taken away, but their lives were prolonged for a season and a time.'

In the historical or meta-historical aspects of Daniel there is no comparison to the confusion of peoples and regions of the ZWY (reminiscent of the Sib. Or., especially the last four books). The author of this sequence in the Danielic text knew well, and the messianic expectancy of the Son of Man, however Jewish it was (again, the parallels

---

[45] Regarding the nature of the last animal – which is entirely incompatible to anything seen or conceived by man – David Flusser suggested an ingenious explanation: this animal was the description of an Indian rhinoceros, but the author of this section of Daniel had never seen one in his presence, hence the fantastic depiction of this fourth beast.

> The animal had indeed nothing in common with the others. Current interpretation among scholars is that the animals refer to the same theme of Dn 2, that is to say, to the succession of the world empires. These are normally identified with Babylon, Media, Persia and Alexander's empire plus the Hellenistic kingdoms. The horns are more difficult to identify, but seem to refer to the Diadochi and also, in the subsequent verses, to Anthiocus Epiphanes, whose notorious lack of political ability gave rise to the Maccabean Revolt (167 a.C.).

For a complete discussion of how academical consensus was found on this and other Danielic issues in the middle of the twentieth century, see Rowley. *Darius the Mede*. The theme of the world monarchies, while particularly important in apocalyptic literature, does appear even in ancient historiography. Flusser identified the possible influence of Pseudo-Callisthenes's *Alexander's Romance* (by way of Philostrato's *Life of Apollonius of Tyana*) on the author of the book of Daniel and thus deducted – as a possibility only – that the 'Fourth Beast' may be a rhinoceros (cf. David Flusser. 'The Fourth Empire – an Indian Rhinoceros?' in: *Judaism and the Origins of Christianity*. Jerusalem: Magnes Press, 1988). The passage, reworked, reads thus:

> And then appeared a beast of an unusual kind, larger than an elephant, armed on its forehead by three horns, which the Indians used to call *odontotyrannos*, (having a dark colour similar to that of a horse). After having drunk water, it gazed at our camp and attacked us suddenly and was not hindered by the thick flames of fire.

More discussions on that are found in Wilhelm Kroll. *Historia Alexandri Magni*. Berlin: Weidmann, 1926; the Armenian version, which has some curiosities on that theme, was edited by Albert M. Wolohjan (*The Romance of Alexander the Great by Pseudo-Callisthenes*. New York: Columbia University Press, 1969). Other versions of the passage are also available in Flusser's edition of the *Josippon* (Jerusalem: Bialik, 1980) and in Adolf Ausfeld's edition (*Der griechische Alexanderroman*. Leipzig: /s.ed./, 1907). Cf. Flusser. 'The Fourth Empire', p. 348. Since Apollonius of Tyana is a first-century character, Flusser is not suggesting that Daniel was redacted after that, but merely that both Daniel and Philostrato drew on the same source.

in redeemers in Zoroastrianism are possible but less likely, and not only due to dating issues – Zoroastriasnism has three redeeming stages, versions that differ from one another when it comes to soteriology: successive redeemers, the two stallions, the *Činwad* bridge), blended in very well with the lengthy historical discourse in chapter 11 and, more importantly, with the real events of the Maccabbean Revolt.

§5 History and matter: Time as process and the role of the enemies of the *dēn* in more detail

As has been discussed, I do not think these schemes are opposite or incompatible with each other. Some look less understandable (as in the Sib. Or.), but then they are less frequent too. Regarding the precedence of the sevenfold structure, it looks unlikely but rather derived from a more primitive fourfold structure, closer to Hesiodic and Vedic schemes.[46] Another feature to be observed in the time block scheme is the relation between metals ranging from five to twelve and also related to different peoples (ZWY 4.57–9, already quoted and discussed above, esp. n. 7 in this chapter).

> The earth, Spandarmad, will open <her> mouth and all gems and metals, like gold, silver, copper, tin and lead [the gloss seen above on n. 7 in this chapter], will be revealed. And lordship and sovereignty will go to those of non-*Ērānian* origin, such as the *Hyōn*, the *Turk*, the *Xadur*, the *Tōbīd*, such as the *Hindūg*, the *Kōfyār*, the *Čynig*,[47] the *Kābulīg*, the *Subdīg*, the *Hrōmāyīg*, the *Karmīr Hyōn* and the *Spēd Hyōn*. They will be rulers over the *Ērānian* lands which I, <Ohrmazd, have created>; their orders and wishes will be current in the world. Authority will go from those with the leather girdle [again], the *Tāzig*, and from the *Hrōmāyīg* to them.

Some brief notes about these people are necessary since it is no longer mandatory to interpret apocalyptic texts as expressions of resistance against foreign invaders: the translation offered by Samuel Eddy[48] goes in this direction, which is the same in essence as the one proposed by Edward West.[49] We must take into account West's hermeneutical limitations at the end of the nineteenth century: 'For the Pahlavi text, of the *Bahman*

---

[46] Nick Allen. 'The Wheel of Existence' in: Marco V. García Quintela, Francisco J. González García and Felipe Criado Boado (eds). *Anthropology of the Indo-European World and Material Culture: Proceedings of the 5th International Colloquium of Anthropology of the Indo-European World and Comparative Mythology*. Budapest: Archaeolingua, 2006, pp. 221–2 n. 2; West. *The Hymns of Zaraθuštra*, Kindle locs 126–30.
[47] Their presence is especially nonsensical, given the very warm reception given to the last Sasanians. Cf. Compareti. 'The Last Sasanians in China', pp. 199–200; Domenico Agostini. 'Their Evil Rule Must End! A Commentary on the Iranian Bundahišn 33:17-28' in: Hagit Amirav, Emmanouela Grypeou and Guy Stroumsa (eds). *Apocalypticism and Eschatology in Late Antiquity*. Leuven: Peeters, 2017; Todd Godwin. *Persian Christians at the Chinese Court: The Xi'an Stele and the Early Medieval Church of the East*. London: I.B. Tauris, 2018.
[48] Eddy. *The King Is Dead*, p. 343.
[49] SBE, 1897.

Yašt [sic] the translator [i.e. West] has to rely upon the single old manuscript K20, already described,[50] from which he also takes numbering and divisions; in ZWY 4.5 Ohrmazd leaves a kind of 'puzzle' to Zaraθuštra, saying that the 'origin of those born of *xēšm* seed is not revealed'; but it may be objected that this is about their offspring, not about *xēšm* itself. Eddy suggests that their Western origin is indicated in the preceding verses (4.2–4), or they may come from Armenia (but Xwarāsān is explicitly mentioned; cf. also Bd 33.25).

Carlo Cereti, following Mary Boyce,[51] suggests that in an original version the term should refer to the Macedonians, but that is not what the internal evidence of ZWY, as it came to us, suggests.[52] In short, it would be a bold speculation to pull back the dating of ZWY far enough to be able to speak of Khorasan as referring to Bactria and the '*xēšm* race' as the descendants of Greek colonization, Alexandrian and even prior to Alexander.[53]

Notwithstanding all the unsolved problems above, it seems fair to say that we have already in the ZWY a vision sufficiently detached of human history from the mythical lore, so it can be considered as a process more human than divine.

This means that long before the so-called philosophies of history, later vulgarized by Voltaire,[54] a Zoroastrian predecessor, whose *Urtext* could have been a proto-ZWY, in its crudest layer could be previous to the Common Era and be the first text where history has both a sense (redemption) and a direction (future times). All this is hypothetical, but it both serves to underline the importance of the ZWY and related material in the Dk, GrBd, AWN and even later material, and also as a warning to those used to Eddy – like readings of cultural resistance to Hellenism – that it could well have happened; to take for granted a 'Bahman Yasht' from, say, the second century BCE is just not acceptable anymore. We have all the essential components in the ZWY in a much clearer fashion than in Dan 2, with particular regard to the episode of 'mixed metal': the Danielic author mixes iron with clay in order to explain the vagaries of Seleucid and Lagid diplomacy.[55]

---

[50] Kindle locs 906–7.
[51] 'The Poems of the Persian Sybil', p. 73.
[52] Cereti. ZWY, p. 174.
[53] I.e. the already quoted Branchidae, cf. n. 7 above.
[54] Karl Löwith. *Meaning in History*. Chicago: University of Chicago Press, 1949, pp. 1, 104.
[55] On this issue, the now old thesis of Jewish apocalyptic flowing and defining the Zoroastrian one, sustained by Philippe Gignoux and Jacques Duchesne-Guillemin, has a complete abstract and rebuttal by Boyce. 'On the Antiquity of Zoroastrian Apocalyptic', p. 71:

> Recently [1982], however, an attempt has been made to set its adoption later, on the assumption that the Iranians learnt of the Greek concept from a Jewish source, namely a passage in the Book of Daniel [2:31]. The argument runs as follows: in Daniel Nebuchadnezzar sees in a dream an image made in five descending stages of gold, silver, bronze, iron and 'part iron, part clay', i.e. 'the feet and toes were part potter's clay and part iron'. This last feature, it has been said, is not to be regarded as an arbitrary invention. 'To cast a metal statue a clay core was needed. The clay was then removed. But in order to stabilize very massive hollow metal pieces or their appurtenances, such as the feet of Nebuchadnezzar's colossus, on completion the clay cores were sometimes retained.' This realistic detail, it is suggested, was then taken over unthinkingly by the Iranian apocalypts [sic], and applied by them to the lowest branch of their symbolic tree, 'où il est hors de place, trahissant ainsi que Daniel était leur modèle, non l'inverse'. Such a relationship here between

It may be objected – with good reason – that the ZWY comes in sets of four or seven and is also dealing with mythical kingdoms (cf. Vištasp – ZWY 1.8; 3:23; Ardaxšir, the Kayanid – ZWY 1.9; 3:24) mixed with historical episodes (Ardaxšir ī Pāpagān, Šābuhr II, Ādurbad ī Mahraspandān – all in ZWY 3:24 – and Wahrām V in ZWY 3:26) – but does this not happen even more confusedly in Herodotus's first pages? And what about the proem of the Peloponnesian War of Thucydides referring to the Argives fleet during the Trojan War that causes embarrassment even to the most zealous supporters of the Athenian *Realpolitik*?

One could ask why the last of the kingdoms of 'sons of the race of wrath' was not included among the mythical kingdoms or between historical periods. In this regard, there are two problems that make this last race very special and difficult to determine: first, the magical attributes of the people 'of the wrath race', most notably the fact that they urinate poison in ZWY 4.4; second, the eternal discussion regarding the location of hostile populations – whether Eastern, in the Khorasan (as posited by Eddy i.e. descendants of the Greeks settled by Alexander, or by the Greeks and their Seleucid successors) or Arab invaders (a thesis more favoured by contemporary scholars, who tend to propose a recent ZWY dating and, by extension, the impossibility of a proto-ZWY BCE). The status of the mss and their quantity are insufficient to arrive at any definite conclusion.

What we have therefore is a final 'race' which appears on the threshold between an undesirable and terrifying present and a frightening future for the land that Ohrmazd created, namely Ērān. However, a comparative exegesis with Second Temple apocalypses yields very meagre results regarding the identification of the last eschatological enemies of the Persian texts.

This happens because, by comparison to Persian material, Jewish apocalyptic texts look far more explicit, although by their own parameters they may appear cryptic, for example, 4 Ezra 11–12 regarding the succession of Roman emperors. A more difficult proposition is the dating of Revelation just on an internal basis: almost no one believes

---

the two traditions is by no means as clear or certain, however, as this statement suggests. On the one hand, learned and ingenious though the explanation of the Daniel passage is, it does not appear to fit the interpretation which is offered of the king's dream. 'As in your vision, the feet and toes were part potter's clay and part iron, it shall be a divided kingdom. Its core shall be partly of iron, just as you saw iron mixed with the common clay: as the toes were part iron and part clay, the kingdom shall be partly strong and partly brittle.' A core of clay within hollow iron feet would if anything have added to their strength and resistance; it was because the two substances were actually mixed that the feet were the weak part of the great image, so that when the stone struck them they shattered, and the whole statue fell and was broken. If then we turn, on the other hand, to the Pahlavi texts, it is to find that they in contrast specify no substance but iron, with the qualification 'intermixed'. They speak of 'the time of intermixed iron' (*āhan-abar-gumēxt āwām*) [cf. Dk 9.8], or 'the branch ... of intermixed iron' (*azg ... ī āhan-abar-gumēxt*) [which Boyce takes the trouble to link to the much later *Zarātušt Nāme* as a similar *šāx-i āhan kumīxt*, translated by Rosenberg as 'la branche en alliage de fer' (Frédéric Rosenberg. *Le livre de Zoroastre (Zarâtusht Nâma)*. St Petersburg: Académie Impériale des Sciences, 1904, p. 68)], concluding the argument that following Duchesne-Guillemin's 'technological' arguments, it should be added that 'no iron alloys are known, it seems, from ancient Iran'.

In this respect it is useful to take a look at the monograph by James W. Allan. *Persian Metal Technology, 700–1300 A.D.* Oxford: Oriental Institute Monographs (no. 2), 1979.

in Neronian dating anymore, and a setting during the times of Domitian looks far more likely;[56] in both cases, we can be sure that the enemy, as hermetic as it may appear in the texts concerned, is the Roman Empire. The same goes for 2 Bar. 6, where both setting and theme can convincingly be dated after the fall of the Temple.[57]

§6 Trees, trunks, empires

The problem[58] I will tackle in this chapter is that of the relationship between vines, trees and gardens, on the one hand, and Baruch and Daniel apocalyptic material, on the other.[59] This seems to be especially important because it is a crossover between the apocalyptic visionary traditions of Baruch and Daniel, following the steps of Andrei Orlov.[60] But I am taking this in another direction, relating it to the vines of 2 Baruch and 3 Baruch, on the one hand (and, by extension, to prophetic and Pentateuch material), and to the trees, forests and the like in that very same material, on the other, which is more strictly in the tradition of apocalyptic visionaries (not just in the canonical Daniel text but mostly in the DSS fragments related to him).

The Syriac Apocalypse of Baruch (2 Baruch) seems very important in this respect, but first let us examine another Baruch apocalypse because of the link it provides to Edenic material.

Orlov drew attention to Edenic traditions preserved only in the Greek texts (as opposed to the Slavonic ones) of the Greek Apocalypse of Baruch (3Br), and this is quite important for the whole argument presented here because of the issues related to the vine in the latter (3 Bar. 4:7–16):[61]

This should suffice as a brief introduction to the main problems to be dealt with regarding the relation between mythical trees, trunks, empire sequences and metal ages; there are further developments. As Orlov himself said, 'the depiction conveys several rare traditions about the garden, of which two are especially important for this

---

[56] Collins. *Combat Myth*, p. 198.
[57] Following a theme of 'voices' (angelic and in any case sacred) found in 2 Bar. 7 also found in 4 Bar. 4:1, BJ 6.300 and Tacitus. *Histories* 5.13.
[58] Most of the discussion below follows closely Dobroruka. 'On Trees and Visionaries'.
[59] As a reminder, it should be noted that not all Danielic material is apocalyptic – the canonical text of Daniel, in itself, has long court tales, wisdom literature or otherwise 'edifying' material that cannot be classified as apocalyptic in the strict sense of the term, for example, as in the now famous division proposed in *Semeia* 14 (1979) because it is 'contained' in a book that came to be known (mostly due to chs 2 and 7–12) as an apocalypse.
[60] Andrei A. Orlov. 'The Flooded Arboretums: The Garden Traditions in the Slavonic Version of 3 Baruch and in the Book of Giants' in: *CBQ* 65 (2003).
[61] It is noteworthy that for 3 Baruch, as Harry E. Gaylord wrote back in 1983, 'we only have two manuscripts in Greek and they are both derived from a highly reworked [Slavonic] version'. This translation is that of Gaylord himself, in *OTP* 1, pp. 653–79. Cf. also Harry E. Gaylord. 'Redactional Elements behind the *Petrisov Zbornik* of the Greek Apocalypse of Baruch' in: *Slovo* 37 (1987): 91. The *Petrisov Sbornik*, or *Zbornik*, is composed of an aggregation of stories dated from 1468; it includes a romance about Troy, translated into Croatian from an Italian source. The whole material probably stems from the late Middle Ages; it also contains the famed *Visio Tugdali* ('Vision of Tundal', which contains, as discussed in Chapter 4 of this book, probably the most graphic detail on the horrors of Hell).

Greek text	Slavonic text
7 Baruch said, 'And how is that?' And the angel said, 'Listen, the Lord God made 360 rivers, the primary ones of them being the Alphias, the Aburos, and the Gerikos, and because of these the sea is not diminished.' 8 And I said, 'I pray you, show me which is the tree which caused Adam to stray.' And the angel said, 'It is the vine which the angel Samael planted by which the Lord God became angered, and he cursed him and his plantling. For this reason he did not permit Adam to touch it. And because of this the devil became envious, and tricked him by means of his vine.' 9 And I Baruch said, 'And since the vine became the cause of such evil and was cursed by God and (was) the destruction of the first formed, how is it now of such great use?' 10 And the angel said, 'Rightly you ask; when God caused the Flood over the earth and destroyed all flesh and 409,000 giants,' and the water rose over the heights 15 cubits, the water entered Paradise and killed every flower, but it removed the sprig of the vine completely and brought it outside.' 11 'And when the earth appeared from the water and Noah left the ark, he started to plant (some) of the discovered plants. 12 He also found the sprig, and taking it, he considered in his mind what it was. And I came and told him about it. 13 And he said, 'Should I plant it, or what (should I do with it)? Since Adam was	7 And the angel said to me, 'When God made the garden and commanded Michael to gather two hundred thousand and three angels so that they could plant the garden, Michael planted the olive and Gabriel, the apple; Ariel, the nut; Raphael, the melon; and Satanael, the vine. For at first his name in former times was Satanael, and similarly all the angels planted the various trees[62].' 8 And again I Baruch said to the angel, 'Lord, show me the tree through which the serpent deceived Eve and Adam.' And the angel said to me, 'Listen, Baruch. In the first place, the tree was the vine, but secondly, the tree (is) sinful desire which Satanael spread over Eve and Adam, and because of this God has cursed the vine because Satanael had planted it, and by that he deceived the protoplast[63] Adam and Eve.' 9 And I Baruch said to the angel, 'Lord, if God has cursed the vine and its seed, then how can it be of use now?' 10 And the angel said to me, 'Rightly you ask me. When God made the Flood upon the earth, he drowned every firstling, and he destroyed 104 thousand giants, and the water rose above the highest mountains 20 cubits above the mountains, and the water entered into the garden, bringing out one shoot from the vine as God withdrew the waters.'

[62] For that episode, useful parallels can be found in the *Midrash of Shemhazai and Azael*:

> One night the sons of Shemhazai, Hiwwa and Hiyya, saw [visions] in dream, and both of them saw dreams. One saw the great stone spread over the earth ... The other [son] saw a garden, *planted* (נטע) whole with [many] kinds of trees and [many] kinds of precious stones. And an angel [was seen by him] descending from the firmament with an axe in his hand, and he was cutting down all the trees, so that there remained only one tree containing three branches. When they awoke from their sleep they arose in confusion, and, going to their father, they related to him the dreams. He said to them: 'The Holy One is about to bring a flood upon the world, and to destroy it, so that there will remain but one man and his three sons.' (cf. Orlov. 'The Flooded Arboretums', p. 189)

And even more importantly, in a Manichaean tradition (in MP) regarding the Kawān fragment of the *Book of Giants* (fragment D), 'Nariman saw a gar[den full of] trees in rows. Two hundred ... came out, the trees...' (cf. Walter B. Henning. 'The Book of the Giants' in: *BSOAS* 11.1 (1943): 57, 60).

[63] Gr., πρῶτον + πλάθω, lit. 'of the first mould'.

Greek text	Slavonic text
destroyed by means of it, will I also encounter the anger of God through this?' And while saying these things, he prayed for God to reveal to him what he should do with this. 14 And in 40 days he completed his prayer and entreating much and crying,[64] he said, 'Lord, I implore you to reveal to me what I should do with this plant.' And God sent the angel Sarasael, and he said to him, 'Rise, Noah, plant the sprig, for the Lord says this: "Its bitterness will be changed into sweetness, and its curse will become a blessing, and its fruit will become the blood of God, and just as the race of men have been condemned through it, so through Jesus Christ Emmanuel in it (they) will receive a calling and entrance into Paradise." 16 Then know, Baruch, that just as Adam through this tree was condemned and was stripped of the glory of God, thus men now who insatiably drink the wine deriving from it transgress worse than Adam, and become distant from the glory of God, and will secure for themselves eternal fire. 17 For (no) good derives from it. For those who drink excessively do these things: Brother does not have mercy on brother, nor father on son, nor children on parents, but by means of the Fall through wine come forth all (these): murder, adultery, fornication, perjury, theft, and similar things. And nothing good is accomplished through it.'	11 And there was dry land, and Noah went out from the ark 12 and found the vine lying on the ground, and did not recognize it having only heard about it and its form. 13 He thought to himself, saying, 'This is truly the vine which Satanael planted in the middle of the garden, by which he deceived Eve and Adam; because of this God cursed it and its seed. So if I plant it, then will God not be angry with me?' 14 And he knelt down on (his) knees and fasted 40 days. Praying and crying, he said, 'Lord, if I plant this, what will happen?' 15 And the Lord sent the angel Sarasael; he declared to him, 'Rise, Noah, and plant the vine, and alter its name, and change it for the better.' 16 'But beware, Baruch: The tree still possesses its evil.'

investigation: the angels planting the garden and the flooding of the garden by the waters of the Deluge'.[65]

And this is why it is important that we have in mind the differences between the Greek and Slavonic versions of 3 Baruch[66] and begin with them before examining other materials.

---

[64] Note the similarity between that passage and the many fastings and grievings of 2 Baruch, for example, 5:1; 9:1; 12:5; 21:1; and 43:1, among others.
[65] Orlov. 'The Flooded Arboretums', p. 188.
[66] Alexander Kulik. *3 Baruch: Greek-Slavonic Apocalypse of Baruch*. Berlin: Walter de Gruyter, 2010, p. 11; and Orlov, 'The Flooded Arboretums', pp. 184–5.

References to the vine, or vineyards, appear fifty-three times in the HB (כרם) plus the NT (ἀμπελών); forests appear another forty-eight times. Most are commonsensical, as expected, and yield nothing special to this research.[67]

A few of them could be linked to symbolic language and thus have special meaning to the apocalyptic texts that are the theme of this research, for 'vines' and 'trees' play very different, although almost permanent roles, in Baruch and Danielic apocalyptic literature. These roles vary from one text to another and we must take into account that the evidence to be used is sometimes unevenly matched (i.e. we have more material for one of the two types than for the other, but that material may be of a more fragmentary nature).

To these preliminary difficulties it should be added that sometimes different recensions or versions of the same text can yield very different results – such is the case of 3 Baruch, with all its variations according to Greek or Slavonic traditions with remarkable differences for the main theme of this book, as stated above and in the footnote quoting Harry E. Gaylord.[68]

For that aspect of the research, vines and trees go almost hand in hand in the Bible and pseudepigrapha, from the outset of their stories. The trees – and also the vine as well – appear in the Garden of Eden, in a variety of forms, guises and mythical roles.[69]

The vine is usually remembered by those of us who study pseudepigrapha as the avenger of the Western (i.e. Roman) wrongs in 2 Bar. 36; however, there are other interesting references before that. One that may have been overlooked is that in 2 Bar. 29:5-6:[70]

> 29:5. Also, the earth will yield its fruits ten-thousandfold. A single vine will have a thousand branches, and a single branch will produce a thousand bunches of grapes, and a single bunch of grapes will produce a thousand grapes, and a single grape will produce a kor[71] of wine. 6. Those who have hungered will rejoice. And furthermore, they will see marvels every day.

---

[67] It should be noted that in the OT the most important symbol for the vine is Israel itself (Ps 80:8–9 is a prime example).

[68] Cf. also Kulik. *3 Baruch*, pp. 7–8, 17.

[69] As seen in the table above, in both the Greek and Slavonic recensions of 3 Baruch the vine is associated with the doom of Adam, and accordingly, a list of vices of sorts appears in 3 Bar. 4:16 Gr. (Slavonic makes it much shorter; it only makes Noah aware of the many evils still present in the vine).

[70] The translation of the Syriac text (and eventually of Greek or Latin fragments) of 2 Baruch follows the work of Michael E. Stone and Matthias Henze. *4Ezra and 2Baruch: Translations, Introductions and Notes*. Minneapolis: Fortress Press, 2013. This work is especially useful in that it offers constant reminders to the reader of similar passages in 4 Ezra and vice versa when reading 4 Ezra (they seem to have been written as one answering the questions posited by the other). I took the occasional glance at Daniel M. Gurtner. *Second Baruch: A Critical Edition of the Syriac Text With Greek and Latin Fragments, English Translation, Introduction, and Concordances*. London: Continuum, 2009. Both were compared with that of Albertus Klijn in *OTP* 1 when needed, throughout this whole book.

[71] BDB, 'מקור': 'spring', 'fountain'; the equivalent measure in the Syriac is called 'shafltha' (880 xestes; 1 xeste is approximately 0.3 litre). 'Xeste' is itself a Greek word of measure: 'ξέστης'.

Something to be recognized as of importance to my argument here is the term used at the end: 'they will see marvels', Syr. ܐܚܪܢ ܐܬܠܟܐ ܗܒܟܐ ܐܬܪܗܢ ܬܘ ܐܢܪ.

This ensures that in 2 Bar. 29 the vine is given its usual role of a plant related to joy, not necessarily to vice; this is all the more important since in the end of times its grapes will yield much more wine, a sign of Edenic 're-composition' (in the Garden of Eden man was one with nature e.g. Gen 1:29–30; 2:8–10).

And in the self-contained apocalypse of the forest, the fountain, the vine and the cedar, this motif will make itself even more important, for here the apparently insignificant vine becomes the avenger of the oppressed (thus associated with the traditional theme of the vengeance of the East against to West). This is important because it parallels the promises made to the resurrected just in Dan 12:10, a cornerstone of apocalyptic promises regarding the world to come and strictly linked to the statue of ch. 2 – in itself, an image of the primordial man or the cosmic pillar.[72]

The flowing of the vine-fruit here is no longer that of the dazzling fruit that got Noah drunk (Gen 9:20; Heb., כרם, 'vineyard', but it could be understood as the vine itself, simply); it is rather the symbol of plenty in a restored world, where it becomes a symbol of eternity (such as trees as a whole – the forest – and then the most stubborn tree of all, the Roman Empire, that, although having a mandate from the God of Heavens, abused it). To exemplify the above, cf. 2 Bar. 36:7–10:

> 36:7. I saw, and see, that vine opened its mouth and spoke and said to that cedar: 'Are you not that cedar that was left from the forest of wickedness, through whom evil persisted and was wrought all these years but never goodness? 8. You seized control over what was not yours, and even over what was yours you never showed compassion. You extended your power over those who were far from you, and those who approached you, you seized in the nets of your wickedness. You have exalted yourself all the time like one who could not be uprooted. 9. Now, then, your time has hastened and your moment has come. 10. Join, then, you too, O cedar, the forest that disappeared before you, and become sand with it, and your dust will be mixed together. Sleep now in sorrow and rest in torment until your last time will come, in which you will come again and be tormented all the more.'[73]

The vine as a symbol for Israel, in contrast to the tree (the 'imperishable' cedar, most likely a reference to the longevity of Rome), poses another striking parallel for the visionary regarding Daniel; it is, in a sense, a cosmic tree, albeit a negative and perverted one.

The abundance of the vine – that ended up occupying all the space previously used up first by the forest and then by the cedar – sums up a sort of 'visionary' promise

---

[72] Cf. Anders Hultgård. 'Mythe et histoire dans l'Iran ancien: Étude de quelques thèmes dans le *Bahman Yast*' in: Geo Widengren et al. *Apocalyptique iranienne et dualisme qoumrânien*. Paris: Adrien Maisonneuve, 1995, pp. 79–81.

[73] A standard apocalyptic motif, present in the Bd, the GrBd, the ZWY and AWN, among others: hatred for invaders knows no limits, hence punishment to them is never harsh enough.

already found in the OT (Gen 15:18; Deut 30:3-5; Josh 1:4; and Isa 43, among many other reminders of that promise); at the same time it gets 'leaked' by the fact that in Gen 9:15-21 it was after the covenant of God with Noah that the vine makes its hurtful appearance. God renewed his alliance in unequivocal terms: never again would His Creation be submerged, and the growing of the vine together with drinking its final product, wine, is linked to the whole episode.[74] This world of plenty, a consequence of God's promises, is described in 2 Bar. 38.1-40:4.

The topics related to trees discussed in the previous pages point us to two quite different - but related - contexts. This relation, as it will be shown, will be resumed at the end of this chapter.

On the one hand, we have a literary *topos* where the seer visualizes the trees as part of a larger mythical complex, namely that of the 'cosmic tree' and its derivatives; such is the case with Danielic visions. On the other, trees can be seen as representing past or present oppression by the powers that be, usually Greeks or Romans.

A third possibility, which looks intermingled with the last one, is that of another branch, or another plant (e.g. the vine in 2 Baruch) growing together or replacing the tree(s), which is precisely what we saw in 2 Bar. 38-40:4.

But these cases should be seen through the eyes of the seers, and this taxonomy is merely a didactic device to illustrate things in an easier way for us. It is my opinion that from the seer's point of view we are talking about the same thing here.

From the seer's 'point of view' different things can *apparently* be seen in the visions of trees and vines, but they all convey similar ideas - which are basically two: one is that of the tree-vine as the cosmic pillar and the other that, more fantastic and more akin to Revelation, which is the one to be found in the speaking vine from 2 Baruch.

This last one shows astounding resemblances in the episodes in the Sib. Or., with their double tradition of allegedly having a woman as a mouthpiece for divine prophecies and their scattered anti-Roman and Greek bias: this would be Sib. Or. 2.15-24,[75] among other passages - if the reader is patient enough with the crescendo of worsened Greek, redaction and meaning that are the hallmark of the Sib. Or. when read from their 'Prologue' up to Sib. Or. 13.

These are traits, both visionary and related to the meaning of history, again referred to justice and uproar regarding imperial oppression but again showing to the visionary,

---

[74] This is one possible reason for the popularity of the ἐκπύρωσις theme; a purge by fire would be in full accord with the divine promises and, in this sense, more acceptable to apocalyptic visionaries. Such a doctrine of two world cycles seems to be implicit in Hesiod's WD 106-201 and is explicit in Heraclitus and Plato - see especially *Politicus* 273 b-c. For such a belief in Judaism, see especially Josephus, in his *Vita* 49; AJ 1.2.3; cf. also Joseph Chaine. 'Cosmogonie aquatique et conflagration finale d'apres la secunda Petri' in: *Revue Biblique* 46 (1937): 207-16.

[75] Alfons Kurfess. *Sibyllinische Weissagungen: Urtext und Übersetzung.* Berlin: Heimann, 1951, pp. 27-8:

δὴ τότε καὶ δεκάτη γενεὴ μετὰ ταῦτα φανεῖται /ἀνθρώπων, ὁπόταν σεισίχθων ἀστεροπητής / εἰδώλων ζῆλον θραύσει λαόν τε τινάξει / Ῥώμης ἑπταλόφοιο, μέγας δέ τε πλοῦτος ὀλεῖται / δαιόμενος πυρὶ πολλῷ ὑπὸ φλογὸς Ἡφαίστοιο. / καὶ τότε δ᾽ αἱματόεσσαι ἀπ᾽ οὐρανίου καταβᾶσαι (?) / αὐτὰρ κόσμος ὅλος περ ἀπειρεσίων ἀνθώπων / ἀλλήλους κτείνουσι μεμηνότες, ἐν δὲ κυδοιμῷ / λιμοὺς καὶ λοιμοὺς θήσει θεὸς ἠδὲ κεραυνούς /ἀνθρώποις, οἳ ἄτερθε δίκης κρίνουσι θέμιστας.

as in 2 Baruch, 3 Baruch and in Danielic material, a world turned upside down by Nature itself. The theme of the world destruction by fire parallels that of the submerging of the forest in 2 Baruch (an image that would have been quite understandable to the public of the Sib.Or.).

So much for the vines and its fruits in the episodes described; essentially, they can be categorized in two broad groups that may overlap, one related to the intoxicating effects of the כרם, another related to the vine as a symbol of plenty which, in this case, can affront the might of powers apparently much more powerful and harder (maybe the cedar in 2 Bar. 36 – but this may also be a thinly veiled reference to the might of the many tribes of Israel against a united foe, with a 'hardened heart' as in Exod 7:3 – קשה את־לב, the property of wood as long-living as cedar[76]). Conversely, for a text written as a theological explanation for the disaster of 70 CE,[77] it can also double as referring to the Diaspora and the future role of the several 'branches' of Jews, once again to be reunited.[78] However, when it comes to the metaphors of trees and woods in Para-Danielic texts, a different picture appears, in many respects, to that of the post-Diluvian vine or the avenging vine.

To begin with, the sources are less straightforward; whereas the vine symbolizes, grossly speaking, one of the main themes depicted above (essentially two, the vine as Israel and the vengeance of the East against the West), the tree or wood is far more complex in its presentation to the visionary in the next fragments to be examined. It can appear on either side (e.g. the cedar in 2 Bar. 36 that bears more than a superficial resemblance to the trees in 4Q552–553 ['Four Kingdoms']).

Then 4Q242 is accepted as part of a 'cycle of Danielic writings' and may yield information that confirms part of our reasoning about the theme of the world empires and its constituents:[79]

> *Frags* 1–3 *1* Words of the pr[ay]er which Nabonidus, king of [the] la[nd of Baby]lon, the [great] king, prayed [when he was afflicted] *2* by a malignant inflammation, by decree of the G[od Most Hi]gh, in Teiman. [I, Nabonidus,] was afflicted [by a malignant inflammation] *3* for seven years, and was banished far [from men, until I prayed to the God Most High] *4* and an exorcist forgave my sin. He was a Je[w] fr[om the exiles, who said to me:] *5* «Make a proclamation in writing, so that glory, exal[tation and hono]ur be given to the name of [the] G[od Most High». And I wrote as follows: «When] *6* I was afflicted by a ma[lignant] inflammation [...] in Teiman, [by decree of the God Most High,] *7* [I] prayed for seven years [to all]

---

[76] Crowfoot and Baldensperger. *From Cedar to Hyssop.*
[77] Goodman. *The Ruling Class of Judaea*, pp. 19, 21, 30; and for a slightly different point of view on the subject, David M. Rhoads. *Israel in Revolution: 6–74 C.E.: A Political History Based on the Writings of Josephus*. Philadelphia: 1976; and Albertus F. J. Klijn. '2 (Syriac Apocalypse of) BARUCH: A New Translation and Introduction' in: *OTP* 1, p. 615.
[78] It should be noted that an 'Enochic fr. of the Dead Sea Scrolls deals with the same myth of the relation between angels and the planting of the garden, although in an Enochic direction: I mean 4Q530', about which these observations were first made by Orlov ('The Flooded Arboretums', p. 188).
[79] Cf. also, for 4Q521, Puech. *Discoveries the Judaean Desert*, pp. 1–38; Geza Vermes. 'Qumran Forum Miscellanea I' in: *Journal of Jewish Studies* 43 (1992): 303–4.

the gods of silver and gold, [of bronze and iron,] *8* of wood, of stone and of clay, because [I thoug]ht that t[hey were] gods' [...]

> *Frag. 4 1* ... [a]part from (?) them. I was healed *2* ... from it he caused to p[as]s. The peace of ... [...] *3* [...] ... my friends. I could not [...] *4* [...] how are you like [...] *5* [...] ... [...][80]

This is strongly similar to some passages in the Apoc. Ab. (preserved only in Slavonic, the *Urtext* dating from approximately 900 CE).[81]

In 4Q243-245, only 244 is of interest here, due to the reference to the Flood in connection with Daniel, mentioned earlier (4Q243 Fr. 13):

4Q244

> *Frag. 1 1* [...] before the ministers of the King, and the Assyrians [...]
> *Frag. 8 1* [...] ... [...] *2* [...] after the flood *3* [...] Noah from [Mount] Lubar [...] *4* [...] a city [...]
> *Frag. 12* (= 4Q242 13) *1* [...] the children of Israel preferred their presence above [God's presence] *2* [and they sacrificed their sons to] the devils of delusion.
> God grew angry against them and or[dered them to be given] *3* [into the hand of Nebuchadnezzar, king of Ba]bylon, and to make their land desolate of them because [...] *4* [...] ... [...] the exiles [...]

4Q245

> *Frag. 1 col. i 1* [...] ... *2* [...] ... and what *3* [...] Daniel *4* [...] a book that was given *5* [...] Qahat *6* [...] Bukki, Uzz[iah] *7* [... Zado]k, A[bia]thar *8* [...] Hi[l]kiah *9* [...] and Onias *10* [... Jona]than, Simeon *11* [...] David, Solomon *12* [...] Ahazia[h ...] *13* [...] ... [...]
> *Frag. 2 1* [...] ... [...] *2* [...] in order to eradicate wic[ked]ness *3* [...] those in their blindness, and they have gone astray *4* [... th]ey then shall arise *5* [...] the [h]oly, and they will return *6* [...] wickedness. *Blank*

There are more fragments of interest: 4Q552 Fr. I Col. 2 is one of those, because of the use made, respectively, of the cypress and of the cedar[82] in an apocalyptic context.

> *Frag. 9 col. ii 1* [...] ... [...] *2* not [...] ... to establish there the tent of me[eting] [...] *3* of the times. For, behold, a son is born to Jesse, son of Perez, son of Ju[dah ...] *4* the Rock of Zion, and he will drive out from there /all/ the

---

[80] For 4Q242, 'Prayer of Nabonides', see József T. Milik. 'Prière de Nabonide et autres écrits d'un cycle de Daniel' in: *RB* 63 (1956): 407–11; Geza Vermes. *Jesus the Jew*. London: Collins, 1973, pp. 67–8.

[81] Apoc. Ab. : 1-3. Translation and commentary by Rubinkiewicz and Hunt in *OTP* 1:

> On the day I was guarding the gods of my father Terah and the gods of my brother Nahor, while I was testing (to find out) which god is in truth the strongest, I (then) Abraham, at the time when my lot came, when I was completing the services of my father Terah's sacrifice to his gods of wood, of stone, of gold, of silver, of copper, and of iron [...].

[82] Heb., Aram. ארז.

Amorites, from [...] *5* to build the house for yhwh, God of Israel. Gold and silver [...] *6* he will bring cedar and cypress [from] Lebanon for its construction; but his son, the younger, [...] *7* he will officiate there first [...] ... [...] and to him [...] *8* [in al]l the [re]sidence from the heaven[s, because] the beloved of yhw[h] will dwell in safety [...] *9* [the] days, [and] his people will dwell forever. But now, the Amorites (are) there, and the Canaan[ites ...] *10* dwellers who have made them sin, because I have not inquired [the jud]gment of [...] *11* from you. And the Shilonite, and be[ho]ld, I have made him the servant of the pe[ople of] ...] *12* And now, let us establish the t[ent of mee]ting far from [...] *13* Eleazar [and Joshu]a the t[ent of me]eting from Beth[el] ...] *14* Joshua [... [ch]ief of the army ... [...]

In all the contexts shown above, it must be concluded that trees and plants in general played a special role in visionary experiences both in Baruch and Danielic-type apocalypses. This may have stemmed from two different sources – the tree as a derivative of the 'tree of life' scheme, although sometimes in an entirely negative role (see the trees in general and especially the cedar i.e. the Roman Empire in 2 Bar. 36).

On another note, the vine seems especially important and in a sense may be understood as representing the same role – Israel can be seen as a sort of 'cosmic pillar' too, although apparently humble and modest; an altogether distinct theme is that of the destiny of the vine, whose nature, purposes and uses are linked to an interesting theme of the fallen angels in 3 Baruch (it has a suspicious origin but has to fit the post-Diluvian world somehow, hence the troubles caused to Noah and also the joy it can give when its fruit is used correctly).

In the end, the role of the vine is not the same as that played in, for example, 4 Ezra 9:23–25 (interdiction of drinking wine as part of fasting), or even more interestingly, that in 4 Ezra 14:38 – part of the visionary process itself:

So I took five men, as he commanded me, and we proceeded to the field, and remained there. And on the next day, behold, a voice called me, saying, 'Ezra, open your mouth and drink what I give you to drink.' Then I opened my mouth, and behold, a cup was offered to me; it was full of something like water, but its color was like fire. And I took it and drank; and when I had drunk it, my heart poured forth understanding, and wisdom increased in my breast, for my spirit retained its memory; and my mouth was opened, and was no longer closed. And the Most High gave understanding to the five men, and by turns they wrote what was dictated, in characters which they did not know. They sat forty days, and wrote during the daytime, and ate their bread at night. As for me, I spoke in the daytime and was not silent at night. So during the forty days ninety-four books were written.[83]

---

[83] Translation by Metzger in *OTP* 1.

The same intoxicating role would be found in non-Jewish texts of apocalyptic flavour, especially Persian ones,[84] where intoxicants of many different types are linked to mystical experiences, mixed with wine or not. But this would take us too far away from the purposes of this chapter.[85]

So, as concluding remarks and ideas for future development of the theme, I think it is fair enough to divide our conclusions in this chapter in three main groups:

1. The first group is composed by what I can call 'the Deluge motif'. It appears in distinctive, if not opposite, roles in the HB and in 2 Baruch and 3 Baruch. Let us remember that once the 'original Deluge' was over, God promised to Noah never to destroy His Creation again by such means.[86] In the case of 2 Baruch, a sort of Deluge marks the end of history and the beginning of another αἰών; it is, in a way, a contradiction to the promise made to Noah in Gen 8:21-22.

Nonetheless, its purpose is good (not the fruit of God distasteful with His sons) and can, of course, be interpreted metaphorically – in fact, that is the reason why it appears placed inside a dream and why the visionary asks for its significance (2 Bar. 36:1: 'And when I had said these things I fell asleep there, and I saw a vision in the night ... 37.1: And surely I awoke and arose'[87]). In fact it can be classified as just another variant of the traditional theme of the East avenging itself on the abuse of the West, that is, it is a rereading of the Danielic theme of the world empires[88] together with the ages of the world.[89]

As a consequence, this kind of destruction takes place, first of all, in the mind of the visionary; it is not a 'fact', as the Deluge supposedly was. This is an important

---

[84] As discussed in Chapter 5, these come basically from eight Persian texts, the JN, the WD, the ZN, the 'Conversion of Vishtaspa', the ZWY, parts of the Dk, the AWN and the Vd. For more information on these texts as related to the whole of Zoroastrian output, cf. Widengren. *Die Religionen Irans*; and also Hartman. 'Datierung der Jungavestischen Apokalyptik', pp. 61–76.

[85] Cf. my article on the subject, Dobroruka. 'Chemically-Induced Visions in the Fourth Book of Ezra in Light of Comparative Persian Material', pp. 9–10.

[86] But this sort of 'new Deluge' could well be a reworked rendering of the Hebrew idea of 'upper' and 'lower' waters (e.g. in Ps 42; cf. Reuven Kiperwasser and Dan D. Y. Shapira. 'Irano-Talmudica I: The Three-Legged Ass and Ridyā in B. Ta'anith. Some Observations about Mythic Hydrology in the Babylonian Talmud and in Ancient Iran' in: *AJS Review* 32.1 (2008): 106).

[87] Such dream-visions could be a by-product of tensions inside the community, and these tensions may have provided the experimental dimension behind the visions (for that prospect cf. Stone. 'Apocalyptic', p. 420). Cf. also Pierre Bogaert. *Apocalypse de Baruch: Introduction, tradutcion du syriaque et commentaire*. Sources Chrétiennes. Paris: Les Éditions du CERF, 1969 (2 vols), vol. 1, p. 487, and vol. 2, pp. 71–3, where Bogaert reminds us that the visionary of 2 Baruch wakes up in a valley of flowers similar to that of 4 Ezra 9:24–26 and 12:51.

[88] For a general view, cf. Charles W. Fornara. *The Nature of History in Ancient Greece and Rome*. Berkeley: Yale University Press, 1983, p. 5; the basic polemics on the theme can be found in Joseph W. Swain. 'The Theory of the Four Monarchies: Opposition History under the Roman Empire' in: *Classical Philology* 35.1 (1940); and in the (late) reply to the many problems posed by Swain's hypothesis in Doron Mendels. 'The Five Empires: A Note on a Propagandistic *Topos*' in: *American Journal of Philology* 102 (1981).

[89] For an entirely different proposal on how to examine the issue of the four ages/empires/metals, cf. Yuhan S.-D. Vevaina. 'Miscegenation, "Mixture" and "Mixed Iron": The Hermeneutics, Historiography and Poesis of the "Four Ages" in Ancient Zoroastrianism' in: Peter Schäfer et al. (eds). *Texts and Studies in Ancient Judaism. Vol. 146, Revelation, Literature, and Community in Late Antiquity*. Tübingen: Mohr, 2010. P. 254 is of special interest.

distinction, lest we would end up with a text where God 'breaks' His promise.[90] We could also see the event described in the small apocalypse of the forest and the vine as a kind of 'proto-scientific lore', where the text tells us data about the causes and reasons for the rain.[91] So, the Deluge of that apocalypse within the text of 2Br may have been, quite simply, misunderstood.[92]

2. The second important theme tackled in this chapter is that of the different meanings that 'trees' and 'gardens' may have for the visionary processes involved; this is especially true when taken into account 2 Baruch and 3 Baruch in comparison to the Para-Danielic material of the DSS.

In the canonical Dan 2 (and, arguably, chs 4 and 7 too), the varied and colourful imagery used may represent, to some extent, the same basic *topos* – the 'Tree of Life'[93] or the 'Cosmic Tree'.[94]

If this is correct, we face the same idea here, ultimately non-Jewish but rather Indo-European or Indo-Iranian, of a development of Iranian[95] or Indian ideas.[96] This would be in itself a theme too great to explore in a summary, but suffice it to say that the hypothesis above is far from unanimous,[97] facing fervent opposition[98] as well as radical defenders.[99] In a fragment of the DSS not examined here, 4Q385, the vine, the tree and blood come altogether – but this is only a fragment.[100]

---

[90] Stone and Henze. *4 Ezra and 2 Baruch*, Kindle loc. 1539, and the 'Introduction' as a whole (e-book); see also Klijn. '2 (Syriac Apocalypse of) BARUCH', pp. 615–16; and Bogaert. *Apocalypse de Baruch*, vol. 2, pp. 12–13, 54 and especially 56. For the history of the mss tradition, I would argue, very tentatively, that this very strange passage (as it is compared to others more 'orthodox' in 2 Baruch, such as the Letter of 78:1–87:1) is one factor to be considered in the comparative smaller popularity of 2 Baruch versus 4 Ezra, as attested by the number of mss available.

[91] Cf. Kiperwasser and Shapira. 'Irano-Talmudica I', p. 105, n. 23 (2 Bar. 59:5; 1 En. 41:3–4; T. Levi 2:7; and Ps 42:8).

[92] Frederick J. Murphy. *The Structure and Meaning of Second Baruch*. Dissertation Series/Society of Biblical Literature 78. Atlanta: Scholars Press, 1985, pp. 76–7, 84; cf. also Kiperwasser and Shapira. 'Irano-Talmudica I', pp. 108–9.

[93] Cf. George Lechler. 'The Tree of Life in Indo-European and Islamic Cultures' in: *Ars Islamica* 4 (1937): 369–420; and Simo Parpola. 'The Assyrian Tree of Life: Tracing the Origins of Jewish Monotheism and Greek Philosophy' in: *J NES* 52.3 (1993): 161–208.

[94] Odette Viennot. *Le cult de l'arbre dans l'Inde ancienne*. Paris: P.U.F., 1954.

[95] Cereti. ZWY, pp. 1–2; Geo Widengren. 'Leitende Ideen und Quellen der iranischen Apokalyptik' in: Daniel Hellholm (ed.). *Apocalypticism in the Mediterranean World and the Near East: Proceedings of the International Colloquium on Apocalypticism, Uppsala, August 12–17, 1979*. Tübingen: Mohr, 1983, pp. 77–80.

[96] Marc Philonenko. 'Introduction generale' in: Geo Widengren et al. (eds). *Apocalyptique iranienne et dualisme qoumrânien*. Paris: Adrien Maisonneuve, 1995, pp. 1, 24–7.

[97] Philippe Gignoux. 'Nouveaux regards sur l'Apocalyptique iranienne' in: *Comptes-rendus des séances de l'Académie des Inscriptions et Belles-Lettres*. Paris: Diffusion de Boccard, 1986, pp. 334–46; Duchesne-Guillemin, 'Apocalypse juive et apocalypse iranienne', pp. 753–6.

[98] Gignoux. 'L'apocalyptique iranienne est-elle vraiment la source d'autres apocalypses?', pp. 71–6, for the most consistent arguments against the thesis of Iranian precedence in apocalyptic *topoi*.

[99] Boyce, 'On the Antiquity of Zoroastrian Apocalyptic'.

[100] Cf. Basil Lourié. 'The Calendar Implied in *2 Baruch* and *4 Ezra*: Two Modifications of the One Scheme', paper presented at the 'Sixth Enoch Meeting in Milan (in memory of Hanan Eshel)', 27 June 2011. Footnote 19 reminds us that, in the author's own words, 'for the full dossier of this prophecy about "the blood from wood", including, beside such widely known texts as the *Epistle of Barnabas* and 4QDeutero-Ezekiel (4Q385), a still unpublished Coptic letter by Horsiesius (late 4th cent.), the Slavonic apocrypha *The Ladder of James* and the *Inscription on the Chalice of Solomon*'.

But there is more than one meaning necessarily involved, because, if the *topos* is the same both in Daniel, the Sib. Or. and in 2 Baruch and 3 Baruch, the use of the imagery is very different.

In each case the idea conveyed is the same, that of the East against West theme, be the Western villain the Hellenistic world or Rome, and it does not really matter, for political propaganda purposes, if the symbol used to denigrate them is a statue or a tree. However, trees and gardens at large play a very different role in 2 Baruch – they are, as a whole, the 'enemy', and one of them is signalled out as the worst, and that is the cedar.

The interpretation of the dream makes it clear that we are still dealing with the 'sequence of four' *topos*:

2 Bar. 39:1. And he answered and said to me: 'Baruch, this is the interpretation of the vision that you saw. 2. As you saw that vast forest that was surrounded by high mountains and steep [rocks], this is the word: 3. See, days are coming and this kingdom will be destroyed that once destroyed Zion. And it will be subjected to the one that is coming after it. 4. Furthermore, this one, too, after a while will be destroyed. And another, a third, will arise, and it, too, will rule in its time, and it will be destroyed. 5. And after these, a fourth kingdom will rise, whose power is harsher and more evil than that of those that were before it. And it will rule many times like the forest of the plain, and it will hold fast for [some] times and exalt itself more than the cedars of Lebanon. 6. And truth will be hidden in it, and all those flee to it who are soiled in iniquity, as evil beasts are fleeing and sneaking into the forest. 7. And when the time of its consummation has drawn near that it should fall.[101] Then the reign of my Messiah will be revealed, which is like the fountain of the vine, and when it is revealed it will uproot the multitude of its hosts.'

But the essence of the idea has, so to speak, surpassed the imagery. In 3 Baruch, by contrast, we find ourselves much closer to Enochic material,[102] since a lot of the themes discussed here have to do with the fallen angels (*the* Enochic theme *par excellence*); the flooding of the Garden of Eden happens due to them,[103] and after the Deluge itself

---

Of interest to the reader is also Basil Lourié. 'Лурье, -Чаша Соломона и скиния на Сионе. Часть 1. Надпись на Чаше Соломона: текст и контекст [The Chalice of Solomon and the Tabernacle in Sion. Part 1: Inscription on the Chalice of Solomon: Text and Context]' in: *Byzantinorossica* 3 (2005): 8-74, especially 14-19; the parallels show that the 'wood' in this prophecy which was originally meant is the tree of vine.

[101] I have followed Hintze's edition as close as possible, but this is a difficult passage – Klijn's translation flows better: 'in which it will fall'. Gurtner explains that he is using Charles's translation, but it is wrong nonetheless. Charles's translation reads, 'And it will come to pass when the time of its consummation that it should fall has approached' (also a strange rendering by the translator in that chapter, Charles himself), in: Robert H. Charles. *The Apocrypha and Pseudepigrapha of the Old Testament*. London: Oxford University Press, 1913, vol. 2, p. 501.

[102] Kulik. *3 Baruch*, pp. 36, 39, 42, 53, 90, 94-6, 117, 122, 124-7, 130; Orlov. 'The Flooded Arboretums', pp. 184-5.

[103] Orlov. 'The Flooded Arboretums', pp. 186-7.

Noah is left with a plant that has after-effects so dangerous that it led to the fall of the primeval man, Adam:

> And I Baruch said, 'Since also the vine has been the cause of such great evil, and is under the judgment of the curse of God, and [was] the destruction of the first created, how is it so in use now?' (3 Bar. 4:9, Gr. recension)

And this takes us to the very last issue to be discussed – the vine.

3. The vine appears both in the HB and in the pseudepigrapha examined in a variety of roles. In the one that matters to this analysis, it is linked to one of its most useful, old and dangerous derivatives: wine.

Wine was the cause of the fall of Adam, so we read in 3 Baruch; wine of good quality is reserved for the Elect, but the dregs will be drunk by the (Roman) oppressors in 2 Baruch:

> 13:8 you shall say to them: 'You who have drunk strained wine, drink also from its dregs!' For [this is] the judgment of the Most High, who shows no partiality.[104]

The imagery is the same, but with markedly different intentions in 3 Baruch from the rest of the texts compared in this article; this may be due, to a certain measure, to the proximity of 3 Baruch with Enochic themes.

But as in everything else in apocalyptic imagination, vines can cause damage or blessing. The same plant that caused Adam to fall, according to 3 Baruch, can be a metaphor for the primordial trees present in Danielic literature and, by way of derivation, in 2 Baruch too. The problem discussed in this part of this chapter is that of the relationship between vines, trees and gardens as material entities, on the one hand, and Baruch and Daniel apocalyptic material, on the other;[105] this seems to be especially important because it seems that here there is a kind of crossover between the apocalyptic visionary traditions of Baruch and Daniel, following the steps of Orlov's analysis.[106]

Resuming the trajectory of this chapter, in terms of chronological external evidence, it has been seen that Hesiod comes first. The scheme of Hesiod does not deal with empires, but after a few centuries the scheme of Herodotus does and is a candidate for the first mention of sequences of 'world empires' (a term still difficult to understand wherever it appears, since it always leaves outside other great powers of the era in question).[107]

---

[104] 'Dregs', Syr. ܫܘܡܪܐ; and Bogaert. *Apocalypse de Baruch*, vol. 2, p. 37.

[105] As a reminder, it should be noted that not all Danielic material is apocalyptic – the canonical text of Daniel, in itself, has long court tales, wisdom literature or otherwise 'edifying' material that cannot be classified as apocalyptic in the strict sense of the term, for example, as in the now famous division proposed in *Semeia* 14 (1979) because it is 'contained' in a book that came to be known (mostly due to chs 2 and 7–12) as an apocalypse.

[106] Orlov. *Apocalypse de Baruch*.

[107] *Histories*, 1.95, 130:

> When the Assyrians had ruled Upper Asia for five hundred and twenty years their subjects began to revolt from them: first of all, the Medes. These, it would seem, proved their valour in fighting for freedom against the Assyrians; they cast off their slavery and won

§7 A last note on resurrection in a concrete context: 2 Macc 12:39–45 in relation to Dan 12:2

When the turmoil[108] that followed the Romans, in the person of ambassador Gaius Popilius Laenas, began to mess around Seleucid affairs in earnest after Antiochus IV's manipulating the Lagids' kingship,[109] so to speak, Antiochus IV Epiphanes had a serious issue to contend with – money, still owed by his predecessor Antiochus III to the Romans after the Peace of Apamaea (187 BCE). Most of this has been presented in other parts of this book.

As per usual, Antiochus left to his *filobasilei* (let us remember that Hellenistic administration can be defined, in opposition to Roman rule, as constituted by *basilika pragmatika* vs *res publica*). Remember that Hellenistic states did not have the elaborate bureaucracy that characterized Roman affairs, at least regarding taxpaying,[110] but rather relied on impulsive decision making.[111]

> freedom. Afterwards the other subject nations too did the same as the Medes / Ἀσσυρίων ἀρχόντων τῆς ἄνω Ἀσίης ἐπ' ἔτεα εἴκοσι καὶ πεντακόσια, πρῶτοι ἀπ' αὐτῶν Μῆδοι ἤρξαντο ἀπίστασθαι, καί κως οὗτοι περὶ τῆς ἐλευθερίης μαχεσάμενοι τοῖσι Ἀσσυρίοισι ἐγένοντο ἄνδρες ἀγαθοί, καὶ ἀπωσάμενοι τὴν δουλοσύνην ἐλευθερώθησαν. μετὰ δὲ τούτους καὶ τὰ ἄλλα ἔθνεα ἐποίεε τὠυτὸ τοῖσι Μήδοισι.
>
> This means a sequence of Assyria–Media–Persia (the next universal power, mentioned elsewhere by Herodotus. In Book I.130 too:
>
> Thus Astyages was deposed from his sovereignty after a reign of thirty-five years: and the Medians were made to bow down before the Persians by reason of Astyages' cruelty. They had ruled all Asia beyond the Halys for one hundred and twenty-eight years, from which must be taken the time when the Scythians held sway. At a later time they repented of what they now did, and rebelled against Darius; but they were defeated in battle and brought back into subjection. But now, in Astyages' time, Cyrus and the Persians rose in revolt against the Medes, and from this time ruled Asia. As for Astyages, Cyrus did him no further harm, and kept him in his own house till Astyages died. This is the story of the birth and upbringing of Cyrus, and thus he became king; and afterwards, as I have already related, he subdued Croesus in punishment for the unprovoked wrong done him; and after this victory he became sovereign of all Asia. / Ἀστυάγης μέν νυν βασιλεύσας ἐπ' ἔτεα πέντε καὶ τριήκοντα οὕτω τῆς βασιληίης κατεπαύσθη, Μῆδοι δὲ ὑπέκυψαν Πέρσῃσι διὰ τὴν τούτου πικρότητα, ἄρξαντες τῆς ἄνω Ἅλυος ποταμοῦ Ἀσίης ἐπ' ἔτεα τριήκοντα καὶ ἑκατὸν δυῶν δέοντα, πάρεξ ἢ ὅσον οἱ Σκύθαι ἦρχον. ὑστέρῳ μέντοι χρόνῳ μετεμέλησέ τέ σφι ταῦτα ποιήσασι καὶ ἀπέστησαν ἀπὸ Δαρείου, ἀποστάντες δὲ ὀπίσω κατεστράφθησαν μάχῃ νικηθέντες. τότε δὲ ἐπὶ Ἀστυάγεος οἱ Πέρσαι τε καὶ ὁ Κῦρος ἐπαναστάντες τοῖσι Μήδοισι ἦρχον τὸ ἀπὸ τούτου τῆς Ἀσίης. Ἀστυάγεα δὲ Κῦρος κακὸν οὐδὲν ἄλλο ποιήσας εἶχε παρ' ἑωυτῷ, ἐς ὃ ἐτελεύτησε. Οὕτω δὴ Κῦρος γενόμενός τε καὶ τραφεὶς ἐβασίλευσε καὶ Κροῖσον ὕστερον τούτων ἄρξαντα ἀδικίης κατεστρέψατο, ὡς εἴρηταί μοι πρότερον, τοῦτον δὲ καταστρεψάμενος οὕτω πάσης τῆς Ἀσίης ἦρξε.
>
> Why is this so important to repeat in the whole passage? Because although the HB does not have this sequence, the book of Tobit does, even if we have it only in Gk.: Tob 14:4: 'Go to Media, my son, for I fully believe what Jonah the prophet said about Nineveh, that it will be overthrown. But in Media there will be peace for a time'/'ἄπελθε εἰς τὴν Μηδίαν τέκνον ὅτι πέπεισμαι ὅσα ἐλάλησεν Ιωνας ὁ προφήτης περὶ Νινευην ὅτι καταστραφήσεται ἐν δὲ τῇ Μηδίᾳ ἔσται εἰρήνη', suggesting also that another power is to take its place in due time.

---

[108] A small part the following paragraphs was originally presented at the meeting of the British Association for Jewish Studies in Dublin, 2013.
[109] Polybius. *History*, 29.27.
[110] Rostovtzeff. *The Social & Economic History of the Hellenistic World*, p. 1053.
[111] Goodman. *The Ruling Class of Judaea*, p. 10.

This all seems quite straightforward and even more so when we take into account that even among the Jews, with the treasure-rich Temple in Jerusalem, there were many in favour of 'Hellenization' – a word that had a very different meaning in the second century BCE than today (mostly because of Droysen's efforts in the nineteenth century).[112]

In spite of semantic changes, the text of 1 and 2 Maccabees (not to mention other sources, like Josephus or Philo) are unanimous in stating that Palestinian Jews, that is, those, on the one side, directly affected by the dispute between Antiochus Epiphanes and the partisans of 'Hellenization', and those, on the other side, who wanted to make no concessions – or so they thought – faced a common problem.

For the first time in Jewish history people were being killed not because of their rebelliousness, their refusal to pay tribute, to join military ranks of service or for any known, familiar issue.[113] They were being killed on the grounds of willing to follow one faith (their native one) and of not making concessions to 'foreign' ways that would radically alter the Judaism some knew, or the Judaism they were brought up with.[114] And it will not suffice – at least not to the historian – to say that religion was in this case, as in many others after, a pretext: that is a much later, and anachronistic, reading of events.

For Jews who were on the receiving end of the revolt against Antiochus Epiphanes and his followers, a new problem arose: in a religion which highly regarded duties to God and corresponding rewards (e.g. Gen 49:10; Mic 3:11; 1 Sam 10:11; Ezra 16:34; Eccl 4:9; Isa 3:11), what happened to those who were 'martyred', executed because of 'stubbornness' in their religious ways and practices? It appeared that this matter – together with other issues – sparked the plug that maybe *šeol*, as it appears in all the examples examined and also in other key passages (like Job 17:16), was just not enough anymore. Too much suffering was involved, and a new concept found the ideal ground in the killings that happened during the Revolt – namely that the righteous dead may, after all, get a 'different' *šeol* or, to put it in a more sophisticated way, deserved a better world beyond. Moreover, even those in need of atonement but could no longer do so in this life (2 Macc 12:43–44) would have another opportunity in a different afterlife.

Again, the promises in Daniel – not to mention 4Q521, 4QPseudo-Ezekiel, Second Isaiah and all the messianic promises in the DSS and Second Temple Jewish literature plus the NT – relate twofold as survival of the soul as well as the end of history as we know it.

A final suggestion after examining a variety of possibilities of *topoi* of 'four' sequences, their convergences, uses and differences is that they are not necessarily related to cultural-political resistance. That is surely not the case in Hesiod, whose worries are very far away from that – but the world empires appear first in Herodotus, then Tobit, and Daniel is the earliest attested source where the theme appears joining the three mythical complexes in one single narrative, and, moreover, given the time of Daniel's final redaction (around 167–164 BCE), it fit perfectly in the new theological

---

[112] Hengel. *Jews, Greeks and Barbarians*, p. 52.
[113] Ibid., p. 95.
[114] 2 Macc 4:7–10.

doubts posed by Antiochus Epiphanes and his minions in Judaea. A hypothetical pre-CE ZWY, or even a hypothetical pre-CE BY, might have done the same thing earlier; but as we have it, with so many layers – sometimes contradictory in the very text, sometimes different among the few mss left – this idea is no more than a gamble. Again, the best there can be sensed here are parallels (quite a lot for the purposes of this book) that all hang on the same proposition: that Zoroastrianism was 'founded', whether Zaraθuštra existed individually or not, much earlier than the three big kings of united Israel (Saul, David and Solomon), earlier than the Exile and that could only have been captivated and adopted by Jews during the Second Temple period.

Conclusion: Towards a great future

This part is a relatively quick reflection on what was discussed above: the positive conclusions to be drawn, the shady areas, the parallels that do not prove influence but that exist, nonetheless. It is also dedicated to the long future Zoroastrian ideas would have regarding the meaning the history and the afterlife.[1]

§1 A great future, regardless of how old Zoroastrianism can be

Considering our own times, the indirect impact of Zoroastrianism is in an inverse proportion to the number of its adherents. If the majority of scholars is correct and Zoroastrianism was already, in its essentials, a living faith from the Late Bronze Age onwards (put in 'order' by Tansar and then by Kirdēr in the third century CE) there would still be the need to prove how this religion was 'exclusive' in the Achaemenid world and then how Jews in Exile had contact with it and incorporated its core ideas.

Most of this has been examined above. Second Isaiah and, even more so, Daniel display traces of very peculiar notions of the destiny of the soul, of the role of God orchestrating not just the usual neighbours that are displayed in pre-Exilic texts in the Deuteronomic-pattern but also a God that takes care of all the geographic boundaries of post-Exilic and Hellenistic times, and whose promises turned the old notion of *šeol* obsolete. Now rewards were greater – they were eternal.

Again, the issue of dualism is present: in Second Isaiah mostly in God's insistence in strict monotheism (and here the fact that Cyrus is His anointed should not scandalize: even a Pagan can be the tool of His will); in Daniel, both in the fourfold schemes in chs 2 and 7 that for the first time in HB texts state human history as a divinely controlled process and in the related theme of the resurrection of the dead and the portion of the just, as well as of the wicked.

This language permeates to a very large extent many important texts in the DSS; 4Q521 presents a fascinating puzzle with the similarity to the Činwad bridge, and 4Q386 is one of a cluster of texts that deal with future life linked to the reunion of flesh and bones; this goes together with promises of healing and related issues, and, to be

---

[1] Foltz. *Spirituality in the Land of the Noble*, pp. 40–1.

fair, they are previous to Second Isaiah (e.g. Isaiah 35). However, this is the shamanistic theme par excellence and will make itself present even in Islam.

We can end this book with the promises made in the Introduction. No 'influence' can be defined, and for several reasons it is very unwise to talk about influence at face value. However, the purpose of this book was not to jump into that directly (as Norman Cohn, Mary Boyce and a host of other scholars did) but is rather more modest and, hopefully, more feasible: to trace parallels when they are too close either in plot or in vocabulary to be ignored.

These occasions, so to speak, are as follows:

1. Strict monotheism instead of monolatry (Second Isaiah and Daniel, who insist there is a 'God in Heaven' who can reveal both a dream he never had in the first place and give its meaning[2]).
2. At least one Second Temple apocalypse – and an important one for that matter – 4Ezra displays clear traces of ASC-inducing techniques present in a great number of Zoroastrian texts. Given the paucity of Zoroastrian texts compared to the plethora of Second Temple texts at large, this is a very surprising piece of information: the proportion here, again, is inverse.
3. The schemes regarding temporal historical sequences present first in Daniel and then in other Second Temple texts (mostly apocalypses but in DSS fragments too) are found in 'proto-forms' (i.e. in forms that look cruder to Danielic or even the ZWY) that again periodize world history in phases of four stages, as examined in Chapter 6.
4. The promise of everlasting rewards appear in Daniel and Zoroastrian literature, but both 4Q521 / the Činwad bridge and purely Zoroastrian ways of separating the good from the bad turn these parallels closer.
5. Finally, the role of Tansar and Kirdēr put Zoroastrian material – perhaps in a less-organized form – from the third century BCE onwards: time enough for this material to be simultaneous to most, if not the whole, of the DSS (doubtless 4Q521) and to Second Temple Judaism at large. This should be taken as a possibility, not as a definite, proven fact.

All that is abridged in the five points above hang on the the mss dating problem, to which Tansar and Kirdēr shed a new light – but this light is not enough. Even the Pahlavi Psalter fragment, by comparison much earlier, only puts us backwards a couple of centuries closer to Second Temple Judaism. Not nearly sufficient to talk about influence but as a reinforcement to the antiquity of the Pahlavi script and, thus, to the ZA.

Of all the five points listed above, the one that would have the more lasting influence is undoubtedly the fourfold scheme of the ZWY, so similar to the Danielic one or that present in 4Ezra. It seems very unwise to speak – as former scholars did – of a BY that

---

[2] Ironically, in so doing Daniel saves not only his own life and that of his three companions but also of the other diviners from other religions that Nebuchadnezzar swore to kill.

existed as a form of spiritual resistance against Hellenization. What we have is the *zand* of a purported Yt, called ZWY. And as it stands, it hardly looks as a Yt at all but rather like other ZA texts where Zaraθuštra receives wisdom concerning the end of times and final judgement.

Here we have a mixture of older notions, common to almost every religion – that of propitiation. In that sense Zoroastrianism is not that different from other cults: sacrifice correctly, live a decent life according to a certain collection of rules (note how the term 'text' is avoided) and you will have your portion of happiness on Earth, in this life; this is what sapiential literature in the HB is all about (and it just takes one look at the questions posed to Job and to Ezra in 4Ezra to realize that the similarities between them are considered seriously). In some rare cases even in the world to come, status differences were to be observed: in Egyptian religion, social hierarchy was scrupulously observed; a pharaoh could expect a much better afterlife than a peasant, with all shades of class and occupation in between.

This takes a twist in Zoroastrianism when Zaraθuštra sees what lies in the world beyond: as a matter of fact others get that chance too (Vištasp and Kirdēr are the important names here, even if there is no agreement that the first existed historically as Zaraθuštra's patron). Observation of correct religious practices (the *dēn*) would generate two parallel processes that had the same purpose: individual judgement (preferably going to *Garōdman*, 'Paradise', than *Dosōx*, 'Hell') and a cosmic struggle where individuals would be judged – according to their deeds – and the whole of Creation will become perfect. This perfection, as seen, was foretold by Ohrmazd just before his Creation and the attack of Ahriman. One interesting parallel here is that like in other religious systems, the Devil, the Opponent, the Evil One or whatever be the name is more ignorant of the outcomes than the 'good' side.

With Zoroastrianism, the range of Salvation is universal in scope, in time and matter; and the novelty is that these two processes lead to a definitive future. The same thing appears in Second Isaiah and in Daniel – but nowhere else in the HB. Promises in the HB take the shape of agreements between God and a man, or some men (Adam, Noah, Abraham, Moses and more), and the Covenant with His people (again, the scope is limited in time, in space and future perspectives).

The horizon of the religion of the Hebrews can be seen as broadening its limits from Genesis to the later pre-Exilic prophets, but nothing compared to the continuum defined first by Cyrus and his successors (including the weird 'Darius the Mede') and the awakening of the dead from the dust in Daniel and the promises of Second Isaiah (to be fair, some already present before ch. 40, e.g. Isa 35). With Hellenism and the broadened geographical promises it brought Second Temple Judaism and its future derivative, Christianity – especially apocalyptic literature – it also widened its horizons, in this world and in the world to come. This fact alone could hardly have been the lone invention of the author of Second Isaiah or the one from the ending of Daniel. Given the fact that together with all its Late Bronze Age features Zoroastrianism has plenty of references to history as a process, and to fine rewards, even with all the mss problems it is very difficult to imagine such concepts having been first devised by a small group of post-Exilic Jews (the author of Second Isaiah, the authors of Daniel, the authors of many texts among the DSS that deal with a final and definite messianic stage in human history). It would take a leap of faith to figure out how characteristics so old would be mimicked by a people that is already living in the last half of the first millenium BCE.

§2 Usage by Pagan and Jewish-Christian late sources

After the discussion in the last paragraph, it seems apparent that there are two ways in which to move forward with the issue of how, where and when such syncretistic processes took place.

The usual guess for a place is Asia Minor, the place of choice of almost every author dealing with syncretic issues in Antiquity.[3] It is not an unfounded suspicion: one need only to take a look at the life of Mithridates, however exceptional it was, to see how many different religious elements were concocted in it. While it would seem naive to accept Asia Minor as the only place for this to happen, it also seems unwise to reject it straightforwardly: being in the crossroads between East and West and having been conquered and reconquered over centuries, if not millennia, of peoples that had the most varied backgrounds – ethnically, linguistically and genetically – it also provided room for different cults in different places, due to its sheer extent. As a melting pot, it could prove bigger and more important than a city like Alexandria.

In modern parlance we refer to the characters created during that period using the epithet of 'pseudo-' before their names, which are usually Hellenized. So it came to be that we refer, however fragmentally, to Pseudo-Hystaspes, Pseudo-Ostanès, Pseudo-Zoroaster.[4] But it should be noted that neither in Jewish apocalyptic tradition nor in Greek usage of half-historical characters is the choosing of names random. There is to me a somewhat obvious connection between authorship and text (or at least one that was obvious in ancient times, as we saw before while discussing the role of 'patron saints' for each type of apocalyptic text).

Now, in order to discuss properly the phenomenon of syncretism of Zoroastrianism with other sources in Antiquity – especially Late Antiquity – one should look not directly into Zoroastrian literature (given the many dating problems that remain unsolved[5]) but rather to the other end, that is, to the consumption, adaptation and usages of what we would call today pseudo-Zoroastrian lore. This would be especially true of the many tales attributed to Zoroaster (or, for that matter, to any other non-Greek source) by the Greeks themselves,[6] in the Barbarian world fashioned according to their custom. This was – partly only, to be true – in the chapter discussing the *Oracles of Hystaspes*, but much more remains to be done.[7]

---

[3] Marek. *In the Land of a Thousand Gods*, pp.180–308.
[4] Bidez and Cumont. *Mages Helenisées*.
[5] Bailey. *Zoroastrian Problems*.
[6] James S. Romm. *The Edges of the Earth in Ancient Thought*. Princeton: Princeton University Press, 1992, pp. 82–120.
[7] De Jong. *Traditions of the Magi*, pp. 12–28. This remains the standard work to deal with Zoroastrianism as perceived in the Graeco-Roman world view, especially in late Hellenistic-Early Roman periods.

This use is far from disrespectful or offensive per se; as a matter of fact, it was part of a double-patterned common behaviour by the Greeks to attribute to non-Greeks some kinds of knowledge, wisdom or just more antiquity in terms of plain years passed.[8] The attribution to Eastern (or even Western) characters of some kind of sacred lore fits into the same pattern.[9] What matters to us here is that practice in a very specific stance, namely Late Antiquity literature that became a sort of 'final product'[10] of that kind of usage. After some more time, this became less and less necessary in a Mediterranean world that was by the end of the sixth century CE essentially Christian.[11]

§3 Shape of meaning in history

As we saw above, all this came to a dead end when it was no longer necessary to recur to the ancient, alleged or invented wisdom of Pagans as proof of the antiquity and thus truthfulness of the Christian revelation. It may have been very important as a means of propaganda, but at some point it was no longer necessary.

On the other hand, the sheer variety of texts of the apocalyptic type, namely the ones denominated by scholars as the 'historical type'[12] would have a very long career. The number of apocalypses attributed to Daniel would be sufficient proof of that – and here I am not mentioning new translations, recensions or versions: I mean complete texts, in languages that range from Old Icelandic to Sogdian.[13]

The same could be said about Revelation: it provided, as Cohn indicated, the most influential prophetic system until the advent of 'secular' philosophies of history in the eighteenth century.[14] How much these philosophies owe to old patterns such as the Danielic world ages scheme has already been discussed many times over; the same can be said about the role of Revelation in prophetic systems such as mediaeval ones, especially the one created and developed by Joachim of Fiore.[15]

---

[8] E.g. the 'Proemium' in: Diogenes Laertius's *Lives of Eminent Philosophers*.
[9] FrGH 115F64a: (71) Diog. Laert. I 8–9:

> Ἀριστοτέλης δ' ἐν πρώτωι Περὶ φιλοσοφίας (F6 Rose) καὶ πρεσβυτέρους εἶναι τῶν Αἰγυπτίων (sc. τοὺς Μάγους)· καὶ δύο κατ' αὐτοὺς εἶναι ἀρχάς, ἀγαθὸν δαίμονα καὶ κακὸν δαίμονα· καὶ τῶι μὲν ὄνομα εἶναι Ζεὺς καὶ Ὡρομάσδης, τῶι δὲ Ἅιδης καὶ Ἀρειμάνιος. φησὶ δὲ τοῦτο καὶ Ἕρμιππος ἐν τῶι πρώτωι Περὶ Μάγων (IV) καὶ Εὔδοξος ἐν τῆι Περιόδωι (V) καὶ Θεόπομπος ἐν τῆι ὀγδόηι τῶν Φιλιππικῶν· ὃς καὶ ἀναβιώσεσθαι κατὰ τοὺς Μάγους φησὶ τοὺς ἀνθρώπους καὶ ἔσεσθαι ἀθανάτους, καὶ τὰ ὄντα ταῖς αὐτῶν ἐπικλήσεσι διαμένειν. ταῦτα δὲ καὶ Εὔδημος ὁ Ῥόδιος ἱστορεῖ. (Fragments from Greek historians taken from Felix Jacoby. *Die Fragmente der griechischen Historiker*. Leiden: Brill, 2003. CD-ROM edition)

[10] Pier Franco Beatrice. *Anonymi Monophysitae Theosophia: An Attempt at Reconstruction*. Leiden: Brill, 2001, p. xxiv.
[11] Vicente Dobroruka. 'The Christian Conversion of Pagan Figures in Late Antique Oracles' in: Lorenzo DiTommaso, Matthias Henze and William Adler (eds). *The Embroidered Bible: Studies in Biblical Apocrypha and Pseudepigrapha in Honour of Michael E. Stone*. Leiden: Brill, 2017.
[12] Collins. 'Apocalypse: The Morphology of a Genre', pp. 5–8.
[13] DiTommaso. *The Book of Daniel and the Apocryphal Daniel Literature*.
[14] Norman Cohn. *The Pursuit of the Millenium*. Oxford: Oxford University Press, 1970, Kindle loc. 1828.
[15] Ibid.

As has been noted, although it may be very difficult to trace the dating of manuscripts, the location of communities and how cultural interchange might have taken shape, it is fair to consider that Zoroastrian ideas shaped Jewish and then Christian thought. It would also be an interesting exercise in counterfactual history to think that, were it not for the consuming fight between the Byzantine Empire and the Sasanian Empire, Islam might not have taken hold of the Near East and Central Asia the way it did, and we would have an entirely different historical course to be taken by Zoroastrianism. As it was, in time Zoroastrianism became a minority group, that is, a very active but small religious group.[16] Our debt towards Zoroastrianism is so pervasive as to be difficult to trace; and in this sense it can be said that no other system of thought, religious or secular, played a more important role in shaping our own concepts of time, history and personal and collective destinies.

§4 Co-joining of individual and collective judgement: The greatest permanence

The novelty brought by Second Temple Judaism was that individual and collective judgements were put together, and although it can be very difficult to trace how this process occurred, it is only fair to say that it did during the Exile and afterwards – this is the equivalent of saying it was with Dan 2, 7 and 12 that a shift occurred joining individual and collective resurrection.

The same can be said regarding the Qumran community – and here we are on a much better footing. The variety of datings that can be given to the DSS is much more secure than the manyfold issues we have when dating Zoroastrian material. It might be argued also that we are uncertain about who constituted that community; taking scepticism to extreme conclusions one might argue that there is no relation whatsoever between the scrolls (which, in turn, also displays a broad variety of theological positions), the caves and the ruins of what some say was the housing of the community.

Be that as it may, as another extreme conclusion we can argue that at a minimum some Qumranic texts – and here the importance of 4Q521 and the GŠR theme comes to the forefront – show a constant worry about the end of the world and the judgement of the dead in the New World to come. These are ideas that are not to be found before the Exile; if we should avoid circular reasoning by trying to date Zoroastrian texts via Danielic and similar literature, the scrolls are of the utmost importance in displaying lines of thought very similar to Zoroastrian ones.

This book is, in a sense, long overdue – the 'grey area' between Zoroastrianism and the West, with its in-between chain links of Daniel, the resurrection themes in the New Testament and, above all, the idea that human history has a sense, a purpose, captivated

---

[16] Almut Hintze. 'A Zoroastrian Vision' in: WILLIAMS, Alan V., STEWART, Sarah, and HINTZE, Almut (eds). *The Zoroastrian Flame. Exploring Religion, History and Tradition*. London: I.B. Tauris, 2016, pp. 77 ff.

me since my late undergraduate years. That was mainly due to my fascination with the possibilities of investigating the ties between Persians and the Jewish communities, both in Exile as in the Diaspora offered. In recent years another challenge had been put forward to me: to view Eastern history, for example, Parthian or Sasanian, from the point of view of Persians themselves and not just as an addendum to a Western history that would be heir apparent to the Graeco-Roman tradition.[17]

Then, already in the specific field of studies related to religious thought and/or experience linked to political resistance, the most important authors for me were Samuel K. Eddy, Anders Hultgård and, most of all, John J. Collins and Martin Goodman.[18] Others helped me shape my interest in all things related to the prevalence and/or influence between Persian and Semitic-speaking peoples, which meant to me, mostly, the relationship between Zoroastrian ideas and the accepted notion that history is a process, with a beginning, an end and a goal to be fulfilled.[19]

And since this is a conclusion of sorts, it is appropriate to say a few words about the job of researching and writing it in itself, and the place it took, for good or bad, in my life. This book remains but a fraction of my interest on the subjects outlined above and is thus formatted accordingly as a series of chapters dealing with the most important aspects of the interaction of Persian and Jewish thought in the Second Temple period – that is to say, in the formative years of Jewish apocalyptic literature, one of the main themes in this book.

As stated in the Introduction, this is *not* a social, economic or cultural history of a given period[20] but rather an attempt at a history of the ideas that shaped religious thinking of a given people ethnically self-identified (the Jews) in a somewhat loose time frame (the Second Temple period i.e. from the commonly established date of the return of the Exile[21] in Babylon in *c*.520 BCE to roughly 100 CE). It is also a work that deals not only with the mainstream and successful ideas but also with some sidelines too – for example, with DSS content. The matter of 'coming back' from Exile cannot

---

[17] Daryaee. *Sasanian Iran*, pp. xiii–xvii.
[18] Eddy. *The King Is Dead*; Hultgård. 'Ecstasy and Vision'; and Goodman. *The Ruling Class of Judaea*.
[19] A few others could be listed here, but as a last important footnote I should mention Carlo Ginzburg. He is, arguably, the historian who can follow the trail of a mythical complex better than most of us do. The most important text by him in my early years was, no doubt, *Storia notturna: Una decifrazione del sabba*. Torino: Einaudi, 1989. It was important in many ways but also because it put me in contact with the works of Karl Meuli, Geo Widengren and Philippe Gignoux, who would all be very important to me due to their work regarding *Männerbünde*.
[20] For that, general and broader titles in the field are still Schürer. *The History of the Jewish People*; and *The Cambridge History of Iran*. Cambridge: Cambridge University Press, 1968–2008 (8 vols).
[21] For the subtleties on the matter, cf. Lester L. Grabbe. 'The Reality of the Return: The Biblical Picture versus Historical Reconstruction' in: Stökl and Waerzeggers, *Exile and Return*, pp. 292–300:

> We could say that the 'biblical picture' is derived from all the biblical texts, the book of Ezra actually tends to be the perspective followed, with the other biblical texts fitted into that outline ... One of the gaps in our knowledge of the ancient Near East is information on how groups travelled, whether under their own volition or under forced conditions. We have some iconographic images of peoples being deported by the Assyrians, and we would assume that travel under normal conditions involved wheeled vehicles, animals (horses and donkeys), walking, and even boats. What we do not know is the arrangements for those journeying from Babylonia to Judah on their own initiative.

> See also by Grabbe, '"They shall come rejoicing to Zion" – or Did They?'.

be taken easily; the differences between professed faith and daily life,[22] formation of something resembling a canon and how,[23] when and by which means a part of Jews settled in Babylonia came back leaves much room for discussion.[24]

In a sense, this is a work that follows in the steps of earlier scholars like Henning, Gershevitch or Boyce: on the other hand, I have found out that many of their propositions are unverifiable or just untenable. This also means that this book is more about similarities and thoughts about them than as a full-fledged and complete attack to solve, once and for all, the dilemmas involved in dealing with 'influence' on Judaism by Zoroastrianism.

§5 Final words

No pun is intended here although we are dealing with final judgement, ordeals and, summing it all up, final endings. After all, regardless of the dating of the texts or even the endless debate on who influenced whom, Zoroastrianism remains the religion of endings by definition; I still believe that both direct and indirect evidence point to its antiquity and thus to the originality of many of its ideas that can be traced to one branch of *PIE languages.

That this branch is better or worse because it constituted in the course of time a genetic pool is, in my view, racism at its worst. But the opposite cannot be denied: communities living together and speaking the same dialects would, in the course of time, constitute themselves a genetic pool by the mere fact of living together and thus 'intermarrying'.

That this community, or their inheritors, passed along – in forms that are perhaps lost forever, but that would be suitable for an investigation à la Quentin Skinner, discussed in this book's introduction – seems beyond doubt to me. The influence, for the lack of a better word, of Persian ideas regarding the conclusion of this world and the judgement that awaits good and bad alike is a motif that remains Zoroastrian par excellence.

In this sense, Second Temple Judaism – that is, the Judaism that Jesus knew and in which he was embedded – has, especially regarding apocalyptic literature, a strong Zoroastrian flavour of 'definitivity'. By its turn, this flavour can be sensed in the Gospels, in Pauline literature and in the book of Revelation – and this is restricting ourselves only to the texts that made it to the Canon that would constitute one day the Canon of Christianity, with one text here and there added or subtracted after Reformation and, before that, the forming and split of Eastern churches.

---

[22] Although this deals with a later period, see the work of Edward P. Sanders. *Judaism – Practice & Belief 63 BCE–66 CE*. London: SCM Press, 1992.
[23] Cf. Eugene Ulrich. 'The Jewish Scriptures: Texts, Versions, Canons' in: John J. Collins and Daniel C. Harlow (eds). *Early Judaism: A Comprehensive Overview*. Michigan: William B. Eerdmans, 2012, pp. 120–2.; in the same book, James L. Kugel's 'Early Jewish Interpretation' reminds us that not all returnees were of the same mind (p. 155).
[24] Shaye D. J. Cohen discusses this all too briefly, in my opinion, in his book *From the Maccabees to the Mishnah*. Louisville: John Knox Press, 2006, p. 86.

If we go beyond that, it will be clear to the reader by now that even contemporary atheism cannot do without Zoroastrian ideas: that is to say that even the so-called philosophies of history need some sort of 'drive' that can only be found outside of themselves. This means that who or what drives history forward may or may not be a religious entity, since it makes no difference to the systems themselves – although the entities are meta-historical, that is, they stand above the historical events proper.

So it is fair enough to say that the heritage of Zoroastrianism to our day became apparent only through two filters: the first one, Second Temple Judaism and, the second, Christianity itself. I hope to have shown some of the aspects, at least the most important ones in my view, regarding the relationship between Zoroastrianism (or perhaps even older ideas) and the Judaism that Jesus knew. Regarding the relationship between Zoroastrian ideas, communities and regulations and the Diaspora Judaism, it remains the subject for other investigations and, hopefully, for another book.

Bibliography

ABDI, Kamyar. 'The Iranian Plateau from Paleolithic Times to the Rise of the Achaemenid Empire' in: DARYAEE, Touraj (ed.). *The Oxford Handbook of Iranian History*. New York: Oxford University Press, 2012. (*OHIR*, Kindle edition)

AGOSTINI, Domenico. 'Their Evil Rule Must End! A Commentary on the Iranian Bundahišn 33:17-28' in: AMIRAV, Hagit, GRYPEOU, Emmanouela, and STROUMSA, Guy (eds). *Apocalypticism and Eschatology in Late Antiquity*. Leuven: Peeters, 2017.

AGOSTINI, Domenico, and THORPE, Samuel (ed. and trans.). *The Bundahišn: The Zoroastrian Book of Creation*. New York: Oxford University Press, 2020.

ALBERTZ, Rainer. 'The Social Setting of the Aramaic and Hebrew Book of Daniel' in: COLLINS, John J., and FLINT, Peter W. (with the assistance of Cameron VANEPPS) (eds). *The Book of Daniel: Composition and Reception*. Leiden: Brill, 2001.

ALBRECHT, Wagner. *Tundale: Das Mittelenglische Gedicht über die Vision des Tundalus*. Halle: Max Niemeyer, 1893.

ALLAN, James W. *Persian Metal Technology, 700-1300 A.D.* Oxford: Oriental Institute Monographs (no. 2), 1979.

ALLEGRO, John. *The Sacred Mushroom and the Cross; a Study of the Nature and Origins of Christianity within the Fertility Cults of the Ancient Near East*. London: Hodder & Stoughton, 1970.

ALLEN, Nick. 'The Wheel of Existence' in: GARCÍA QUINTELA, Marco V., GONZÁLEZ GARCÍA, Francisco J., and CRIADO BOADO, Felipe (eds). *Anthropology of the Indo-European World and Material Culture: Proceedings of the 5th International Colloquium of Anthropology of the Indo-European World and Comparative Mythology*. Budapest: Archaeolingua, 2006.

ALONSO-NUÑEZ, José. 'Die Abfolge der Weltreiche bei Polybios und Dionysios von Halikarnassos' in: *Historia* 32 (1983): 411–26.

ALONSO-NUÑEZ, José. 'Appian and the World Empires' in: *Athenaeum* 62 (1984): 640-4.

ALONSO-NUÑEZ, José. 'Die Weltreichsukzession bei Strabo' in: *Zeitschrift für Religions- und Geistesgeschichte* 36 (1984): 53-4.

ALONSO-NUÑEZ, José. 'The Emergence of Universal Historiography from the 4th to the 2nd Centuries B.C.' in: VERDIN, Herman, SCHEPENS, Guido, and KEYSER, Els de (eds). *Purposes of History: Studies in Greek Historiography from the 4th to the 2nd Centuries B.C.* Leuven: Orientaliste, 1990.

ANDERSON, Bernhard W. *Creation versus Chaos: The Reinterpretation of Mythical Symbolism in the Bible*. Minneapolis: Fortress Press, 1987.

ANDRÉ, Gunnel. 'Ecstatic Prophesy in the Old Testament' in: HOLM, Nils (ed.). *Religious Ecstasy: Based on Papers read at the Symposium on Religious Ecstasy held at Åbo, Finland, on the 26th-28th of August 1981*. Stockholm: Almqvist and Wiksell, 1982.

ANDREAS, Friedrich C., and BARR, Kay. *Bruchstücke einer Pehlevi-Übersetzung der Psalmen*. Berlin: Sonderausgabe aus den Sitzungsberichten der Preussischen Akademie der Wissenshaften, 1933.

ANDRÉS-TOLEDO, Miguel A. *The Zoroastrian Law to Expel the Demons: Widewdad 10-15. Critical Edition, Translation and Glossary of the Avestan and Pahlavi Texts*. Iranica 23. Wiesbaden: Harrassowitz, 2016.

ANKLESARIA, Behamgore T. *Zand-Akasih: Iranian or Greater Bundahishn*. Bombay: Published for the Rahnumae Mazdayasnan Sabha by its Honorary Secretary Dastur Framroze A. Bode, 1956.

ANKLESARIA, Behramgore T. *Zand ī Vohûman Yasn and two Pahlavi Fragments with Text, Transliteration and Translation in English*. Bombay: K.R. Cama Oriental Institute, 1957.

ANON. *Mādigān ī Hazār Dādistān*. (The Book of a Thousand Judgements; A Sasanian Law Book. Introduction, transcription and translation of the Pahlavi text, notes, glossary and indexes by Anahit Perikhanian; translated from Russian by Nina Garsoïan), ed. Anahit PERIKHANIAN. New York: St. Petersburg Branch of the Institute of Oriental Studies, Russian Academy of Sciences, Center for Iranian Studies, Columbia University, 1997.

ARBMAN, Ernst. *Ecstasy or Religious Trance: In the Experience of the Ecstatics and from the Psychological Point of View*. Stockholm: Bokförlaget, 1963-70. (3 vols)

ASMUSSEN, Jan P. 'The Pahlavi Psalm 122 in English' in: *Dr. Unvala Memorial Volume*. Bombay: Published by Kaikhusroo M. Jamaspasa for Dr. J.M. Unvala Memorial Volume Sub-Committee, 1964.

ASSMANN, Jan. 'Cultural Memory and the Myth of the Axial Age' in: BELLAH, Robert N., and JOAS, Hans (eds). *The Axial Age and Its Consequences*. Cambridge, MA: Harvard University Press, 2012. Pp. 366-408.

ASSMANN, Jan. *The Mind of Egypt: History and Meaning in the Time of the Pharaohs*. New York: Metropolitan Books, 1996.

ASSMANN, Jan. *The Price of Monotheism*. Stanford: Stanford University Press, 2009.

ASSMANN, Jan. *Zeit und Ewigkeit im Alten Ägypten: Ein Beitrag zur Geschichte der Ewigkeit*. Heidelberg: Carl Winter, 1975.

AUSFELD, Adolf. *Der griechische Alexanderroman*. Leipzig: /s.ed./, 1907.

BAILEY, Harold W. 'Iranian Studies' in: *BSOAS* 6.4 (1932): 945-55.

BAILEY, Harold W. *Zoroastrian Problems in the Ninth-Century Books*. Oxford: Clarendon Press, 1943.

BAILEY, Harold W. 'Hārabhunā' in: SCHUBERT, Johannes, and SCHNEIDER, Ulrich (hrgs). *Asiatica. Festschrift Friedrich Weller. Zum 65 Geburtstag gewindet von seinen Freunde, Kollegen und Schülern*. Leipzig: Harrassowitz, 1954.

BAR, Shaul. *A Letter That Has Not Been Read: Dreams in the Hebrew Bible*. Cincinnati: Hebrew Union College Press, 2001.

BARR, James. 'The Question of Religious Influence: The Case of Zoroastrianism, Judaism, and Christianity' in: *JAAR* 53.2 (1985): 201-35.

BARTHOLOMAE, Christian. *Altiranisches Wörterbuch*. Berlin: Walter de Gruyter, 1961. (Original edition from 1904)

BAUMGARTEN, Albert. 'Who Cares and Why Does It Matter? Qumran and the Essenes, Once Again!' in: *Dead Sea Discoveries* 11.2 (2004): 174-90.

BEATRICE, Pier Franco. *Anonymi Monophysitae Theosophia: An Attempt at Reconstruction*. Leiden: Brill, 2001.

BECKER, Adam H. 'Political Theology and Religious Diversity' in: HERMAN, Geoffrey (ed.). *Jews, Christians and Zoroastrians: Religious Dynamics in a Sasanian Context*. Piscataway: Gorgias Press, 2014. Pp. 7-26.

BECKER, Michael. '"4Q521" und die Gesalbten' in: *Revue de Qumrân* 18.1(69) (1997): 73–96.

BELARDI, Walter. *The Pahlavi Book of the Righteous Viraz*. Rome: University Department of Linguistics and Italo-Iranian Cultural Centre, 1979.

BELLAH, Robert N., and JOAS, Hans (eds). 'Bibliography: Works on the Axial Age' in: *The Axial Age and Its Consequences*. Cambridge, MA: Harvard University Press, 2012. Pp. 469–538.

BERGSMA, John S. 'The Persian Period as Penitential Era: The "Exegetical Logic" of Daniel 9.1-27' in: KNOPPERS, Gary N., and GRABBE, Lester L., with FULTON, Deirdre N. (eds). *Exile and Restoration Revisited: Essays on the Babylonian and Persian Periods in Memory of Peter R. Ackroyd*. London: T&T Clark, 2009. Pp. 50–64.

BERQUIST, Jon. *Judaism in Persia's Shadow*. Minneapolis: Fortress Press, 1995.

BEYERLE, Stefan. 'The "God in Heaven" in Persian and Hellenistic Times' in: NICKLAS, Tobias, VERHEYDEN, Joseph, EYNIKEL, Erik M. M., and GARCÍA-MARTÍNEZ, Florentino (eds). *Other Worlds and Their Relation to This World: Early Jewish and Ancient Christian Traditions*. Leiden: Brill, 2010.

BIANCHI, Ugo. 'Dualism' in: ELIADE, Mircea (ed.). *Encyclopedia of Religion*, vol. 1. New York: Macmillan, 1987.

BIDEZ, Joseph, and CUMONT, Franz. *Les Mages Hellenisés: Zoroastre, Ostanès et Hystaspe d'après la tradition grecque*. Paris: Belles Lettres, 1973. (2 vols) (Several reprints from the 1939 edition, sometimes reunited in one single volume but the text remains the same)

BLENKINSOPP, Joseph. *Isaiah 40–55: A New Translation with Introduction and Commentary*. New York: Doubleday, 2002.

BLENKINSOPP, Joseph. *Isaiah 56–66: A New Translation with Introduction and Commentary*. New York: Doubleday, 2003.

BOGAERT, Pierre. *Apocalypse de Baruch. Introduction, tradutcion du syriaque et commentaire*. Sources Chrétiennes. Paris: Les Éditions du CERF, 1969. (2 vols)

BONGARD-LEVIN, Grigorii M., and GRANTOVSKII, Ėdvin A. *Ot Skifii do Indii: Zagadki istorii drev. ariev* ('From Scythia to India: Mysteries of the History of the Ancient Aryans', in Russian). Moscow: Academy of Sciences, 1974. (A later French translation from 1981: *De la Scythie à l'Inde: Énigmes de l'histoire des anciens Aryens*. Paris: Klincksieck, 1981)

BOYCE, Mary. *The Letter of Tansar (translation)*. Roma: Istituto Italiano per il Medio ed Estremo Oriente, 1968.

BOYCE, Mary. 'Iconoclasm among the Zoroastrians' in: NEUSNER, Jacob (ed.). *Studies for Morton Smith at Sixty*. Leiden: Brill, 1975.

BOYCE, Mary. *A Persian Stronghold of Zoroastrianism: Based on the Ratanbai Katrak Lectures, 1975*. Oxford: Oxford University Press, 1977.

BOYCE, Mary. *Zoroastrians, Their Religious Beliefs and Practices*. London: Routledge & Kegan Paul, 1979.

BOYCE, Mary. 'On the Antiquity of Zoroastrian Apocalyptic' in: *BSOAS* 47 (1984).

BOYCE, Mary. *Textual Sources for the Study of Zoroastrianism*. Manchester: Manchester University Press, 1984.

BOYCE, Mary. 'The Poems of the Persian Sybil' in: *Études Irano-aryennes offertes à Gilbert Lazard*. Studia Iranica, Cahier 7. Paris: Association pour l'avancement des études iranniennes, 1989.

BOYCE, Mary. 'Some Further Reflections on Zurvanism' in: AMIN, Dina, and KASHEFF, Manuchehr (eds). *Iranica Varia: Papers in Honor of Professor Ehsan Yarshater*. Acta Iranica 30. Leiden: Brill, 1990.

BOYCE, Mary, and GRENET, Frantz. *A History of Zoroastrianism*. Leiden: Brill, 1975–91 (3 vols).
BRANDON, Samuel G. F. 'The Weighing of the Soul' in: KITAGAWA, Joseph M. and LONG, Charles H. (eds). *Myths and Symbols: Studies in Honor of Mircea Eliade*. Chicago: University of Chicago Press, 1969.
BREECH, Earle. 'These Fragments I Have Shored against My Ruins: The Form and Function of 4 Ezra' in: *JBL* 92 (1973).
BROSHI, Magen. 'Beware the Wiles of the Wicked Woman' in: *Biblical Archaeological Review* 9.4 (1983).
BULTMAN, Christoph. 'Deuteronomy' in: BARTON, John, and MUDDIMAN, John (eds). *Oxford Bible Commentary*. Oxford: Oxford University Press, 2001.
BULTMANN, Rudolf. *Die Geschichte der synoptischen Tradition*. Göttingen: Vandenhoeck und Ruprecht, 1921.
BURKERT, Walter. *Ancient Mystery Cults*. Cambridge, MA: Harvard University Press, 1987.
CANEPA, Matthew P. 'Unceasing Embassies' in: CANEPA, Matthew P. (ed.). *The Two Eyes of the Earth: Art and Ritual of Kingship between Rome and Sasanian Iran*. Berkeley: University of California Press, 2009.
CANTERA GLERA, Alberto. 'Los viajes al más allá en la tradición irania preislámica' in: *Cicle de Conferències sobre Religions del Món Antic (4º. 2003. Palma de Mallorca)*. Salamanca: Gredos, 2004.
CANTERA GLERA, Alberto. *Studien Zur Pahlavi-Ubersetzung Des Avesta*. Wisbaden: Harrassowitz, 2004.
CANTERA GLERA, Alberto. '*Abastāg ud Zand*: Das Avesta und dessen Pahlavi-Übersetzung' in: *Studien zur Pahlavi-Übersetzung des Avesta*. Wiesbaden: Harrassowitz, 2006.
CANTERA GLERA, Alberto. 'Die Überlieferung des Avesta und dessen schriftliche Fixierung' in: *Studien zur Pahlavi-Übersetzung des Avesta*. Wiesbaden: Harrassowitz, 2006.
CANTERA GLERA, Alberto. 'Ethics' in: STAUSBERG, Michael, VEVAINA, Yuhan S.-D., and TESSMANN, Anna (eds). *The Wiley Blackwell Companion to Zoroastrianism*. Malden: Wiley-Blackwell, 2015. (*WBCZ*)
CARR, David M. 'Changes in Pentateuchal Criticism' in: SÆBØ, Magne, SKA, Jean L., and MACHINIST, Peter (eds). *Hebrew Bible / Old Testament. Vol.III: From Modernism to Post-Modernism. Part II: The Twentieth Century – From Modernism to Post-Modernism*. Göttingen: Vandenhoeck & Ruprecht, 2014.
CERETI, Carlo G. (ed.). *The Zand-i Wahman Yasn: A Zoroastrian Apocalypse*. Roma: Istituto italiano per il Medio ed Estremo Oriente, 1995. [ZWY]
CERETI, Carlo G. '*Padīriftan ī dēn* and the Turn of the Millennium' in: *East and West* 45.1/4 (1995).
CERETI, Carlo G. 'Central Asian and Eastern Iranian Peoples in Zoroastrian Apocalyptic Literature' in: BÁLINT, Csánad (hrg.). *Kontakte zwischen Iran, Byzanz und der Steppe in 6.-7. Jh*. Budapest: Archäeologisches Institut der UAW, 2000.
CERETI, Carlo G. *La letteratura pahlavi*. Milano: Mimesis, 2001.
CERETI, Carlo G. 'Sconfiggere il demone della menzogna: Guerra santa, guerra giusta nell'Iran preislamico' in: *Studi Storici* 43.3 (2002).
CERETI, Carlo G. *Guerra santa e guerra giusta dal mondo antico alla prima età moderna*. 2002.

CERETI, Carlo G. 'Personal Names Ending in ت in the *Šāhnāma*' in: DARYAEE, Touraj, and OMIDSALAR, Mahmoud (eds). *The Spirit of Wisdom [Mēnōg ī Xrad]: Essays in Memory of Ahmad Tafazzoli*. Costa Mesa: Mazda, 2004.

CERETI, Carlo G. 'Some Notes on the *Škand Gumanig Wizār*' in: WEBER, Dieter (ed.). *Languages of Iran: Past and Present*. Ranian Studies in Memoriam David Neil Mackenzie. Wiesbaden: Harrassowitz, 2005.

CERETI, Carlo G. "And the *frawahrs* of the men [...] agreed to go into the material world": Zoroastrian Cosmogony in the 3rd Chapter of the *Greater Bundahišn*' in: MACUCH, Maria, MAGGI, Mauro, and SUNDERMANN, Werner (eds). *Iranian Languages and Texts from Iran and Turan: Ronald E. Emmerick Memorial Volume*. Iranica 13. Wiesbaden: Harrasowitz, 2007.

CERETI, Carlo G., and MACKENZIE, David N. 'Except by Battle: Zoroastrian Cosmogony in the 1st Chapter of the *Greater Bundahishn*' in: CERETI, Carlo G., MAGGI, Mauro and PROVASI, Elio (eds). *Religious Themes and Texts of Pre-Islamic Iran and Central Asia: Studies in Honour of Professor Gherardo Gnoli on the Occasion of his 65th Birthday on 6th December 2002*. Wiesbaden: Reichert, 2003.

CHAINE, Joseph. 'Cosmogonie aquatique et conflagration finale d'apres la secunda Petri' in: *RB* 46 (1937): 207–16.

CHARLES, Robert H. *The Apocrypha and Pseudepigrapha of the Old Testament*. London: Oxford University Press, 1913. (2 vols)

CHARPENTIER, Jarl. 'The date of Zoroaster' in: *BSOAS* 3 (1925): 4.

CHRISTENSEN, Arthur. *Les types du premier homme et du premier roi dans l'histoire légendaire des Iraniens, pt. I Gajōmard, Masjay et Masjānay, Hōšang et Taxmōruw*, vol. 1. Leiden: Brill, 1918–34.

CHRISTENSEN, Arthur. *L'Iran sous les Sassanides*. Copenhague: Ejnar Munksgaard, 1944.

COHEN, David (in collaboration with François Bron and Antoine Lonnet). *Dictionnaire de Racines Sémitiques ou attestées dans les langues sémitiques. Comprenant um fichier comparatif de Jean Cantineau*. Brussels: Peeters, 1993.

COHEN, Shaye D. J. 'Alexander the Great and Jaddus the High Priest according to Josephus' in: *AJSR* 7.8 (1982–3).

COHEN, Shaye D. J. *From the Maccabees to the Mishnah*. Louisville: John Knox Press, 2006.

COHN, Norman. *The Pursuit of the Millenium*. Oxford: Oxford University Press, 1970.

COHN, Norman. *Cosmos, Chaos and the World to Come*. New Haven: Yale University Press, 2001.

COLLINS, Adela Y. *The Combat Myth in the Book of Revelation*. Missoula: Scholars Press, 1976.

COLLINS, John J. 'The Court-Tales in Daniel and the Development of Apocalyptic' in: *JBL* 94.2 (1975).

COLLINS, John J. 'The Mythology of Holy War in Daniel and the Qumran War Scroll: A Point of Transition in Jewish Apocalyptic' in: *VT* 25.3 (1975): 596–612.

COLLINS, John J., and FLINT, Peter W. (with the assistance of Cameron VANEPPS) (eds). *The Book of Daniel: Composition and Reception*. Leiden: Brill, 2001. (2 vols)

COLLINS, John J. 'Apocalypse: The Morphology of a Genre' in: *Semeia* 14 (1979).

COLLINS, John J. *Daniel, with an Introduction to Apocalyptic Literature*. Grand Rapids: William B. Eerdmans, 1984.

COLLINS, John J. 'Daniel, Book of' in: FREEDMAN, David N. (ed.). *The Anchor Bible Dictionary*. Yale: Yale University Press, 1992.

COLLINS, John J. *Daniel: A Commentary on the Book of Daniel*. Hermeneia. Minneapolis: Fortress Press, 1993.

COLLINS, John J. *The Apocalyptic Imagination*. Grand Rapids: William B. Eerdmans, 1998.

COLLINS, John J. *The Bible after Babel: Historical Criticism in a Postmodern Age*. Grand Rapids: William B. Eerdmans, 2005.

COLLINS, John J., and STERLING, Gregory E. (eds). *Hellenism in the Land of Israel*. Christianity and Judaism in Antiquity Series 13. Notre Dame: University of Notre Dame, 2001.

COMPARETI, Matteo. 'The Last Sasanians in China' in: *Eurasian Studies* 2.2 (2003).

COOK, David. *Studies in Muslim Apocalyptic*. Princeton: Darwin Press, 2002.

CROSS, Frank M. 'The Development of the Jewish Scripts' in: WRIGHT, George E. (ed.). *The Bible and the Ancient Near East: Essays in Honor of W. F. Albright*. New York: Doubleday, 1961.

CROWFOOT, Grace M. H., and BALDENSPERGER, Louise. *From Cedar to Hyssop: A Study in the Folklore of Plants in Palestine*. London: Sheldon Press, 1932.

DARMESTETER, James. *Sacred Books of the East*, vol. 23. Oxford: Oxford University Press, 1897. (*SBE*)

DARYAEE, Touraj. *Sasanian Iran. 224–651 CE: Portrait of a Late Antique Empire*. Costa Mesa: Mazda, 2008.

DARYAEE, Touraj (ed.). *The Oxford Handbook of Iranian History*. New York: Oxford University Press, 2012. (*OHIR*)

DARYAEE, Touraj. 'The Sasanian Empire 224–651 CE' in: *The Oxford Handbook of Iranian History*. New York: Oxford University Press, 2012. (*OHIR*)

DARYAEE, Touraj. 'From Zoroastrian to Islamic Iran: A Note on the Christian Intermezzo' in: *Vicino Oriente* 23 (2019).

DAVIS, Kipp, BAEK, Kyung S., FLINT, Peter W., and PETERS, Dorothy M. (eds). *The War Scroll, Violence, War and Peace in the Dead Sea Scrolls and Related Literature: Essays in Honour of Martin G. Abegg on the Occasion of His 65th Birthday*. Leiden: Brill, 2015.

DECLERCQ, Georges. *Anno Domini. The Origins of the Christian Era*. Turnhout: Brepols, 2000.

DHALLA, Maneckji N. *History of Zoroastrianism*. New York: Oxford University Press, 1938.

DITOMMASO, Lorenzo. *The Book of Daniel and the Apocryphal Daniel Literature*. Leiden: Brill, 2005.

DOBRORUKA, Vicente. 'Chemically-Induced Visions in the *Fourth Book of Ezra* in Light of Comparative Persian Material' in: *Jewish Studies Quarterly* (2006).

DOBRORUKA, Vicente. 'Hesiodic Reminiscences in Zoroastrian-Hellenistic Apocalypses' in: *BSOAS* 75 (2012).

DOBRORUKA, Vicente. 'The Order of Metals in Daniel 2 and in Persian Apocalyptic' in: *ARAM Periodical* 26.1 (2014).

DOBRORUKA, Vicente. 'Zoroastrian Apocalyptic and Hellenistic Political Propaganda' in: *ARAM Periodical* 26.1–2 (2014).

DOBRORUKA, Vicente. 'On Trees and Visionaries: The Role of the Cosmic Tree and Related Material in Baruch, Daniel and Pseudo-Danielic Literature' in: KNIGHT, Jonathan, and SULLIVAN, Kevin (eds). *The Open Mind: Essays in Honour of Christopher Rowland*. London: Bloomsbury, 2015.

DOBRORUKA, Vicente. 'The Christian Conversion of Pagan Figures in Late Antique Oracles' in: DITOMMASO, Lorenzo, HENZE, Matthias, and ADLER, William (eds).

The Embroidered Bible: Studies in Biblical Apocrypha and Pseudepigrapha in Honour of Michael E. Stone. Leiden: Brill, 2017.

DOBRORUKA, Vi(n)cente [sic]. 'Mithridates and the *Oracle of Hystaspes*: Some Dating Issues' in: *JRAS*, forthcoming.

DOBRORUKA, Vicente, and REZAKHANI, Khodadad. 'apocalyptic and eschatology, Zoroastrian' in: NICHOLSON, Oliver (ed.). *The Oxford Dictionary of Late Antiquity*. Oxford: Oxford University Press, 2018. (2 vols) (*ODLA*)

DOBRORUKA, Vicente, and KRAFT, Robert A. 'Oracles of Hystaspes: A New Translation and Introduction' in: DAVILA, James R., BAUCKHAM, Richard, and PANOYATOV, Alexander (eds). *Old Testament Pseudepigrapha: More Noncanonical Scriptures*, vol. 2. Grand Rapids: Eerdmans, forthcoming.

DOWNING, Francis G. 'Cosmic Eschatology in the First Century: "Pagan", Jewish and Christian' in: *L'antiquité classique* 64 (1995): 99–109.

DRIJVERS, Jan W. 'Ammianus Marcelinus' Image of Sasanian society' in: WIESEHÖFER, Josef, and HUYSE, Philip (Hg.). *Ērān und Anērān: Studien zu den Beziehungen zwischen dem Sasanidenreich und der Mittelmeerwelt*. München: Franz Steiner, 2006.

DUCHESNE-GUILLEMIN, Jacques. 'Apocalypse juive et apocalypse iranienne' in: BIANCHI, Ugo, and VERMASEREN, Maarten J. (eds). *La soteriologia dei culti orientali nell'Impero romano: Atti del Colloquio internazionale su la soteriologia dei culti orientali nell'Impero romano, Roma, 24–28 settembre 1979*. Etudes préliminaires aux religions orientales dans l'Empire romain 92. Leiden: Brill, 1982.

DUCHESNE-GUILLEMIN, Jacques. 'Zoroastrian Religion: Iranian Religion under the Selucids and Arsacida' in: YARSHATER, E. (ed.). *CHIr, Vol. 3: The Selucid, Parthian and Sasanid Periods, Part 2*. Cambridge: Cambridge University Press, 1983. Pp. 866–908.

DUHAIME, Jean. *The War Texts: 1QM and Related Manuscripts*. Companion to the Qumran Scrolls 6. London: T&T Clark, 2004.

DUMÉZIL, Georges. *Naissance d'archanges (Jupiter, Mars, Quirinus III): Essai sur la formation de la théologie zoroastrienne*. Paris: Gallimard, 1945.

DUMÉZIL, Georges. *Heur et malheur du guerrier: Aspects mythiques de la fonction guerrière chez les indo-européens*. Paris: P.U.F., 1969.

DUMÉZIL, Georges. *Romans de Scythie et d'alentours*. Paris: Payol, 1978.

EDDY, Samuel K. *The King Is Dead: Studies in the Near Eastern Resistance to Hellenism 334-31 B.C.* Lincoln: University of Nebraska Press, 1961.

EGO, Beate. 'Death and Burial in the Tobit Narration in the Context of the Old Testament Tradition' in: NICKLAS, Tobias, REITERER, Friedrich V., and VERHEYDEN, Joseph (in collaboration with Heike Braun) (eds). *The Human Body in Death and Resurrection*. Berlin: De Gruyter, 2009. Pp. 87–103.

EISSFELDT, Otto. 'Der gegenwärtige Stand der Erforschung der in Palästina neu gefundenen hebraischen Handschriften' in: *ThLZ* 75 (1950): 23–6.

ELIADE, Mircea. 'Ancient Scythia and Iran' in: ANDREWS, George, and VINKENOOG, Simon (eds). *The Book of Grass; an Anthology of Indian Hemp*. Harmondsworth: Penguin Books, 1972.

ELIADE, Mircea. *Shamanism: Archaic Techniques of Ecstasy*. Princeton: Princeton University Press, 1962.

ELMAN, Yaakov. '"Up to the Ears" in Horses Necks (B.M. 108a): On Sasanian Agricultural Policy and Private "Eminent Domain"' in: *JSIJ* 3 (2004).

ELMAN, Yaakov. 'Does Pollution Fill Space?' in: *ARAM Periodical* 25.1-2 ('Zoroastrianism in the Levant and the Amorites') (2014).

EMBODER, WILLIAM A., Jr. 'Ritual Use of the *Cannabis Sativa* L.: A Historical-Ethnographic Survey' in: FURST, Peter (ed.). *Flesh of the Gods: The Ritual Use of Hallucinogens*. London: Allen & Unwin, 1972.

ERCIYAS, Deniz B. *Wealth, Aristocracy and Royal Propaganda under the Hellenistic Kingdom of the Mithradatids in the Central Black Sea Region of Turkey*. Leiden: Brill, 2006.

ESKENAZI, Tamara C. 'From Exile and Restoration to Exile and Reconstruction' in: KNOPPERS, Gary N., and GRABBE, Lester L., with FULTON, Deirdre N. (eds). *Exile and Restoration Revisited: Essays on the Babylonian and Persian Periods in Memory of Peter R. Ackroyd*. London: T&T Clark, 2009.

FARNSWORTH, Norman R. 'Hallucinogenic Plants' in: *Science*, New Series, 162.3858 (1968).

FLATTERY, David S., and SCHWARTZ, Martin. *Haoma and Hermaline: The Botanical Identity of the Indo-Iranian Sacred Hallucinogen 'Soma' and Its Legacy in Religion, Language, and Middle Eastern Folklore*. Ann Arbor: University of Michigan Press, 1989.

FLECK, Ludwig. *Genesis and Development of a Scientific Fact*. Chicago: University of Chicago Press, 1979.

FLEMING, Daniel E. 'The Day of Yahweh in the Book of Amos: A Rhetorical Response to Ritual Expectation' in: RB 110 (2010).

FLINT, Peter. 'The Daniel Tradition at Qumran' in: COLLINS, John J., and FLINT, Peter W. (with the assistance of Cameron VANEPPS) (eds). *The Book of Daniel: Composition and Reception*. Leiden: Brill, 2001.

FLUSSER, David. 'The Fourth Empire – an Indian Rhinoceros?' in: *Judaism and the Origins of Christianity*. Jerusalem: Magnes Press, 1988.

FLUSSER, David. *Josippon*. Jerusalem: Bialik, 1980. (Hebrew)

FOLTZ, Richard C. *Spirituality in the Land of the Noble: How Iran Shaped the World's Religions*. London: Oneworld, 2004.

FOLTZ, Richard C. (ed.). *Environmentalism in the Muslim World*. New York: Nova Science, 2005.

FOLTZ, Richard C. *Animals in Islamic tradition and Muslim Cultures*. Oxford: Oneworld, 2006.

FOLTZ, Richard. 'Buddhism in the Iranian World' in: *Muslim World* 100 (2010).

FORNARA, Charles W. *The Nature of History in Ancient Greece and Rome*. Berkeley: Yale University Press, 1983.

FORSMANN, Bernard. 'Apaosha, der Gegner des Tishtriia' in: *Zeitschrift für vergleichende Sprachforschung* 82 (1968): 42–9.

FORTSON IV, Benjamin W. *Indo-European Language and Culture: An Introduction*. Second edition. Chicester: Wiley Blackwell, 2010.

FOSS, Clive. 'The Persians in Asia Minor and the End of Antiquity' in: *The English Historical Review* 90.357 (1975).

FREI, Peter. 'Persian Imperial Authorization: A Summary' in: WATTS, James (ed.). *Persia and Torah: The Theory of Imperial Authorization of the Pentateuch*. Atlanta: SBL Press, 2001.

FRENSCHKOWSKI, Marco. 'Christianity' in: STAUSBERG, Michael, VEVAINA, Yuhan S.-D., and TESSMANN, Anna (eds). *The Wiley Blackwell Companion to Zoroastrianism*. Malden: Wiley-Blackwell, 2015. (WBCZ)

FRYE, Richard N. 'A Brief Note on the Pahlavi Psalter and Bare Ideogramms' in: *Sir J. J. Zarthoshti Madressa Centenary Volume*. Bombay: Trustees of the Parsi Punchayet Funds and Properties, 1967.
FURST, Peter. *Hallucinogens and Culture*. San Francisco: Chandler & Sharp, 1976.
GARDINER, Eileen. 'An Edition of the Middle English "Vision of Tundale"'. PhD diss., Fordham University, 1980.
GARDINER, Eileen (ed.). *Greek & Roman Hell: Visions, Tours and Descriptions of the Infernal Otherworld*. New York: Italica Press, 2019.
GAVRILOV, Aleksandr K. 'Techniques of Reading in Classical Antiquity' in: *The Classical Quarterly*, New Series, 47.1 (1997).
GAYLORD, Harry E. 'Redactional Elements behind the *Petrisov Zbornik* of the Greek Apocalypse of Baruch' in: *Slovo* 37 (1987).
GEFFCKEN, Johannes. *Komposition und Entstehungszeit der Oracula Sybillina*. Leipzig: C.H. Hinrichs, 1902.
GELDNER, Karl F. *Avesta: The Sacred Books of the Parsis*. Stuttgart: W. Kohlhammer, 1896.
GIGNOUX, Philippe. 'Notes sur la rédaction de l'Ardāy Virāz Nāmag' in: *Zeitschrift der Deutschen Morgenländischen Gesellschaft*, Supplementa 1 (1969).
GIGNOUX, Philippe. 'L'inscription de Kirdīr a Naqš-i Rustam' in: *SIr* 2 (1972).
GIGNOUX, Philippe. 'La signification du voyage extra-terrestre dans l'eschatologie mazdéenne' in: LASSIER, Suzanne (ed.). *Mélanges d'histoire des religions offerts à Henri-Charles Puech*. Paris: Presses Universitaires de France, 1974.
GIGNOUX, Philippe. '"Corps osseux et âme osseuse": Essai sur le chamanisme dans l'Iran ancien' in: *JA* 267.1-2 (1979): 41-79.
GIGNOUX, Philippe. 'Les voyages chamaniques dans le monde iranien' in: *AI* 21 (1981).
GIGNOUX, Philippe. 'Middle Persian Inscriptions' in: YARSHATER, E. (ed.). *CHIr, Vol. 3: The Selucid, Parthian and Sasanid Periods, Part 2*. Cambridge: Cambridge University Press, 1983. Pp. 1205-15.
GIGNOUX, Philippe. 'The Private Inscriptions of Kirdir' in: *CHIr* 3.2 (1985).
GIGNOUX, Philippe. 'Nouveaux regards sur l'Apocalyptique iranienne' in: *Comptes-rendus des séances de l'Académie des Inscriptions et Belles-Lettres*. Paris: Diffusion de Boccard, 1986.
GIGNOUX, Philippe. 'Sur l'inexistence d'un *Bahman Yasht* avestique' in: *JAAS* 32 (1986): 53-64.
GIGNOUX, Philippe. 'Apocalypses et voyages extra-terrestres dans l'Iran mazdéen' in: KAPPLER, Claude (ed.). *Apocalypses et voyages dans l'au-delà*. Paris: CERF, 1987.
GIGNOUX, Philippe. 'Dietary Laws in pre-Islamic and post-Sasanian Iran' in: *JSAI* 17 (1987): 16-42.
GIGNOUX, Philippe. 'L'apocalyptique iranienne est-elle vraiment la source d'autres apocalypses?' in: ActAnt 31.1-2 (1988): 67-78.
GIGNOUX, Philippe. *Le mage Kirdīr et ses quatre inscriptions*. Paris: Diffusion de Boccard, 1989.
GIGNOUX, Philippe. *Les quatre inscriptions du Mage Kirdir: Textes et concordances, Collection des sources pour l'histoire de l'Asie centrale pré-islamique II/I*. Studia Iranica 9. Leuven: Association pour l'avancement des études iraniennes, 1991.
GIGNOUX, Philippe. 'On the Notion of Good Measure (paymān) and Other Related Philosophical Concepts from the Dēnkard III' in: *K.R. Cama Oriental Institute, Third International Congress*. Bombay: 2001.

GIGNOUX, Philippe (ed.). *Mazdéens et chrétiens en terre d'Iran à l'époque sassanide*. Serie Orientale Roma. Roma: ISMEO, 2014.

GIGNOUX, Philippe. 'Anērān' (entry originally published 15 December 1985 and last updated 3 August 2011). Available online: http://www.iranicaonline.org/articles/achaemenid-religion (accessed 18 November 2019).

GINZBURG, Carlo. *Storia notturna: una decifrazione del sabba*. Torino: Einaudi, 1989.

GLESSNER, Uwe. 'Die "vier Reiche" aus Daniel in targumischen Literatur' in: COLLINS, John J., and FLINT, Peter W. (with the assistance of Cameron VANEPPS) (eds). *The Book of Daniel: Composition and Reception*. Leiden: Brill, 2001.

GNUSE, Robert K. *No Other Gods: Emergent Monotheism in Israel*. London: Continuum, 1997.

GODWIN, Todd. *Persian Christians at the Chinese Court: The Xi'an Stele and the Early Medieval Church of the East*. London: I.B. Tauris, 2018.

GOLDEN, Leon. 'Hamartia, Ate, and Oedipus' in: *The Classical World* 72.1 (1978): 3–12.

GOLDINGAY, John. *God's Prophet, God's Servant: A Study in Jeremiah and Isaiah 40–55*. Carlisle: Paternoster Press, 1994.

GOLDINGAY, John. *The Message of Isaiah 40–55: A Literary-Theological Commentary*. London: Continuum, 2005. (2 vols)

GOLDINGAY, John, and PAYNE, David. *A Critical and Exegetical Commentary on Isaiah 40–55*. London: T&T Clark, 2007. (2 vols)

GOODMAN, Martin. *The Ruling Class of Judaea: The Origins of the Jewish Revolt against Rome, A.D. 66-73*. Cambridge: Cambridge University Press, 1987.

GOODMAN, Martin, and VERMÈS, Geza. *The Essenes according to the Classical Sources*. Sheffield: Oxford Centre Textbooks, 1990.

GRABBE, Lester L. 'A Dan(iel) for All Seasons: For Whom Was Daniel Important?' in: COLLINS, John J., and FLINT, Peter W. (with the assistance of Cameron VANEPPS) (eds). *The Book of Daniel: Composition and Reception*. Leiden: Brill, 2001.

GRABBE, Lester L. '"They shall come rejoicing to Zion" – or Did They? The Settlement of Yehud in the Early Persian Period" in: KNOPPERS, Gary N. and GRABBE, Lester L., with FULTON, Deirdre N. (eds). *Exile and Restoration Revisited: Essays on the Babylonian and Persian Periods in Memory of Peter R. Ackroyd*. London: T&T Clark, 2009.

GRABBE, Lester L. 'Was Jerusalem a Persian Fortress?' in: KNOPPERS, Gary N., GRABBE, Lester L., with FULTON, Deirdre N. (eds). *Exile and Restoration Revisited: Essays on the Babylonian and Persian Periods in Memory of Peter R. Ackroyd*. London: T&T Clark, 2009.

GRABBE, Lester L. 'The Reality of the Return: The Biblical Picture versus Historical Reconstruction' in: STÖKL, Jonathan, and WAERZEGGERS, Caroline (eds). *Exile and Return: The Babylonian Context*. Berlin: Walter de Gruyter, 2015.

GRAPOW, Hermann. 'Die Welt vor der Schöpfung' in: *Zeitschrift für ägyptische Sprache und Altertumskunde* 67 (1931): 34–8.

GREEN, Alberto R.W. *The Storm-God in the Ancient Near East*. Winona Lake: Eisenbrauns, 2003.

GRENET, Frantz. "Crise et sortie de crise em Bactriane-Sogdiane aus IVe-Ve siècles: De l'heritage antique à l'adoption de modèles sassanides" in: VVAA. *La Persia e L'Asia centrale da Alessandro al X secolo*. Roma: 1996.

GRENET, Frantz. "Pour une nouvelle visite à la 'Vision de Kerdir'" in: *Studia Asiatica* 3, 2002.

GRUENWALD, Ithamar. *Apocalyptic and Merkavah Mysticism*. Leiden: Brill, 1980.

GUNKEL, Hermann. *Die Psalmen*. Göttingen: Vandenhoeck & Ruprecht, 1929.
GURTNER, Daniel M. *Second Baruch: A Critical Edition of the Syriac Text with Greek and Latin Fragments, English Translation, Introduction, and Concordances*. London: Continuum, 2009.
HAMMER, Raymond. *The Book of Daniel*. Cambridge: Cambridge University Press, 1976.
HARNER, Michael. 'The Role of Hallucinogenic Plants in European Witchcraft' in: HARNER, Michael (ed.). *Hallucinogens and Shamanism*. New York: Oxford University Press, 1970.
HARTMAN, Sven. 'Datierung der Jungavestischen Apokalyptik' in: HELLHOLM, Daniel (ed.). *Apocalypticism in the Mediterranean World and the Near East: Proceedings of the International Colloquium on Apocalypticism, Uppsala, August 12-17, 1979*. Tübingen: Mohr, 1983.
HARTNER, Willy. 'Die Störungen der Planeten in Gyldénschen Koordinaten als Funktionen der mittleren Länge' in: *Mitteilungen der Universitäts-Sternwarte Frankfurt am Main, Stück 5, Arbeiten d. Planeteninstituts* 6 (1928): 1–51.
HARTNER, Willy. 'Old Iranian Calendars' in: GERSHEVITCH, I. (ed.). *CHIr, Vol. 2, The Median and Achaemenian Periods*. Cambridge: Cambridge University Press, 1985. Pp. 714-92.
HARTNER, Willy. 'The Pseudoplanetary Nodes of the Moon's Orbit in Hindu and Islamic Iconographies' in: *Ars Islamica* 5 (1938): 113–54.
HARTNER, Willy. 'The Young Avestan and Babylonian Calendars and the Antecedents of Precession' in: *Journal for the History of Astronomy* 10 (1979): 1–22, 144–65.
HASEL, Gerhard. 'The Four World Empires of Daniel 2 against its Near Eastern Environment' in: *JSOT* 12 (1972): 17–29.
HAUG, Martin. *The Pahlavi Language. [From the Pahlavi-Pazand Glossary Edited by Destur Hoshangji and M. Haug]*. Stuttgart: Carl Grüninger, 1870.
HEISER, Michael S. 'Monotheism, Polytheism, Monolatry, or Henotheism? Toward an Assessment of Divine Plurality in the Hebrew Bible' in: *Bulletin for Biblical Research* 18.1 (2008): 1–30.
HENGEL, Martin. *Judaism and Hellenism*. Philadelphia: Fortress Press, 1974.
HENGEL, Martin. *Jews, Greeks and Barbarians*. Philadelphia: Fortress Press, 1980.
HENGEL, Martin. 'Judaism and Hellenism Revisited' in: COLLINS, John J., and STERLING, Gregory E. (eds). *Hellenism in the Land of Israel*. Christianity and Judaism in Antiquity Series 13. Notre Dame: University of Notre Dame, 2001.
HENNING, Walter B. 'The Great Inscription of Šāpūr I' in: *BSOAS*, 9.4 (1939).
HENNING, Walter B. 'The Book of the Giants' in: *BSOAS*, 11.1 (1943).
HENNING, Walter B. 'Notes on the Great Inscription of Sapur I' in: BOYCE, Mary, and GERSHEVITCH, Ilya (eds). *W. B. Henning Memorial Volume*. London: Lund Humphries, 1970.
HINTZE, Almut. 'Avestan Literature' in: EMMERICK, Ronald E., and MACUCH, Maria (eds). *The Literature of Pre-Islamic Iran: Companion Volume I to A History of Persian Literature*. London: Taurus, 2009.
HINTZE, Almut. 'Zarathustra's Time and Homeland: Linguistic Perspectives' in: STAUSBERG, Michael, VEVAINA, Yuhan S.-D., and TESSMANN, Anna (eds). *The Wiley Blackwell Companion to Zoroastrianism*. Malden: Wiley-Blackwell, 2015. (*WBCZ*)
HINTZE, Almut. 'A Zoroastrian Vision' in: WILLIAMS, Alan V., STEWART, Sarah, and HINTZE, Almut (eds). *The Zoroastrian Flame. Exploring Religion, History and Tradition*. London: I.B. Tauris, 2016.

HINZ, Walther. 'Mani and Kardēr' in: VVAA. *La Persia nel Medioevo. Atti del Convegno Internazionale sul Tema*. Roma: Accademia Nazionale dei Lincei, 1971.

HOBBINS, John F. 'Resurrection in the Daniel Tradition and Other Writings at Qumran' in: COLLINS, John J., and FLINT, Peter W. (with the assistance of Cameron VANEPPS) (eds). *The Book of Daniel: Composition and Reception*. Leiden: Brill, 2001.

HOFFMAN, Karl. 'The Avesta Fragment FrD.3' in: *IIJ* 10.4 (1968).

HOLT, Frank L. *Into the Land of Bones: Alexander the Great in Afghanistan*. Berkeley: University of California Press, 2005.

HORNUNG, Erik. 'Licht und Finstemis in der Vorstellungswelt Altägyptens' in: *Studium Generale* 18 (1965): 73–83.

HOWARD-JOHNSTON, James. *The Armenian History Atrributed to Sebeos*. Liverpool: Liverpool University Press, 1999.

HOWES, Llewellyn. '"Who will put my soul on the scale?" Psychostasia in Second Temple Judaism' in: *Old Testament Essays* 27.1 (2014).

HUFFMAN, Carl (org.). *A History of Pythagoreanism*. Cambridge: Cambridge University Press, 2014.

HULTGÅRD, Anders. 'Ecstasy and Vision' in: HOLM, Nils (ed.). *Religious Ecstasy: Based on Papers Read at the Symposium on Religious Ecstasy Held at Åbo, Finland, on the 26th-28th of August 1981*. Stockholm: Almqvist and Wiksell, 1982.

HULTGÅRD, Anders. 'Forms and Origins of Iranian Apocalypticism' in: HELLHOLM, Daniel (ed.). *Apocalypticism in the Mediterranean World and the Near East: Proceedings of the International Colloquium on Apocalypticism, Uppsala, August 12-17, 1979*. Tübingen: Mohr, 1983.

HULTGÅRD, Anders. 'Mythe et histoire dans l'Iran ancien: Étude de quelques thèmes dans le *Bahman Yast*' in: WIDENGREN, Geo, et al. (eds). *Apocalyptique iranienne et dualisme qoumrânien*. Paris: Adrien Maisonneuve, 1995.

HULTGÅRD, Anders. 'Persian Apocalypticism' in: COLLINS, John J. (ed.). *The Encyclopedia of Apocalypticism*, vol. 1. New York: Continuum, 1998. Pp. 39–83.

HULTGREN, Stephen. '4Q521, the Second Benediction of the "'Tefilla", the "Ḥasîdîm", and the Development of Royal Messianism' in: *Revue de Qumrân* 23.3(91) (2008): 313–40.

HUMBACH, Helmut. *The Gāthās of Zarathustra and Other Old Avestan Texts. Part I – Introduction – Text and Translation*. Heidelberg: Carl Winter Universitätsverlag, 1991.

HUMBACH, Helmut. *The Gāthās of Zarathustra and Other Old Avestan Texts. Part II – Commentary*. Heidelberg: Carl Winter Universitätsverlag, 1991.

HUMBACH, Helmut (in collaboration with Josef ELFENBEIN and Prods O. SKJÆRVØ). *The Gāthās of Zarathustra and the Other Old Avestan Texts. Part I – Introduction – Text and Translation*. Heidelberg: Carl Winter – Universitätsverlag, 1994.

HUMBACH, Helmut. 'Interpretations of Zarathustra and the *Gāthās*' in: STAUSBERG, Michael, VEVAINA, Yuhan S.-D., and TESSMANN, Anna (eds). *The Wiley Blackwell Companion to Zoroastrianism*. Malden: Wiley-Blackwell, 2015. (*WBCZ*)

HUMBACH, Helmut. 'The *Gāthās*' in: STAUSBERG, Michael, VEVAINA, Yuhan S.-D., and TESSMANN, Anna (eds). *The Wiley Blackwell Companion to Zoroastrianism*. Malden: Wiley-Blackwell, 2015. (*WBCZ*)

HUMBACH, Helmut, and ICHAPORIA, Pallan. *The Heritage of Zarathustra: A New Translation of his Gāthās*. Heidelberg: Carl Winter – Universitätsverlag, 1994.

HUMPHREYS, W. Lee. 'A Life-Style for the Diaspora: A Study of the Tales of Esther and Daniel' in: *JBL* 92 (1973): 211–15.

HUTTER, Manfred. 'The Impurity of the Corpse (*nasā*) and the Future Body (*tan ī pasēn*): Death and Afterlife in Zoroastrianism' in: NICKLAS, Tobias, REITERER, Friedrich V., and VERHEYDEN, Joseph (in collaboration with Heike Braun) (eds). *The Human Body in Death and Resurrection*. Berlin: de Gruyter, 2009. Pp. 13–26.
IBN WARRAQ. *Defending the West: A Critique of Edward Said's Orientalism*. New York: Prometheus Books, 2007.
INSLER, Stanley. *The Gāthās of Zarathustra*. Iranica 8. Leiden: Brill, 1975.
IRVING-PEASE, Evan, et al. 'Paleogenomics of Animal Domestication' in: LINDQVIST, Charlotte, and RAJORA, Om P. (eds). *Paleogenomics: Genome-Scale Analysis of Ancient DNA*. Cham: Springer, 2018.
JACKSON, Abraham V. W. 'On the date of Zoroaster' in: *JAOS* 17 (1896): 1–22.
JASPERS, Karl. *The Origin and Goal of History*. New Haven: Yale University Press, 1953.
JASPERS, Karl. *Vom Ursprung und Ziel der Geschichte*. Frankfurt am Main: Fischer, 1955.
JOHNSON, Paul. *Jesus: A Biography from a Believer*. New York: Penguin, 2010.
JONG, Albert de. *Traditions of the Magi: Zoroastrianism in Greek and Latin Literature*. Leiden: Brill, 1997.
JUNKER, Heinrich F. J. *The Frahang I Pahlavīk*. Heidelberg: Carl Winters, 1912. (2 vols)
JUSTI, Ferdinand. *Iranisches Namenbuch*. Marburg: N. G. Elwertsche Verlagsbuchhandlung, 1895.
KASSOCK, Zeke. *Dādestān ī Mēnōg ī Xrad.A Pahlavi Student's 2013 Guide*. Fredericksburg: Author's edition, 2013.
KELLENS, Jean. 'Les frauuashis dans l'art sassanide' in: *IrAnt* 10 (1972).
KELLENS, Jean. *Fravardin Yast (1-70)*. Wiesbaden: Reichert, 1975.
KELLENS, Jean. 'Avesta' in: *Encyclopaedia Iranica*, vol. 3. New York: Routledge and Kegan Paul, 1987. Pp. 35–44.
KELLENS, Jean. 'Yima et la mort' in: JAZAYERY, Mohammad Ali, and WINTER, Werner (eds). *Languages and Cultures. Studies in Honor of Edgar C. Polomé*. Berlin: Mouton de Gruyter, 1988.
KELLENS, Jean. *Essays on Zarathustra and Zoroastrianism*. Costa Mesa: Mazda, 2000.
KELLENS, Jean, and PIRART, Eric. '*Yazamaidē, nāmēni, āpō; Yazamaiē, nāmēni, urvarō*' in: *Les textes vieil-avestiques*, vol. 1. Wiesbaden: Reichert, 1988. (3 vols)KING, Richard. 'Mysticism and Spirituality' in: HINNELLS, John (ed.). *The Routledge Companion to the Study of Religion*. Second edition. Abingdon: Routledge, 2010.
KINGSLEY, Peter. 'Meetings with Magi: Iranian Themes among the Greeks, from Xanthus of Lydia to Plato's Academy' in: *JRAS*, Third Series, 5.2 (1995): 173–209.
KIPERWASSER, Reuven, and SHAPIRA, Dan D.Y. 'Irano-Talmudica I: The Three-Legged Ass and Ridyā in B. Ta'anith. Some Observations about Mythic Hydrology in the Babylonian Talmud and in Ancient Iran' in: *AJSR* 32.1 (2008): 101–16.
KIPPENBERG, Hans G. "Die Geschichte der Mittelpersischen apokalytischen Tradizionen" in: *SIr* 7 (1978).
KLIJN, Albertus F. J. '2 (Syriac Apocalypse of) BARUCH: A New Translation and Introduction' in: *OTP* 1.
KLOOS, Carlos. *Yhwh's Combat with the Sea: A Canaanite Tradition in the Religion of Ancient Israel*. Leiden: Brill, 1986.
KOENEN, Ludwig. *Die Prophezeiungen des 'Töpfers'*. Bonn: Habelt, 1968.
KOESTER, Craig R. *Revelation: A New Translation with Introduction and Commentary*. New Haven: Yale University Press, 2014.

KÖNIG, Fridrich-Wilhelm. *Relief und Inschrift des Koenigs Dareios I. am Felsen von Bagistan.* Leiden: Brill, 1938.

KÖNIG, Friedrich-Wilhelm. *Die Persika des Ktesisas von Knidos.* Graz: Archiv für Orientforschung, Beiheft 18, 1972.

KOSMIN, Paul J. *The Land of the Elephant Kings: Space, Territory, and Ideology in the Seleucid Empire.* Cambridge, MA: Harvard University Press, 2014.

KOTWAL, Dastur F. M., and BOYD, James W. *A Persian Offering. The Yasna: A Zoroastrian High Liturgy.* Studia Iranica – Cahier 8. Paris: Association pour l'avancement des études iraniennes, 1991.

KRATZ, Reinhard. 'The Visions of Daniel' in: COLLINS, John J., and FLINT, Peter W. (with the assistance of Cameron VANEPPS) (eds). *The Book of Daniel: Composition and Reception.* Leiden: Brill, 2001.

KROLL, Wilhelm. *Historia Alexandri Magni.* Berlin: Weidmann, 1926.

KUEHN, Sara. 'The Dragon-Fighter: The Influence of Zoroastrianism Ideas on Judaeo-Christian and Islamic Iconography' in: *ARAM Periodical* 26.1–2 (2014).

KUGEL, James L. 'Early Jewish Interpretation' in: COLLINS, John J., and HARLOW, Daniel C. (eds). *Early Judaism: A Comprehensive Overview.* Cambridge: William B. Eerdmans, 2012.

KULIK, Alexander. *3 Baruch: Greek-Slavonic Apocalypse of Baruch.* Berlin: Walter de Gruyter, 2010.

KURFESS, Alfons. *Sibyllinische Weissagungen: Urtext und Übersetzung.* Berlin: Heimann, 1951.

KUZMINA, Elena E. *The Prehistory of the Silk Road.* Encounter with Asia. Philadelphia: University of Pennsylvania Press, 2008.

KVANVIG, Helge S. *Roots of Apocalyptic: The Mesopotamian Background of the Enoch Figure and of the Son of Man.* Neukirchen-Vluyn: Neukirchen Verlag, 1988.

LACOQUE, André. *Daniel in His Time.* Columbia: University of South Carolina Press, 1996.

LAMBERT, Wilfred G. 'Destiny and Divine Intervention in Babylon and Israel' in: WOUDE, Adam S. Van der (ed.). *The Witness of Tradition.* Leiden: Brill 1972.

LAMBERT, Wilfred G. 'Trees, Snakes and Gods in Ancient Syria and Anatolia' in: *BSOAS* 48.3 (1985).

LAMBERT, Wilfred G. *The Background of Jewish Apocalyptic.* London: Athlone Press, 1978.

LANDAU, Brent. *Revelation of the Magi: The Lost Tale of the Wise Men's Journey to Bethlehem.* New York: HarperOne, 2010.

LECHLER, George. 'The Tree of Life in Indo-European and Islamic Cultures' in: *Ars Islamica* 4 (1937): 369–420.

LEUNER, H. 'Die toxische Ekstase' in: SPOERRI, Theodor (ed.). *Beiträge zur Ekstase.* Bibliotheca psychiatrica et neurologica. Basel: Karger, 1968.

LEWIS, Ioan M. *Ecstatic Religion: An Anthropological Study of Spirit Possession and Shamanism.* Harmondsworth: Penguin, 1971.

LOMMEL, Herman. *Die Religion Zarathustras: Nach den Awesta dargestellt.* Tübingen: Verlag von J. C. B. Mohr (Paul Siebeck), 1930.

LOURIÉ, Basil. 'The Calendar Implied in 2 Baruch and 4 Ezra: Two Modifications of the One Scheme'. Paper presented at the 'Sixth Enoch Meeting in Milan (in memory of Hanan Eshel)', 27 June 2011.

LOURIÉ, Basil. 'Лурье, -Чаша Соломона и скиния на Сионе. Часть 1. Надпись на Чаше Соломона: текст и контекст [The Chalice of Solomon and the Tabernacle in Sion. Part 1: Inscription on the Chalice of Solomon: Text and Context]' in: *Byzantinorossica* 3 (2005): 8–74.

LOUW-KRITZINGER, Ellie Marie. *Die Eskatologiese/Apokaliptiese Oorlog Tussen Goeden Kwaad in die Zoroastrisme, die Judaïsme (Qumran) en'n Vroeg-Christelike Geskrif (Die Apokalyps)*. PhD diss., Stellenbosch, 2009.

LÖWITH, Karl. *Meaning in History*. Chicago: University of Chicago Press, 1949.

LURKER, Manfred. 'Hermaphróditos' in: *The Routledge Dictionary of Gods and Goddesses, Devils and Demons*. London: Routledge, 1987.

MACKENZIE, David N. '*Bundahišn*' (entry originally published 15 December 1989 and last updated 15 December 1989). Available online: http://www.iranicaonline.org/artic les/achaemenid-religion (accessed 18 November 2019).

MACUCH, Maria. 'Law in Pre-Modern Zoroastrianism' in: STAUSBERG, Michael, VEVAINA, Yuhan S.-D., and TESSMANN, Anna (eds). *The Wiley Blackwell Companion to Zoroastrianism*. Malden: Wiley-Blackwell, 2015. (*WBCZ*)

MACUCH, Maria. 'Pahlavi Literature' in: EMMERICK, Ronald E., and MACUCH, Maria. *A History of Persian Literature*, volume 17. London: I.B. Tauris, 2009.

MALLORY, James P., and ADAMS, Douglas Q. *The Oxford Introduction to Proto-Indo European and the Proto-Indo-European World*. New York: Oxford University Press, 2008.

MAREK, Christian (in collaboration with Peter Frei). *In the Land of a Thousand Gods: A History of Asia Minor in the Ancient World*. Princeton: Princeton University Press, 2016.

MAY, Herbert G. 'Some cosmic connotations of Mayim Rabbim, "Many Waters"' in: *JBL* 74 (1955): 9–21.

MAYOR, Adrienne. *The Poison King: The Life and Legend of Mithradates, Rome's Deadliest Enemy*. Princeton: Princeton University Press, 2010.

MAYRHOFER, Manfred. *Zum Namengut des Avesta*. Vienna: Verlag der Österreichischen Akademie der Wissenschaften, 1977.

MAYRHOFER, Manfred. *Die altiranischen Namen, Iranisches Personennamenbuch*. Band I, Fascs. I-II-III. Wien: Österreichisches Akademie der Wissenschaften, 1979.

MEARNS, Rodney. *The Vision of Tundale, Edited from the B.L. MS Cotton Caligula A II*. (Text in Middle English). Heidelberg: Carl Winter, 1985.

MENASCE, Jean de. *Une apologétique Mazdéene du IXe Siècle. Škand-Gumānīk Vičār. La Solution Décisive des Doutes*. Fribourg: Librairie de l'Université, 1945.

MENASCE, Jean de. *Le Troisième Livre du Dēnkart: Traduit du pehlevi*. Paris: Klincksieck, 1973.

MENDELS, Doron. 'The Five Empires: A Note on a Propagandistic *Topos*' in: *American Journal of Philology* 102 (1981).

METZGER, Bruce. 'Forgeries and Canonical Pseudepigrapha' in: *JBL* 91.1 (1972).

METZGER, Bruce. '4 Ezra: A New Translation and Introduction' in: *OTP* 1.

MEULI, Karl. 'Scythica' in: *Hermes* 70.2 (1935): 133–4.

MILIK, Józef T. 'Prière de Nabonide et autres écrits d'un cycle de Daniel' in: *RB* 63 (1956): 407–11.

MILLS, Lawrence H. *Avesta – Yasna: Sacred Liturgy and Gathas / Hymns of Zarathushtra*. Oxford: Oxford University Press, 1887. (*SBE*)

MILLS, Lawrence H. et alii. *The Zend Avesta*. Oxford: Clarendon Press, 1895. (3 vols) (*SBE*)

MILLS, Lawrence H. '*Yasna XXX* as the Document of Dualism' in: *JRAS* (1912).

MOAZAMI, Mahnaz. 'The Dog in Zoroastrian Religion: "*Vidēvdād*" Chapter XIII' in: *IIJ* 49.1/2 (2006): 127–49.
MOJSOV, Bojana. 'The Ancient Egyptian Underworld in the Tomb of Sety I: Sacred Books of Eternal Life' in: The Massachusetts Review 42.4 (2001): 489–506.
MOLÉ, Marijan. *La légende de Zoroastre: selon les textes Pehlevis*. Paris: Klincksieck, 1967.
MOMIGLIANO, Arnaldo. 'Time in Ancient Historiography' in: MOMIGLIANO, Arnaldo (ed.). *Essays in Ancient and Modern Historiography*. Middletown: Wesleyan University Press, 1987.
MORGENSTIERNE, Georg G. *Indo-Iranian Frontier Languages II: Iranian Pamir Languages*. Oslo: 1938.
MOWINCKEL, Sigmund. *Psalmen Studien II, Das Thronbesleigungsfest Jäawäs*. Kristiania: SNVAO, 1922.
MURPHY, Frederick J. *The Structure and Meaning of Second Baruch*. Dissertation Series/Society of Biblical Literature 78. Atlanta: Scholars Press, 1985.
NARTEN, Johanna. 'Avestisch frauuaši-' in: *IIJ* 28 (1985).
NEUSNER, Jacob. 'Zoroastrianism in the Comparison of Religions' in: Acta Iranica 25 (1985): 436–7.
NEUSNER, Jacob. *A History of the Jews in Babylonia II: The Early Sasanian Period, III: From Shapur I to Shapur II*. Leiden: Brill, 1999.
NIDITCH, Susan. *Chaos to Cosmos: Studies in Biblical Patterns of Creation*. Missoula: Scholars Press, 1985.
NISKANEN, Paul. *The Human and the Divine in History: Herodotus and the Book of Daniel*. London: Continuum, 2004.
NÖLDEKE, Theodor. 'Syrische Polemik gegen die persische Religion' in: KUHN, Ernst (ed.). *Der Festgruß an Robert von Roth zum Doctor-Jubiläum 24. August 1893*. Stuttgart: W. Kohlhammer, 1893.
NOTH, Martin. *Überlieferungsgeschichtliche Studien: Die sammelnden und bearbeitenden Geschichtswerke im Alten Testament*. Tübingen: M. Niemeyer, 1957.
NYBERG, Henrik S. *Frahang i Pahlavīk, Ed. with Transliteration, Transcription and Commentary from the Posthumous Papers of Henrik Samuel Nyberg by Bo Utas with the Collaboration of Christopher Toll*. Wiesbaden: Harrassowitz, 1988.
O'BRIEN, Elmer. *Varieties of Mystic Experience: An Anthology and Interpretation*. New York: Holt, Rinehart and Winston, 1964.
OLSSON, Tord. 'The Apocalyptic Activity: The Case of Jāmāsp Nāmag' in: HELLHOLM, Daniel (ed.). *Apocalypticism in the Mediterranean World and the Near East: Proceedings of the International Colloquium on Apocalypticism, Uppsala, August 12-17, 1979*. Tübingen: Mohr, 1983.
OMIDSALAR, Mahmoud, OMIDSALAR, Teresa P., BOYCE, Mary, and DIGARD, Jean-Pierre. 'Dog' (entry originally published 15 December 1995 and last updated 29 November 2011). Available online: http://www.iranicaonline.org/articles/dog#pt2 (accessed 20 November 2019).
ORLOV, Andrei A. 'The Flooded Arboretums: The Garden Traditions in the Slavonic Version of 3 Baruch and in the Book of Giants' in: *CBQ* 65 (2003).
PANAINO, Antonio. 'Astral Characters of Kingship in the Sasanian and Byzantine Worlds' in: VVAA. *La Persia e Bisanzio. Atti dei convegni Lincei (Roma), 201*. Bologna: Università degli Studi di Bologna, 2002.
PANAINO, Antonio. 'Iniziazione e dimensione esoterica nella tradizione mazdaica. Riti e simboli' in: *Sulla soglia del sacro: Esoterismo ed iniziazione nelle grandi religioni e nella*

tradizione massonica. Firenze 1-3 marzo 2002. Atti del Convegno di Studi, a cura di A. Panaino. Milano: Mimesis, 2002.

PANAINO, Antonio. 'Trends and Problems Concerning the Mutual Relations between Pre-Islamic and Jewish Cultures' in: PANAINO, Antonio, and PIRAS, Andrea (eds). *Melammu Symposia IV. Schools of Oriental Studies nd the Development of Modern Historiography. Proceedings of the Fourth Annual Symposium of the Asasyrian and Babylonian Intellectual Heritage Project held in Ravenna, Italy, October 17-21, 2001.* Milano: Università di Bologna & ISIAO, 2004.

PANAINO, Antonio. 'Cosmologies and Astrology' in: STAUSBERG, Michael, VEVAINA, Yuhan S.-D., and TESSMANN, Anna (eds). *The Wiley Blackwell Companion to Zoroastrianism*. Malden: Wiley-Blackwell, 2015. (*WBCZ*)

PARPOLA, Simo. 'The Assyrian Tree of Life: Tracing the Origins of Jewish Monotheism and Greek Philosophy' in: *J NES* 52.3 (1993): 161–208.

PAUL, Ludwig (ed.). *Handbuch der Iranistik*. Wiesbaden: Reichert, 2013.

PAYNE, Richard E. *A State of Mixture: Christians, Zoroastrians and Iranian Political Culture in Late Antiquity*. Oakland: University of California Press, 2015.

PEARCE, Laurie E. 'Identifying Judaeans and Judaean Identity in the Babylonian Evidence' in: STÖKL, Jonathan, and WAERZEGGERS, Caroline (eds). *Exile and Return: The Babylonian Context*. Berlin: Walter de Gruyter, 2015.

PENGLASE, Charles. 'Foundations' in: *Greek Myths and Mesopotamia: parallels and influence in the Homeric hymns and Hesiod*. London: Routledge, 1994.

PENNACCHIETTI, Fabrizio A. 'Gli Acta Archelai ed il viaggio di Mani nel Bēt ʿArbāyē' in: *Rivista di Storia e Letterattura Religiosa* 24.3 (1988): 503–14.

PEZZOLI-OGLIATI, Daria. 'Approaching Afterlife Imagery: A Contemporary Glance at Ancient Concepts of Otherworldly Dimensions' in: NICKLAS, Tobias, VERHEYDEN, Joseph, EYNIKEL, Erik M. M., and GARCÍA-MARTÍNEZ, Florentino (eds). *Other Worlds and Their Relation to This World. Early Jewish and Ancient Christian Traditions*. Leiden: Brill, 2010.

PHILONENKO, Marc. 'Introduction generale' in: WIDENGREN, Geo, et al. (eds). *Apocalyptique iranienne et dualisme qoumrânien*. Paris: Adrien Maisonneuve, 1995.

POCOCK, John G. A. *Politics, Language, and Time: Essays on Political Thought and History*. New York: Athenaeum, 1971.

POPOVIČ, Mladen. 'Bones, Bodies and Resurrection in the Dead Sea Scrolls' in: NICKLAS, Tobias, REITERER, Friedrich V., and VERHEYDEN, Joseph (in collaboration with Heike Braun) (eds). *The Human Body in Death and Resurrection*. Berlin: de Gruyter, 2009. Pp. 221–42.

PORTIER-YOUNG, Anathea E. *Apocalypse against Empire: Theologies of Resistance in Early Judaism*. Grand Rapids: Eerdmans, 2013.

POURSHARIATI, Parvaneh. *Decline and Fall of the Sasanian Empire: The Sasanian-Parthian Confederacy and the Arab Conquest of Iran*. London: I.B. Tauris, 2011.

PRITCHARD, James B. *Ancient Near Eastern Texts related to the Old Testament*. Princeton: Princeton University Press, 1969.

PROPP, Vladimir I. *Morphology of the Folktale*. Austin: University of Texas Press, 2009.

PUECH, Émile. 'Une apocalypse messianique (4Q521)' in: *Revue de Qumrân* 15 4(60) (1992).

PUECH, Émile. *La croyance des Esséniens*. Paris: J. Gabalda et Cie., 1993.

PUECH, Émile. *Discoveries in the Judaean Desert. Textes Hébreux (4Q521-4Q528, 4Q576-4Q579). Qumrân Grotte 4. Vol.XXV [continued in XXVII]*. Oxford: Clarendon Press, 1998.

RAD, Gerhard von. *Theologie des Alten Testaments*. Munich: Christian Kaiser Verlag, 1960.
RAEI, Sharokh. *Die Endzeitvorstellungen der Zoroastrier in iranischen Quellen.* Wiesbaden: Harrasowitz, 2010.
RAPHAEL, Simcha P. *Jewish Views of the Afterlife*. Lanham: Rowman & Littlefield, 2009.
REZAKHANI, Khodadad. *Re-Orienting the Sasanians: East Iran in Late Antiquity.* Edinburgh: Edinburgh University Press, 2017.
REZANIA, Kianoosh. 'Zurvan: Limitless Time or Endless Time? The Question of Eternity and Time in Zoroastrianism' in: *JKR* 68 (2008).
RHOADS, David M. *Israel in Revolution: 6–74 C.E.: A Political History Based on the Writings of Josephus*. Philadelphia: Fortress Press, 1976.
RICHTER, Sandra L. *The Deuteronomistic History and the Name Theology*. Berlin: Walter de Gruyter, 2002.
RINGGREN, Helmer. 'Akkadian Apocalypses' in: HELLHOLM, Daniel (ed.). *Apocalypticism in the Mediterranean World and the Near East: Proceedings of the International Colloquium on Apocalypticism, Uppsala, August 12-17, 1979.* Tübingen: Mohr, 1983. Pp. 379–86. (*AMWNE*)
ROBINSON, Andrew. *The Last Man Who Knew Everything*. Oxford: Oneworld, 2006.
ROBINSON, Andrew. *Cracking the Egyptian Code: The Revolutionary Life of Jean-François Champollion*. Oxford: Oxford University Press, 2012.
ROFÉ, Alexander. *Introduction to the Composition of the Pentateuch*. Sheffield: Sheffield Academic Press, 1999.
ROFÉ, Alexander. *Deuteronomy: Issues and Interpretation*. London: T&T Clark, 2002.
RÖMER, Thomas C. 'Du Temple au Livre: L'idéologie de la centralisation dans l'historiographie deutéronomiste' in: MCKENZIE, Steven L., and RÖMER, Thomas (in collaboration with Hans Heinrich Schmid) (eds). *Rethinking the Foundations. Historiography in the Ancient World and in the Bivle. Essays in Honour of John Van Seeters*. Berlin: Walter de Gruyter, 2000.
ROMM, James S. *The Edges of the Earth in Ancient Thought*. Princeton: Princeton University Press, 1992.
ROSE, Herbert J. *Concerning Parallels*. Oxford: Frazer Lecture, 1934.
ROSENBERG, Frédéric. *Le livre de Zoroastre (Zarâtusht Nâma)*. St Petersburg: Académie Impériale des Sciences, 1904.
ROSTOVTZEFF, Mikhail. *The Social & Economic History of the Hellenistic World*, vol. 2. New York: Oxford, 1941.
ROWLAND, Christopher. 'The Book of Daniel and the Radical Critique of Empire: An Essay in Apocalyptic' in: COLLINS, John J., and FLINT, Peter W. (with the assistance of Cameron VANEPPS) (eds). *The Book of Daniel: Composition and Reception*. Leiden: Brill, 2001.
ROWLEY, Harold H. *Darius the Mede and the Four World Empires in the Book of Daniel*. Cardiff: University of Wales Press Board, 1959.
ROZIK, Eli. *The Roots of Theatre: Rethinking Ritual and Other Theories of Origin*. Iowa City: University of Iowa Press, 2002.
RUSSELL, David S. *The Method and Message of Jewish Apocalyptic*. Philadelphia: The Westminster Press, 1964.
RUSSELL, James. 'Kartīr and Mānī: A Shamanistic Model of Their Conflict' in: AMIN, Dina, and KASHEFF, Manuchehr (eds). *Iranica Varia: Papers in Honor of Professor Ehsan Yarshater*. Acta Iranica 30. Leiden: Brill, 1990.
RUSSELL, James. *Zoroastrianism as the State Religion of Ancient Iran*. Bombay: K.R. Cama Oriental Institute, 1984.

SAID, Edward. *Orientalism*. Harmondsworth: Penguin, 1985.
SANDERS, Edward P. *Judaism – Practice & Belief 63 BCE–66 CE*. London: SCM Press, 1992.
SANJANA, Darab D. P. *The Zand ī Javīt Shēda Dād or the Pahlavi Version of the Avesta Vendidād the Text Prescribed for the B.A. and M.A. Examinations of the University of Bombay. Edited, with an Introduction, Critical and Philological Notes, and Appendices on the History of Avestan Literature*. Bombay: Education Society's Steam Press, 1895.
SANJANA, Peshotan D. B. (trans. Ratanshah E.KOHIYAR). *Denkard, Book 3. Vol. 7*. Avestan compilation by Joseph Peterson Available online: http://www.avesta.org/denkard/dk3s.html. (Original, Bombay: 1894)
SARACHEK, Bernard. 'Greek Concepts of Leadership' in: *The Academy of Management Journal* 11.1 (1968).
SATRAN, David. 'Daniel: Seer, Philosopher, Holy Man' in: NICKELSBURG, George W. E., and COLLINS, John J. (eds). *Ideal Figures in Ancient Judaism: Profiles and Paradigms*. Chico: Scholars Press, 1980.
SCHIPPMANN, Klaus. *Die iranischen Feuerheiligtümer*. Berlin: Walter de Gruyter, 1971.
SCHMID, Hans H. *Gerechtigkeit als Weltordnung: Hintergrund und Geschichte des alttestamentlicher Theologie*. Zurich: NZN Burchverlag, 1974.
SCHMITT, Rüdiger. (Entry originally published 20 July 2002 and last updated 20 July 2002). Available online: http://www.iranicaonline.org/articles/achaemenid-religion (accessed 18 November 2019).
SCHULTES, Richard E., and HOFFMAN, Albert. *Plants of the Gods: Origins of Hallucinogenic Use*. New York: McGraw-Hill, 1979.
SCHULTZ, Brian. *Conquering the World: The War Scroll (1QM) Reconsidered*, STDJ 76. Leiden: Brill, 2009.
SCHÜRER, Emil. *The History of the Jewish People in the Age of Jesus Christ (175 B.C – A.D. 135)*. Rev. by Geza Vermes, Fergus Millar, Martin Goodman and Matthew Black. Edinburgh: T&T Clark, 1979. (3 vols)
SCHWAB, Raymond. *Vie d'Anquetil-Duperron: Suivie des usages civils et religieux des Parses*. Paris: Librairie Ernest Leroux, 1934.
SCHWAB, Raymond. *La renaissance orientale*. Paris: Payot, 1950.
SCHWARTZ, Martin. 'Dimensions of the *Gāthas* as Poetry' in: STAUSBERG, Michael, VEVAINA, Yuhan S.-D., and TESSMANN, Anna (eds). *The Wiley Blackwell Companion to Zoroastrianism*. Malden: Wiley-Blackwell, 2015. (*WBCZ*)
SHAHBAZI, Alireza S. 'The Achaemenid Persian Empire (550–330 BCE)' in: DARYAEE, Touraj (ed.). *The Oxford Handbook of Iranian History*. Oxford: Oxford University Press, 2012. (*OHIR*)
SHAKED, Shaul. *The Wisdom of the Sasanian Sages (Denkard VI)*. Boulder: Persian Heritage Series, 1979.
SHAKED, Shaul. 'Iranian Influence on Judaism: First Century B.C.E. to Second Century C.E.' in: DAVIES, W. D., and FINKELSTEIN, Louis (eds). *CHJ Vol. 1, Introduction: The Persian Period*. Cambridge: Cambridge University Press, 1984. Pp. 308-25.
SHAKED, Shaul. *Dualism in Transformation: Varieties of Religion in Sasanian Iran*. London: University of London, 1994.
SHAKED, Shaul. 'Jewish and Iranian Visions in the Talmudic Period' in: GAFNI, Isaiah M. et al. (eds). *The Jews in the Hellenistic-Roman World: Studies in Memory of Menahem Stern*. Jerusalem: The Zalman Shazar Center for Jewish History, 1996. (Hebrew).

SHAKED, Shaul. 'Eschatology i. In Zoroastrianism and Zoroastrian Influence' in: *EIr* 8.6 (1998): 565–9.
SHENKAR, Michael. 'Rethinking Sasanian Iconoclasm' in: *Journal of the American Oriental Society* 135.3 (2015): 471–98.
SINT, Josef A. *Pseudonymität im Altertum; ihre Formen und ihre Gründe.* Innsbruck: Universitätsverlag Wagner, 1960.
SKINNER, Quentin. 'Meaning and Understanding in the History of Ideas' in: TULLY, James (ed.). *Meaning & Context: Quentin Skinner and his Critics.* New Jersey: Princeton University Press, 1988.
SKJÆRVØ, Prods O. ' "Kirdir's Vision": Translation and Analysis' in: *Archäologische Mitteilungen aus Iran* 16 (1983).
SKJÆRVØ, Prods O. 'Praise and Blame in the Avesta: The Poet Sacrificer and His Duties' in: *JSAI* 26 (2002).
SKJÆRVØ, Prods O. 'The Antiquity of Old Avestan' in: *IJAIS* 3.2 (2003–4): 15–41.
SKJÆRVØ, Prods O. 'The Avestan Yasna: Ritual and Myth' in: PEDERSEN, Claus V., and VAHMAN, Fereydun (eds). *Religious Texts in Iranian Languages: Symposium Held in Copenhagen May 2002.* Copenhagen: Det Kongelige Danske Videnskabernes Selskab, 2007.
SKJÆRVØ, Prods O. *The Spirit of Zoroastrianism.* New Haven: Yale University Press, 2011.
SKJÆRVO, Prods O. 'The *Gāthās* as Myth and Ritual' in: STAUSBERG, Michael, VEVAINA, Yuhan S.-D., and TESSMANN, Anna (eds). *The Wiley Blackwell Companion to Zoroastrianism.* Malden: Wiley-Blackwell, 2015. (*WBCZ*)
SKJÆRVØ, Prods O. 'Kartir' (entry originally published 15 December 2011 and last updated 24 April 2014). Available online: http://www.iranicaonline.org/articles/kartir (accessed 18 November 2019).
SONSINO, Rifat, and SYME, Daniel B. (eds). *What Happens after I Die? Jewish Views of Life after Death.* New York: URJ Press, 1990.
SPARKS, Kenton L. 'Form Criticism' in: PORTER, Stanley E. (ed.). *Dictionary of Biblical Criticism and Interpretation.* New York: Routledge, 2007.
SPERBER, Daniel. 'Bab Nahara' in: *IrAnt* 8 (1968).
SPIEGEL, Friedrich. *Êrânische Alterthumskunde.* Leipzig: Wilhelm Engelmann 1871. (3 vols)
SPRENGLING, Martin. 'Kartīr, Founder of Sasanian Zoroastrianism' in: *The American Journal of Semitic Languages and Literatures* 57.2 (1940).
STAUSBERG, Michael. 'Zoroastrian Purity Rules and Purification Rituals' in: STAUSBERG, Michael (ed.). *Die Religion Zarathustras: Geschichte – Gegenwart – Rituale.* Band 3. Stuttgart: Kohlhammer, 2004.
STAUSBERG, Michael. 'Zarathustra Post-Gathic Trajectories' in: STAUSBERG, Michael, VEVAINA, Yuhan S.-D., and TESSMANN, Anna (eds). *The Wiley Blackwell Companion to Zoroastrianism.* Malden: Wiley-Blackwell, 2015. (*WBCZ*)
STINTON, Tom C. W. 'Hamartia in Aristotle and Greek Tragedy' in: *The Classical Quarterly* 25.2 (1975): 221–54.
STÖKL, Jonathan. ' "A youth without blemish, handsome, proficient in all wisdom, knowledgeable and intelligent": Ezekiel's Access to Babylonian Culture' in: STÖKL, Jonathan, and WAERZEGGERS, Caroline (eds). *Exile and Return: The Babylonian Context.* Berlin: Walter de Gruyter, 2015.
STONE, Michael E. 'Apocalyptic – Vision Or Hallucination?' in: *Selected Studies in Pseudepigrapha and Apocrypha with Special Reference to the Armenian Tradition.* Leiden: Brill, 1991.

STONE, Michael E., and HENZE, Matthias. *4Ezra and 2Baruch: Translations, Introductions and Notes*. Minneapolis: Fortress Press, 2013.
STONE, Michael E. *Fourth Ezra: A Commentary on the Book of Fourth Ezra*. Hermeneia. Minneapolis: Fortress Press, 1990.
STOYANOV, Yuri. *The Other God*. New Haven: Yale University Press, 2000.
SWAIN, Joseph W. 'The Theory of the Four Monarchies: Opposition History under the Roman Empire' in: *Classical Philology* 35.1 (1940).
TAFFAZOLĪ, Aḥmad. 'Činwad Puhl' (entry originally published 15 December 1991 and last updated 11 October 2011). Available online: http://www.iranicaonline.org/articles/cinwad-puhl-av (accessed 25 November 2019).
TARDIEU, Michel. *Manichaeism*. Urbana: University of Illinois Press, 2008.
THORPE, Samuel. 'Zoroastrian Exegetical Parables in the Škand Gumānīg Wizār' in: *Iran and the Caucasus* 17.3 (2013).
TORM, Frederik. 'Die Psychologie der Pseudonimität im Hinblick auf die Literatur des Urchristentums' in: BROX, Norbert (ed.). *Pseudepigraphie in der Heidnischen und Jüdisch-Christlichen Antike*. Darmstadt, Wissenschaftliche Buchgesellschaft, 1977. (Original chapter from 1932)
TROMP, Johannes. 'Can These Bones Live? Ezekiel 37:1-14 and Eschatological Resurrection' in: JONGE, Henk J. de, and TROMP, Johannes (eds). *The Book of Ezekiel and Its Influence*. Aldershot: Routledge, 2007. Pp. 61–78.
TULLY, James (ed.). *Meaning & Context: Quentin Skinner and his Critics*. New Jersey: Princeton University Press, 1988.
ULRICH, Eugene. 'The Jewish Scriptures: Texts, Versions, Canons' in: COLLINS, John J., and HARLOW, Daniel C. (eds). *Early Judaism A Comprehensive Overview*. Michigan: William B. Eerdmans, 2012.
VAHMAN, Fereydun. *Arda Wiraz Nāmag: The Iranian 'Divina Commedia'*. London: Curzon Press, 1986.
VAUX, Roland de. 'La grotte des manuscrits hébreux' in: *RB* 56 (1949).
VAUX, Roland de. *Archaeology and the Dead Sea Scrolls*. Schweich Lectures. London: Oxford University Press, 1973.
VERMES, Geza. *Jesus the Jew*. London: Collins, 1973.
VERMES, Geza. 'Qumran Forum Miscellanea I' in: *Journal of Jewish Studies* 43 (1992).
VEVAINA, Yuhan S.-D. 'Textual Taxonomies, Cosmological Deixis, and Canonical Commentaries in Zoroastrianism' in: *History of Religions* 50.2 (2010): 111–43.
VEVAINA, Yuhan S.-D. 'Miscegenation, "Mixture", and "Mixed Iron": The Hermeneutics, Historiography, and Cultural Poesis of the 'Four Ages' in Zoroastrianism' in: TOWNSEND, Philippa, and VIDAS, Moulie (eds). *Revelation, Literature, and Community in Late Antiquity*. Tübingen: Mohr Siebeck, 2011. Pp. 237–69.
VEVAINA, Yuhan S.-D. 'Theologies and Hermeneutics' in: STAUSBERG, Michael, VEVAINA, Yuhan S.-D., and TESSMANN, Anna (eds). *The Wiley Blackwell Companion to Zoroastrianism*. Malden: Wiley-Blackwell, 2015. (*WBCZ*)
VIENNOT, Odette. *Le cult de l'arbre dans l'Inde ancienne*. Paris: P.U.F., 1954.
WAKEMAN, Mary K. *God's Battle with the Monster*. Leiden: Brill, 1973.
WASSON, Robert G. 'What Was the Soma of the Aryans?' in: FURST, Peter (ed.). *Flesh of the Gods: The Ritual Use of Hallucinogens*. London: Allen & Unwin, 1972.
WATKINS, Calvert. *How to Kill a Dragon*. New York: Oxford University Press, 1995.
WEBER, Max. *The Sociology of Religion*. London: Methuen, 1965.
WEST, Edward W. *Sacred Books of the East*, vol. 5. Oxford: Oxford University Press, 1897. (*SBE*)

WEST, Martin L. *Works and Days*. Oxford: Oxford University Press, 1977.
WEST, Martin L. *Indo-European Poetry and Myth*. New York: Oxford University Press, 2008.
WEST, Martin L. *Old Avestan Syntax and Stylistics: With an Edition of the Texts*. Berlin: De Gruyter, 2011.
WEST, Martin L. *The Hymns of Zaraθuštra: A New Translation of the Most Ancient Sacred Texts of Iran*. London: I.B. Tauris, 2010.
WESTERGAARD, Niels L. *Zendavesta or The Religious Books of the Zoroastrians. Vol.I: The Zend Texts*. Wiesbaden: Reichert, 1993.
WHITBY, Michael, and WHITBY, Mary (eds). *The History of Theophylact Simocatta*. Oxford: Oxford University Press, 1986.
WHITCOMB, Donald. 'The City of Istakhr and the Marv Dasht Plain' in: *Akten des VII. Internationalen Kongresses für Iranische Kunst und Archäologie, München, 7-10 September 1976*. Berlin: D. Reimer, 1979. Pp. 363–70.
WIDENGREN, Geo. 'Leitende Ideen und Quellen der iranischen Apokalyptik' in: HELLHOLM, Daniel (ed.). *Apocalypticism in the Mediterranean World and the Near East: Proceedings of the International Colloquium on Apocalypticism, Uppsala, August 12-17, 1979*. Tübingen: Mohr, 1983.
WIDENGREN, Geo. 'Les ages du monde selon hésiode' in: WIDENGREN, Geo, et al. (eds). *Apocalyptique iranienne et dualisme qoumrânien*. Paris: Adrien Maisonneuve, 1995.
WIDENGREN, Geo. *Die Religionen Irans*. Stuttgart: W. Kohlhammer, 1965.
WIESEHÖFER, Josef. *Ancient Persia*. London: I.B. Tauris, 2011.
WILLIAMS, Alan V. *The Zoroastrian Myth of Migration from Iran and Settlement in the Indian Diaspora: Text, Translation and Analysis of the 16th Century Qesse-ye Sanjan 'The Story of Sanjan'*. Leiden: Brill, 2003.
WILLIAMS, Alan V. 'Purity and Pollution: The Body' in: STAUSBERG, Michael, VEVAINA, Yuhan S.-D., and TESSMANN, Anna (eds). *The Wiley Blackwell Companion to Zoroastrianism*. Malden: Wiley-Blackwell, 2015. (*WBCZ*)
WILSON, Edmund. *Os Manuscritos do Mar Morto*. São Paulo: Companhia das Letras, 2009.
WIMSATT, William K., and BEARDSLEY, Monroe C. *Hateful Contraries: Studies in Literature and Criticism*. Lexington: University Press of Kentucky, 1965.
WINDISCH, Hans. *Die Orakel des Hystaspes*. Amsterdam: Koninklijke Akademie van Wetenschappen te Amsterdam, 1929.
WINSTON, David. 'The Iranian Component in the Bible, Apocrypha and Qumran: A Review of the Evidence' in: *History of Religions* 5 (1966): 183–216.
WOLOHJAN, Albert M. *The Romance of Alexander the Great by Pseudo-Callisthenes*. New York: Columbia University Press, 1969.
WYBRAY, Roger N. *The Second Isaiah*. Sheffield: JSOT Press, 1983.
XERAVITS, Géza G. (ed.). *Dualism in Qumran*. London: T&T Clark, 2010.
XERAVITS, Géza G., and PORZIG, Peter. *Einführung in die Qumranliteratur: Die Handschriften vom Toten Meer*. Berlin: de Gruyter, 2015.
YAMAUCHI, Edwin M. *Persia and the Bible*. Grand Rapids: Baker Book House, 1990.
YARDLEY, John C. *Justin and Pompeius Trogus: A Study of the Language of Justin's Epitome of Trogus*. Toronto: University of Toronto Press, 2003.
ZAEHNER, Robert C. *Zurvan: A Zoroastrian Dilemma*. Oxford: Clarendon Press, 1955.

Index of passages

Hebrew Bible / Old Testament

Genesis
          14, 18, 19, 37, 41, 47, 70, 177, 201
1:29–30   186
2:8–10   186
7:1   41
8:21–22   191
9:12–13   97
9:15–21   187
9:20   186
15:18   187
17:10   97
35:37   47
37:34   117
37:35   5, 47
49:10   73, 196

Exodus
6:5   97
7:3   188
9:24   74
19:10   97
20:5   69

Leviticus
11:13   60
11:47   60

Deuteronomy
          46, 61, 84, 170, 199
14:12   60
14:21   60
30:3–5   187
32:8   43

Joshua
          ix, 190
13   117
1:4   187

1 Samuel
9:7   47
9:24   47
10:11   73, 196
18   117
26:19   88
28:3–25   124
28:7   47

2 Samuel
3   117
13   117
14   117

2 Kings
5:17   88

1 Chronicles
2   117

Ezra
          ix, x, 24, 89, 141, 142, 143, 144, 145, 146, 147, 148, 150, 157, 158, 159, 190, 201, 205
1:1–8   80
2:70   61
3:1   61
3:7   80
4:3   80
16:34   73, 196

Nehemiah
          ix, x, 24, 89
8:2   61

Esther
          x, 74

Job
          47, 61, 62, 201
17:16   73, 196

Index of Passages

Psalms		49:8–9	88
29:3	43, 61	51:4	88
37	47		
74:12–14	47	**Jeremiah**	
93	43, 61	25:15–16	146
		30:7	74
Ecclesiastes / Qohelet			
	5, 7	**Ezekiel**	
1:22–11	46		ix, 23, 81
4:9	73, 196	2:8–3:3	146
9:3–5	5	14:14	62, 84
10	5	34:17	175
		37	116
Song of Songs		37:1–14	119, 124
	x	38:11	41
Isaiah		**Daniel**	
	22, 24, 48, 81, 82, 83,		x, 5, 9, 17, 18, 19, 21,
	85, 86, 87, 88, 89, 93,		23, 24, 40, 43, 44, 45,
	97, 100, 103, 116, 199,		47, 49, 50, 51, 61, 62,
	200, 201		64, 66, 71, 72, 74, 80,
1–39	ix, 83		81, 83, 84, 85, 87, 89,
1–55	89		93, 100, 102, 103, 108,
2:2–4	88		116, 125, 126, 131, 134,
3:11	73, 196		141, 142, 144, 148,
5:20	47		160, 161, 162, 166, 167,
10:5	86		171, 173, 174, 175, 178,
19:24–25	88		181, 182, 185, 186, 187,
27:1	87		188, 189, 190, 191, 193,
35	200, 201		194, 196, 199, 200, 201,
40–48	87		203, 204
40–54	ix, 83, 84, 87	1:6	4, 5, 80, 84, 85
41	116	1:8–15	140
42	116	2	54, 62, 66, 80, 85, 101,
41:8–20	8		108, 136, 162, 165, 171,
42:4	88		172, 176, 177, 180,
43	187		192, 204
43:1–7	86	2:1–19	173
43:8–20	85	2:31	180
43:14–21	86	2:34	142
44:18	86	2:41	171
44:24–45:7	86	2:42	172
45:1	ix	2:43	162
45:1–3	84	3	142
45:5	60	5:31	162
45:6	87	7	50, 62, 101, 143, 165,
45:7	47		175, 204
45:23–49:23	88	7:1	40
49:6	88, 116	7–12	66, 84, 131, 175, 177–8

8	175	18:3, 21–35	112
9:3	142	19:14, 23–24	112
10:20	44, 85	20:1–16	112
10:21	74	21:19	60
11	85, 176	22:1–14	112
11:1–41	176–7	22:14	52
11:7–11	162	23:15	22
12	204	24:21	68, 74
12:1–3	74	25:1–30	112
12:1–14	116		
12:2	7, 41, 46, 50, 67, 68, 70, 71, 124, 136, 186, 195	Mark	
		4:26–34	112
		5:13	60
12:2–3	6	8:23	48
12:2–6	129	10:14, 23	112
12:10	116, 136	10:38	146
		11:20	60
Amos		13:19	74
5:18	170	13:26–15:31	68
		14:36	146
Jonah		15:39	68
	195		
		Luke	
Zechariah		7:21–22	48, 123
10:3	175	8:10	112
		8:32	60
2 Maccabbees		18:29–30	112
	74, 196	21:32	68
4:7–10	196		
12:39–45	74, 195	John	
12:43–44	73, 196		xi
		3:3	112
Tobit		5:3	48
	24, 161, 174, 195, 196	9:2	69
14:4	195	12:35	xi
		13:18	52
New Testament		Acts	
Matthew			24
	24	2:9–11	159
1:24	74		
3:2	112	1 John	
4:17	112	2:18	68
5:3, 10	112		
9:27–28	48	Revelation	
10:7	112		135
11:2–5	123	1:13–15	68
12:22	48	16:18	74
13:24–52	112		
16:19	112		

Index of Passages

APOCRYPHA AND PSEUDEPIGRAPHA

1 En.
1:2	123
5:8–10	45
9:27–28	48
11:1	123
12:22	48
13:6–10	142
18:10	123
39:3	123
39:9–14	142
41:3–4	192
42:1	123
47:2	123
54:7–8	123
55:2	123
60:1	123
61:9	123
71:1–5	123
84:2–4	123
93:12	123
98:6	123

2 En.
1–68	123

3 En.
5:11	123
12:4	123
17:1–3	123
18:1–2, 25	123
19:1	123
22:3–4	123
26:5–6, 10	123
38:1	123
44:7	123
46:13, 14	123
48:1	123

2 Bar.
1–6	40
6	182
7	182
6:4–9	61
29	186
29:5–6	185
36	185, 188, 190
36:1	191
36:7–10	186
38:1–40:4	187
39:1–7	193
59:5	192

3 Bar.
2:1	123
3:1	123
7:2	123
10:1	123
11:1	123

4 Bar.
4:1	182

4 Ezra
	40, 49, 51, 61, 68, 110, 132, 139, 140, 141, 142, 144, 146, 149, 150, 151, 152, 153, 154, 156, 157, 158, 159, 160, 166, 185, 192
3–14	90
3:1	142
3:28	61
4–6	40
7:19–30	40
8:1–2	40
9	143, 157, 158
9:23–25	141, 155, 190
9:23–29	140, 145, 155
9:24–26	191
9:26	141, 142
9:38	142
10:19–59	40
11	40
11–12	181
12	157, 158
12:10–12	166
12:38–39	143
12:39	143
12:41	141
12:51	140, 141, 143, 145, 148, 155, 191
13	143
14	147, 148, 158
14:27	52
14:38	144, 190

14:38–42	157	4Q174	176
14:38–48	140, 143, 145, 150, 153	4Q184	137, 138
16:15	119	4Q242	188, 189
		4Q243 Fr.	13 189
Apoc. Ab.		4Q243–245	189
	189	4Q244	189
1:3	189	4Q245	189
9:7	143	4Q266:8	138
		4Q385	123, 192
Ascen. Isa.		4Q385–388	41
6:11	123	4Q386	123, 199
		4Q388	123
Mart. Isa.		4Q521	110, 114, 116, 117, 120,
2:7–11	140		121, 122, 123, 124, 125,
5:14	146		134, 135, 136, 137, 196,
			199, 200, 204
Sib. Or.		4Q530	188
	178, 179, 187, 188, 193	4Q552 Fr.I Col.2	189
1:387–400	169	4Q552–553	188
2:15–24	187		
3:156–161	169	Persian Sources	
3:156–196	165	AiP	174
4:88–101	165		
8	169	AWN	
9	169		48, 49, 50, 65, 97, 110,
13	187		111, 112, 117, 120, 128,
			133, 138, 146, 175, 180,
T. 12 Patr.			186, 191
2:3–6	142	1–4	134
		2.25–31	149
T. Levi		3.15	148
2:7	192		
		Bd	
Oracles of Hystaspes			52, 57, 95, 96, 109, 167,
	3, 16, 24, 107, 148, 150,		170, 186
	151, 202	1.3	105
		1.12–13	39
Dead Sea Scrolls		1.21–23	67–8
CD 45		1.44	101
CD xv, 6	137	3.10	101
Cd xv.15–17	138	3.27	105
1Q28	138	9.9	109
1Q28a	137	19.21–24	62
1QH 6:34		19–25	39
1QM	45, 48, 120	23	101
1QM 1–9	121	24.31–36	62
1QM 10–19	121	26.28	109
1QS	120	26.53	109
1QS 2; 4:7–8	174	29–33	60

30	96	KIns	
30.17–19	115		99, 137, 174
30.20	168		
30.26	115	KKZ	
33	174		99, 111
33.25	180	18–19	112
34.24	123		
35.4–5	70	KSM	
48	109		99, 114
		38–40	137
GrBd		41	127
	55, 57, 59, 71, 95, 96,	45	116
	97, 102, 167, 170, 171,	47	116
	180, 186	50	116
1a.1–13	55		
1a.6	67	KNRb	
1.14	168		99, 114
4.10–11	59		
27	168	KNRm	
28	168		99, 114
32	168	63–64	137
30	96	65	127
30.4–17	128		
33	171	JN	
34.10	52, 54, 60		49, 146, 151, 191
		17.14	155
CV			
	49, 98, 146, 148, 191	MX	
47	150		97, 132
		1.49	106
DD		2.115	127
1.21	132	2.124	132
Dk		OAv.	
	49, 97, 102, 111, 112,		31
	133, 135, 146, 147,		
	180, 191	PahRiv	
I.12	133	47	148
III	32		
IV	32	YAv.	
IV.7	111		94, 131
VI.634	41		
VII.4	148, 150	Y	
IX.8	181		92
		1.31	38
FrYt		1.32	38
13.79	28	18	64
		23.1	101

26	102	2:1	64
32.1	54	3	101, 165, 166, 167, 173, 174
43	102		
45.2	55	3:3	104
51.9	95	3:7–8	111
		3:11	104
YH		3:15	101
37.2	38	3:15–18	77
41.3	41	3:23	181
		3:24	181
Yt		3:26	181
	10, 27, 87, 92, 201	3:20–26	133
5.85	38	3:29	64, 66, 170
5.109	4	4	65, 104, 166
13	98, 102, 105	4:1	77
13.22	101	4:1–4	170
13.28	101	4:2–4	64
13.94	10	4:4	181
14	87	5:5	180
19	102, 103	4:57–59	166, 174, 179
19.80–81	10	5:1	77
42	127	5:6	168
27.13	10	6:1	77
		6:5	163
ZN		7:1	77
	49, 66, 146, 147, 150, 191	6:10	64

CLASSICAL SOURCES

Aristophanes
Frogs

	118

Hesiod
Works and Days

	101, 163, 166, 167
8–10	167
106–201	187

ZWY

	xx, 16, 48, 49, 51, 59, 63, 64, 65, 66, 67, 78, 80, 101, 102, 111, 112, 120, 128, 134, 146, 148, 150, 152, 161, 162, 163, 166, 167, 168, 170, 171, 172, 173, 174, 178, 181, 186, 191, 192, 197, 200, 201
1	101, 108, 165, 167, 174
1–3	104, 166
1–4	63
1:1–5	172
1:3	101
1:8	166, 181
1:8–11	166
1:11	66
1	166

Plato
Symposium
189 D–191 E 42–3
Politicus

273 b–c	187

Republic

2	26

www.ingramcontent.com/pod-product-compliance
Lightning Source LLC
Chambersburg PA
CBHW062132300426
44115CB00012BA/1891